Empire an

Partha Chatterjee
Empire and Nation
Selected Essays

with an Introduction by
NIVEDITA MENON

Columbia University Press   New York

Columbia University Press
Publishers Since 1893
New York   Chichester, West Sussex
Copyright © 2010 Partha Chatterjee
All rights reserved

Library of Congress Cataloging-in-Publication Data

Chatterjee, Partha, 1947–
Empire and nation : selected essays / Partha Chatterjee ;
with an Introduction by Nivedita Menon.
p. cm.
Includes index.
ISBN 978-0-231-15220-4 (cloth : alk. paper)—
ISBN 978-0-231-15221-1 (pbk. : alk. paper)—
ISBN 978-0-231-52650-0 (ebook)
1. Chatterjee, Partha, 1947– 2. Nationalism.
3. Democracy. 4. Nationalism—India. 5. India—
Politics and government. I. Title.

JC251.C44 2010
320.954—dc22
2010005439

Columbia University Press books are printed on permanent
and durable acid-free paper.
This book is printed on paper with recycled content.
Printed in the United States of America

References to Internet Web sites (URLs) were accurate at the
time of writing. Neither the author nor Columbia University
Press is responsible for URLs that may have expired or
changed since the manuscript was prepared.

Contents

Contents

PART III: CAPITAL AND COMMUNITY

Acknowledgements

The essays in this book first appeared in various books and journals, or were given as talks, as listed below. Copyright over them belongs to the author. As a matter of courtesy, the originating publishers whose addresses were available have been informed. Should any omissions in this regard be brought to our notice, they will be rectified in future printings of this book.

PART I: EMPIRE AND NATION

1   'Whose Imagined Community?', *Millennium*, 20, 3 (Winter 1991)

2   'The Constitution of Indian Nationalist Discourse', in Bhikhu Parekh and Thomas Pantham, eds, *Political Discourse: Explorations in Indian and Western Political Thought* (New Delhi: Sage, 1987)

3   'History and the Nationalization of Hinduism', *Baromas*, April 1991 (translated from the Bengali)

4   'The Fruits of Macaulay's Poison Tree', in Ashok Mitra, ed., *The Truth Unites: Essays in Tribute to Samar Sen* (Calcutta: Subarnarekha, 1985)

5   'Of Diaries, Delirium and Discourse', *Biblio*, August 1996

6   'The Nationalist Resolution of the Women's Question', in Kumkum Sangari and Sudesh Vaid, eds, *Recasting Women* (New Delhi: Kali for Women, 1989)

7   'Our Modernity', Srijnan Haldar Memorial Lecture, 1994 (translated from the Bengali)

8   'A Tribute to the Master' (unpublished)

9   'Those Fond Memories of the Raj', *Times of India*, 20 July 2005

10   'Beyond the Nation? Or Within?' *Economic and Political Weekly*, 32, 1–2 (4–11 January 1997)

EMPIRE AND NATION

Introduction

NIVEDITA MENON

As the old joke goes:

Why did the chicken cross the road?

Karl Marx: Given the material stage of development of the road, it was a historical inevitability.

Jacques Derrida: Any number of contending discourses construct the meaning of that act and the authorial intention can never be discerned, because the Author is DEAD, DAMMIT, DEAD!

To introduce a set of essays that one has not selected is to risk misreading the curatorial intention. Nevertheless, secure in the knowledge that Author/Curator is dead-dammit-dead, I draw my legitimacy from the simple fact that I am one of those whose engagement with the contemporary has been utterly transfigured by reading Partha Chatterjee's work over the years.

The reader familiar with his work should know that this collection is a new *arrangement* of some of his essential writings. It is also not surprising, for anyone who has followed Chatterjee's slow building up of arguments over the years, to find here earlier versions of some of the most influential of such conceptual innovations as have now passed into common shorthand—'our' modernity, the inner/outer in nationalist thought, and the dyad of civil society/modernity, political society/democracy.

What this collection of essays does, then, is to set some of Chatterjee's key writings within the framework of *Empire and Nation*, thus enabling a particular counternarrative of modernity to emerge—not an alternative modernity nor a non-modernity (both terms leaving untouched European modernity as the norm)—but rather, an account that reveals *both* 'our' modernity as well as European modernity to be particular cases of a general history of modernity.

Modernity: Consumers and Producers

In an interview a few years ago, Chatterjee said that he comes to Western social theory 'at a tangent':

> there was a time early in my career when . . . I probably would have said that . . . if one was approaching political theory, one should approach it irrespective of one's cultural or geographical location . . . I am far more aware now of the ways in which my location in India influences the questions about politics and society that seem more urgent . . . In trying to approach those concerns, I often find myself in a position of relative remoteness from the body of Western social theories . . . Even when Western social theory approaches these issues, it actually misrepresents, often misidentifies, the problem . . .
>   The theory that will explain Indian democracy or the theory that will explain China's capitalism today will actually be a far more general theory of which Western theory will just be a particular case.[1]

Chatterjee began his travels in theory from the late 1970s when, as a young Marxist, he was armed with certainty and the confidence to advance 'on behalf of a class, an alliance or the people as a whole, a rival claim to rule.' Today he is certain only of his scepticism of utopias, even while his central concern remains the same—the 'politics of the governed'.[2] His perspective: 'oppositional, negative, resolutely critical'.[3] For many who came to scholarship in the 1990s, in a period already deeply marked by the tracks of such troubled journeys—those of Chatterjee of course, but also of Ashis Nandy and writers in the early Subaltern Studies volumes (Susie Tharu, Sudipta Kaviraj, and Dipesh Chakrabarty in particular)—there was never that moment of innocence, the assumption that 'one could approach political theory irrespective of one's cultural or geographical location.'

Chatterjee's work foregrounds the question of location, a move that has been often misunderstood to mean something like indigenism, as

---

[1] Interview with Rudrangshu Mukherjee, *Sephis e-Magazine*, vol. 1, no. 1, 2004.
[2] Partha Chatterjee, *A Possible India. Essays in Political Criticism* (New Delhi: Oxford University Press, 1997), p. vii.
[3] Ibid., p. ix.

for example when Sarah Joseph, terming Chatterjee and Nandy 'critics of modernity',[4] reads their argument as counterposing 'Indian communitarianism' against 'Western individualism'. This conflation of Nandy and Chatterjee's positions is unsustainable. Nandy could certainly be called a neo-Gandhian 'critic of modernity', or at least of 'actually existing' modernity, if I may so term it—a particular strain of modernity that triumphed in Europe and was then exported all over the globe on the back of imperialism. Chatterjee on the other hand is not so much a *critic* of modernity as a *historian* of modernity. The position Joseph attributes to him is this: 'His thesis is that the introduction of alien, modern institutions, values and concepts into a traditional society like the Indian led to consequences that were unexpected and different from . . . [those] on European societies. This he attributes to the persistence of indigenous life forms and practices in India . . .'[5]

However, when Chatterjee invokes location it is not about 'India versus the West' (with the imputation of greater authenticity to the Indian side of the equation); nor does he frame the question within the tradition/modernity framework, and certainly not in terms of 'persistence' of the traditional. The idea of persistence assumes a teleological journey from traditional to modern, an assumption alien to Chatterjee. His project, rather, is to map the various formations of modernity 'in most of the world', thus showing both Europe and 'us' to be particular cases of a general history.

Chatterjee's insistence on location is a productive conceptual development inflected by later scholars in their different ways. I suggest that location in the sense in which Chatterjee uses it must be understood as gesturing towards the materiality of spatial and temporal co-ordinates that inevitably suffuse all theorizing. A sensitivity to location invariably leads to a productive contamination of the purity of empty universalist categories and challenges their claim to speak about everywhere from nowhere. Pradeep Jeganathan has argued that the question of location does not refer to some 'more authentic' point of epistemic access, but rather underlines the need to engage with the

---

[4] Sarah Joseph, 'Modernity and its Critics: A Discussion of Some Contemporary Social and Political Theorists', in V.R. Mehta and Thomas Pantham, *Political Ideas in Modern India: Thematic Explorations*, vol. x, pt 7 (New Delhi: Sage Publications, 2006), p. 422.

[5] Ibid., p. 428.

'density of arguments within a lived community'.[6] Satish Deshpande, seeking a 'sense of location that can maintain a critical distance from both cosmopolitanism and patriotism', points us towards the range of intellectual and political 'oppositional stances'—the '"Asianism" movement in Japan, China, and other parts of Asia at the turn of the [nineteenth] century; the "Negritude" movement associated with the names of Aimé Césaire and Leopold Senghor', the Bandung project of the mid-twentieth century 'and its various avatars', and so on.

So Chatterjee's invocation of locality must be grounded within a larger global political/intellectual field of reworkings of the question of modernity, of colonial modernity in particular. In such a field, other kinds of engagements with the problematic of location become visible; to cite a few random examples—Dipesh Chakrabarty of course; but also Tejaswini Niranjana on translation; Mahmood Mamdani deconstructing the slogan 'Out of Iraq and into Darfur' as the denial of a history and a politics to the non-West; the journal *Inter-Asia Cultural Studies*, founded in 2000, which assumes a pan-Asian location for exploring the relationship between cultural theory and political/cultural movements; Achille Mbembe's exploration of the modernity into which Africa was thrust by colonialism, so that after its conquest Africa has served as 'the supreme receptacle of the West's obsession with, and circular discourse about, the facts of "absence", "lack" . . .'[7]

To insist on location is precisely to contest 'lack' as the predominant way of characterizing Europe's Other, and there is no doubt that Chatterjee's contribution here has been formative. In 'Our Modernity' (essay 7 in the present volume), moving between sceptical nineteenth-century Bengali responses to the transformations brought by modernity and Kant's celebratory 'What is Enlightenment' as an instance of 'Western modernity representing itself', Chatterjee says:

[6] Malathi De Alwis, *et al.*, 'The Postnational Condition', *Economic and Political Weekly* (*EPW*), 7 March 2009, vol. XLIV, no. 10.

[7] Achille Mbembe, *On the Postcolony* (Berkeley: University of California Press, 2001), p. 4; see also Dipesh Chakrabarty, *Provincializing Europe* (Princeton: Princeton University Press, 2000), key parts of which were published in journals and edited volumes throughout the 1990s; Tejaswini Niranjana, *Siting Translation: History, Post-Structuralism and the Colonial Context* (Berkeley: University of California Press, 1992); Mahmood Mamdani, 'The Politics of Naming: Genocide, Civil War, Insurgency', *London Review of Books*, vol. 29, no. 5, 8 March 2007.

There must be something in the very process of our becoming modern that continues to lead us, even in our acceptance of modernity, to a certain scepticism about its values and consequences . . .

My argument is that because of the way in which the history of our modernity has been intertwined with the history of colonialism, we have never quite been able to believe that there exists a universal domain of free discourse, unfettered by differences of race or nationality. Somehow from the very beginning we have made a shrewd guess that given the close complicity between modern knowledges and modern regimes of power, we would forever remain consumers of universal modernity; never would we be taken seriously as its producers. It is for this reason that we have tried, for over a hundred years, to take our eyes away from this chimera of universal modernity and clear up a space where we might become the creators of our own modernity . . .

. . . There is no promised land of modernity outside the network of power. Hence one cannot be for or against modernity; one can only devise strategies for coping with it.

A lingering question here in my mind plays with the 'our' of 'our modernity'—is there a way in which this pronoun acts as a homogenizing move, dissolving counter-identities within the nation for whom 'their' (European) modernity was far preferable to 'our' non-modernity? A little later there occurs this claim:

[W]hereas Kant, speaking at the founding moment of Western modernity, looks at the present as the site of one's escape from the past, for us it is precisely the present from which we feel we must escape. This makes the modality of our coping with modernity radically different from the historically evolved modes of Western modernity.

Rajnarayan Basu may well have contrasted the decline to ill-health and selfishness in '*e kal*' (these days) from the compassion, genuineness, and good health of '*se kal*' (those days), but for many middle-class women and historically untouchable castes of that same nineteenth century it was in fact the present which worked as the 'site of escape' from the past. The nostalgia of upper-caste men could not, it seems to me, ever have been available to women and Dalits who rebelled against illiteracy, untouchability, forced and early marriage, and the fetters of Hinduism—the features of their *se kal*.

Rajnarayan Basu wrote *Se kal ar e kal* in 1873. About two decades earlier, in 1855, the Marathi journal *Dnyanodaya* carried an essay written by 11-year-old Muktabai, a Dalit student at the school in Pune established by Savitribai and Jotiba Phule:

> Earlier, Gokhale, Apate, Trimkaji [a series of other Brahmin surnames] . . . who showed their bravery by killing rats in their homes, persecuted us, not even sparing pregnant women, without any rhyme or reason. That has stopped now . . . Harassment and torture of mahars and mangs, common during the rule of Peshwas in Pune, has stopped. Now, human sacrifice for the foundation of forts and mansions has stopped . . . Now, our population is growing in numbers. Earlier, if any mahar or mang wore fine clothes, they would say that only brahmans could wear such clothes . . . they would tie them to trees and punish them. But under British rule, anybody with money can buy and wear clothes . . .[8]

And so it goes on: 'Earlier' (*se kal*) was hell; 'now' (*e kal*) is the time of liberation.

Or take Pandita Ramabai at the turn of the nineteenth century, challenging the authorities of the Church of England: 'I have a conscience and a mind of my own . . . I have with great effort freed myself from the yoke of the Indian priestly tribe so I am not at present willing to place myself under another similar yoke by accepting everything that comes from priests as the authorized command of the Most High.'[9] 'At present' is the time in which Ramabai sees herself entering the adulthood of Kant's enlightenment. Crucially, she finds this adulthood denied her by the English priesthood, but she challenges it fiercely. *Now*—now that she has broken free of one kind of fetter, a new kind is intolerable. For many like Muktabai and Ramabai, it was *e kal* that offered some promise of escape from suffocating and humiliating pasts.

I draw attention to these voices that complicate Chatterjee's narrative of 'our' modernity precisely in order to acknowledge his conclusion that 'to fashion the terms of our own modernity, we need to have the courage at times to reject the modernities established by others.'

There is now a great deal of self-reflexivity about Eurocentrism among Western scholars. So, for instance, Charles Taylor's warning against the easy transposing of the state–civil society opposition derived from the experience of Western Europe to other parts of the world

---

[8] Braj Ranjan Mani and Pamela Sardar, trans. and eds, *A Forgotten Liberator: The Life and Struggle of Savitribai Phule* (New Delhi: Mountain Peak, n.d.), pp. 74–5.

[9] Cited in Uma Chakravarty, *Rewriting History: The Life and Times of Pandita Ramabai* (Delhi: Kali for Women, 2000), p. 322.

and his proposal to enrich the concept of civil society by including within its purview other forms of state–society interaction in non-European contexts. However, in his response to Taylor (essay 16), Chatterjee points out that the central assumption of Taylor's proposal continues to be an understanding that 'it is only the concepts of European social philosophy that contain within them the possibility of universalization.' His own project, therefore, is to explore the specificity of the European concept of civil society and demonstrate the ways in which 'that concept could be shown to be a particular form of a more universal concept'; in other words, 'to send the concept of civil society back to where I think it properly belongs— the provincialism of European social philosophy.'

The four essays in the final section, 'Capital and Community', including this response, explore in different and tangential ways, through studies of peasant resistance and linguistic and religious nationalisms in Bengal (essays 18 and 19) and a history of Subaltern Studies (essay 17), Chatterjee's assertion in his response to Taylor:

> If there is one great moment that turns the provincial thought of Europe to universal philosophy, the parochial history of Europe to universal history, it is the moment of capital—capital that is global in its territorial reach and universal in its conceptual domain. It is the narrative of capital that can turn the violence of mercantilist trade, war, genocide, conquest and colonialism into a story of universal progress, development, modernization and freedom.

For this narrative to take shape, the destruction of community is fundamental, says Chatterjee; yet community could not entirely be suppressed either. Therefore, '[n]otwithstanding its universal scope, capital remained parasitic upon the reconstructed particularism of the nation.' At the same time, community is not easily appropriated within narratives of capital and the contradictions between the two are seen clearly in histories of anti-colonial nationalist movements. Indeed, one might say that the core of Chatterjee's explorations is precisely this tension posed by the contradiction between capital and community in, so to speak, the rest of the world.

'History and the Nationalization of Hinduism' (essay 3) is an analysis of the break marked by the advent of the idea of universal history via modern historiography, in indigenous ways of telling stories of the past. On the other hand the oblique and witty response to 'Dronacharya' (Ranajit Guha) from 'the third Pandava' (Partha Chatterjee), wickedly titled 'Tribute to the Master' (essay 8), is a sharp questioning of Guha's critique of universal history in *History at the Limit of World-history*. Chatterjee charges Guha with 'assimilating all forms of proto-historical narrative in India to the *Mahabharata*' and with applying 'the conditions of antiquity or tradition and succession or continuous retelling in order to privilege the two Brahmanical epics over all other narrative specimens.' Ouch.

Essays 1, 2, 4, and 6, including two pieces now seen as classics, 'The Nationalist Resolution of the Women's Question' and 'The Constitution of Indian Nationalist Discourse', lay out Chatterjee's controversial and much-debated argument on anti-colonial nationalism, familiar now from *Nationalist Thought and the Colonial World: A Derivative Discourse?* and *The Nation and its Fragments*, which I will not go into here.[10]

There are in addition four short pieces—a playful review of Sudipta Kaviraj's *Unhappy Consciousness,* a sharp attack on Prime Minister Manmohan Singh's 'fond memories of the Raj', a defence of Rushdie's *Satanic Verses,* and a demolition of anti-reservation arguments in the post-Mandal scenario.

Civil and Political Society

Chatterjee's conceptual innovation of 'political society' has captured the imaginations of many scholars who have struggled to understand that domain where democracy seems to be actually in action, but which meets none of the standards set by political theory for what is permitted to count as democracy—rationality, deliberation, reasonable justification, control over excess, non-violence. What is exciting about

---

[10] To name just a few serious engagements with Chatterjee's argument on nationalism: Sumit Sarkar, 'Indian Nationalism and the Politics of Hindutva', in David Ludden, ed., *Contesting the Nation: Religion, Community and the Politics of Democracy in India* (Philadelphia: University of Pennsylvania Press, 1996); Ayesha Jalal, 'Nation, Reason and Religion: Punjab's Role in the Partition of India', *EPW*, vol. 33, no. 32, 8 August 1998; Aamir R. Mufti, *Enlightenment in the Colony: The Jewish Question and the Crisis of Postcolonial Culture* (Princeton: Princeton University Press, 2007); and the following three essays in Pradeep Jeganathan and Qadri Ismail, eds, *Unmaking the Nation. The Politics of Identity and History in Modern Sri Lanka* (Colombo: Social Scientists Association, 1995): Pradeep Jeganathan and Qadri Ismail, 'Introduction: Unmaking the Nation'; Qadri Ismail, 'Unmooring Identity: The Antinomies of Elite Muslim Self-representation in Modern Sri Lanka'; and Malathi de Alwis, 'Gender, Politics and the "Respectable Lady"'.

the concept is precisely that political society seems to 'raise the spectre of pure politics', and that there, in its messy spaces, 'the foundations of a new democratic order' may be coming into being (essay 11).

In this now well-known and well-developed argument (here represented in essays 10 and 11), Chatterjee suggests that in order to escape the confines of the modernization narrative, in which the conceptual domains of state and society are either sharply distinguished (with the central state institutions carrying the burden of an interventionist modernizing project) or collapsed entirely (so that state practices are seen as completely under the influence of social institutions), we need to think of a field of practices mediating between state institutions and civil society. In essay 11 Chatterjee says he thinks of civil society in Hegelian/Marxist terms as 'an actually existing arena of institutions and practices inhabited by a relatively small section' of people, marked by the 'characteristic institutions of modern associational life originating in Western societies' and based on equality, freedom of entry and exit, contract, deliberative procedures of decision-making, recognized rights, and so on. Civil society is thus the sphere of modernity.

In terms of the formal structure of the state as given by the constitution, all of society is civil society. But in actual fact 'most of the inhabitants of India are only tenuously, and even then ambiguously and contextually, rights-bearing citizens in the sense imagined by the constitution.' However, they are not excluded from the domain of politics; rather, as 'populations' they have to be both looked after and controlled by various governmental agencies. This is the zone of 'political society', distinct from both state and civil society, the domain of democracy.

The 'hiatus' between civil and political society thus defined (essay 10) is 'the mark of non-Western modernity', in which 'modernization' is an always incomplete project, to be carried out by an enlightened elite 'engaged in a pedagogical mission in relation to the rest of society.' So, what lies outside civil society/modernity is not tradition but a realm 'relegated to the zone of the traditional', that is, political society, which copes with the modern in ways that often do not conform to the Western bourgeois secularized Christian principles of modern civil society. Civil social institutions, if they are to conform to the model presented by Western modernity, must necessarily exclude from their scope the vast mass of the population. But this does not lead Chatterjee to expand the definition of civil society, as neo-liberal discourse does, in whose rhetoric every non-state organization is consecrated 'as the precious flower of the associative endeavours of free members of civil society.' Rather, he prefers to retain the older, restrictive idea of civil society, and to introduce the idea of political society in order 'to capture some of the conflicting desires of modernity that animate' contemporary debates in places such as India.

In a recent development of the idea he has suggested that 'civil society is where corporate capital is hegemonic, whereas political society is the space of management of non-corporate capital', corporate capital being distinguished by the profit-maximization logic while non-corporate capital is governed by livelihood needs.[11]

Now that the concept has been developed by Chatterjee for the past decade, and has implicitly or explicitly influenced a number of scholars,[12] questions needing clarification have begun to emerge. To begin with, as we saw above, Chatterjee himself conceives of civil and political society as *empirical spaces*. Further, he makes a distinction between 'civil society as an ideal' which extends to the entire nation, and civil society as an actually existing form which is 'demographically limited' (essay 11). However, if civil/political society is treated as mapping actual configurations on the ground—civil society consisting of *citizens* with legal rights, composed of urban middle classes, and the zone of corporate capital; political society marked by *populations* which are the object of development policies, people with no legal rights, consisting of largely urban but some rural poor, the zone of management of non-corporate capital—such a neat picture is bound to founder on empirical data. That is, people located within civil society (the urban middle classes) can also be viewed as 'populations' by

[11] Partha Chatterjee, 'Democracy and Economic Transformation in India', *EPW*, 19 April 2008, vol. XLII, no. 16, p. 58.

[12] For instance, Lawrence Liang, 'Porous Legalities and Avenues of Participation', *Sarai Reader 05: Bare Acts* (Delhi: Sarai Media Lab, 2005); Aditya Nigam, 'Civil Society and its "Underground": Explorations in the Notion of Political Society', in Rajeev Bhargava and Helmut Reifeld, eds, *Civil Society, Public Sphere and Citizenship: Dialogues and Perceptions* (Delhi: Sage, 2005); Nivedita Menon and Aditya Nigam, *Power and Contestation: India After 1989* (London: Zed Books, 2007); Rajarshi Dasgupta, 'The CPI(M) "Machinery" in West Bengal: Two Village Narratives from Kochbihar and Malda', *EPW*, vol. XLIV, no. 9, 28 February 2009; Dwaipayan Bhattacharya, 'Of Control and Factions: The Changing "Party-Society" in Rural West Bengal', in ibid.; Solomon Benjamin, 'Governance, Economic Settings and Poverty in Bangalore', *Environment and Urbanization*, vol. 12, no. 1, 2000.

the state (for instance, Residents' Welfare Associations of middle-class housing colonies in relation to local government; or up-market traders' associations that have to negotiate the same network of municipality structures and police at a higher level, as street hawkers have to at a lower).

Conversely, people in political society (urban and rural poor) often invoke rights, contracts, and the discourse of equality in addressing the state. Thus, for instance, participants in the Narmada Bachao Andolan do not make 'claims on the state for governmental benefits' but insist as citizens of India that they have a right to their lands. Chatterjee argues that the claims of people in political society are a matter of constant political negotiation and are never permanent, their entitlements never become rights. But as far as 'political society'-type negotiations are concerned this is as true for upscale Khan Market in Delhi as for street hawkers. For instance, it is common to find the normal parking arrangements in posh markets suddenly turned upside down, with cars being fined or towed away by the traffic police when a new police officer takes over the area, at which point reciprocally beneficial 'gifts and services' have to be renegotiated with him even by powerful and wealthy traders' associations. Illegal practices among the urban middle classes are thus no less constitutive of everyday life than those of political society, and while Chatterjee readily concedes this when it comes up as a critique, he immediately distinguishes between illegality among the well off (civil society) and the poor (political society) with the argument that the latter still has broad moral legitimacy while the former does not.[13] This is debatable; certainly it remains unproductively trapped within the framework of 'governmentality', a point I will come to later.

Thus, running away with the ball Chatterjee has thrown us, it seems to me that the two terms should be understood as conceptual distinctions rather than as actual empirical groupings. I wonder if it is not more productive to think of civil and political society as two *styles of political engagement* that are available to people—the former style is

[13] Partha Chatterjee, 'Classes, Capital and Indian Democracy' (a reply to three critical responses to 'Democracy and Economic Transformation in India', op cit.), *EPW*, 15 November 2008, vol. XLIII, no. 46, pp. 91–2. This particular response was to Amita Baviskar and Nandini Sundar, 'Democracy versus Economic Transformation?', ibid.

more available to an urbanized elite, the latter to the rest. The availability is fluid and contextual, not fixed by class.

One of the consequences of treating civil and political society as empirical spaces is that as more and more instances emerge of actual groupings that do not fit into those categories, the categories themselves appear to be in need of multiplication. For example, in essay 11 Chatterjee makes a distinction between (a) the modernizing elite/ civil society/governing classes; (b) the 'natural leaders' of governed populations,[14] for example, the Shiv Sena; and (c) the 'thicket of contestations', i.e. political society. This suggests that (b), i.e. political parties, are outside both civil and political society as well as the state. But in an earlier piece (essay 10) he spells out 'parties, movements, non-party political formations' as constituting political society. Then again, he has recently posited another grouping outside (or as the 'underside' of) political society: marginal groups marked by their exclusion from peasant society such as low castes who do not participate in agriculture, or tribal people who depend on forest products and pastoral activities.[15] Excluding such groups from political society becomes necessary because, in Chatterjee's own understanding, the term is limited to those sections of the poor that can form organizations and petition the state. Because 'Political society and electoral democracy have not given these groups the means to make effective claims on governmentality',[16] they cannot be seen as part of political society. This last point leads us directly to a second set of questions that arise from the troubling restriction by Chatterjee of the potential of his radically innovative conceptual move, which happens when he limits political society within the framework of a narrow understanding of governmentality: 'As populations, within the territorial jurisdiction of the state, they have to be both looked after and controlled by various government agencies' (essay 11). And: 'The major instrumental form here in the postcolonial period is that of the developmental state which seeks to relate to different sections of the population through the governmental function of welfare' (essay 10).

This perspective also emerges from the passage cited earlier, in which he seems to see 'civil society' ('the governing classes') as the agent determining 'the project of democratic modernity'. They have two

---

[14] Chatterjee puts the phrase 'natural leaders' within quotation marks.
[15] 'Democracy and Economic Transformation', op. cit., p. 61.
[16] Ibid.

choices: that of suspending the modernization project, 'walling in the protected zones of bourgeois civil society and dispensing the governmental functions of law and order and welfare through the "natural leaders" of the governed populations' (such as the Shiv Sena); or the 'less cynical' yet more pragmatic option of not abandoning the project of enlightenment but attempting to steer it through 'the thicket of contestations' in political society. This is the zone, Chatterjee says, where the project of democratic modernity has to operate 'slowly, painfully, unsurely' (essay 11).

This is the startling and productive insight—that democratic aspirations often violate institutional norms of liberal civil society. However, Chatterjee's addressee appears to be 'civil society'; he seems to be advising it on how it ought to conduct itself—'taking seriously the functions of direction and leadership of a vanguard' (essay 11)—much as Machiavelli addresses his prince.

I have chosen to reread 'political society' in the sense that I believe to be more true to Chatterjee's own phrase describing it—as a 'thicket of contestations'. I would like also to highlight the point he makes that 'the practices that activate the forms and methods of mobilization and participation in political society are not always consistent with the principles of association in civil society.' The addressee, then, cannot be 'civil society' in his sense, i.e. the governing classes, but must be movements and political practices. If we accept this understanding, then it is clear that politics, the struggle to reclaim and produce meaning, will have to be waged in this uncomfortable realm, that of political society, and not in the sanitized spaces of civil society. This is an understanding we have had to come to terms with, painfully, as far as secularism is concerned, for example.[17]

In reading 'political society' in this way, I unhitch Chatterjee's notion of this concept from its link in his argument to the welfare function of government. I find that his emphasis on this function reduces the initial potential offered by 'political society' for understanding a hitherto untheorized realm.

Of course, the problem with 'political society' understood in this way is that political society-type activities would not necessarily conform to our understanding of what is progressive or emancipatory.

[17] Nivedita Menon, 'Living with Secularism', in Anuradha Dingwaney Needham and Rajeswari Sunder Rajan, eds, *The Crisis of Secularism in India* (Durham: Duke University Press, and Ranikhet: Permanent Black, 2007).

These could be the struggles of squatters on government land to claim residence rights (which could include illegally tapping electricity lines, for example), or the effort of a religious sect to preserve the corpse of their leader on account of their belief in his imminent resurrection. Both these are Chatterjee's own examples, and he views both exclusively from the perspective of the state and civil society as problems requiring intervention and resolution—as against the perspective of the groups challenging the rule of law. Political society-type interventions can also, as we have too often seen, be the decisions of village panchayats to kill women accused of adultery. I have no intention, therefore, of romanticizing this style of political engagement, nor do I think of it as uniformly 'subaltern'. Rather, 'political society' in this sense involves many new loci of power and new elites. The point I take from Chatterjee is that any project of radical democratic transformation would have to engage and collide with the ideas, beliefs, and practices that this style of engagement enables. It cannot remain in the rarefied realms of 'civil society' where, in fact, the struggles of both 'unauthorized' squatters and those of religious sects may be dismissed as uncivilized. From the point of view of civil society norms, the large grey realm of survival strategies among the urban poor (what Lawrence Liang terms 'porous legalities'[18]) can only be dismissed as plainly 'illegal'. Thus, I would suggest that their only hope of survival is to remain invisible to the state, and to be *not* brought within its governmentalizing drive.

Such a reading of political society is what makes it an 'unprecedented opportunity for thinking the unthinkable . . . Unfortunately, it is precisely these explosive possibilities . . . that are relegated [by Chatterjee] to the "outside", thus domesticating and taming political society . . .'[19] In his recent development of the idea, referred to earlier, Chatterjee makes this taming even more explicit:

> Interestingly, even though the claims made by different groups in political society are for governmental benefits, these cannot often be met by standard application of rules . . . Thus when a group of people living in or cultivating illegally occupied land or selling goods on the street claim the

[18] Lawrence Liang, 'Porous Legalities', op. cit.
[19] Aditya Nigam, 'Political Society and the Fable of Primitive Accumulation', in http://kafila.org/2008/06/15/political-society-and-the-fable-of-primitive-accumulation/

right to continue with their activities, or demand compensation for moving somewhere else, they are in fact inviting the state to declare their case as an exception to the universally applicable rule. They do not demand that the right to private property in land be abolished or that the regulations on trade licences and sales tax be set aside. Rather, they demand that their cases be treated as exceptions.[20]

From the reformulation of the concept of political society that I urge, based on taking seriously Chatterjee's idea that it invokes 'the spectre of pure politics', the account above is deeply troubling, taking for granted as it does that political society consists exclusively of groups making claims on government benefits; that these groups consciously choose not to challenge property rights and regulations on sales tax; that they understand they are asking to be treated as 'exceptions' to universally applicable rules. I would think, rather, that ideas such as structures of property rights and sales tax regimes have no place in their intellectual horizon; and they probably have no conception of 'universally applicable rules', never having encountered such a thing in their lives. These are constructs of the capitalist imagination completely alien to vast tracts of the population 'in most parts of the world', constructs which states continually struggle to 'teach' their populations. Chatterjee shows as much in 'Development Planning and the Indian State' (essay 14) when he argues that planning 'in its legitimizing role', constituted as a domain outside politics, 'was to become an instrument of politics'; but once again this insight is harnessed to the framework of governmentality.

As Timothy Mitchell (who also seems to read Chatterjee's 'political society' in the way I do), demonstrates, the success of Hernando de Soto—Peruvian entrepreneur and economist—and his Institute of Liberty and Democracy, working closely with governments in several countries in Africa, Asia, and Latin America, lies in their cataloguing of the forms of wealth and material activity that lie outside the capitalist economy, diagnosing the nature of the barriers that keep them out, and proposing techniques for bringing them in.[21] In other words, far

---

[20] 'Democracy and Economic Transformation', op. cit. p. 61.
[21] Timothy Mitchell, 'The Properties of Markets', in *Do Economics Make Markets: On the Performativity of Economics*, ed. Donald MacKenzie, Fabian Muniesa, and Lucia Siu (Princeton: Princeton University Press, 2007).

from being exclusively formed by governmentality, the large majority of people in most parts of the world are in a sense 'ungovernable', and inaccessible to capital, to the state, and to governmentality.

I would prefer, thus, to think of a 'political society style' as *escaping governmentality* rather than making people the *objects of governmentality*. Not necessarily only through conscious political acts, but also simply through myriad everyday practices: from 'public' and visible acts such as squatting on public land, to 'private' and invisible acts such as same-sex love—continuously, unselfconsciously, embodying breached boundaries and unrespected limits.

If one reformulates political society in this way, then the actual sections of people Chatterjee describes as inhabiting it—the labouring poor—would be recognized as adopting civil and political society styles at different points and in different contexts; and so would the urban elites. It would also be possible to see that the attitude of the state towards the poor can be characterized as having gone through different stages. The transformations in the 1990s are not taken adequately into account by Chatterjee, the period when the state withdrew more and more from its 'development' obligations. He does recognize the 'cleaning up' of Indian cities of the poor by citizens' rights groups and an activist judiciary,[22] but still claims that mobilizations in political society make demands for governmental welfare, and that agencies of the state and NGOs deal with these people not as citizens but as population groups deserving welfare. This was true enough till the 1980s, but it needs to be rethought. Demands from these sections are no longer in the form of demanding welfare; nor do government agencies assume that they 'deserve welfare'. The development in the 1990s has been that the poor are seen now as an obstacle to civil society-type conceptions of democracy and development rather than as the target of that development. Meanwhile the poor themselves, whether in Nandigram, or on the streets of Seelampur in Delhi protesting the sealing of their small commercial establishments,[23] are militantly claiming spaces and livelihoods as their own, not as largesse from the state.

---

[22] Partha Chatterjee, 'Are Indian Cities Becoming Bourgeois at Last?', in Indira Chandrasekhar and Peter Seel, eds, *body.city: Siting Contemporary Culture in India* (New Delhi: Tulika, 2003).

[23] Nivedita Menon and Aditya Nigam, 'Lambs at the Law's Guillotine', *Tehelka*, 7 October 2006.

And finally, a third stage may have emerged in the late 1990s and the early 2010s. In this period, determinations of citizenship are made not only by the state but by the corporate sector. Paula Chakravartty, for instance, argues that corporations have now made the poor the targets of corporate governance, their claim being that—unlike the government which renders the poor as objects of charity—they unleash agency among the poor.[24]

This third stage of citizenship is, of course, well in keeping with Chatterjee's account in 'Democracy and Economic Transformation in India', where he argues that 'the capitalist class has come to acquire a position of moral-political hegemony . . . The dominance of the capitalist class within the state structure as a whole can be inferred from the virtual consensus among all major political parties about the priorities of rapid economic growth led by private investment, both domestic and foreign.'[25]

The Parthovian Resolution of the Women's Question?[26]

In 'The Nationalist Resolution of the Women's Question' (essay 6) Chatterjee argued that the nationalist elite resolved this question by adopting the understanding that while in the outer material realm 'we' (Indians) are the same as 'them' (the British), in the inner cultural realm we are different. We are equal as citizens in the outer material realm, but in the inner realm we are different, being essentially spiritual. In this realm our women will be remade as appropriately modern, but that is *our* task. The colonial state may not enter this inner realm. With this insightful essay Chatterjee appears to have theoretically resolved the 'Women's Question' to his satisfaction in his own work. Thus, even

---

[24] Paula Chakravartty, 'Brand India, Citizen Microsoft and the Rise of Entrepreneurial Civil Society', paper presented at the conference 'Beyond Good Governance: Rethinking Civil Society, Human Rights and Democracy Promotion', Watson Institute, Brown University, 14–16 May 2009.

[25] 'Democracy and Economic Transformation in India', op. cit., p. 57.

[26] This subtitle is of course inspired both by the title of Chatterjee's famous paper as well as by his trademark use of question marks in his titles, thus producing the intriguing effect of non-closure. (In this volume alone, see essays 10 and 13 with two each in their titles, and essay 1 with one, not to mention his well-known books, *Nationalist Thought and the Colonial World: A Derivative Discourse?*, and *A Princely Impostor? The Kumar of Bhawal and the Secret History of Indian Nationalism*.)

while engaging closely with discourses around Indian secularism, at the heart of which lies the identity demarcated as 'Woman', Chatterjee maintains silence on this question, in effect assuming the contradiction between Democracy and Modernity to be ungendered.

In 'Secularism and Toleration' (essay 12) Chatterjee argues that a collective cultural right is the right *not* to offer a reason for not being different, provided that the group explains itself adequately to its own chosen forum. Unlike many of his critics, I agree that, though difficult, this is the democratic path to follow, and this is also the kind of understanding that the women's movement in India has come to since the late 1990s.[27] What I am disappointed by is Chatterjee's silence on the crucial fact that this chosen forum marks itself as 'different' precisely by the defining of 'its' women. It is after all, not fortuitous that the debate on cultural rights in India is the debate on the Uniform Civil Code. What is at stake in this debate is not differences in cultural practices as such, but the manner in which cultural practices are implicated in notions of the self, *constituted as male.* That is, the self recognized by different cultural/religious groups—the self endowed with selfhood— is male. Thus, what is happening in this debate is that while the 'Hindu' male identity is claimed as devoid of all distinguishing marks (like the 'citizen' in the public sphere defined by the Indian constitution), all other religious identities are seen from this perspective, and by themselves, as having a specific maleness that distinguishes them from the Other. Without ever explicitly recognizing and engaging with the gendered self in these discourses, Chatterjee takes for granted that personal laws are 'at the heart of religious practice'—why should this be so? Why does the heart of religious practice necessarily have to involve constructing gendered selves? I would have expected Chatterjee to directly ask these questions rather than let them be raised by designated feminists.

But his silence is also more than merely an absence of questioning. It leads to positive assertions such as his characterization of the codification of Hindu law as embodying the 'reformist urge' of the Indian parliament, and as being 'far-reaching in their departure from traditional brahmanical principles'. On the contrary, the Hindu Code Bills, passed in 1955 and 1956, did not reform Hindu personal laws, they

---

[27] Nivedita Menon, 'Women and Citizenship', in *Wages of Freedom*, ed. Partha Chatterjee (New Delhi: Oxford University Press, 1998).

merely codified them, that is, brought them into conformity with what was assumed to be the 'Indian' norm: North Indian upper-caste practices. Other practices were explicitly characterized during the debates in parliament as being un-Indian. Several scholars have shown that ending the diversity of Hindu law as it was practised in various regions destroyed, in many cases, more liberal existing provisions for women.[28]

Similarly, Chatterjee sees devadasi abolition and the transformation of matrilineal practices unproblematically, as located within the 'reformist' worldview. However, both these instances offer us the opportunity to track a different trajectory of 'our' modernity, enabling us to sense the complex negotiations of colonial modernity made by male nationalist elites in different situations. It is revealing that it is precisely in the late nineteenth century, when the Women's Question had been 'resolved', that the state is called upon to legislate in both these instances. Could it be that when the 'inner' is already marked by female autonomy of some sort (as with the devadasi tradition,[29] and with matriliny), male nationalist desire to protect 'cultural difference' is necessarily complicated? As I have argued elsewhere, this situation produces a cruel paradox for the modernizing male elite—to continue to be different and autonomous from the colonial order is to repudiate proper masculine roles; but to be properly modern and masculine is to be subjugated to colonial values.[30] Eventually in the case of both matriliny and devadasi *pratha*, the desire to be 'properly modern' won out, and this proper modernity also just happened to establish the proper patriarchal order.

---

[28] Nivedita Menon, 'The Historian and "His" Others. A Response to Ram Guha', *EPW*, vol. 43, 4–10 October 2008.

[29] The work of feminist scholars has shown that devadasis had rights to property and the space to make decisions about their lives that 'respectable' Hindu women did not have. These rights were ended by the abolition of the institution, often reducing former devadasis to the very 'prostitution' which the reform movements had claimed to rescue them from, leaving them with little control over whom they could sell sex to. See Amrit Srinivasan, 'Reform and Revival: The Devadasi and Her Dance', *EPW*, vol. xx, no. 44, 2 November 1985; Janaki Nair, 'The Devadasi, Dharma and the State', *EPW*, 10 December 1994, vol. xxix; Kalpana Kannabiran, 'Judiciary, Social Reform and Debate on "Religious Prostitution" in Colonial India', *EPW*, vol. xxx, 8 October 1995.

[30] Introduction in *Sexualities*, ed. Nivedita Menon (Delhi: Women Unlimited, 2007).

Conclusion

So, why *did* the chicken cross the road?

Partha Chatterjee: The posing of the question in these terms reveals the parochialism of human social theory. A close reading of *Murgija-tir Itihash* reveals that the straight, smooth and bi-directional 'road' was used by very few chickens. The real foci of chicken activity were the unruly, dark, and mysterious thickets on the margins of the road. If it had ever been suggested to the chicken that 'crossing the road' was a meaningful activity, it is doubtful that it would have understood.

I

Empire and Nation

1

Whose Imagined Community?
(1991)

Nationalism has once more appeared on the agenda of world affairs. Almost every day, state leaders and political analysts in Western countries declare that with 'the collapse of communism' (that is the term they use; what they mean is presumably the collapse of Soviet socialism), the principal danger to world peace is now posed by the resurgence of nationalism in different parts of the world. Since in this day and age a phenomenon has first to be recognized as a 'problem' before it can claim the attention of people whose business it is to decide what should concern the public, nationalism seems to have regained sufficient notoriety for it to be liberated from the arcane practices of 'area specialists' and made once more a subject of general debate.

However, this very mode of its return to the agenda of world politics has, it seems to me, hopelessly prejudiced the discussion on the subject. In the 1950s and 1960s, nationalism was still regarded as a feature of the victorious anticolonial struggles in Asia and Africa. But simultaneously, as the new institutional practices of economy and polity in the postcolonial states were disciplined and normalized under the conceptual rubrics of 'development' and 'modernization', nationalism was already being relegated to the domain of the particular histories of this or that colonial empire. And in those specialized histories defined by the unprepossessing contents of colonial archives, the emancipatory aspects of nationalism were undermined by countless revelations of secret deals, manipulations, and the cynical pursuit of private interests. By the 1970s, nationalism had become a matter of ethnic politics, the reason why people in the Third World killed each other—sometimes in wars between regular armies, sometimes, more distressingly, in cruel and often protracted civil wars, and increasingly, it seemed, by technologically sophisticated and virtually unstoppable acts of terrorism. The leaders of the African struggles against colonialism and racism had spoiled their records by becoming heads of corrupt, fractious, and often brutal regimes; Gandhi had been appropriated by such marginal cults as pacifism and vegetarianism; and even Ho Chi Minh in his moment of glory was caught in the unyielding polarities of the Cold War. Nothing, it would seem, was left in the legacy of nationalism to make people in the Western world feel good about it.

This recent genealogy of the idea explains why nationalism is now viewed as a dark, elemental, unpredictable force of primordial nature threatening the orderly calm of civilized life. What had once been successfully relegated to the outer peripheries of the earth is now seen picking its way back towards Europe, through the long-forgotten provinces of the Habsburg, the Czarist, and the Ottoman empires. Like drugs, terrorism, and illegal immigration, it is one more product of the Third World that the West dislikes but is powerless to prohibit.

In light of the current discussions on the subject in the media, it is surprising to recall that not many years ago nationalism was generally considered one of Europe's most magnificent gifts to the rest of the world. It is also not often remembered today that the two greatest wars of the twentieth century, engulfing as they did virtually every part of the globe, were brought about by Europe's failure to manage its own ethnic nationalisms. Whether of the 'good' variety or the 'bad', nationalism was entirely a product of the political history of Europe. Notwithstanding the celebration of the various unifying tendencies in Europe today and of the political consensus in the West as a whole, there may be in the recent amnesia on the origins of nationalism more than a hint of anxiety about whether it has quite been tamed in the land of its birth.

In all this time, the 'area specialists', the historians of the colonial world, working their way cheerlessly through musty files of administrative reports and official correspondence in colonial archives in

London or Paris or Amsterdam, had of course never forgotten how nationalism arrived in the colonies. Everyone agreed that it was a European import; the debates in the 1960s and 1970s in the historiographies of Africa or India or Indonesia were about what had become of the idea and who was responsible for it. These debates between a new generation of nationalist historians and those whom they dubbed 'colonialists' were vigorous and often acrimonious, but they were largely confined to the specialized territories of 'area studies'; no one else took much notice of them.

Ten years ago, it was one such area specialist who managed to raise once more the question of the origin and spread of nationalism in the framework of a universal history. Benedict Anderson demonstrated with much subtlety and originality that nations were not the determinate products of given sociological conditions such as language or race or religion; they had been, in Europe and everywhere else in the world, imagined into existence.[1] He also described some of the major institutional forms through which this imagined community came to acquire concrete shape, especially the institutions of what he so ingeniously called 'print-capitalism'. He then argued that the historical experience of nationalism in Western Europe, in the Americas, and in Russia had supplied for all subsequent nationalisms a set of modular forms from which nationalist elites in Asia and Africa had chosen the ones they liked.

Anderson's book has been, I think, the most influential in the last few years in generating new theoretical ideas on nationalism, an influence that of course, it is needless to add, is confined almost exclusively to academic writings. Contrary to the largely uninformed exoticization of nationalism in the popular media in the West, the theoretical tendency represented by Anderson certainly attempts to treat the phenomenon as part of the universal history of the modern world.

~

I have one central objection to Anderson's argument. If nationalisms in the rest of the world have to choose their imagined community from certain 'modular' forms already made available to them by Europe

---

[1] Benedict Anderson, *Imagined Communities: Reflections on the Origin and Spread of Nationalism* (London: Verso, 1983).

and the Americas, what do they have left to imagine? History, it would seem, has decreed that we in the postcolonial world shall only be perpetual consumers of modernity. Europe and the Americas, the only true subjects of history, have thought out on our behalf not only the script of colonial enlightenment and exploitation, but also that of our anticolonial resistance and postcolonial misery. Even our imaginations must remain forever colonized.

I object to this argument not for any sentimental reason. I object because I cannot reconcile it with the evidence on anticolonial nationalism. The most powerful as well as the most creative results of the nationalist imagination in Asia and Africa are posited not on an identity but rather on a *difference* with the 'modular' forms of the national society propagated by the modern West. How can we ignore this without reducing the experience of anticolonial nationalism to a caricature of itself?

To be fair to Anderson, it must be said that he alone is not to blame. The difficulty, I am now convinced, arises because we have all taken the claims of nationalism to be a *political* movement much too literally and much too seriously.

In India, for instance, any standard nationalist history will tell us that nationalism proper began in 1885 with the formation of the Indian National Congress. It might also tell us that the decade preceding this was a period of preparation, when several provincial political associations were formed. Prior to that, from the 1820s to the 1870s, was the period of 'social reform', when colonial enlightenment was beginning to 'modernize' the customs and institutions of a traditional society and the political spirit was still very much that of collaboration with the colonial regime: nationalism had still not emerged. This history, when submitted to a sophisticated sociological analysis, cannot but converge with Anderson's formulations. In fact, since it seeks to replicate in its own history the history of the modern state in Europe, nationalism's self-representation will inevitably corroborate Anderson's decoding of the nationalist myth. I think, however, that as history, nationalism's autobiography is fundamentally flawed.

By my reading, anticolonial nationalism creates its own domain of sovereignty within colonial society well before it begins its political battle with the imperial power. It does this by dividing the world of social institutions and practices into two domains—the material and the spiritual. The material is the domain of the 'outside', of the economy and of statecraft, of science and technology, a domain where the

West had proved its superiority and the East had succumbed. In this domain, then, Western superiority had to be acknowledged and its accomplishments carefully studied and replicated. The spiritual, on the other hand, is an 'inner' domain bearing the 'essential' marks of cultural identity. The greater one's success in imitating Western skills in the material domain, therefore, the greater the need to preserve the distinctness of one's spiritual culture. This formula is, I think, a fundamental feature of anticolonial nationalisms in Asia and Africa.[2]

There are several implications. First, nationalism declares the domain of the spiritual its sovereign territory and refuses to allow the colonial power to intervene in that domain. If I may return to the Indian example, the period of 'social reform' was actually made up of two distinct phases. In the earlier phase, Indian reformers looked to the colonial authorities to bring about by state action the reform of traditional institutions and customs. In the latter phase, although the need for change was not disputed, there was a strong resistance to allowing the colonial state to intervene in matters affecting 'national culture'. The second phase, in my argument, was already the period of nationalism.

The colonial state, in other words, is kept out of the 'inner' domain of national culture; but it is not as though this so-called spiritual domain is left unchanged. In fact, here nationalism launches its most powerful, creative, and historically significant project: to fashion a 'modern' national culture that is nevertheless not Western. If the nation is an imagined community, then this is where it is brought into being. In this, its true and essential domain, the nation is already sovereign, even when the state is in the hands of the colonial power. The dynamics of this historical project is completely missed in conventional histories in which the story of nationalism begins with the contest for political power.

In order to define my main argument, let me anticipate a few points that will be discussed more elaborately later. I wish to highlight here several areas within the so-called spiritual domain that nationalism transforms in the course of its journey. I will confine my illustrations to Bengal, with whose history I am most familiar.

---

[2] This is a central argument of my book *Nationalist Thought and the Colonial World: A Derivative Discourse?* (London: Zed Books, 1986).

The first such area is that of language. Anderson is entirely correct in his suggestion that it is 'print-capitalism' which provides the new institutional space for the development of the modern 'national' language.[3] However, the specificities of the colonial situation do not allow a simple transposition of European patterns of development. In Bengal, for instance, it is at the initiative of the East India Company and the European missionaries that the first printed books are produced in Bengali at the end of the eighteenth century and the first narrative prose compositions commissioned at the beginning of the nineteenth. At the same time, the first half of the nineteenth century is when English completely displaces Persian as the language of bureaucracy and emerges as the most powerful vehicle of intellectual influence on a new Bengali elite. The crucial moment in the development of the modern Bengali language comes, however, in mid-century, when this bilingual elite makes it a cultural project to provide its mother tongue with the necessary linguistic equipment to enable it to become an adequate language for 'modern' culture. An entire institutional network of printing presses, publishing houses, newspapers, magazines, and literary societies is created around this time, *outside* the purview of the state and the European missionaries, through which the new language, modern and standardized, is given shape. The bilingual intelligentsia came to think of its own language as belonging to that inner domain of cultural identity, from which the colonial intruder had to be kept out; language therefore became a zone over which the nation first had to declare its sovereignty and then transform in order to make it adequate for the modern world.

Here the modular influences of modern European languages and literatures did not necessarily produce similar consequences. In the case of the new literary genres and aesthetic conventions, for instance, whereas European influences undoubtedly shaped explicit critical discourse, it was also widely believed that European conventions were inappropriate and misleading in judging literary productions in modern Bengali. To this day there is a clear hiatus in this area between the terms of academic criticism and those of literary practice. To give an example, let me briefly discuss Bengali drama.

Drama is the one modern literary genre that is the least commended on aesthetic grounds by critics of Bengali literature. Yet it is the form

---

[3] Anderson, *Imagined Communities*, pp. 17–49.

in which the bilingual elite has found its largest audience. When it appeared in its modern form in the middle of the nineteenth century, the new Bengali drama had two models available to it: one, the modern European drama as it had developed since Shakespeare and Molière, and two, the virtually forgotten corpus of Sanskrit drama, now restored to a reputation of classical excellence because of the praises showered on it by Orientalist scholars from Europe. The literary criteria that would presumably direct the new drama into the privileged domain of a modern national culture were therefore clearly set by modular forms provided by Europe. But the performative practices of the new institution of the public theatre made it impossible for those criteria to be applied to plays written for the theatre. The conventions that would enable a play to succeed on the Calcutta stage were very different from the conventions approved by critics schooled in the traditions of European drama. The tensions have not been resolved to this day. What thrives as mainstream public theatre in West Bengal or Bangladesh today is modern urban theatre, national and clearly distinguishable from 'folk theatre'. It is produced and largely patronized by the literate urban middle classes. Yet their aesthetic conventions fail to meet the standards set by the modular literary forms adopted from Europe.

Even in the case of the novel, that celebrated artifice of the nationalist imagination in which the community is made to live and love in 'homogeneous time',[4] the modular forms do not necessarily have an easy passage. The novel was a principal form through which the bilingual elite in Bengal fashioned a new narrative prose. In the devising of this prose, the influence of the two available models—modern English and classical Sanskrit—was obvious. And yet, as the practice of the form gained greater popularity, it was remarkable how frequently in the course of their narrative Bengali novelists shifted from the disciplined forms of authorial prose to the direct recording of living speech. Looking at the pages of some of the most popular novels in Bengali, it is often difficult to tell whether one is reading a novel or a play. Having created a modern prose language in the fashion of the approved modular forms, the literati, in its search for artistic truthfulness, apparently found it necessary to escape as often as possible the rigidities of that prose.

[4] Ibid., pp. 28–40.

The desire to construct an aesthetic form that was modern and national, and yet recognizably different from the Western, was shown in perhaps its most exaggerated shape in the efforts in the early twentieth century of the so-called Bengal school of art. It was through these efforts that, on the one hand, an institutional space was created for the modern professional artist in India—as distinct from the traditional craftsman—for the dissemination through exhibition and print of the products of art and for the creation of a public schooled in the new aesthetic norms. Yet this agenda for the construction of a modernized artistic space was accompanied, on the other hand, by a fervent ideological program for an art that was distinctly 'Indian', that is, different from the 'Western'.[5] Although the specific style developed by the Bengal school for a new Indian art failed to hold its ground for very long, the fundamental agenda posed by its efforts continues to be pursued to this day, namely, to develop an art that would be modern and at the same time recognizably Indian.

Alongside the institutions of print-capitalism was created a new network of secondary schools. Once again, nationalism sought to bring this area under its jurisdiction long before the domain of the state had become a matter of contention. In Bengal, from the second half of the nineteenth century, it was the new elite that took the lead in mobilizing a 'national' effort to start schools in every part of the province and then to produce a suitable educational literature. Coupled with print-capitalism, the institutions of secondary education provided the space where the new language and literature were both generalized and normalized—outside the domain of the state. It was only when this space was opened up, outside the influence of both the colonial state and the European missionaries, that it became legitimate for women, for instance, to be sent to school. It was also in this period, from around the turn of the century, that the University of Calcutta was turned from an institution of colonial education to a distinctly national institution, in its curriculum, its faculty, and its sources of funding.[6]

[5] The history of this artistic movement has recently been studied in detail by Tapati Guha-Thakurta, *The Making of a New 'Indian' Art: Artists, Aesthetics and Nationalism in Bengal, 1850–1920* (Cambridge: Cambridge University Press, 1992).

[6] See Anilchandra Banerjee, 'Years of Consolidation: 1883–1904'; Tripurari Chakravarti, 'The University and the Government: 1904–24'; and Pramathanath

Another area in that inner domain of national culture was the family. The assertion here of autonomy and difference was perhaps the most dramatic. The European criticism of Indian 'tradition' as barbaric had focused to a large extent on religious beliefs and practices, especially those relating to the treatment of women. The early phase of 'social reform' through the agency of the colonial power had also concentrated on the same issues. In that early phase, therefore, this area had been identified as essential to 'Indian tradition'. The nationalist move began by disputing the choice of agency. Unlike the early reformers, nationalists were not prepared to allow the colonial state to legislate the reform of 'traditional' society. They asserted that only the nation itself could have the right to intervene in such an essential aspect of its cultural identity.

As it happened, the domain of the family and the position of women underwent considerable change in the world of the nationalist middle class. It was undoubtedly a new patriarchy that was brought into existence, different from the 'traditional' order but also explicitly claiming to be different from the 'Western' family. The 'new woman' was to be modern, but she would also have to display the signs of national tradition and therefore would be essentially different from the 'Western' woman.

The history of nationalism as a political movement tends to focus primarily on its contest with the colonial power in the domain of the outside, that is, the material domain of the state. This is a different history from the one I have outlined. It is also a history in which nationalism has no option but to choose its forms from the gallery of 'models' offered by European and American nation-states: 'difference' is not a viable criterion in the domain of the material.

In this outer domain, nationalism begins its journey (after, let us remember, it has already proclaimed its sovereignty in the inner domain) by inserting itself into a new public sphere constituted by the processes and forms of the modern (in this case, colonial) state. In the

Banerjee, 'Reform and Reorganization 1904–24', in Niharranjan Ray and Pratulchandra Gupta, eds, *Hundred Years of the University of Calcutta* (Calcutta: University of Calcutta, 1957), pp.129–78, 179–210, and 211–318.

beginning, nationalism's task is to overcome the subordination of the colonized middle class, that is, to challenge the 'rule of colonial difference' in the domain of the state. The colonial state, we must remember, was not just the agency that brought the modular forms of the modern state to the colonies; it was also an agency that was destined never to fulfil the normalizing mission of the modern state because the premise of its power was a rule of colonial difference, namely, the preservation of the alienness of the ruling group.

As the institutions of the modern state were elaborated in the colony, especially in the second half of the nineteenth century, the ruling European groups found it necessary to lay down—in lawmaking, in the bureaucracy, in the administration of justice, and in the recognition by the state of a legitimate domain of public opinion—the precise difference between the rulers and the ruled. If Indians had to be admitted into the judiciary, could they be allowed to try Europeans? Was it right that Indians should enter the civil service by taking the same examinations as British graduates? If European newspapers in India were given the right of free speech, could the same apply to native newspapers? Ironically, it became the historical task of nationalism, which insisted on its own marks of cultural difference with the West, to demand that there be no rule of difference in the domain of the state.

In time, with the growing strength of nationalist politics, this domain became more extensive and internally differentiated and finally took on the form of the national, that is, postcolonial, state. The dominant elements of its self-definition, at least in postcolonial India, were drawn from the ideology of the modern liberal-democratic state.

In accordance with liberal ideology, the public was now distinguished from the domain of the private. The state was required to protect the inviolability of the private self in relation to other private selves. The legitimacy of the state in carrying out this function was to be guaranteed by its indifference to concrete differences between private selves—differences, that is, of race, language, religion, class, caste, and so forth.

The trouble was that the moral-intellectual leadership of the nationalist elite operated in a field constituted by a very different set of distinctions—those between the spiritual and the material, the inner and the outer, the essential and the inessential. That contested field over which nationalism had proclaimed its sovereignty and where it had imagined its true community was neither coextensive with nor coincidental to the field constituted by the public/private distinction.

In the former field, the hegemonic project of nationalism could hardly make the distinctions of language, religion, caste, or class a matter of indifference to itself. The project was that of cultural 'normalization', like, as Anderson suggests, bourgeois hegemonic projects everywhere, but with the all-important difference that it had to choose its site of autonomy from a position of subordination to a colonial regime that had on its side the most universalist justificatory resources produced by post-Enlightenment social thought.

The result is that autonomous forms of imagination of the community were, and continue to be, overwhelmed and swamped by the history of the postcolonial state. Here lies the root of our postcolonial misery: not in our inability to think out new forms of the modern community but in our surrender to the old forms of the modern state. If the nation is an imagined community and if nations must also take the form of states, then our theoretical language must allow us to talk about community and state at the same time. I do not think our present theoretical language allows us to do this.

Writing just before his death, Bipinchandra Pal (1858–1932), the fiery leader of the Swadeshi movement in Bengal and a principal figure in the pre-Gandhian Congress, described the boarding houses in which students lived in the Calcutta of his youth:

> Students' messes in Calcutta, in my college days, fifty-six years ago, were like small republics and were managed on strictly democratic lines. Everything was decided by the voice of the majority of the members of the mess. At the end of every month a manager was elected by the whole 'House', so to say, and he was charged with the collection of the dues of the members, and the general supervision of the food and establishment of the mess. . . . A successful manager was frequently begged to accept re-election; while the more careless and lazy members, who had often to payout of their own pockets for their mismanagement, tried to avoid this honour.
>
> . . . Disputes between one member and another were settled by a 'Court' of the whole 'House'; and we sat night after night, I remember, in examining these cases; and never was the decision of this 'Court' questioned or disobeyed by any member. Nor were the members of the mess at all helpless in the matter of duly enforcing their verdict upon an offending

colleague. For they could always threaten the recalcitrant member either with expulsion from the mess, or if he refused to go, with the entire responsibility of the rent being thrown on him. . . . And such was the force of public opinion in these small republics that I have known of cases of this punishment on offending members, which so worked upon him that after a week of their expulsion from a mess, they looked as if they had just come out of some prolonged or serious spell of sickness. . . .

The composition of our mess called for some sort of a compromise between the so-called orthodox and the Brahmo and other heterodox members of our republic. So a rule was passed by the unanimous vote of the whole 'House', that no member should bring any food to the house . . . which outraged the feelings of Hindu orthodoxy. It was however clearly understood that the members of the mess, as a body and even individually, would not interfere with what anyone took outside the house. So we were free to go and have all sorts of forbidden food either at the Great Eastern Hotel, which some of us commenced to occasionally patronise later on, or anywhere else.[7]

The interesting point in this description is not so much the exaggerated and obviously romanticized portrayal in miniature of the imagined political form of the self-governing nation, but rather the repeated use of the institutional terms of modern European civic and political life (republic, democracy, majority, unanimity, election, House, Court, and so on) to describe a set of activities that had to be performed on material utterly incongruous with that civil society. The question of a 'compromise' on the food habits of members is really settled not on a principle of demarcating the 'private' from the 'public' but of separating the domains of the 'inside' and the 'outside', the inside being a space where 'unanimity' had to prevail, while the outside was a realm of individual freedom. Notwithstanding the 'unanimous vote of the whole House', the force that determined the unanimity in the inner domain was not the voting procedure decided upon by individual members coming together in a body but rather the consensus of a community—institutionally novel (because, after all, the Calcutta boarding house was unprecedented in 'tradition'), internally differentiated, but nevertheless a community whose claims preceded those of its individual members.

[7] Bipinchandra Pal, *Memories of My Life and Times* (1932; rpnt. Calcutta: Bipinchandra Pal Institute, 1973), pp. 157–60.

But Bipinchandra's use of the terms of parliamentary procedure to describe the 'communitarian' activities of a boarding house standing in place of the nation must not be dismissed as a mere anomaly. His language is indicative of the very real imbrication of two discourses, and correspondingly of two domains, of politics. The attempt has been made in recent Indian historiography to talk of these as the domains of 'elite' and 'subaltern' politics.[8] But one of the important results of this historiographical approach has been precisely the demonstration that each domain has not only acted in opposition to and as a limit upon the other but, through this process of struggle, has also shaped the emergent form of the other. Thus, the presence of populist or communitarian elements in the liberal constitutional order of the postcolonial state ought not to be read as a sign of the inauthenticity or disingenuousness of elite politics; it is rather a recognition in the elite domain of the very real presence of an arena of subaltern politics over which it must dominate and yet which also had to be negotiated on its own terms for the purposes of producing consent. On the other hand, the domain of subaltern politics has increasingly become familiar with, and even adapted itself to, the institutional forms characteristic of the elite domain. The point, therefore, is no longer one of simply demarcating and identifying the two domains in their separateness, which is what was required in order first to break down the totalizing claims of a nationalist historiography. Now the task is to trace in their mutually conditioned historicities the specific forms that have appeared, on the one hand, in the domain defined by the hegemonic project of nationalist modernity, and on the other, in the numerous fragmented resistances to that normalizing project.

This is the exercise I wish to carry out. Since the problem will be directly posed of the limits to the supposed universality of the modern regime of power and with it of the post-Enlightenment disciplines of knowledge, it might appear as though the exercise is meant to emphasize once more an 'Indian' (or an 'Oriental') exceptionalism. In fact, however, the objective of my exercise is rather more complicated, and considerably more ambitious. It includes not only an identification of

---

[8] Represented by the various essays in Ranajit Guha, ed., *Subaltern Studies*, vols I–VI (Delhi: Oxford University Press, 1982–90). The programmatic statement of this approach is in Ranajit Guha, 'On Some Aspects of the Historiography of Colonial India', in Guha, ed., *Subaltern Studies I* (Delhi: Oxford University Press, 1982), pp. 1–8.

the discursive conditions that make such theories of Indian exceptionalism possible, but also a demonstration that the alleged exceptions
actually inhere as forcibly suppressed elements even in the supposedly
universal forms of the modern regime of power.

The latter demonstration enables us to make the argument that the
universalist claims of modern Western social philosophy are themselves
limited by the contingencies of global power. In other words, 'Western
universalism' no less than' Oriental exceptionalism' can be shown to be
only a particular form of a richer, more diverse, and differentiated
conceptualization of a new universal idea. This might allow us the
possibility not only to think of new forms of the modern community, which, as I argue, the nationalist experience in Asia and Africa has
done from its birth, but, much more decisively, to think of new forms
of the modern state.

The project then is to claim for us, the once-colonized, our freedom
of imagination. Claims, we know only too well, can be made only as
contestations in a field of power. To make a claim on behalf of the
fragment is also, not surprisingly, to produce a discourse that is itself
fragmentary. It is redundant to make apologies for this.

2

The Constitution of Indian Nationalist Discourse

(1987)

On the Autonomy of Nationalist Discourse

Antonio Gramsci's writings have prompted some Indian Marxist scholars to reconceptualize the relation between nationalism and capitalism in India. Following Marx's ideas on the relationship between base and superstructure, his view of the state as 'coercion plus hegemony', and of the struggle for power as the struggle for 'domination plus intellectual-moral leadership', these Indian Marxists have examined afresh the so-called 'renaissance' in nineteenth-century India in terms of the aspirations of a new class to assert its intellectual-moral leadership over a modernizing Indian nation and stake its claim to power in opposition to its colonial masters.[1] It has been demonstrated that under the specific conditions of the economy and polity of a colonial country, this domination necessarily rests on extremely fragile foundations and that the intellectual-moral leadership of the dominant classes over the new nation remains fragmented.

[1] See the contributions of Sumit Sarkar, Asok Sen, Barun De, and Pradyumna Bhattacharya in V.C. Joshi, ed., *Rammohun Roy and the Process of Modernization in India* (Delhi: Vikas, 1975). See also Sumit Sarkar, 'The Complexities of Young Bengal', *Nineteenth Century Studies*, vol. 4 (1973), pp. 504–34; Barun De, 'A Historiographical Critique of Renaissance Analogues for Nineteenth Century India', in B. De, ed., *Perspectives in the Social Sciences I: Historical Dimensions* (Calcutta: Oxford University Press, 1977); Asok Sen, *Iswar Chandra Vidyasagar and His Elusive Milestones* (Calcutta: Riddhi-India, 1977); Ranajit Guha, '*Neel Darpan:* The Image of a Peasant Revolt in a Liberal Mirror', *Journal of Peasant Studies*, vol. 2, no. 1 (October 1974).

Gramsci's writings help us to clarify and explain the apparently deviant cases of the formation of capitalist nation-states. In his famous 'Notes on Italian History',[2] he outlines an argument about the 'passive revolution of capital'. Contrasting the history of the formation of the Italian state in the period of the Risorgimento with the classic political revolution in France in 1789, Gramsci says that the new claimants to power in Italy, lacking the social strength to launch a full-scale political assault on the old dominant classes, opted for a path in which the demands of a new society would be 'satisfied by small doses, legally, in a reformist manner—in such a way that it was possible to preserve the political and economic position of the old feudal classes, to avoid agrarian reforms, and, especially, to avoid the popular masses going through a period of political experience such as occurred in France in the years of Jacobinism.' Thus, in situations where an emergent bourgeoisie lacks the social conditions for establishing complete hegemony over the new nation, it resorts to a 'passive revolution' by attempting a 'molecular transformation' of the old dominant classes into partners in a new historical bloc and only a partial appropriation of the popular masses, in order first to create a state as the necessary precondition for the establishment of capitalism as the dominant mode of production.

Gramsci's ideas provide only a general, and somewhat obscurely stated, formulation of this problem. To sharpen it, one must examine several historical cases of 'passive revolutions' in their economic, political, and ideological aspects. On the face of it, the Indian case seems a particularly good example, but the examination of modern Indian history in terms of this problematic has only just begun. What I propose to outline here is an analytical framework in which the ideological history of the Indian state can be studied. The framework attempts to locate, within a historical context of 'passive revolution', the problem of the autonomy of nationalist discourse as a discourse of power.

Nationalist texts were addressed both to 'the people' who were said to constitute the nation and to the colonial masters whose claim to rule nationalism questioned. To both, nationalism sought to demonstrate the falsity of the colonial claim that the backward peoples were culturally incapable of ruling themselves in the conditions of the modern

---

[2] Antonio Gramsci, *Selections from the Prison Notebooks*, trans. Q. Hoare and G. Nowell Smith (New York: International Publishers, 1971), pp. 44–120.

world. Nationalism denied the alleged inferiority of the colonized people; it also asserted that a backward nation could 'modernize' itself while retaining its cultural identity. It thus produced a discourse in which, even as it challenged the colonial claim to political domination, it accepted the very intellectual premises of 'modernity' on which colonial domination was based. This domination rested not just on military might or industrial strength, but on thought as well. Hence, we need to approach the field of discourse—historical, philosophical, and scientific—as a battleground of political power.

From such a perspective, the problem of nationalist thought becomes the particular manifestation of a much more general problem, namely, the problem of the bourgeois-rationalist conception of knowledge (established in the post-Enlightenment period of European intellectual history) as the moral and epistemic foundation of a supposedly universal framework of thought which perpetuates, in a real and not merely metaphorical sense, a *colonial* domination. It is a framework of knowledge which proclaims its own universality; its validity, it pronounces, is independent of cultures. Nationalist thought, in agreeing to become 'modern', accepts the claim to the universality of this 'modern' framework of knowledge. Yet it also asserts the autonomous identity of a national culture. It thus simultaneously rejects and accepts the dominance, both epistemic and moral, of an alien culture.

Indeed, if nationalism expresses itself in a frenzy of irrational passion, it does so *because* it seeks to represent itself in the image of the Enlightenment, and fails to do so. For Enlightenment itself, to assert its sovereignty as the universal ideal, needs its Other; if it could ever actualize itself in the real world as the truly universal, it would in fact destroy itself. No matter how much the liberal-rationalist may despair, the Cunning of Reason has not met its match in nationalism.[3] On the contrary, it has seduced, apprehended, and imprisoned it.

---

[3] 'Nationalism is the starkest political shame of the twentieth century. . . . The degree to which its prevalence is still felt as a scandal is itself a mark of the unexpectedness of this predominance, of the sharpness of the check which it has administered to Europe's admiring Enlightenment vision of the Cunning of Reason. In nationalism at last, or so it at present seems, the Cunning of Reason has more than met its match.' John Dunn, *Western Political Theory in the Face of the Future* (Cambridge: Cambridge University Press, 1979), p. 55.

The Thematic and the Problematic

In his book *Orientalism,* Edward W. Said has shown how the post-Enlightenment age in Europe produced an entire body of knowledge in which the Orient appeared as a 'system of representations framed by a whole set of forces that brought the Orient into Western learning, Western consciousness, and later, Western empire.'[4] As a style of thought, Orientalism is based upon an ontological and epistemological distinction made between 'the Orient' and (most of the time) 'the Occident'. On this basis, an 'enormously systematic discipline' was created 'by which European culture was able to manage—and even produce—the Orient politically, sociologically, militarily, ideologically, scientifically, and imaginatively during the post-Enlightenment period.' Orientalism *created* the Oriental; it was a body of knowledge in which the Oriental was '*contained* and *represented* by dominating frameworks' and Western power over the Orient was given the 'status of scientific truth'. Thus, Orientalism was 'a kind of Western projection on to and will to govern over the Orient.'

In so characterizing this Western 'dominating framework' of knowledge, Said has relied on the important distinction, drawn by Anouar Abdel-Malek, between the *problematic* and the *thematic* of Orientalism.[5] Relying, presumably, on the distinction between the *problématique* and the *thématique* (or *thétique)* as it has been used in post-War French philosophy, especially in the phenomenological writings of Jean-Paul Sartre or Maurice Merleau-Ponty, Abdel-Malek maintains that there are 'levels' within the structure of a body of knowledge. This gives us a clue to the formulation of our problem here in which nationalist thought appears to oppose the dominating implications of post-Enlightenment European thought at one level (i.e. at the level of the problematic) and yet, at the same time, seems to accept that domination at another level (i.e. at the level of the thematic).

In a social ideology consciously formulated and expressed in terms of a formal theoretical discourse, we would distinguish that part which asserts the existence, and often the practical realizability, of certain historical possibilities from the part which seeks to justify those claims

---

[4] Edward W. Said, *Orientalism* (London: Routledge and Kegan Paul, 1978).

[5] Anouar Abdel-Malek, 'Orientalism in Crisis', *Diogenes,* vol. 44 (Winter 1963), pp. 102–40.

by an appeal to both epistemic and moral principles. That is, we wish to separate the claims of an ideology (i.e. its identification of historical possibilities and the practical or programmatic forms of its realization) from its justificatory structures (i.e. the nature of the evidence it presents in support of those claims, the rules of inference it relies on to logically relate a statement of the evidence to a structure of arguments, the set of epistemological principles it uses to demonstrate the existence of its claims as historical possibilities, and, finally, the set of ethical principles it appeals to in order to assert that those claims are morally justified). The former part of a social ideology we will call its *problematic* and the latter part its *thematic.* The thematic, in other words, refers to an epistemological as well as ethical system which provides a framework of elements and rules for establishing relations between elements; the problematic, on the other hand, consists of concrete statements about possibilities justified by reference to the thematic.

This distinction might seem analogous to the distinction in structural linguistics between *parole* and *langue,* where the latter refers to the language system shared by a given community of speakers while the former is the concrete speech act of individual speakers. It will also appear analogous to the distinction in the analytical philosophy of language between an understanding of meaning in terms of the subjective *intentions* that lie behind particular speech acts, and meaning as codified in linguistic *conventions.* It would be an interesting exercise in itself to explore some of these analogies with reference to the many recent debates concerning the validity and usefulness of these distinctions. For the moment, however, let me point out an important reason why our particular distinction between the thematic and the problematic must serve a purpose which the apparently analogous distinctions in other fields are not designed to serve.

Our study of the ideology of nationalism, and of the nature of the discourse which it produces, is intended to be a critical study. We will therefore wish to bring within the purview of our analysis the truth claims made within that discourse. We are not, in other words, interested simply in understanding the subjective intentions that lie behind the specific texts of specific nationalist writers, or even the larger structure of conventions understood by the community to which the text is addressed. We are also interested in exploring the meaning of nationalist texts in terms of their implicit or explicit reference to things (i.e. their logical and theoretical implications). That is, we must conduct our analysis not just at the level of language, but also at the level of *discourse*. And to do this, we cannot prejudge the issue by declaring that since this discourse is only a product of ideology, its content must be purely tautological and thus unworthy of being studied as content. We will, in fact, argue that it is precisely because nationalist discourse has recourse, whether implicitly or explicitly, to a *cognitive* system which refers to things in quite a specific way that the possibility is opened for a creative play between the problematic and the thematic, for critical points to emerge which can lead to a reformulation of the problematic and then, in turn, to a critical reconsideration of the thematic itself. This would obviate, at least in principle, the difficulties of understanding a particular thinker either solely as the author of a text or solely as the representative voice of a particular historical context. It also gives us, the analysts of discourse, the opportunity to situate ourselves as self-conscious participants in that very process of evolving a discourse, a constant elaboration of the tension between the problematic and the thematic until it produces the critical conditions for superseding the terms of the discourse.

With that brief explication of our terms, let us return to the subject of Orientalism, and its relation to nationalist thought. When one turns from European knowledge of the Orient to nationalist thinking in the East in the nineteenth and twentieth centuries, what stares one in the face is the profound manner in which nationalist thought is itself shaped, indeed contained, by the same dominating framework—the framework of Orientalism. Of course, nationalism in colonial countries is premised on opposition to alien rule, in this case rule by a Western power. But it is vitally important to emphasize that this opposition occurs within a body of knowledge about the East (large parts of it purporting to be scientific) which has the same representational structure and shares the same theoretical framework as Orientalism.

We find, in fact, that the problematic in nationalist thought is exactly the reverse of that in Orientalism. That is, the 'object' in nationalist thought is still the Oriental, who retains the essentialist character depicted in Orientalist discourse. Only he is not passive, non-participating. He is seen to possess a 'subjectivity' which he can himself 'make'. In other words, while his relationships to himself and to others have been 'posed, understood and defined' by others (i.e. by an objective scientific consciousness, by knowledge, by reason), those relationships are *not* acted by others. His subjectivity, he thinks, is active, autonomous, and sovereign.

At the level of the thematic, on the other hand, nationalist thought accepts and adopts the same essentialist conception based on the distinction between 'the East' and 'the West', the same typology, created by a transcendent studying subject, and hence the same 'objectifying' procedures of knowledge constructed in the post-Enlightenment age of Western science.

There is, consequently, an inherent contradiction in nationalist thinking because it reasons within a framework of knowledge whose representational structure corresponds to the very structure of power nationalist thought seeks to repudiate. It is this contradiction in the domain of thought which creates the possibility for several divergent solutions to be proposed for the nationalist problematic. Furthermore, it is this contradictoriness which signifies, in the domain of thought, the theoretical insolubility of the national question in a colonial country or, for that matter, of the extended problem of social transformation in a post-colonial country, within a strictly nationalist framework.

An analysis of nationalist thought which seeks to locate the specific site of that discourse will now require a critical point of view that is, in many ways, quite novel. A simple comparison with the historical models of transition in Europe will no longer be adequate, for this will always highlight the incompleteness, the fragmentation, indeed the inauthenticity of the transition in the non-Western world. This is precisely the point brought out both by the liberal debate about nationalism and by the Marxist debate on the 'Indian renaissance'. And yet, the need to undertake an analysis of nationalist thought not in terms of its *differences* with the paradigmatic European forms, but in its own constitutive terms, is perhaps emphasized more clearly than elsewhere in the case of India. The bourgeoisie in India has not achieved hegemony; there is no organic intelligentsia chiselling out the cultural edifice of the intellectual-moral leadership of a fundamental class. Nonetheless, there has clearly come into existence a specific political structure and process, and a complex and differentiated cultural formation through which this structure of domination is sought to be legitimised—and, it cannot be denied, with some measure of success.

To what extent does this historical experience accord with Gramsci's description of the 'passive revolution' as a process in which an emergent bourgeoisie, unable to overturn and destroy the old structures of dominance, prefers to create a state by constituting a historical bloc with the traditional classes, by sharing power with them in the new ruling structures, by avoiding a thoroughgoing transformation of the economic forms of production, by appropriating for themselves the claim to represent the national-popular will while distancing the popular masses from the direct political processes of the state, and finally by succeeding in getting the traditional intelligentsia to perform many of the organic functions required for the creation of an admittedly fragmented intellectual-moral leadership over the nation? A detailed examination can hardly be attempted here. All I will do is set out, in the context of this problem, the three main steps in the historical constitution of a nationalist discourse in India. I will, in fact, be summarizing an argument that has been elaborated in a longer study;[6] the account here will therefore be extremely sketchy and somewhat schematic. The three steps may be called the moment of departure, the moment of manoeuvre, and the moment of arrival. I illustrate these moments by reference, respectively, to the writings of Bankimchandra, Gandhi, and Nehru.

The Moment of Departure

The moment of departure lies in the encounter of a rationalist consciousness with the framework of knowledge created by Orientalism. Colonialism asserted that the culture of the Indian people, though ancient, was incompatible with the requirements of power in the modern world. It was a culture which assigned the greatest social virtue to what were essentially other-worldly values. Early nationalist consciousness, through its encounter with post-Enlightenment European knowledge, came to accept this rationalist critique of traditional Indian culture. Bankimchandra Chattopadhyay (1838–94), for instance, located the primary cause of India's subjection in the emphasis on *vairagya* which characterized the overwhelming part of religious beliefs in India. Indeed, Bankim's argument proceeded from the acceptance of this essential cultural difference between East and West: modern European culture possessed certain attributes which made the European culturally equipped for power and progress, while the Indian, lacking these attributes, was doomed to poverty and subjection. Thus, Bankim undertook the same classificatory project as the Orientalist, scrupulously following the rationalist methods laid down by the Great Science of Society of

[6] Partha Chatterjee, *Nationalist Thought and the Colonial World* (Delhi: Oxford University Press; London: Zed Books, 1986).

which, to him, the greatest architects were Auguste Comte, John Stuart Mill, and Herbert Spencer. He arrived at precisely the same typologies under which the Oriental was stamped with an essentialist character signifying in every aspect his difference from modern Western man.

But Bankim did not accept the immutability of this character. That is what made him a nationalist. There was, he argued, a subjectivity that could *will* a transformation of this culturally determined character. This was the national will, which could be summoned into existence by the nation acting collectively. The traditional culture of India, unsuited to the requirements of power in the modern world, could be transformed by a modern intelligentsia. How? An obvious answer was by imitating the West, by adopting all the modern attributes of European culture. But then, how would Indian culture still remain Indian? Would it not lose those very marks of national identity which make Indian culture essentially different from Western culture? Bankim's answer to this question is characteristic of nationalist discourse at its moment of departure. It is an answer that can be found within the thematic and problematic of nationalist thought. It does no violence to its theoretical framework where the thematic of Orientalism is dominant, while it still provides a specific subjectivity to the East in which it is active, autonomous, and undominated.

The superiority of the West was in the materiality of its culture. The West had achieved progress, prosperity, and freedom because it had placed reason at the heart of its culture. The distinctive culture of the West was its science, its technology, and its love of progress. But culture did not consist only of the material aspect of life. There was the spiritual aspect too, and here the European Enlightenment had little to contribute. In the spiritual aspect of culture, the East was superior—and, hence, undominated. This answer did not conflict in any way with the fundamental classificatory scheme of Orientalist thought. All it did was assert a cultural domain of superiority to the East, and, in time, it tied this assertion with the national struggle against Western political domination.

The nationalist project, therefore, was to build a new cultural ideal—the national religion, as Bankim called it—which was more complete and more perfect than the fundamentally agnostic, and hence strictly materialistic, Western concept of culture. The task was indeed 'to unite European industries with Indian *dharma*'. That would be a cultural ideal which retained what was thought to be distinctively

Indian while subsuming what was valuable in the culture of the West. The aim was to produce the complete and perfect man—learned, wise, agile, religious, and refined—a better man than the merely efficient and prosperous Westerner.

But, once again, the striking fact here is not so much the distinction between the material and the spiritual domains of culture. What is remarkable is that Bankim defends this distinction on the most thoroughly rationalist grounds afforded by nineteenth-century European philosophy: the positivist critique of Christianity, Darwin's theory of evolution, Kantian epistemology. All of these are summoned to prove the inadequacy of modern European religion as a 'complete system of culture' and the superiority of a pure Indian dharma as a philosophy of modern man.

Bankim's concept of dharma attempts to reconcile a philosophy of spirit with a rational doctrine of power. In the process, the interplay between the thematic and the problematic of nationalist thought results in a curious transposition of the supposed relation between a puritan ethic and the rationalization of social life in the modern age. Bankim's nationalism leads him to the claim that a purified and regenerated Hindu ideal is far superior as a rational philosophy of life than anything that Western religion or philosophy has to offer.

We have in Bankim a reversal of the Orientalist problematic, but within the same general thematic. It is only in this sense that nationalist thought is opposed to imperialist (Orientalist) thought. Bankim then seeks a specific subjectivity for the nation but within an essentialist typology of cultures in which this specificity can never be truly historical. Within the domain of thought thus defined, however, it seems a valid answer. The West has a superior culture, but only partially; spiritually, the East is superior. What is needed now is the cultivation of a cultural ideal in which the industries and the sciences of the West can be learnt and emulated while retaining the spiritual greatness of Eastern culture. This is the national-cultural project.

An elitism now becomes inescapable because the act of cultural synthesis can in fact be performed only by a supremely cultivated and refined intellect. It is a project of national-cultural regeneration in which the intelligentsia leads and the nation follows. The national-cultural ideal of the complete and perfect man was to be aspired for and approximated by practice, that is, *anusilana*. And it was not likely, as Bankim himself acknowledged, that large masses of people would reach this perfection.

Further, this project could also not be realized through mere political reform. Bankim was an unsparing opponent of the principal form of elite nationalist politics of his times (namely, social reform through the medium of legislative institutions of the colonial state). This state was founded on a superiority of force; its *raison d'être* lay in the maintenance and extension of British imperial power. The original superiority of force was the product of a superior culture which shaped and directed the British national project in the world. To match and overcome that superiority, Indian society would have to undergo a similar transformation. And the key to this transformation must lie in a regeneration of national culture embodying, in fact, an unrivalled combination of material and spiritual values. To Bankim, therefore, the remedy for cultural backwardness was not reform but the total regeneration of a 'national religion'. Indeed, mere reform negates the nationalist problematic itself, for it assumes that the Oriental is non-autonomous, passive, historically non-active, indeed, for that very reason, ahistorical, and therefore ever in need to be acted upon by others. Bankim's doctrine of power was premised on a reversal of this historical relationship.

This elitism of the intelligentsia, rooted in the vision of a radical regeneration of national culture, did not find any viable political means to actualize itself in Bankim's time—the heyday of colonial rule. Indeed, the divergence between the modern and the national was not really resolved in Bankim in any historically specific way: the specificity of the modern and the specificity of the national remained distinct and opposed. The contradiction served as a basis for divergent political programmes in the early phase of nationalism. An emphasis on the modern meant arguing for a period of tutelage until the country had been sufficiently 'modernized'. This meant a continuation of colonial rule, a sharing of power between colonial officials and a modernized elite, and an emphasis on state action to reform traditional institutions and bring into being modern ones. On the other hand, an emphasis on the distinctively national elements of culture has meant the growth of revivalist or fundamentalist cultural movements, usually of a religious-communal type. Both possibilities are inherent in Bankim's unresolved problem.

The Moment of Manoeuvre

This narrow elitism of the intelligentsia could hardly resolve the central problem of nationalist politics in a large agrarian country under colonial rule. To represent the nation as a political entity within a colonial state process which clearly possessed considerable resources to broaden its bases of legitimacy by intervening directly in the agrarian class struggle, it was necessary above all to take nationalist politics to the peasantry. Without this, an emergent Indian bourgeoisie could never hope to pose an adequate challenge to colonial rule. Similarly, without devising suitable ways of establishing an intellectual-moral leadership over the vast masses of the peasantry, the organic functions of the new intelligentsia in building a national consensus for self-government was doomed to failure.

role of peasantry

The problem, however, lay precisely in the insurmountable difficulty of reconciling the modes of thought characteristic of a peasant consciousness with the rationalist forms of an 'enlightened' nationalist politics. Either peasant consciousness would have to be transformed, or else it would have to be appropriated. The former would require a total transformation of the agrarian economy, the abolition of pre-capitalist forms of production, and the virtual dissolution of the peasantry as a distinct form of the social existence of labour. Given the conditions of the colonial economy even in the early twentieth century, this would hardly seem a viable political possibility. The other possibility, then, was an appropriation of peasant support for the historic cause of creating a nation-state in which the peasant masses would be represented, but of which they would not be a constituent part. In other words, passive revolution.

This is where the moment of manoeuvre occurs. To understand the significance of this moment in the historical constitution of a nationalist discourse, we must extricate the problem from questions of subjective motivations, influences, manipulations, who used whom to gain what, etc. Those are valid historical questions, but they lie at an entirely different analytical level. It is at this moment of manoeuvre—this critical moment in the task of constituting a historical bloc to achieve a 'passive revolution of capital' in India—that we examine the significance of the Gandhian intervention in Indian politics.

Gandhi's intervention occurs from a position which rejects both the problematic and the thematic of nationalism. His fundamental text, *Hind Swaraj*, is not concerned with the question of how India can become modern while retaining its essential cultural identity. It proceeds by rejecting modernity itself and all the claims made on its behalf. *Hind Swaraj* is an attack on every constituent aspect of modern bourgeois society: its continually expanding and prosperous economic life, based on individual property, the social division of labour, and the impersonal laws of the market; its political institutions based on a dual notion of sovereignty in which the people in theory rule themselves, but are only allowed to do so through the medium of their representatives; its spirit of innovation, adventure, and scientific progress; its rationalization of philosophy and ethics and secularization of art and education.

In demonstrating the fundamental immorality of 'modern civilization', Gandhi does not resort to the conceptual frameworks or the modes of reasoning and inference adopted by the nationalists of his day. In fact, he quite emphatically rejects their rationalism, scientism, and historicism. Not only that, his critique of modernity, though overtly directed against the modern civilization of the West, is not, like Bankim's, an attempt to establish the essential inferiority of Western culture. In fact, Gandhi's charge against the West is not that its religion is inferior, but that by wholeheartedly embracing the doubtful virtues of modern civilization it had forgotten the true teachings of the Christian faith. Not only does Gandhi reject the thematic of nationalism, in *Hind Swaraj* he is not operating with its problematic either.

Politically, Gandhi counterposed against the nationalist conception of representative government an undivided concept of popular sovereignty, where the community is self-regulating and political power is dissolved into the collective moral will. In its form, this political ideal is not meant to be a consensual democracy with complete and continual participation by every member of the polity. The utopia is Ramarajya, a patriarchy in which the ruler, by his moral quality and habitual obedience to truth, always expresses the collective will. It is also a utopia in which the economic organization of production, arranged according to a perfect fourfold varna scheme of specialization and a perfect system of reciprocity in the exchange of commodities and services, always ensures that there is no spirit of competition and no difference in status between different kinds of labour. The ideal conception of Ramarajya, in fact, encapsulates the critique of all that is morally reprehensible in the economic and political organization of civil society.

From this basis, the Gandhian intervention in Indian politics is built around the central concept of satyagraha. Satyagraha is not mere passive resistance. It means intense political activity by large masses of people. It was a legitimate, moral, and truthful form of political resistance to unjust rule. It was not aimed at the destruction of the state, nor was it—as yet—conceived as part of a political process intended to replace the functionaries of the state. To use a Gramscian phrase, we could say that satyagraha expressed a purely 'negative consciousness'. It articulated that aspect of peasant consciousness which, at moments of insurgency, seeks to negate the signs of domination.[7] It is therefore easy to recognize why it could express so effectively the characteristic modes of peasant-communal resistance to oppressive state authority.

But this is not where the Gandhian intervention ended. It was also very much an intervention in the elite nationalist politics of his time. Historically, it was as a consequence of Gandhi's intervention in the Indian National Congress that nationalist politics was taken to the masses and, reciprocally, the masses brought into nationalist politics. This presents a great historical paradox. How could a text which rejected the very problematic as well as the thematic of nationalism become part of a nationalist discourse? How could the Gandhian ideology become a nationalism—a nationalism which stood upon a critique of the very idea of civil society, a movement supported by the bourgeoisie which rejected the idea of progress, the ideology of a political organization fighting for the creation of a modern national state which accepted at the same time the ideal of an 'enlightened anarchy'?

Clearly, there are many contradictory aspects to Gandhism, and a large measure of ambiguity in its meaning. The moment of manoeuvre must be understood by identifying that terrain of ambiguity. The concept of *ahimsa* is crucial in the attempt to reconcile the 'negative' notion of satyagraha with the requirements of a nationalist politics. Ahimsa was not so much about resistance as the modalities of resistance, about organizational principles, rules of conduct, strategies, and tactics. Ahimsa was the necessary complement to the concept of satyagraha which both limited and, at the same time, made it something more than 'purely and simply civil disobedience'. Ahimsa was the rule for concretizing the 'truth' of satyagraha.

Ahimsa indeed was the concept —both ethical and epistemological because it was defined within a moral and epistemic practice that was wholly 'experimental'—which supplied Gandhism with a theory

[7] For a detailed discussion on this, see Ranajit Guha, *Elementary Aspects of Peasant Insurgency in Colonial India* (Delhi: Oxford University Press, 1983).

of politics, enabling it to become the ideology of a national political movement. It was the moral framework for solving every *practical* problem of the organized political movement. Consequently, it dealt with questions such as the requirements for being a political satyagrahi, his rules of conduct, his relations with the political leadership as well as with the masses, questions about the structure of decision-making, lines of command, political strategies and tactics, and about the practical issues of breaking as well as obeying the laws of the state.

The political employment of ahimsa did not depend upon everyone accepting it as a creed. It was possible for it to be regarded as a valid political theory even without its religious core. This, in fact, was the only way it could become a general guide for solving the practical problems of an organized political movement. Ahimsa then was premised on a disjuncture between morality and politics, between private conscience and public responsibility, indeed between noble folly and *realpolitik*. It was a disjuncture which the 'experimental' conception of ahimsa was meant to bridge. And yet, it was a disjuncture the steadfast denial of whose very existence had been the foundation of the original conception of *Hind Swaraj*. Now, however, with the Gandhian ideology inserting itself into the political process of a nationalist movement, the concept of ahimsa itself became a means by which wholly ambiguous meanings could be produced within nationalist discourse and reconciled in different ways at various levels of an already differentiated political structure.

Thus, the failure of politics to reach utopia could be attributed to the loftiness of the ideal, noble, truthful, but inherently unreachable, or else, equally credibly, to the imperfections of the human agency. The vision of a non-violent India could be 'a mere day-dream, a childish folly'. Or else, one could argue with equal validity that the problem lay not with the ideal but with one's own deficiencies.

The result, of course, was that under the moral umbrella of the quest for utopia, the experimental conception of politics could accommodate a potentially limitless range of imperfections, adjustments, compromises, and failures. Gandhi could say, on the one hand, 'I shall retain my disbelief in legislatures as an instrument for obtaining *swaraj* in terms of masses', and in the same breath talk about those Congressmen who were wanting to enter the legislatures: 'But I see that I have failed to wean some of the Congressmen from their faith in council-entry. . . . I have no doubt that they must have the recognition they want. Not to give it will be to refuse to make use of the talents we possess.' If Congressmen, on becoming ministers were getting corrupt, Gandhi would say: either 'purge' the Congress of these elements, or else 'secede from it'. While satyagraha had claimed that the masses knew the true dharma and were quite capable of resisting injustice on their own, now the concept of ahimsa would assert that the model peasant movements were those in which the masses 'surrendered their hearts' to their leader. Thus the peasantry was meant to become willing participants in a struggle wholly conceived and directed *by others*.

The moment of manoeuvre required an ideology which would legitimize a national framework of politics in which the peasants are mobilized but do not participate, of a nation of which they are a part but a national state from which they are forever distanced. This is how the Gandhian intervention coincided with the requirements of a 'passive revolution of capital' in India.

Of course, the manoeuvre depended crucially on the great ambiguity of meanings which nationalist discourse could produce at this moment in its constitution. The message of the Mahatma meant different things to different sections of the people. Shahid Amin has attempted a detailed analysis of what the Mahatma's message meant to the peasants of Chauri Chaura.[8] These meanings were entirely different from the way they were interpreted by the literati. The real historical achievement of the nationalist leadership in India was to reconcile those ambiguities within a single differentiated political structure, to appropriate all of them in the body of the same discourse.

The Moment of Arrival

At its moment of arrival, nationalist discourse reconstitutes itself into a legitimate state ideology. The specific form of the passive revolution in India is an *étatisme*, explicitly recognizing a central, autonomous, and directing role of the state and legitimizing it by a specifically nationalist marriage between the ideas of progress and social justice. It is an ideology of which the central organizing principle is the autonomy of the state. The legitimizing principle is a conception of social justice. The argument then runs as follows. Social justice for all cannot be

---

[8] Shahid Amin, 'Gandhi as Mahatma: Gorakhpur 1918', in Ranajit Guha, ed., *Subaltern Studies III* (Delhi: Oxford University Press, 1984).

provided within the old framework because it is antiquated, decadent, and incapable of dynamism. What is necessary is to create a new framework of institutions which can embody the spirit of progress or, a synonym, modernity. Progress or modernity, according to the terms of the twentieth century, means giving primacy to the sphere of the economic, because it is only by a thorough reorganization of the systems of economic production and distribution that enough wealth can be created to ensure social justice for all.

This mature ideological form of nationalist thought in India can be clearly demonstrated in the writings of Jawaharlal Nehru. In *The Discovery of India*, Nehru returns to the nationalist thematic. Only now, the difference between East and West is reduced from the essential to the conjunctural. Every civilization, Nehru argued, has its periods of growth and periods of decay. There is nothing organic or essential in European civilization which has made it dynamic and powerful. It is just that at a certain point in history, the dawn of the modern age, it suddenly found a new spirit, new sources of energy and creativity. Similarly, there is nothing organic or essential in Asian civilizations which has made them static and powerless. After a long period of magnificent growth, the old springs of vitality and innovation had gradually dried up. It was at this historical conjuncture that the clash had occurred between West and East: the West conquered, the East submitted. The cultural values, or the 'spirit', which go with a particular sort of growth are capable of being extracted from their particular civilizational context and made universal historical values. Then they are no longer the 'property' of any particular culture, nor are they essentially or organically tied with that culture.

What was this 'spirit of the age'? It was everything that post-Enlightenment rationalist thought claimed for itself. It was scientific and rational, practical rather than metaphysical. But to Nehru the 'scientific method' and the 'scientific approach to life' meant something much more specific. It meant the primacy of the economic in all social questions. This was the distinctively modern or twentieth-century way of looking at history and society. Whether it was a question of political programmes or economic policy or social and cultural issues, a 'scientific' analysis must always proceed by relating it to the basic economic structure of society. The correct solutions to such problems must also be searched for in terms of a restructuring of those economic arrangements of society.

This now becomes the new theoretical framework for a reconstituted nationalism. It supplies to it the key to a whole new series of rationalist positions on the vital political questions facing it. From these positions, it is even able to appropriate for purely nationalist purposes 'the scientific method of Marxism' as the most advanced expression yet of the rationalism of the European Enlightenment.

Within the ideological framework of mature nationalism, then, the path of economic development was clearly set out in terms of the 'scientific' understanding of society and history. There were three fundamental requirements: 'a heavy engineering and machine-making sector, scientific research institutes and electric power'. All that remained was to identify the political forces, and the policies, which were in favour of or against such industrialization. The fundamental obstacle was the colonial state. Whatever industries had grown under Indian ownership had had to struggle against the interests of the colonial power. So the task was, first of all, to replace the colonial state with a truly national state; second, to eradicate feudalism in the countryside; and, third, to carefully plan the industrial development of the country, under the central co-ordinating aegis of the state and by using the best available scientific and technical expertise.

If this was the national project, where did Gandhi fit in? To Nehru, Gandhi's economic and social ideas were obsolete, often idiosyncratic, and in general 'reactionary'. 'But the fact remains that this "reactionary" knows India, understands India, almost *is* peasant India, and has shaken up India as no so-called revolutionary has done.' Gandhi's appeal was not primarily to the faculty of reason; on the contrary, the appeal was essentially hypnotic, calling for a suspension of reason. In a remarkable passage in his *Autobiography,* Nehru says of Gandhi:

> I used to be troubled sometimes at the growth of this religious element in our politics. . . . I did not like it at all. . . . [The] history and sociology and economics appeared to me all wrong, and the religious twist that was given to everything prevented all clear thinking. Even some of Gandhiji's phrases sometimes jarred upon me—thus his frequent reference to *Rama Raj* as a golden age which was to return. But I was powerless to intervene, and I consoled myself with the thought that Gandhiji used the words because they were well known and understood by the masses. He had an amazing knack of reaching the heart of the people.
> . . . he was a very difficult person to understand, sometimes his language was almost incomprehensible to an average modern. But we felt

that we knew him well enough to realize he was a great and unique man and a glorious leader, and having put our faith in him we gave him an almost blank cheque, for the time being at least. Often we discussed his fads and peculiarities among ourselves and said, half-humorously, that when *swaraj* came these fads must not be encouraged.

This passage lays down in the space of a few sentences the entire strategy of the passive revolution in India. To start with, it sets out the contrast between 'we' on the one hand, and 'Gandhi' on the other. Thus, on the one hand, it states that

(*a*) we know the correct history, sociology and economics, but
(*b*) we are powerless to intervene.

On the other hand,

(*c*) Gandhi operates with a religious element (i.e. he has the wrong history, sociology, and economics). He has fads and peculiarities. His language is almost incomprehensible.

But,

(*d*) Gandhi uses words that are well known and understood by the masses. He has an amazing knack of reaching the heart of the people.

Therefore,

(*e*) Gandhi is a great and unique man and a glorious leader.

It follows as an unstated deduction that

(*f*) [Gandhi has the power to mobilize the masses towards swaraj.]

The strategy then follows:

(*g*) We know him well enough.
(*h* We give him an almost blank cheque for the time being.
(*i*) After swaraj, his fads and peculiarities must not be encouraged.

The argument, in other words, is that whereas our very knowledge of society tells us that 'we' are powerless, Gandhi's unique and incomprehensible knack of reaching the people makes him powerful; however, for that very reason, our knowledge of the consequences of Gandhi's power enables us to let him act on our behalf for the time being but to resume our own control afterwards.

From its own understanding of Indian society, the emerging state leadership recognized the historical limits of its powers of direct intervention. It was a 'progressive' leadership, with its own conception of the sort of changes that were necessary if Indian society was to progress. It identified the chief obstacle to these changes in the existence of a colonial state power, and looked towards its replacement by a national state power as the central agency of change. But it also knew that a successful movement to create a new national state would require the incorporation of the vast mass of the peasantry into the political nation. And here its own understanding of society had made it conscious of the great inconsistencies that existed between the real objective interests of the peasants and their unreasonable subjective beliefs. It also knew, and this is what distinguished them as an emerging state leadership, that given its historical circumstances it could not realistically hope for a transformation of the social and cultural conditions of Indian agrarian society before the political objective was reached. The colonial state was an insurmountable impediment to all such attempts at a transformation. Rather than wasting one's energies in futile projects like 'constructive work in the villages', it was necessary first of all to concentrate on the immediate political task of winning self-government. The task of transforming the countryside could be taken up afterwards.

And yet the colonial state itself could not be overthrown unless the peasantry was mobilized into the national movement. How could this be done if the peasantry did not see that it was in its objective interest to join in the struggle for an independent and united national state? This could be done by 'reaching into their hearts', by speaking a language which they understood. One must have a 'knack' for this, because it was not a language that would emerge out of a rational understanding of objective interests. It would have to be a very special 'knack', and only a great and unique man like Gandhi had it.

Once Gandhism had acknowledged that the sinfulness of political life might finally force it to save its morality by withdrawing from politics, the path was opened for a new state leadership to appropriate the political consequences of the Gandhian intervention at the same time as it rejected its Truth. The critical point of Gandhism's ideological intervention was now pushed back into the zone of the 'purely religious' or the metaphysical; only its political consequences were 'real'. It now became possible for Jawaharlal Nehru, prime minister of India, to inaugurate on Gandhi's birthday a new factory for making railway coaches and say, 'I am quite sure that if it had been our good fortune to have Gandhiji with us today he would have been glad at the opening of this factory.' For now, Gandhi's Truth had surrendered the specificity of its moral critique: it had been cleansed of its religious idiom and subsumed under the rational monism of historical progress. Indeed, once the Truth of Gandhism had been retrieved from the irrational trappings of its 'language', the possibilities were endless: it could justify everything that was 'progressive'. Thus: '[The Congress] formulated a policy of land reform and social justice, and took some steps towards the formulation of a public sector. The whole philosophy of Gandhiji, although he did not talk perhaps in a modern language, was not only one of social justice, but of social reform and land reform. All these concepts were his.'

Now the final stage of the nationalist project was defined. No matter how imperfect the preparation, how difficult the circumstances, or even how incomplete and fragmented the final result, the struggle was now one of building the new national state.

> . . . it is a race between the forces of peaceful progress and construction and those of disruption and disaster. . . . We can view this prospect as optimists or as pessimists, according to our predilections and mental make-up. Those who have faith in a moral ordering of the universe and in the ultimate triumph of virtue can, fortunately for them, function as lookers on or as helpers, and cast the burden on God. Others will have to carry that burden on their own weak shoulders, hoping for the best and preparing for the worst.

This was the epitaph, wondrous and yet condescending, put up on the grave of Gandhian politics by the new nationalist state leadership. The relentless thrust of its rationalist thematic turned the Gandhian intervention into a mere interlude in the unfolding of the real history of the nation. And thus it was that the political consequences of that intervention were fully appropriated within the monistic progression of 'real' history.

The tasks before the new state were clear: to achieve industrialization and equality. Neither of these were innately political questions to be resolved on the battlefield of politics. The universal principle and the world standards had already been set by history: there was no room for choice on those matters. Only the specific national path remained to be determined. But this was now a technical problem, a problem of balancing and optimization. It was a job for experts.

This now became the new utopia, a realist's utopia, a utopia here and now. It was a supremely *étatist* utopia, where the function of government was wholly abstracted out of the messy business of politics and established in its pristine purity as rational decision-making conducted through the most advanced operational techniques provided by the sciences of economic management. The world of the concrete, of differences, of conflict, of the struggle between classes, of history and politics, now finds its unity in the life of the state.

Was there, then, no violence in the life of the state? Was it not in itself an institution which exercised power over the various parts of society? What if there were impediments in the path of progress? Would not the state, acting on behalf of society as a whole, be required to exercise power to remove those impediments? 'Everything that comes in the way will have to be removed, gently if possible, forcibly if necessary. And there seems to be little doubt that coercion will often be necessary. But [and this is a significant 'but'] . . . if force is used it should not be in the spirit of hatred or cruelty, but with the dispassionate desire to remove an obstruction.' The coercion of the state was itself a rational instrument for the achievement of progress by the nation. It was to be used by the state with surgical dispassion, and would be justified by the rationality of its own ends.

Nationalism has now constituted itself into a state ideology. It has appropriated the life of the nation into the life of the state. It is rational and progressive, a particular manifestation of the universal march of reason. It has accepted the global realities of power, accepted the fact that world history resides elsewhere. Only now has it found its place within that universal scheme of things.

Has the history of nationalism then exhausted itself? Such a conclusion is unwarranted. For hardly anywhere in the post-colonial world has it been possible for the nation-state to fully appropriate the life of the nation into its own. Everywhere the intellectual-moral leadership of the ruling classes is based on a spurious ideological unity. The fissures are clearly marked on its surface.

Where then will the critique emerge of nationalism? How will nationalism supersede itself? A historical discourse, unfortunately, can only struggle with its own terms. Its evolution will be determined by history itself.

3

History and the Nationalization of Hinduism

(1991)

History is today, not implicitly but in the most explicit way possible, the pretext for violent political conflict in India, a conflict which threatens to tear apart what was for several decades taken to be the consensus about the fundamental character of the nation-state which the constitution calls 'India, that is Bharat'. For almost three years now, the most contentious debate that has preoccupied the very centre of organized political life in India—as distinct from the continuing insurgencies in Punjab, Kashmir, and Assam which to a large extent have been kept to the margins—is a dispute over the status of a certain mosque in a small town called Ayodhya in the state of Uttar Pradesh. The reason why this dispute continues to produce such shattering reverberations in the central corridors of Indian politics is that it has become implicated in the increasingly powerful claims now being made by the organized proponents of political Hinduism. The central demand of this political campaign, spearheaded by the Bharatiya Janata Party (BJP) and a 'cultural' organization called the Viswa Hindu Parishad (VHP), is that the past, present, and future of the Indian nation be constituted around a notion of *hindutva*, Hinduness.

I will not go into the question of why this case, which as a legal dispute over the proprietorial status of the mosque has existed unresolved for more than fifty years, should have acquired such a momentous significance at this particular time in Indian politics.[1] I will also not

---

[1] For details on the dispute, see S. Gopal, ed., *Anatomy of a Confrontation: The Babri Masjid–Ram Janmabhumi Issue* (Delhi: Penguin India, 1991); J.C. Aggarwal

discuss here the complex question of the evolution of 'communalist' politics in India, the contradictions in the politics of 'secularism', and the problematic involvement of the state and the 'secular' political parties in the politics of religious identity.[2] My focus will be on the construction of the historical claims of hindutva. My argument will be that such claims become possible only within the modern forms of historiography, a historiography which is necessarily constructed around the complex identity of a people-nation-state. To the extent that the genealogy of modern historiography in India is deeply implicated in the encounter with British colonialism, these historical claims of political Hinduism are also a product of contestations with the forms of colonial knowledge. Finally, I will show that many of the themes that run through the contemporary rhetoric of Hindu extremist politics were in fact part and parcel of the historical imagining in the nineteenth century of 'India' as a nation. This implies that, with respect to the fragile consensus over 'nationness' in India today, the tendency which emphasizes the singularity of a historically constituted national formation called 'India, that is Bharat', a singularity often demanded by the need to legitimize the centralized apparatuses of a modern nation-state, will always have available for its sectarian use the common resources of a single 'national' history of 'the Hindus'.

I will use as my material a set of school textbooks on Indian history from nineteenth-century Bengal.[3] None of these books were written by major historians, and none claimed any great originality in historical interpretation. But for that very reason they are good indicators of the main features of a commonly shared discursive formation within which Indian nationalist historiography made its appearance.

But before I present this material from the middle and late nineteenth century, let me begin with a text from the very early years of the century. This will give us an idea of how radical a transformation was effected in the forms of recounting the political events of the past.

---

and N.K. Chowdhry, *Ram Janmabhoomi through the Ages: Babri Masjid Controversy* (New Delhi: S. Chand, 1991).

[2] For a recent discussion of these issues, see Gyanendra Pandey, *The Construction of Communalism in Northern India* (Delhi: Oxford University Press, 1989).

[3] I have made a fuller discussion of these sources in my essay 'Itihaser Uttaradhikar', *Baromas* (Calcutta), 12 (April 1991): 1–24. Large parts of the present article are translated from this earlier essay.

A Puranic History

The first three books of narrative prose in Bengali commissioned by the Fort William College in Calcutta for use by young officials of the Company learning the local vernacular were books of history. Of these, *Rajabali* (1808) by Mrityunjay Vidyalankar,[4] was a history of India—the first such history in the Bengali language that we have in print. Mrityunjay (*c.* 1762–1819) taught Sanskrit at Fort William College and was the author of some of the first printed books in Bengali. When he decided to set down in writing the story of 'the Rajas and Badshahs and Nawabs who have occupied the throne in Delhi and Bengal', it does not seem that he had to undertake any fresh 'research' into the subject; he was only writing down an account that was already in circulation at the time among the Brahman literati and their land-owning patrons.[5] His book was, we might say, a good example of the historical memory of elite Bengali society as exemplified in contemporary scholarship.

The book starts with a precise reckoning of the time at which it is being written:

> In course of the circular motion of time, like the hands of a clock, passing through the thirty *kalpa* such as Pitrkalpa etc., we are now situated in the Svetavaraha kalpa. Each kalpa consists of fourteen *manu*; accordingly, we are now in the seventh manu of Svetavaraha kalpa called Vaivasvata. Each manu consists of 284 *yuga*; we are now passing through the one hundred and twelfth yuga of Vaivasvata manu called Kaliyuga. This yuga consists of 432,000 years. Of these, up to the present year 1726 of the Saka era, 4905 years have passed; 427,095 years are left.[6]

The calendrical system is also precisely noted. For the first 3044 years of Kaliyuga, the prevailing era (*saka*) was that of King Yudhisthira. The next 135 years comprised the era of King Vikramaditya. These two eras are now past:

<hr>

[4] Mrtyunjaya Sarmanah, *Rajabali* (Serampore: Baptist Mission Press, 1908) [hereafter *R*]. All translations from the Bengali sources are mine.

[5] R.C. Majumdar has discussed some of the dynastic lists in circulation among prominent landed families in eighteenth-century Bengal in Rameschandra Majumdar, 'Samskrta Rajabali Grantha', *Sahitya Parisat Patrika*, 46 (1953): 232–9. I am grateful to Gautam Bhadra for this reference.

[6] *R*, pp. 3–4.

Now we are passing through the era of the king called Salivahana who lived on the southern banks of the river Narmada. This Saka will last for 18,000 years after the end of the Vikramaditya era. After this there will be a king called Vijayabhinandana who will rule in the region of the Citrakuta mountains. His *saka* will last for 10,000 years after the end of the Salivahana era.

After this there will be a king called Parinagarjuna whose era will last until 821 years are left in the Kaliyuga, at which time will be born in the family of Gautabrahmana in the Sambhala country an *avatara* of Kalkideva. Accordingly, of the six eras named after six kings, two are past, one is present and three are in the future.[7]

Whatever one might say of this system of chronology, lack of certitude is not one of its faults. Mrityunjay is equally certain about identifying the place where the historical events in his narrative take place:

Of the five elements—space (*akasa*), air, fire, water and earth—the earth occupies eight *ana* [i.e. half] while the other four occupy two *ana* [i.e. one-eighth] each. . . . Half of the earth is taken up by the seas, north of which is Jambudvipa. . . . There are seven islands on earth of which ours is called Jambudvipa. Jambudvipa is divided into nine *varsa* of which Bharatavarsa is one. Bharatavarsa in turn is divided into nine parts (*khanda*) which are called Aindra, Kaseru, Tamraparna, Gavastimata, Naga, Saumya, Varuna, Gandharva and Kumarika. Of these, the part in which the *varnasrama* [caste] system exists is the Kumarikakhanda.

The other parts [of Bharatavarsa] are inhabited by the *antyaja* people [those outside caste].[8]

Thus *Rajabali* is the history of those who ruled over the earth in which there are seven islands of which the one called Jambudvipa has nine parts of which Bharatavarsa is one, etc., etc. Where does this history begin?

In the Satyayuga, the Supreme Lord [*paramesvara*] had planted in the form of an Asvathva tree a king called Iksaku to rule over the earth. The two main branches of this tree became the Surya and the Candra *vamsa*. The kings born in these two lineages have ruled the earth in the four *yuga*. Of these, some were able to acquire the greatest powers of righteousness [dharma] and thus ruled over the entire earth consisting of the seven islands. Others had lesser powers and thus ruled over only Jambudvipa or only Bharatavarsa or, in some cases, only the Kumarikakhanda. If a king from one

[7] *R*, p. 8.
[8] *R*, pp. 4–5.

lineage became the emperor [*samrata*], then the king of the other lineage would become the lord of a *mandala*. The accounts of these kings are recorded in the branches of knowledge [*sastra*] called the Purana and the Itihasa.[9]

A few things may be clarified at this point. In Mrityunjay's scheme of history, the rulers on earth are, as it were, appointed by divine will. They enjoy that position to the extent, and as long as, they acquire and retain the powers of righteousness. By attaining the highest levels of dharma, one could even become the ruler of the entire earth. We may wish, in order to distinguish this variety of history-writing from those with which we are more familiar today, to call Mrityunjay's narrative a Puranic history. Mrityunjay would not have quarrelled with this description, not because he was aware of the distinction we are making but because *puranetihasa* was for him the valid form of retelling the political history of Bharatavarsa.

We cannot, however, accuse the discipline of Puranic history of being sloppy in its counting of dynasties and kings. 'In the 4267 years since the beginning of the Kaliyuga, there have been 119 Hindus of different *jati* who have become *samrat* on the throne of Delhi.'[10] The count begins with King Yudhisthira of the *Mahabharata* who heads a list of twenty-eight Ksatriya kings who ruled for a total of 1812 years. 'After this the actual reign of the Ksatriya *jati* ended.' Then came fourteen kings of the Nanda dynasty, starting with 'one called Mahananda born of a Ksatriya father and a Sudra mother', who ruled for a total of five hundred years. 'The Rajput *jati* started with this Nanda.' After this came the Buddhist kings: 'Fifteen kings of the Nastika faith, from Viravahu to Aditya, all of the Gautama lineage, ruled for four hundred years. At this time the Nastika views enjoyed such currency that the Vaidika religion was almost eradicated.' We then have a curious list of dynasties—nine rulers of the Mayura dynasty, sixteen of the Yogi dynasty, four of the Bairagi dynasty, and so on. Of course, there are 'the Vikramadityas, father and son, who ruled for ninety-three years.' We are also told of 'thirteen kings, from Dhi Sena to Damodara Sena, of the Vaidya *jati* of Bengal who ruled for 137 years and one month'— from, let us remember, 'the throne in Delhi'! The rule of the 'Chohan Rajput *jati*' ends with

[9] *R*, pp. 6–7.
[10] *R*, p. 10.

Prthoray who ruled for fourteen years and seven months. . . . This is as far as the empire [*samrajya*] of the Hindu kings lasted.

After this began the *samrajya* of the Musalmans. From the beginning of the empire of the Yavanas [Muslims] to the present year 1726 of the Saka era, fifty-one kings have ruled for 651 years three months and twenty-eight days.[11]

What is interesting about this chronology is the way in which its dynastic sequence passes ever so smoothly from the kings of the *Mahabharata* to the kings of Magadha and ends with the Mughal emperor Shah Alam II, 'of the lineage of Amir Taimur', occupying the throne in Delhi at the time of Mrityunjay's writing. Myth, history, and the contemporary—all become part of the same chronological sequence; one is not distinguished from another; the passage from one to another, consequently, is entirely unproblematic. There is not even an inkling in Mrityunjay's prose of any of the knotty questions about the value of Puranic accounts in constructing a 'proper' historical chronology of Indian dynasties which would so exercise Indian historians a few decades later. Although Mrityunjay wrote at the behest of his colonial masters, his historiographic allegiances are entirely precolonial.

It would therefore be of some interest to us to discover how a Brahman scholar such as Mrityunjay describes the end of 'the Hindu dynasties' and the accession to the throne at Delhi of 'the Yavana emperors'. Our curiosity is aroused even further when we discover that the story of the defeat of Prithviraj Chauhan at the hands of Shihabuddin Muhammad Ghuri takes the form of a Puranic tale. The story is as follows.

Prithviraj's father had two wives, one of whom was a demoness (*raksasi*) who ate human flesh. She had also introduced her husband into this evil practice. One day the demoness ate the son of the other queen who, taken by fright, ran away to her brother. There she gave birth to a son who was called Prthu. On growing up, Prthu met his father. At his request, Prthu cut off his father's head and fed the flesh to twenty-one women belonging to his *jati*. Later, when Prthu became king, the sons of those twenty-one women became his feudatories (*samanta*). 'Because Prthu had killed his father, the story of his infamy

[11] *R*, pp. 12–13.

spread far and wide. Kings who paid tribute to him stopped doing so.' In other words, Prithviraj was not a ruler who enjoyed much respect among his subjects.

It was at this time that Shihabuddin Ghuri threatened to attack Prithviraj:

> When the king heard of the threatening moves of the Yavanas, he called a number of scholars learned in the Vedas and said, 'O learned men! Arrange a sacrifice which will dissipate the prowess and the threats of the Yavanas.' The learned men said, 'O King! There is such a sacrifice and we can perform it. And if the sacrificial block [*yupa*] can be laid at the prescribed moment, then the Yavanas can never enter this land.' The king was much reassured by these words and arranged for the sacrifice to be performed with much pomp. When the learned men declared that the time had come to lay the block, much efforts were made but no one could move the sacrificial block to its assigned place. Then the learned men said, 'O King! What the Supreme Power [*isvara*] desires, happens. Men cannot override his wishes, but can only act in accordance with them. So, desist in your efforts. It seems this throne will be attacked by the Yavanas.'

Hearing these words, Prithviraj was greatly disheartened and 'slackened his efforts at war'. His armies were defeated by Shihabuddin, who arrived triumphantly at Delhi. Then Prithviraj

> emerged from his quarters and engaged Sahabuddin in a ferocious battle. But by the grace of Isvara, the Yavana Sahabuddin made a prisoner of Prthuraja. On being reminded that Prthuraja was son-in-law of King Jayacandra [Jaichand, ruler of a neighbouring kingdom, had already collaborated with Muhammad Ghuri], he did not execute him but sent him as a prisoner to his own country of Ghazna.[12]

Let us remember that in Mrityunjay's scheme of history, dynasties are founded by the grace of the divine power and kingdoms are retained only as long as the ruler is true to dharma. The Chauhan dynasty was guilty of such heinous offenses as cannibalism and patricide. That Prithviraj had lost divine favour was already revealed at the sacrificial ceremony. His defeat and the establishment of 'Yavana rule' by Muhammad Ghuri were, therefore, acts of divine will. Half a century later, when Puranic history would be abandoned in favour of rational historiography, this account of the battle of Thanesar would undergo

---

[12] This account is in *R*, pp. 109–10.

a complete transformation. English-educated Brahman scholars would not accept with such equanimity the dictates of a divine will.

Mrityunjay has a few more things to say about the reasons for the downfall of the Chauhan dynasty. These remarks are prefaced by the following statement: 'I will now write what the Yavanas say about the capture of the throne of Delhi by the Yavana Sahabuddin.'[13] Mrityunjay then goes back to the earlier raids into various Indian kingdoms by Nasruddin Sabuktagin, father of Mahmud Ghaznavi:

> When Nasruddin came to Hindustan, there was no harmony among the kings of Hindustan. Each thought of himself as the emperor [*badsah*]; none owed fealty to anyone else and none was strong enough to subjugate the others. On discovering this, the Yavanas entered Hindustan. The main reason for the fall of kingdoms and the success of the enemy is mutual disunity and the tendency of each to regard itself as supreme. When Sekandar Shah [Alexander] had become emperor in the land of the Yavanas, he had once come to Hindustan, but seeing the religiosity and learning of the Brahmans, he had declared that a land whose kings had such advisers [*hakim*] could never be conquered by others. Saying this, he had returned to his country and had never come back to Hindustan. Now there were no more such Brahmans and, bereft of their advice, the kings of this country lost divine grace and were all defeated by the Yavanas.[14]

Mrityunjay's accounts of the Sultanate and the Mughal periods were very likely based on the Persian histories in circulation among the literati in late-eighteenth-century Bengal. It is possible that some of these texts contained comments on the disunity among Indian kings and perhaps even the statement attributed to Alexander. But the argument that it was because of the failings of the Brahmans that the kings strayed from the path of righteousness and thus lost the blessings of god was undoubtedly formulated by Mrityunjay, the Brahman scholar. It was the duty of the Brahmans to guide the king along the path of dharma. They had failed in that duty and had brought about the divine wrath which ended the rule of the Hindu kings and established the rule of the Yavanas. We will see later that as the role of divine intervention in history becomes less credible, this story of the fall acquires in modern writings the form of a general decay of society and polity.

[13] *R*, pp. 112–13.
[14] *R*, pp. 121–2.

But we are anticipating. We need to note, for purposes of comparison, Mrityunjay's account of the destruction by Mahmud Ghaznavi of the temple at Somnath. The main details of the story are the same as those that would appear in later histories, for they all come from Persian sources such as the *Tarikh-i-Firishta*. But Mrityunjay mentions one 'fact' about the idol at Somnath which is never subsequently mentioned: 'There was a very large sacred idol called Somnath which was once in Mecca. Four thousand years after the time when the Yavanas say the human race was born, this idol was brought by a king of Hindustan from Mecca to its present place.'[15] Mrityunjay's source for this information is uncertain, but it is never mentioned again by any Bengali historian.

Two Mughal emperors are the subjects of much controversy in nationalist historiography. Let us note what Mrityunjay has to say about them. On Akbar, Mrityunjay is effusive. 'Since Sri Vikramaditya, there has never been in Hindustan an emperor with merits equal to those of Akbar Shah.'[16] Apart from possessing a deep sense of righteousness and performing all the required duties to protect his subjects, Akbar also had, according to Mrityunjay, an additional merit: 'Because of his knowledge of many *sastra*, his spiritual views were sceptical of the doctrines of Muhammad and were closer to those of the Hindus. The kings of Iran and Turan often complained about this. . . . He did not eat beef and forbade the slaughter of cows within his fort. To this day, cow-slaughter is prohibited in his fort.'[17] On Aurangzeb, on the other hand, Mrityunjay has this to say: 'He became very active in spreading the Muhammadi faith. And he destroyed many great temples. Many ceremonies of the Hindus such as the worship of the sun and of Ganesa had been performed in the fort of the Badshah since the time of Akbar; [Aurangzeb] discontinued these practices and issued new rules invented by himself.' He then adds: 'Although he destroyed many great temples, he was favoured by the divine powers at Jvalamukhi and Lachmanbala and made sizeable grants of land for the maintenance of those temples. He later lived at Aurangabad for twelve years and, on being cursed by a Brahman, died uttering horrible cries of pain.'[18]

[15] *R*, p. 129.
[16] *R*, p. 195.
[17] *R*, pp. 191, 194.
[18] *R*, p. 221.

Where kings acquire kingdoms and hold power by divine grace, the business of arriving at a verdict on the character of rulers has to be negotiated between kings and gods. The only role that the ordinary *praja* (subject) has in all this is in bearing the consequences of the actions of these superior entities. Of course, the praja knows the difference between a good king and a bad one, which is why he praises a ruler such as Akbar. And when Aurangzeb dies 'uttering horrible cries of pain', perhaps the praja shudders a little at the ferocity of divine retribution, but in the end is reassured by the victory of dharma. In all this, however, the praja never implicates himself in the business of ruling; he never puts himself in the place of the ruler. In recalling the history of kingdoms, he does not look for a history of himself.

If it was ever suggested to Mrityunjay that in the story of the deeds and fortunes of the kings of Delhi might lie the history of a nation, it is doubtful that he would have understood. His own position in relation to his narrative is fixed—it is the position of the praja, the ordinary subject, who is most often only the sufferer and sometimes the beneficiary of acts of government. It is from that position that he tells the story of Prithviraj's misdeeds or of Akbar's righteousness. But the thought would never have occurred to him that because of the associations of 'nationality', he, Mrityunjay Vidyalankar, a Brahman scholar in the employment of the East India Company in Calcutta in the early nineteenth century, might in some way become responsible for the acts of Prithviraj or Akbar. *Rajabali* is not a national history because its protagonists are gods and kings, not people. The bonds of 'nation-ness' have not yet been imagined which would justify the identification of the historian with the consciousness of a solidarity that is supposed to act itself out in history.

History as the Play of Power

This framework changed radically as the Bengali literati were schooled in the new colonial education. Now Indians were taught the principles of European history, statecraft, and social philosophy. They were also taught the history of India as it came to be written from the standpoint of modern European scholarship. The Orientalists had, from the last years of the eighteenth century, begun to 'recover' and reconstruct for modern historical consciousness the materials for an understanding of Indian history and society. The English-educated class in Bengal, from

its birth in the early decades of the nineteenth century, became deeply
interested in this new discipline of Indology.

But, curiously enough, the new Indian literati, while they enthusiasti-
cally embraced the modern rational principles of European historiography, did not accept the history of India as it was written by British
historians. The political loyalty of the early generation of English-
educated Bengalis towards the East India Company was unquestioned,
and in 1857, when most of northern India was in revolt, they were
especially demonstrative in their protestations of loyalty. And yet, by
the next decade, they were engaged in open contestation with the
colonialist interpretation of Indian history. By the 1870s, the principal
elements were already in place for the writing of a nationalist history
of India. It is interesting to trace the genealogy of this new history of
'the nation'.

In 1857-8, with the inauguration of the University of Calcutta, a set
of translations was produced in Bengali, for use in schools, of histories
of India and Bengal written by British historians. The translations ended with a eulogy to the blessings of Providence which had chosen the
East India Company to bring to an end the anarchy and corruption
into which the country had fallen.[19] Only ten years later, however, in
1869, a book of questions and answers based on the same English
textbooks had the following entry:

Q. How did Clive win?

A. If the treacherous Mir Jafar had not tricked the Nawab [Siraj-ud-
daulah], Clive could not have won so easily.[20]

A Bengali textbook of 1872 tells the story of the betrayal of Nawab
Siraj-ud-daulah in much greater detail. Siraj, it says, was a tyrant, but,
contrary to the canards spread by the English, he was not responsible
for the 'black hole of Calcutta'. Although his general Mir Jafar betrayed
him at Plassey, his other generals fought valiantly: 'If this battle had
continued for some time, then Clive would surely have lost. But fortune favoured the English, and weakened by the betrayal of Mir Jafar,

---

[19] For instance, Ramgati Nyayaratna, *Bangalar Itihas, Pratham Bhag, Hindu
Rajadiger Caramabastha Abadhi Nabab Alibarddi Khanr Adhikar Kal Paryyanta*
(Hooghly: 1859), pp. 179–80.

[20] Ramsaday Bhattacharya, *Bangala Itihaser Prasnottar* (Calcutta: 1869), pp. 110–
11.

the Nawab was defeated and Clive was victorious.'[21] Not only in gaining an empire, but even in administering one, the English resorted to conspiracy and force. In the period before and after Clive, says the same book, 'the English committed such atrocities on the people of this country that all Bengalis hated the name of the English.'[22] Because of his intrigues, Hastings 'is despised by all and is condemned in history.'[23] In 1857, just as the soldiers committed atrocities, so did the English: 'At the time of the suppression of the revolt, the English who are so proud of their Christian religion wreaked vengeance upon their enemies by cutting out the livers from the bodies of hanged rebels and throwing them into the fire.'[24] Even the end of the mutiny did not bring peace: 'In no age do the poor and the weak have anyone to protect them. When the disorder died down at other places, a huge commotion began in Bengal. In the areas of Bengal where indigo is grown, the English planters became truculent. The cruelties they perpetrated on the poor tenants will prevent them for all time from being counted among human beings.'[25]

It was in fact in the course of writing the history of British rule in India that English-educated Bengalis abandoned the criteria of divine intervention, religious value, and the norms of right conduct in judging the rise and fall of kingdoms. The recent history of Bengal demonstrated that kingdoms could be won and, what was more, held by resorting to the grossest acts of immorality. The modern historiography seemed to validate a view of political history as simply the amoral pursuit of *raison d'état*.

A popular textbook published in the 1870s portrayed the political success of the British in India as the result of a cynical pursuit of power devoid of all moral principles. Of Clive's intrigues, it said, 'Most people criticize Clive for these heinous acts, but according to him there is nothing wrong in committing villainy when dealing with villains.'[26] The new revenue arrangements of 1772 are described as follows:

[21] Kshetranath Bandyopadhyay, *Sisupath Bangalar Itihas, Bargir Hangam Haite Lard Narthbruker Agaman Paryyanta* (Calcutta: 1872), p. 22.

[22] Ibid., p. 39.

[23] Ibid., p. 59.

[24] Ibid., p. 98.

[25] Ibid., p. 100.

[26] Krishnachandra Ray, *Bharatbarser Itihas, Imrejdiger Adhikarkal*, 9th edn (1859; rpnt. Calcutta: J.C. Chatterjee, 1870), pp. 43–4.

'The land belongs to him who has force on his side.' It is from this time that the Company stopped being a revenue collector and really became the ruler. If the Emperor [in Delhi] had been strong, there would have been a huge incident over this. But there was nothing left [to the Empire]. Whatever Hastings decided, happened.[27]

History was no longer the play of divine will or the fight of right against wrong; it had become merely the struggle for power. The advent of British rule was no longer a blessing of Providence. English-educated Bengalis were now speculating on the political conditions that might have made the British success impossible: 'If this country had been under the dominion of one powerful ruler, or if the different rulers had been united and friendly towards one another, then the English would never have become so powerful here and this country would have remained under the Musalman kings. Perhaps no one in this country would have ever heard of the English.'[28] The book ends with a list of the benefits of British rule. And yet it is clearly implied that this does not establish its claims to legitimacy: 'In any case, whatever be the means by which the English have come to acquire this sprawling kingdom, it must be admitted that infinite benefits have been effected by them to this country.'[29] We have almost reached the threshold of nationalist history.

A book published in 1876 has this announcement by its author in the preface: 'I have written this book for those who have been misled by translations of histories written in English.'[30] The extent to which European historiography had made inroads into the consciousness of the Bengali literati can be judged from the following comment on relations between the European colonial powers: 'The English and the French have always been hostile towards each other. Just as the conflict between the Mughals and the Pathans is proverbial in India, so is the hostility between the English and the French in Europe. Thus it was beyond belief that in India they would not attack each other and instead drink from the same water.'[31] The book ends with the following

---

[27] Ibid., p. 70.

[28] Ibid., p. 214.

[29] Ibid., p. 238.

[30] Kshirodchandra Raychaudhuri, *Samagra Bharater Samksipta Itihas* (Calcutta: 1876).

[31] Ibid., p. 115.

sentences: 'Having come to India as a mere trader, the East India Company became through the tide of events the overlord of two hundred million subjects, and the shareholders of the Company, having become millionaires and billionaires, began to institute the laws and customs of foreign peoples. In no other country of the world has such an unnatural event taken place.'[32]

Elements of a Nationalist History

In relation to Mrityunjay, I said that his position with respect to the political events he was describing was that of an ordinary subject. One could say the same of the authors of the textbooks just mentioned. But these 'subjects' were very different entities. In the seventy years that had passed, the creature known as the educated Bengali had been transmuted. Now he had grown used to referring to himself, like the educated European, as a member of 'the middle class'. Not only was he in the middle in terms of income, but he had also assumed, in the sphere of social authority, the role of a mediator. On the one hand he was claiming that those who had wealth and property were unfit to wield the power they had traditionally enjoyed. On the other hand he was taking upon himself the responsibility of speaking on behalf of those who were poor and oppressed. To be in the middle now meant opposing the rulers and leading the subjects. Our textbook historians, while they may have thought of themselves as ordinary subjects, had acquired a consciousness in which they were already exercising the arts of politics and statecraft.

Simultaneously, the modern European principles of social and political organization had become deeply implanted in their minds. The English-educated middle class of Bengal was by the 1870s unanimous in its belief that the old institutions and practices of society needed to be fundamentally changed. It is useful to remind ourselves of this fact, because we often tend to forget that those who are called 'conservative' or 'traditionalist', and who are associated with the movements of Hindu revivalism, were also vigorous advocates of the reform and modernization of Hindu society. Whatever the differences between 'progressives' and 'conservatives' among the new intellectuals in the nineteenth century, they were all convinced that the old society had to be reformed in order to cope with the modern world.

[32] Ibid., p. 211.

This becomes clear from reading the most commonplace writings of minor writers in the second half of the nineteenth century. A completely new criterion of political judgement employed in these readings is, for instance, the notion of 'impartiality'. We have a text from 1866 by an author who is undoubtedly a 'traditionalist Hindu' because, in a chapter on 'The Treatment of Young Women', he recommends that 'whether indoors or out, no young woman should at any time be left alone and unwatched;'[33] yet he is opposed to polygamy and the practice of dowry. In a chapter on 'The Subject of Political Loyalty', this traditionalist writes:

> In the days when this country was under the rule of the Hindu *jati*, the arbitrariness of kings led to the complete domination by a particular jati over all the others. That jati wielded the power to send others to heaven or hell. . . . When the kingdom was in the hands of the Yavanas, they treated all Hindus as infidels. In all respects they favoured subjects belonging to their own jati and oppressed those who were Hindu. . . . The principles of government followed by the British jati do not have any of these defects. When administering justice, they treat a priest of their own jati as equal to someone of the lowest occupation in this country, such as a sweeper. . . . No praise is too great for the quality of impartiality of this jati.[34]

One step further and we get the next argument in nationalist history: the reason why Hindu society was corrupt and decadent was the long period of Muslim rule. The following is an extract from a lecture at a reformist religious society in 1876:

> The misfortunes and decline of this country began on the day the Yavana flag entered the territory of Bengal. The cruelty of Yavana rule turned this land to waste. Just as a storm wreaks destruction and disorder to a garden, so did the unscrupulous and tyrannical Yavana jati destroy the happiness and good fortune of Bengal, this land of our birth. Ravaged by endless waves of oppression, the people of Bengal became disabled and timid. Their religion took distorted forms. The education of women was completely stopped. In order to protect women from the attacks of Yavanas, they were locked up inside their homes. The country was reduced to such a state that the wealth of the prosperous, the honour of the genteel and the chastity of the virtuous were in grave peril.[35]

---

[33] Tarakrishna Haldar, *Camatkar Svapnadarsan* (Calcutta: 1868), pp. 134–6.

[34] Ibid.

[35] Bholanath Chakravarti, *Sei Ek din Ar Ei Ek Din, Arthat Banger Purbba o Barttaman Abastha* (Calcutta: Adi Brahmo Samaj, 1876), p. 10.

Half of nationalist history has been already thought out here. In the beginning, the nation was glorious; in wealth, power, learning, and religion it had reached the pinnacle of civilization. This nation was sometimes called Bengali, sometimes Hindu, sometimes Arya, sometimes Indian, but the form of its history remained the same. After this came the age of decline. The cause of decline was Muslim rule, i.e. the subjection of the nation. We do not get the rest of nationalist history in this lecture because, although the speaker talks of the need for national regeneration, he also thinks that its possibility lies entirely in the existence of British rule:

> There are limits to everything. When the oppressions of the Musalmans became intolerable, the Lord of the Universe provided a means of escape. . . . The resumption of good fortune was initiated on the day the British flag was first planted on this land. Tell me, if Yavana rule had continued, what would the condition of this country have been today? It must be loudly declared that it is to bless us that *isvara* has brought the English to this country. British rule has ended the atrocities of the Yavanas. . . . There can be no comparison between Yavana rule and British rule: the difference seems greater than that between darkness and light or between misery and bliss.[36]

However, even if this lecturer did not subscribe to it, the remainder of the argument of nationalist history was already fairly current. I have before me the eighteenth edition, published in 1878, of *The History of India* by Tarinicharan Chattopadhyay.[37] Tarinicharan (1833–97) was a product of colonial education—a professor at Sanskrit College and a social reformer. His textbooks on history and geography were extremely popular and the basis of many other less-known textbooks. His *History of India* was probably the most influential textbook read in Bengali schools in the second half of the nineteenth century.

I will recount here some of the stories from Tarinicharan's history in order to point out how the materials of Hindu extremist political rhetoric today were fashioned from the very birth of nationalist historiography.

[36] Ibid., pp. 11–12.
[37] Tarinicharan Chattopadhyay, *Bharatbarser Itihas*, vol. 1 (1858; rpnt. Calcutta, 1878); hereafter *BI*.

The Construction of a Classical Past

The first sentence is striking: 'India [*bharatavarsa*] has been ruled in turn by Hindus, Musalmans, and Christians. Accordingly, the history of this country [*des*] is divided into the periods of Hindu, Muslim and Christian rule [*rajatva*].'[38] We have passed from the 'history of kings' to the 'history of this country'. Never again will *Rajabali* be written; from now on, everything will be the 'history of this des'. This history, now, is periodized according to the distinctive character of rule, and this character, in turn, is determined by the religion of the rulers. The identification here of country (des) and realm (rajatva) is permanent and indivisible. This means that although there may be at times several kingdoms and kings, there is in truth always only one realm, which is coextensive with the country and which is symbolized by the capital or the throne. The rajatva, in other words, constitutes the generic sovereignty of the country, whereas the capital or the throne represents the centre of sovereign statehood. Since the country is *bharatavarsa*, there can be only one true sovereignty which is coextensive with it, represented by a single capital or throne as its centre. Otherwise, why should the defeat of Prithviraj and the capture of Delhi by Muhammad Ghuri signal the end of a whole period of Indian history and the beginning of a new one? Or why should the battle of Plassey mark the end of Muslim rule and the beginning of Christian rule? The identification in European historiography between the notions of country or people, sovereignty and statehood, is now lodged firmly in the mind of the English-educated Bengali.

On the next page, we have another example of the modernity of this historiographic practice. 'All Sanskrit sources that are now available are full of legends and fabulous tales; apart from the *Rajataran-gini* there is not a single true historical account.'[39] The criteria of the 'true historical account' had been, of course, set by then by European historical scholarship. That India has no true historical account was a singular discovery of European Indology. The thought had never occurred to Mrityunjay. But to Tarinicharan, it seems self-evident.

[38] *BI*, p. 1.
[39] *BI*, p. 2.

We then have a description of the inhabitants of India: 'In very ancient times, there lived in India two very distinct communities [*sampraday*] of people. Of them, one resembled us in height and other aspects of physical appearance. The descendants of this community are now called Hindu. The people of the other community were short, dark, and extremely uncivilized. Their descendants are now known as Khas, Bhilla, Pulinda, Saontal, and other primitive [*jangla* = of the bush] jati.'[40] There were others who were the product of the mixing of sampradays. Thus the first three varna among the Hindus are said to be twice-born, but the Sudra are not entitled to that status. 'This shows that in the beginning the former were a separate sampraday from the latter. The latter were subsequently included in the former community, but were given the status of the most inferior class.'[41]

There is also a notion of the gradual spread of 'the Hindu religion' from the north of the country to the south. This spread is the result of the expansion of the realm: 'The south of the country was in the beginning covered by forests and inhabited by non-Hindu and uncivilized jati. Ramacandra was the first to hoist the Hindu flag in that part of India. . . . To this day there are many popular tales of the ancient colonization of the south by the Hindus.'[42] The image of the hero of the *Ramayana* holding aloft the modern symbol of national sovereignty came easily to the mind of this English-educated Bengali Brahman a hundred years ago, although the votaries of political Hinduism today will probably be embarrassed by the suggestion that Rama had subdued the inhabitants of South India and established a colonial rule.

Since there is a lack of authentic sources, the narrative of ancient Indian history is necessarily fragmentary. Gone is the certitude of Mrityunjay's dynastic lists; Tarinicharan states quite clearly the limits to a rational reconstruction of the ancient past. 'European historians have proved by various arguments that the battle of Kuruksetra took place before the fourteenth century BC. For a long period after the battle of Kuruksetra, the historical accounts of India are so uncertain, partial, and contradictory that it is impossible to construct a narrative from them.'[43] The narrative he does construct is not particularly remarkable, because he follows without much amendment the history

[40] *BI*, p. 2.
[41] *BI*, p. 4.
[42] *BI*, p. 27.
[43] *BI*, pp. 16–17.

of ancient India as current at the time among British writers on the subject. The only comment that is interesting in these chapters of Tarinicharan's book is the one he makes on Buddhism: '[The Buddha] became a great enemy of the Hindu religion, which is why Hindus describe him as an atheist and the destroyer of dharma. Nevertheless, the religion founded by him contains much advice of the highest spiritual value. He did not admit anything that was devoid of reason [*yukti*]. No matter how ancient the customs of a jati, if stronger reasons can be presented against the traditional views, then the opinions of at least some people are likely to change.'[44] What is interesting here is that the reasonableness of the religious views of Buddhism is not denied. On the contrary, it is presented as a rationalist critique from within 'the Hindu religion'. Otherwise, in accordance with the criterion of periodization, the period of the Buddhist rulers would have had to be classified as a separate period of ancient Indian history. Now it is given a place within the 'Hindu period'.

Although the historical sources for the ancient period are said to be fragmentary and unreliable, on one subject there seems to be no dearth of evidence. That is 'the civilization and learning of the ancient Indians'. This is the title of chapter six of Tarinicharan's book. The main argument is as follows:

> What distinguishes the giant from the dwarf or the mighty from the frail is nothing compared to the difference between the ancient and the modern Hindu. In earlier times, foreign travellers in India marvelled at the courage, truthfulness, and modesty of the people of the Arya *vamsa*; now they remark mainly on the absence of those qualities. In those days Hindus would set out on conquest and hoist their flags in Tatar, China, and other countries; now a few soldiers from a tiny island far away are lording it over the land of India. In those days Hindus would regard all except their own jati as *mleccha* and treat them with contempt; now those same mleccha shower contempt on the descendants of Aryans. Then the Hindus would sail their ships to Sumatra and other islands, evidence of which is still available in plenty in the adjacent island of Bali. Now the thought of a sea voyage strikes terror in the heart of a Hindu, and if anyone manages to go, he is immediately ostracized from society.[45]

Ancient glory, present misery: the subject of this entire story is 'us'. The mighty heroes of ancient India were 'our' ancestors, and the feeble

[44] *BI*, p. 17.
[45] *BI*, p. 32.

inhabitants of India today are 'ourselves'. That ancient Indians conquered other countries or traded across the seas or treated other people 'with contempt' is a matter of pride for 'us'. And it is 'our' shame that 'the descendants of Aryans' are today subordinated to others and are the objects of the latter's contempt. There is a certain scale of power among the different peoples of the world; earlier, the people of India were high on that scale, while today they are near the bottom.

Not only physical prowess; the achievements of ancient Indians in the field of learning were also universally recognized: 'In ancient times, when virtually the whole world was shrouded in the darkness of ignorance, the pure light of learning shone brightly in India. The discoveries in philosophy which emanated from the keen intellects of ancient Hindus are arousing the enthusiasm of European scholars even today.'[46] It will be noticed that the opinion of European scholars in this matter is extremely important to Tarinicharan. In fact, all the examples he cites on the excellence of ancient Indian learning—in the fields of astronomy, mathematics, logic, and linguistics—were the discoveries of nineteenth-century Orientalists. By bringing forward this evidence, Tarinicharan seems to be suggesting that although Europeans today treat Indians with contempt because of their degraded condition, Indians were not always like this, because even European scholars admit that the arts and sciences of ancient India were of the highest standard. This evidence from Orientalist scholarship was extremely important in the construction of the full narrative of nationalist history.

That Tarinicharan's history is nationalist is also signified by something else. His story of ancient glory and subsequent decline has a moral at the end: reform society, remove all those superstitions which are the marks of decadence, and revive the true ideals of the past. These false beliefs and practices for which Indians are today the objects of contempt did not exist in the past because even Europeans admit that in ancient times 'we' were highly civilized: 'Today we find Hindu women treated like slaves, enclosed like prisoners and as ignorant as beasts. But if we look a millennium and a quarter earlier, we will find that women were respected, educated, and largely unconstrained. Where was child marriage then? No one married before the age of twenty-four.'[47]

[46] *BI*, p. 33.
[47] *BI*, p. 33.

Ancient India became for the nationalist the classical age, while the period between the ancient and the contemporary was the dark age of medievalism. Needless to say, this was a pattern heartily approved by European historiography. If the nineteenth-century Englishman could claim ancient Greece as his classical heritage, why should not the English-educated Bengali feel proud of the achievements of the so-called Vedic civilization?

Narrative Break

The chapter on 'The Civilization and Learning of the Ancient Indians' closes Tarinicharan's history of ancient India. He then takes the reader outside India—to Arabia in the seventh century. It might seem reasonable to ask why it should be necessary, if one is to speak of a change of historical periods in twelfth-century India, to begin the description from seventh-century Arabia. The answer to this question is, of course, obvious. But implicit in that answer is an entire ensemble of assumptions and prejudices of nineteenth-century European historiography:

> Muhammad gave to his followers the name *musalman*, i.e. the faithful, and to all other humans the name *kafir* or infidel. . . . Directing his followers to take the sword in order to destroy the kafir, he said that God had ordained that those Muslims who die in the war against false religion will go to paradise and live in eternal pleasure in the company of doe-eyed nymphs. But if they run away from battle, they will burn in hell. The Arab jati is by nature fearless and warlike. Now, aroused by the lust for plunder in this world and for eternal pleasure in the next, their swords became irresistible everywhere. All of Arabia came under Muhammad's control and only a few years after his death the Muslim flag was flying in every country between Kabul and Spain. Never before in history had one kingdom after another, one land after another, fallen to a conqueror with the speed at which they fell to the Muslims. It was impossible that such people, always delirious at the prospect of conquest, would not covet the riches of India.[48]

The ground is being prepared here for the next episode, which will result from the clash of this distinct history of the Muslims with the history of Indians. This distinct history originates in, and acquires its identity from, the life of Muhammad. In other words, the dynasty

---

[48] *BI*, pp. 36–7.

which will be founded in Delhi at the beginning of the thirteenth century and the many political changes that will take place in the subsequent five centuries are not to be described merely as the periods of Turko-Afghan or Mughal rule in India; they are integral parts of the political history of Islam.

The actors in this history are also given certain behavioural characteristics. They are warlike and believe that it is their religious duty to kill infidels. Driven by the lust for plunder and visions of cohabiting with the nymphs of paradise, they are even prepared to die in battle. They are not merely conquerors, but 'delirious at the prospect of conquest' (*digvijayonmatta*), and consequently are innately covetous.

It is important at this point to note the complex relation of this new nationalist historiography to the histories of India produced by British writers in the nineteenth century. While James Mill's *History of British India*, completed in 1817, may have been 'the hegemonic textbook of Indian history' for European Indology,[49] for the first nationalist historians of India it represented precisely what they had to fight against. Mill did not share any of the enthusiasm of Orientalists such as William Jones for the philosophical and literary achievements of ancient India. His condemnation of the despotism and immorality of Indian civilization was total, and even his recognition of 'the comparative superiority of Islamic civilization' did not in any significant way affect his judgement that until the arrival of British rule India had always been 'condemned to semi-barbarism and the miseries of despotic power'.[50] Nationalist history in India could only be born by challenging such an absolute and comprehensive denial of all claims to historical subjectivity.[51]

[49] Ronald Inden has made this point with much force: *Imagining India* (Oxford: Basil Blackwell, 1990), pp. 45–6.
[50] For a discussion of Mill's comparative treatment of the Hindu and Muslim periods in Indian history, see J.S. Grewal, *Muslim Rule in India: The Assessments of British Historians* (Calcutta: Oxford University Press, 1970), pp. 64–97.
[51] Romila Thapar has argued that Mill's *History* nevertheless remained influential for Indian writers because 'it laid the foundation for a communal interpretation of Indian history and thus provided the historical justification for the two-nation theory'. His severe condemnations 'led to a section of the Orientalists and later to Indian historians having to defend "Hindu civilization" even if it meant overglorifying the ancient past'. 'Communalism and the Writing of Ancient Indian History', in Romila Thapar, Harbans Mukhia, and Bipan Chandra, *Communalism and the Writing of Indian History* (Delhi: People's Publishing House, 1969), p. 4.

Far more directly influential for the nationalist school texts we are looking at was Elphinstone's *History of India* (1841). This was the standard textbook in Indian universities and was the most widely read British history of India until Vincent Smith's books were published in the early twentieth century. The reason why nationalist readers found Elphinstone more palatable than Mill is not far to seek. As E.B. Cowell, who taught in Calcutta and added notes to the later editions of Elphinstone's *History*, explained in a preface in 1866, a 'charm of the book is the spirit of genuine hearty sympathy with and appreciation of the native character which runs through the whole, and the absence of which is one of the main blemishes in Mr. Mill's eloquent work.'[52] In this spirit of sympathy, Elphinstone wrote entire chapters in his volume called 'Hindus' on 'Philosophy', 'Astronomy and Mathematical Science', 'Medicine', 'Language', 'Literature', 'Fine Arts', and 'Commerce'. He also began his volume on 'Mahometans' with a chapter called 'Arab Conquests A.D. 632, A.H. 11 – A.D. 753, A.H. 136', whose first section was 'Rise of the Mahometan Religion'.

Another source often acknowledged in the Bengali textbooks is the series called *The History of India as Told by Its Own Historians*.[53] Compiled by Henry Elliot, and edited and published after his death by John Dowson between 1867 and 1877, these eight volumes comprised translated extracts from over 150 works, principally in Persian, covering a period from the ninth to the eighteenth century. It was a gigantic example of the privilege claimed by modern European scholarship to process the writings of a people supposedly devoid of historical consciousness and render into useful sources of history what otherwise could 'scarcely claim to rank higher than Annals'. The technical qualities of the scholarship of Elliot and Dowson were to be questioned in subsequent decades,[54] but, with the substitution of English for Persian as the language of the state, it was through their mediation that the Persian sources of Indian history would now become available to the modern literati in Bengal.

[52] 'Advertisement to the Fifth Edition', in Mountstuart Elphinstone, *The History of India: The Hindu and Mahometan Periods*, 9th edn (London: John Murray, 1905), p. vii.

[53] H.M. Elliot, *The History of India as Told by Its Own Historians: The Muhammadan Period*, ed. John Dowson, 8 vols (London: Trubner, 1867–77).

[54] The most detailed criticism was in Shahpurshah Hormasji Hodivala, *Studies in Indo-Muslim History: A Critical Commentary on Elliot and Dowson's History of India as Told by Its Own Historians*, 2 vols (Poona: 1939; Lahore: Islamic Book Service, 1979).

The assumptions which regulated the selection and translation of these sources were quite explicitly stated by Elliot:

> In Indian Histories there is little which enables us to penetrate below the glittering surface, and observe the practical operation of a despotic Government. . . . If, however, we turn our eyes to the present Muhammadan kingdoms of India, and examine the character of the princes . . . we may fairly draw a parallel between ancient and modern times. . . . We behold kings, even of our own creation, slunk in sloth and debauchery, and emulating the vices of a Caligula or a Commodus. . . . Had the authors whom we are compelled to consult, portrayed their Caesars with the fidelity of Suetonius, instead of the more congenial sycophancy of Paterculus, we should not, as now, have to extort from unwilling witnesses, testimony to the truth of these assertions. . . . The few glimpses we have, even among the short Extracts in this single volume, of Hindus slain for disputing with Muhammadans, of general prohibitions against processions, worship, and ablutions, and of other intolerant measures, of idols mutilated, of temples razed, of forcible conversions and marriages, of proscriptions and confiscations, of murders and massacres, and of the sensuality and drunkenness of the tyrants who enjoined them, show us that this picture is not overcharged, and it is much to be regretted that we are left to draw it for ourselves from out of the mass of ordinary occurrences. . . .[55]

The fact that even Hindu writers wrote 'to flatter the vanity of an imperious Muhammadan patron' was, Elliot thought, 'lamentable . . . there is not one of this slavish crew who treats the history of his native country subjectively, or presents us with the thoughts, supposed to give vent to. . . .' Elliot also drew for his readers the conclusions from his presentation of these extracts:

> They will make our native subjects more sensible of the immense advantages accruing to them under the mildness and equity of our rule. . . . We should no longer hear bombastic Babus, enjoying under our Government the highest degree of personal liberty, and many more political privileges than were ever conceded to a conquered nation, rant about patriotism, and the degradation of their present position. If they would dive into any of the volumes mentioned herein, it would take these young Brutuses and Phocions a very short time to learn, that in the days of that dark period for whose return they sigh, even the bare utterance of their ridiculous fantasies would have been attended, not with silence and contempt, but with the severer discipline of molten lead or impalement.

[55] 'Sir Henry Elliot's Original Preface', in ibid., vol. 1, pp. xv–xxvii.

Ironically, when the young Brutuses and Phocions did learn Elliot's lessons on Muhammadan rule, their newly acquired consciousness of being 'a long oppressed race' did not stop with a condemnation of Islamic despotism; it was also turned against British rule.

In the second half of the nineteenth century, European Indological scholarship seemed to have agreed that the history of Hinduism was one of a classical age—for some the Vedic civilization, for others the so-called Gupta revival from the fourth to the seventh centuries—followed by a medieval decline from the eighth to the eighteenth centuries.[56] For some, this decline was itself the reason why the country fell so quickly to the Muslim invaders. In any case, the theory of medieval decline fitted in nicely with the overall judgement of nineteenth-century British historians that 'Muslim rule in India' was a period of despotism, misrule, and anarchy—this, needless to say, being the historical justification for colonial intervention.[57]

For Indian nationalists in the late nineteenth century, the pattern of classical glory, medieval decline, and modern renaissance appeared as one that was not only proclaimed by the modern historiography of Europe but also approved for India by at least some sections of European scholarship. What was needed was to claim for the Indian nation the historical agency for completing the project of modernity. To make that claim, ancient India had to become the classical source of Indian modernity, while 'the Muslim period' would become the night of medieval darkness. Contributing to that description would be all the prejudices of the European Enlightenment about Islam. Dominating the chapters from the twelfth century onwards in the new nationalist history of India will be a stereotypical figure of 'the Muslim', endowed with a 'national character': he will be fanatical, bigoted, warlike, dissolute, and cruel.

Muslim Tyranny: Hindu Resistance

The story which begins with the birth of Islam in Arabia does, of course, shift to India, but this happens in stages. Tarinicharan gives long descriptions of the Arab invasions of Sind and the successive raids by Mahmud Ghaznavi into various Indian kingdoms, all of which take place well before the establishment of the so-called Slave Dynasty

[56] The point is discussed in Inden, *Imagining India*, pp. 117–22.
[57] On this, see Grewal, *Muslim Rule*.

84   *Empire and Nation: Essential Writings 1985–2005*

in Delhi in the early thirteenth century. These descriptions have a similar pattern which can be clarified by looking at three examples: Tarinicharan's accounts of the invasion of Sind by Muhammad Ibn Kasim, of Mahmud Ghaznavi's attack on Punjab, and of the victory of Muhammad Ghuri at Thanesar.

Muhammad Kasim began his war on Dahir, the king of Sind, in 712: 'Fortune favoured him. A ball of fire thrown by his soldiers struck King Dahir's elephant which panicked and fled from the battlefield. Dahir's troops, thinking that their king had given up the battle, fell into disarray. Later it will be seen that even when Indians had every chance of victory, similar misfortunes often led to their defeat at the hands of the Muslims.'[58] It must be noted that what Tarinicharan calls 'fortune' (*daiva*) and 'misfortune' (*durddaiva*) are not the same as the daiva that was divine intervention in Mrityunjay's narrative. Misfortune here is mere accident, a matter of chance. There is no suggestion at all of any retribution for immorality. It is the misfortune not of kings but of 'Indians', that, despite deserving to win, they lost repeatedly because of accidents:

> Finally, after displaying much heroism, [King Dahir] was killed at the hands of the enemy. His capital was besieged, but Dahir's wife, displaying a courage similar to her husband's, continued to defend the city. In the end, food supplies ran out. Deciding that it was preferable to die rather than submit to the enemy, she instructed the inhabitants of the city to make the necessary arrangements. Everyone agreed; everywhere, pyres were lit. After the immolations [of the women], the men, completing their ablutions, went out sword in hand and were soon killed by the Muslims.[59]

Later, we will get similar stories of defeat in battle. Two features are worth our notice: one, the courage of Hindu women in resisting aggression, and the other, the death in battle of Hindu men as a ritualized form of self-sacrifice. We thus have narrative indices such as 'everywhere,

[58] *BI*, p. 38. The same description occurs in Elphinstone, *History*, pp. 300–1, minus the last comment.

[59] *BI*, p. 38. These details also appear in Elphinstone, *History*, p. 301, where the source mentioned is James Tod, *Annals and Antiquities of Rajasthan or the Central and Western Rajput States of India*, ed. William Crooke (1829–32; rpnt. London: Oxford University Press, 1920). What is a story from Rajput folklore in Tod, having entered modern historiography in Elphinstone as the slaughter of a 'Rajput tribe by the Mahometans', becomes in Tarinicharan an episode in the history of the resistance by 'Indians' to Muslim conquest.

pyres were lit' and 'completing their ablutions . . . killed by the Muslims'. The corresponding index for Muslim soldiers is 'driven by the prospect of cohabiting with doe-eyed nymphs . . . etc'. The contrast is significant.

Tarinicharan tells another story about Kasim which is part of the same narrative structure:

> On completing his conquest of Sind, Kasim was preparing to drive further into India when the resourcefulness of a woman became his undoing. Among the women who were captured in war in Sind were two daughters of King Dahir. They were not only of high birth but were also outstandingly beautiful. Kasim thought they would make appropriate presents for the Khalifa and accordingly sent them to his master. The ruler of the Muslims was bewitched by the beauty of the elder daughter and began to look upon her with desire. At this, she burst into tears and said, 'It is a pity that I am not worthy of receiving the affections of someone like you, because Kasim has already sullied my dharma.' Hearing of this act of his servant, the Khalifa was enraged and ordered that Kasim be sewn in hide and brought before him. When this order was carried out, the Khalifa showed Kasim's corpse to the princess. Eyes sparkling with delight, she said, 'Kasim was entirely innocent. I had made the allegation only in order to avenge the deaths of my parents and the humiliation of their subjects.'[60]

To the courage of Hindu women is added another element: intelligence. And parallel to the story of self-sacrifice is created another story: vengeance on the enemy for the death of one's kin.

Let us move to the beginning of the eleventh century and the period of Mahmud of Ghazna: 'Of all Muslims, it was his aggressions which first brought devastation and disarray to India, and from that time the freedom of the Hindus has diminished and faded like the phases of the moon.'[61] Tarinicharan mentions some of Mahmud's qualities, such as courage, foresight, strategic skill, and perseverance, but ignores the fact, discussed in Elphinstone, that Mahmud was also a great patron of arts and letters: 'Although he was endowed with these qualities, he was also a great adherent, at least in public, of the Musalman

---

[60] *BI*, p. 39. The story occurs in Elphinstone, *History*, pp. 303–4, which is undoubtedly the source for Tarinicharan. There is a much more detailed account in an extract from 'Chach-nama, or Tarikh-i Hind wa Sind' in Elliot and Dowson, *Own Historians*, vol. 1, pp. 209–11, in which in the end the princess rebukes the Khalifa for passing such peremptory orders against an innocent man.

[61] *BI*, p. 41.

religion, a bitter opponent of the worship of idols and an unyielding pursuer of wealth and fame.'[62] This was another trait of the so-called 'Muslim character': where faith in Islam was a reason for war, it was not true faith but only an apparent adherence to religion.

Mahmud moved against King Anandapal of the Shahiya dynasty:

> 'The Muslims are determined to destroy the independence of all of India and to eradicate the Hindu religion. If they conquer Lahore, they will attack other parts of the country. It is therefore a grave necessity for all to unite in suppressing the mleccha forces.' Saying this, the King [Elphinstone writes the name as Anang Pal; Tarinicharan does the same] sent emissaries to all the principal Hindu kings. His appeal did not go unheeded. The kings of Delhi, Kanauj, Ujjain, Gwalior, Kalinjar and other places joined with Anangapal. Masses of troops arrived in Punjab. Worried by this sudden increase in the strength of the opposition, Mahmud decided, for reasons of safety, to halt near Peshawar. The Hindu forces increased daily. Hindu women from far away sold their diamonds, melted down their gold ornaments and sent supplies for war. . . .[63]

King Anandapal is unlikely to have had the historical foresight to anticipate that the fall of Lahore to Mahmud would lead to 'the destruction of the independence of all of India'. Needless to say, these are Tarinicharan's words. But by putting them on the lips of the ruler of Punjab, he turns this story into a war of the Hindu jati: 'the kings joined with Anangapal', 'the Hindu forces increased daily', 'Hindu women from far away sent supplies', etc. But then came the stroke of misfortune: 'A fire-ball or a sharp arrow flung from the Musalman camp struck the elephant of the Hindu commander Anangapal. The elephant, with the king on its back, fled from the field of battle. At this, the Hindu soldiers fell into disarray.'[64] This episode too ends with a story of vengeance, but this time of another variety: 'The king of Kanauj, who had collaborated with Mahmud, became an object of hatred and contempt in the community of Hindu kings. Hearing this, the ruler of Ghazni entered India for the tenth time to help his protege. But well before his arrival, the king of Kalinjar performed the

---

[62] *BI*, p. 42.

[63] *BI*, pp. 43–4. All these details, once again, are in Elphinstone, *History*, pp. 320–1, where the authority cited is David Price, *Chronological Retrospect, or Memoirs of the Principal Events of Mahommedan History*, vol. 2 (London: 1821).

[64] *BI*, p. 44.

execution of the king of Kanauj.'[65] Needless to say, this too was a ritual; hence, it was not just 'an execution', but the 'performance of an execution'.

Of Muhammad Ghuri, Tarinicharan says that his soldiers were 'inhabitants of the hills, hardy and skilled in warfare. By comparison, the Hindu kings were disunited and their soldiers relatively docile and undisciplined. Consequently, it was only to be expected that Muhammad would win easily. But that is not what happened. Virtually no Hindu ruler surrendered his freedom without a mighty struggle. In particular, the Rajahputa were never defeated. The rise, consolidation and collapse of Muslim rule have been completed, but the Rajahputa remain free to this day.'[66] Not only did the Hindu kings not submit without resistance, but after the first attack by Muhammad they even 'chased the Muslims away for twenty *kros* [forty miles].'[67] On his second attack, the treachery of Jaichand and the unscrupulousness of Muhammad led to the defeat of Prithviraj. This account by Tarinicharan bears no resemblance at all to the narratives of Mrityunjay. There is also a story of revenge at the end. A hill tribe Tarinicharan calls Goksur (Elphinstone calls them 'a band of Gakkars') had been defeated by Muhammad; one night, some of them managed to enter his tent and kill the sultan in revenge.

With the establishment of the Sultanate, the story of the oppression of Hindus by intolerant rulers will be repeated a number of times. For instance, Sikandar Lodi: 'Sekendar prohibited pilgrimage and ritual bathing in the Ganga and other sacred rivers. He also destroyed temples at many places. A Brahman who had declared that "The Lord recognizes every religion if followed sincerely" was called before Sekendar, and when he refused to discard his tolerant views was executed by the cruel ruler. When a Musalman holy man criticized the prohibition of pilgrimages, the king was enraged and shouted, "Rascal! So you support the idolaters?" The holy man replied, "No, that is not what I am doing. All I am saying is that the oppression by rulers of their subjects is unjust."'[68] Tarinicharan's barbs are the sharpest when directed against Aurangzeb. 'Aranjib was deceitful, murderous and

---

[65] *BI*, p. 46.

[66] *BI*, p. 53.

[67] *BI*, p. 54.

[68] *BI*, p. 83. These stories appear in Elphinstone, *History*, pp. 409–10.

plundered the wealth of others.'[69] 'His declaration of faith in the Musalman religion only facilitated the securing of his interests. . . . In truth, Aranjib would never forsake his interests for reasons of religion or justice.'[70] On the other hand, Tarinicharan has praise for Akbar, although his reasons are interesting: 'Akbar attempted to eradicate some irrational practices prescribed in the Musalman religion. He also tried to stop several irrational practices of the Hindus. He prohibited the ordeal by fire, the burning of widows against their wishes and child-marriage. He also allowed the remarriage of widows. . . . Ortho-dox Muslims were strongly opposed to him because of his liberal views on religion. Many called him an atheist.'[71] It was not his impartiality in matters of religion but rather his use of the powers of the state to reform both the Hindu and the Muslim religions that makes Akbar worthy of praise.

History as the Source of Nationhood

It is remarkable how pervasive this framework of nationalist history became in the consciousness of the English-educated middle class in Bengal in the late nineteenth century. In its literary and dramatic productions as well as in its schools and colleges, this narrative of na-tional history went virtually unchallenged until the early decades of the twentieth century.

The idea that 'Indian nationalism' is synonymous with 'Hindu nationalism' is not the vestige of some premodern religious conception. It is an entirely modern, rationalist, and historicist idea. Like other modern ideologies, it allows for a central role of the state in the mod-ernization of society and strongly defends the state's unity and sovereignty. Its appeal is not religious but political. In this sense, the framework of its reasoning is entirely secular. A little examination will show that, compared to Mrityunjay's historiography which revolved around the forces of the divine and sacred, Tarinicharan's is a wholly secular historiography.

In fact, the notion of 'Hindu-ness' in this historical conception cannot be, and does not need to be, defined by any religious criteria at all. There are no specific beliefs or practices which characterize this

[69] *BI*, p. 220.
[70] *BI*, p. 173.
[71] *BI*, p. 141.

'Hindu' and the many doctrinal and sectarian differences among
Hindus are irrelevant to this concept. Indeed, even such anti-Vedic
and anti-Brahmanic religions as Buddhism and Jainism count here as
'Hindu'. Similarly, people outside the Brahmanic religion and outside
caste society are also claimed as part of the Hindu jati. But clearly excluded from this jati are religions like Christianity and Islam.

What then is the criterion for inclusion or exclusion? It is one of
historical origin. Buddhism or Jainism are 'Hindu' because they originate in India, out of debates and critiques that are internal to Hinduism.
Islam and Christianity come from outside and are therefore foreign.
And 'India' here is the generic entity, with fixed territorial definitions,
which acts as the permanent arena for the history of the jati.

What, we may ask, is the place of those inhabitants of India who are
excluded from this nation? There are several answers that are suggested
in the historiography we are looking at. One answer, which assumes
the centrality of the modern state in the life of the nation, is frankly
majoritarian. The majority 'community' is Hindu; the others are
minorities. State policy must therefore reflect this preponderance, and
the minorities must accept the leadership and protection of the majority. This view, which today is being propagated with such vehemence
by Hindu extremist politics, actually has its origin more than a
hundred years ago, at the same time that Indian nationalism was born.

The other answer, which also makes the distinction between
majority and minority 'communities', is associated with what is called
the politics of 'secularism' in India. This view holds that in order to
prevent the oppression of minorities by the majority, the state must
enact legal measures to protect the rights and separate identities of the
minorities. The difficulty is that the formal institutions of the state,
based on an undifferentiated concept of citizenship, cannot allow for
the separate representation of minorities. Consequently, the question of who represents minorities necessarily remains problematic,
and constantly threatens the tenuous identity of nation and state.

There was a third answer in this early nationalist historiography.
This denied the centrality of the state in the life of the nation and instead pointed to the many institutions and practices in the everyday
lives of the people through which they had evolved a way of living with
their differences. These historians argued that the true history of India
lay not in the battles of kings and the rise and fall of empires but in
this everyday world of popular life whose innate flexibility, untouched

by conflicts in the domain of the state, allowed for the coexistence of all religious beliefs. The principal difficulty with this view, which has many affinities with the later politics of Gandhism, is its inherent vulnerability to the overwhelming sway of the modern state. Its only defence against the historicist conception of the nation is to claim for the everyday life of the people an essential and transhistorical truth.

None of these answers, however, can admit that the Indian nation as a whole might have a claim on the historical legacy of Islam. The idea of the singularity of national history has inevitably led to a single source of Indian tradition, namely, ancient Hindu civilization. Islam here is either the history of foreign conquest or a domesticated element of everyday popular life. The classical heritage of Islam remains external to Indian history.

The curious fact is, of course, that this historicist conception of Hindu nationalism has had little problem in claiming for itself the modern heritage of Europe. It is as rightful participants in that globalized domain of the modern state that today's contestants fight each other in the name of history.

4

The Fruits of Macaulay's Poison Tree
(1985)

The time has come once again to talk about the 'Bengal Renaissance'. And also to talk about ourselves.

It was in the age of nationalism that the story of our renaissance was invented. Our nationalism required not only the ennobling memory of an ancient and glorious civilization, it also needed to affiliate itself with a more recent tradition of the authentic rediscovery and reinterpretation of that ancient heritage. For us, the renaissance had to be a modern—and for that reason historically authentic—recreation of our memory of the nation's glorious past.

In their eagerness not to miss out any potentially significant part of this new intellectual tradition, nationalist historians of modern Indian thought cast their nets as wide as possible. Liberal, conservative, rationalist, romantic, westernizing, revivalist, forward-looking, backward-looking—they all became part of the story of our modern rebirth, and nationalist historians were not unduly fussy about the precise quality of modernity which the great figures of the Indian renaissance displayed. The criteria for a more discriminating sense of historical judgement were provided, interestingly enough, from within Indian Marxism. And it was the Bengal case which came to exemplify these criteria.

The Debate Within Marxism

The intellectual history of India in the nineteenth and twentieth centuries, Marxist historians argued, was a history of the struggle between the forces of progress and those of reaction. Progress was represented by those who stood for *modernity*, that is to say by those who fought against the antiquated beliefs and practices of a medieval society, who championed the cause of rationality, science, and enlightenment against scripture, custom, and faith. Progress was also represented by those who took up the cause of the *nation* against the exploitative rule of a colonial power. The criterion of modernity acquired its progressive historical significance in terms of an analogy between the social and intellectual history of nineteenth-century India and the Renaissance, the Reformation, and perhaps also the Enlightenment, in Europe. This analogy then seemed to imply that the social and intellectual history of nineteenth-century India could be interpreted in relation to the economic history of this period in much the same way as the Renaissance or the Reformation in Europe has been interpreted in relation to the class struggles in the age of transition from feudalism to capitalism. That is to say, our renaissance too was thought to go hand in hand with the rise of a historically progressive bourgeoisie. This in turn justified the second analogy which attributed in the Indian case the same progressive significance to the criterion of nationality as in the nationalist struggles in central and southern Europe in the nineteenth century. Taken together, the double analogy sought to encapsulate within a single concept of 'progress' two quite distinct criteria of modernity and nationality. The results were hardly satisfactory.

In fact, the difficulties were apparent almost as soon as this more discriminating history of 'the Bengal Renaissance' began to be written down. Susobhan Sarkar, in his classic 'Notes on the Bengal Renaissance', underlined the two analogies at every available opportunity.[1] Bengal's role in 'the modern awakening of India' was, he thought, 'comparable to the position occupied by Italy in the story of the European Renaissance'. Rammohun Roy's criticism of priestcraft and superstition reminded him of the leaders of the Protestant revolution, and his defence of free speech of Milton's *Areopagitica*, and Madhusudan Dutt seemed to him 'a typical Italian humanist indulging in wild free living'. Surendranath Banerjea, he thought it important to mention, 'made his audience thrill in sympathy with the Italy of the Risorgimento or

---

[1] First published in 1949 and reprinted in Susobhan Sarkar, *Bengal Renaissance and Other Essays* (New Delhi: People's Publishing House, 1970), pp. 1–74. Other examples of this 'orthodox' Marxist interpretation of nineteenth-century thought can be found in A.R. Desai, *Social Background of Indian Nationalism* (Bombay: Popular Prakashan, 1948); Bipan Chandra, *The Rise and Growth of Economic Nationalism in India* (New Delhi: People's Publishing House, 1966); Arabinda Poddar, *Renaissance in Bengal: Search for Identity* (Simla: Indian Institute of Advanced Study, 1977).

Ireland of the Home Rule movement'. Rammohun Roy was, of course, unquestionably the great figure of the renaissance, not merely because he began the struggle to transform 'the stagnant, degraded and corrupt state into which our society had fallen', but because he sought to do so on the basis of a synthesis of 'the best thought of the East and the West'. He was modern, but not denationalized. By contrast, the impact of the Derozians was 'ephemeral and insubstantial'. Even their irreverence for social conventions did not lead to 'sturdy revolt or bold defiance', but to 'mere evasion'. The conservative opponents of Rammohun were traditionalists, unable to appreciate the progressive quality of the new ideas that were beginning to challenge many long-standing beliefs. And yet, Sarkar himself admitted, men like Radhakanta Deb or Mrityunjay Vidyalankar were not 'out and out reactionary', for although they opposed Rammohun they were often 'in favour of many progressive reforms'.

On the criterion of nationality, the entire progressive intelligentsia of Bengal, virtually without exception, was on the wrong side during the revolt of 1857. But Sarkar is able to find an alternative conjuncture, a historical point not too distant in time from the Great Indian Revolt, where this anomaly is set right. The Indigo agitations 'swept like a tidal wave over the country in 1859–60 and formed a striking landmark in the growth of Bengal's consciousness.' The significance of this mass upsurge against English planters—carried out by the peasants and fully supported by the city intelligentsia—Sarkar emphasizes by pointing out that even the Royal Institute of International Affairs called it 'a landmark in the history of nationalism'. The rest is a story of the progressive disappearance of illusions about the benefits of British rule and the growing militancy of anti-colonial struggles.

More detailed historical studies, however, easily brought out the main difficulty with this framework. It was obvious that the national was not always secular and modern, and the popular and democratic quite often traditional and sometimes fanatically anti-modern. The 1970s, in fact, saw several attempts by historians to question what had by then become the Marxist orthodoxy on the subject. How much this academic rethinking was prompted by the political turmoil in the Left in West Bengal in this period, and particularly by the quite literal attempts at iconoclasm, remains an interesting question of our own intellectual history. In any event, the earlier Marxist formulations on the nineteenth-century 'renaissance' were severely criticized by these historians. It was all very well, such critics argued, to pick out the many undoubtedly modern elements in the thought of the nineteenth-century social reformers and ideologues, but what significance do these elements of modernity acquire when looked at in the context of the evolving colonial economy of the same period, of massive deindus-trialization and destitution, of unbearable pressure on the land leading to a virtually irreversible process of regressive rent exploitation and stagnation in levels of productivity, of the crushing of peasant resistance, of the growing social gulf rather than bonds of alliance between a modernized, Western-educated urban elite and the rest of the nation? In what sense can this modernity be reconciled with any meaningful conception of the national–popular?

Sumit Sarkar, for instance, showed that Indian Marxists, in inter-preting the evolution of Indian thought as a conflict between two trends, 'westernist' or 'modernist' on the one hand and 'traditionalist' on the other, had, notwithstanding the many analytical intricacies, wholeheartedly plumped for Westernism as the historically progressive trend.[2] He then argued: 'An unqualified equation of the "western-izers" . . . with modernism or progress almost inevitably leads to a more positive assessment of British rule, English education, and the nineteenth-century protagonists of both . . .' In fact, the entire 'tradition–modernization dichotomy' served as a cover under which 'the grosser facts of imperialist political and economic exploitation [were] very often quietly tucked away in a corner.' As facts stand, Ram-mohun Roy's break with tradition was 'deeply contradictory', accom-modating within the same corpus of thinking numerous compromises with orthodox, Hindu elitist, and by his own enlightened standards clearly irrational ways of thought and practice. In any case, it was a break only 'on the intellectual plane and not at the level of basic social transformation.' In his economic thinking, he accepted, *in toto*, the then fashionable logic of free trade and seemed to visualize 'a kind of dependent but still real bourgeois development in Bengal in close

---

[2] Sumit Sarkar, 'Rammohun Roy and the Break with the Past', in V.C. Joshi, ed., *Rammohun Roy and the Process of Modernization in India* (Delhi: Vikas, 1975), pp. 46–68. Similar arguments are put forward in three other articles in the same volume: Asok Sen, 'The Bengal Economy and Rammohun Roy'; Barun De, 'A Biographical Perspective on the Political and Economic Ideas of Rammohun Roy'; Pradyumna Bhattacharya, 'Rammohun Roy and Bengali Prose'; and Barun De, 'A Historiographical Critique of Renaissance Analogues for Nineteenth-Century India', in Barun De, ed., *Perspectives in the Social Sciences I: Historical Dimensions* (Calcutta: Oxford University Press, 1977), pp. 178–218.

collaboration with British merchants and entrepreneurs.' This was an absurd illusion because colonial subjection would never permit full-blooded bourgeois modernity but only 'a weak and distorted caricature'.

The argument therefore was that while there were elements of modernity in the new cultural and intellectual movements in nineteenth-century India, these cannot be meaningful unless they are located in their relation on the one hand to the changing socio-economic structure, and on the other to the crucial context of power, that is, to the reality of colonial subjection. When thus located, the achievements of early-nineteenth-century 'modernizers' such as Rammohun seem limited within a Hindu elitist, colonial, almost comprador, framework.

In another article on the Derozians, Sumit Sarkar once again questioned the simple-minded tendency among Marxists to distinguish between a clear progressive trend and a clear conservative trend among nineteenth-century intellectuals.[3] 'Perhaps we have all been somewhat guilty of a Whig interpretation of our nineteenth-century heritage.' Although the Derozians were seen as the most extreme radicals of their times, Sumit Sarkar showed how there occurred a quite rapid blurring of distinctions between them and other sections of the intelligentsia. On many crucial matters, in fact, they shared the same presuppositions. 'The virtually ubiquitous presence of the concept of Muslim tyranny (and of British rule as a deliverance from the same) is merely one of the most striking features of nineteenth-century "renaissance" thought, and the Derozian acceptance of these assumptions is a reminder that in certain crucial respects our "radicals" were not all that different from the "moderates" or even the "conservatives".' Indeed these, much more than the presence or absence of liberal attitudes and sentiments, were the crucial questions which would have to determine our characterization of nineteenth-century thought. And the answer was clear: 'Dependence on the foreign rulers and alienation from the masses were to remain for long the two cardinal limitations of our entire "renaissance" intelligentsia.'

The same argument was stated at greater length in Asok Sen's study of the career of Iswar Chandra Vidyasagar.[4] Sen placed the problem in the theoretical context of Gramsci's discussion of the relation of

[3] Sumit Sarkar, 'The Complexities of Young Bengal', *Nineteenth Century Studies*, 1, 4 (October 1973), pp. 504–34.

[4] Asok Sen, *Iswar Chandra Vidyasagar and His Elusive Milestones* (Calcutta: Riddhi, 1977). Subsequent bracketed references are to this work.

intellectuals to more fundamental forces of social transformation. The mere acceptance of new ideas or their original structure of assumptions and implications did not in themselves mean much. Major changes in thought and attitude were, in fact, brought about 'by the capacity of nascent social forces to achieve goals of transformation [often] not clarified in the original postulates of reasoning or speculation' (Sen, p. 75). What was crucial, therefore, was a fundamental class striving for class hegemony and the advance of social production. Without such a class, 'the cultural influence of intellectuals is reduced to an essentially abstract phenomenon giving no consistent direction of significant social renewal; their influence is limited to tiny intellectual groups who have no creative bonds with a broader social consensus' (Sen, p. 86). In the specific context of nineteenth-century Bengal, the middle class was not a fundamental class nor were its intellectuals organic to any fundamental project of social transformation or conquest of hegemony. The new middle class was a product of English education. But in an economy under direct colonial control, in which there was little prospect for the release of forces of industrialization, the attempt 'to achieve through education what was denied to the economy' was utterly anomalous.

Vidyasagar's own attempts at social reform, for instance, placed great reliance upon liberal backing by the colonial government. The failure of those attempts showed that his hopes were misplaced. Nor did he find effective support for his schemes within his own class. When arguing for reform Vidyasagar, despite his professed disregard for the sanctity or reasonableness of the *sastra*, felt compelled to search out scriptural support for his programmes. He did not think it feasible to try creating a 'nonconformism outside the bond of canonical orthodoxy'. In fact, this remained a major ideological anomaly in all nineteenth-century attempts to 'modernize' religion and social practices—'a spurious conciliation of Indian idealism and imported liberal sanctions'—which led to a major backlash after 1880 in the form of movements to 'revive tradition', movements that were openly hostile to the earlier decades of 'reason and enlightenment'.

In Sen, therefore, the argument becomes sharper. The nineteenth-century intelligentsia may have genuinely welcomed the new ideas of reason and rationality, and some may even have shown considerable courage and enterprise in seeking to 'modernize' social customs and attitudes. But certain fundamental forces of transformation were absent in colonial society. As a result, the possibility for the emergence of a consistently rational set of beliefs or practices did not exist. Liberalism stood on highly fragile foundations; 'reason dwindled to merely individual means of self-gratification without social responsibility.' The halfheartedness and ambiguity were part of the very process of bourgeois development in a colonial country: 'the dialectics of loyalty and opposition' did not permit 'a clear division among the native bourgeoisie or the entire middle class into two exclusive categories of collaborators and opponents of imperialism.' In India, bourgeois opposition to imperialism was always ambiguous.

The attempt to relate developments in thought to the evolving socio-economic structure of a colonial country inevitably, therefore, led to the problem of power: the subjection of a colonial country and the question of loyalty or opposition to imperial power. And once put in that perspective, the modern and the national seemed to diverge in fundamental ways.

It is the problem of power which is placed at the centre of another critique of the nineteenth-century 'renaissance'—Ranajit Guha's analysis of Dinabandhu Mitra's *Neel Darpan*.[5] This play has long enjoyed a reputation for being a bold indictment of the depredations of British planters in the Indian countryside and a classic portrayal of the bravery and determination of the peasantry in their resistance to colonialism. But Guha shows the innately liberal-humanitarian assumptions underlying Dinabandhu's criticism of the planters, assumptions he shared with virtually the entire new intelligentsia of the nineteenth century. Underlying the criticism of the lawlessness of the planters and of the actions of a few foolish and inconsiderate English officials, there was in the author an abiding faith in the rationality and impartiality of English law and in the good intentions of the colonial administration as a whole. Never did it occur to these newly enlightened gentlemen, despite their fondness for justice and liberty, that the legitimacy of British rule in India might be called in question. In fact, it was the very existence of British power in India that was regarded as the final and most secure guarantee against lawlessness, superstition, and despotism. Not only that; the image of the resolute peasant defending his rights against the predatory planter, as represented in elite accounts such as Dinabandhu's play, is that of an enlightened liberal, conscious of his rights as an individual, willing to go to great lengths to defend these

[5] Ranajit Guha, '*Neel Darpan:* The Image of a Peasant Revolt in a Liberal Mirror', *Journal of Peasant Studies*, 2, 1 (October 1974), pp. 1–46.

rights against recalcitrant officials, even succumbing to 'brief, inter-mittent bursts' of violence, but all the while believing in the fundamen-tal legitimacy of the social order. This was a far cry from any truly revolutionary appreciation by a progressive intelligentsia of the strength of peasant resistance to colonialism and of its potential for the cons-truction of a new 'national-popular' consciousness. What the play does reveal is, in fact, an attitude of collaboration between a colonial government and its educated native collaborators, sealed by the mar-riage of law and literacy. The sympathy of the intelligentsia for victims of the violence of indigo planters, and the support by large sections of the rich and middling in town and countryside to the cause of the peas-ants, are explained by a specific conjuncture of interests and events. In the overall estimate, such opposition only opened up 'an immense hinterland of compromise and reformism into which to retreat from a direct contest for power with the colonial masters. . . . And, thus "improvement", that characteristic ideological gift of nineteenth-century British capitalism, is made to pre-empt and replace the urge for a revolutionary transformation of society.'

The critique of the 1970s seriously damaged the old structure of assumptions about our 'renaissance'. It emphasized at numerous points the impossibility of making the distinction between a progressive and a conservative trend within the nineteenth-century intelligentsia. It showed, in fact, that on most fundamental questions virtually the entire intelligentsia shared the same presuppositions. But those pre-suppositions were neither unambiguously modern nor unambiguous-ly national. Liberal, secular, and rational attitudes were invariably compromised by concessions to scriptural or canonical authority or, even more ignominiously, by succumbing to pressures for conformity or to material enticements. Moreover, sentiments of nationality flowed out of an unconcealed faith in the basic goodness of the colonial order and the progressive support of the colonial state. All this reflected the absence of a fundamental social class infused by a revolutionary urge to transform society and to stamp it with the imprint of its own un-questioned hegemony. Our 'renaissance' had no historical links with the revolutionary mission of a progressive bourgeoisie seeking to create a nation in its own image.

Interestingly, however, even in their critique of the 'renaissance' argument, the historians of the 1970s did not relinquish the analogy with European history as their basic structure of reference. Indeed, the critique was possible only by reference to that analogue. The point of the critique was, in fact, to show that if modern Europe is taken as the classic demonstration of the progressive significance of an intellectual revolution in the history of the emergence of the capitalist economy and the modern state, then the intellectual history of nineteenth-century India did not have this significance. As the harbinger of a bourgeois and national revolution, the Indian 'renaissance' was partial, fragmented; indeed, it was a failure.

The Nationalist Project

The critique of the 'renaissance' could not have avoided an implicit reference to European analogues because the most crucial terms of this discourse—modernity, progress, science, rationality, liberalism, capitalism, nation—could be defined within the domain of historical scholarship only by reference to the classical cases from Europe. The problem, in this case, was compounded by the fact that the great figures of the 'renaissance' themselves thought, spoke, and wrote within more or less the same discursive limits, and in fact consciously set out to emulate the historical experience from which that discourse had been born. As any reader of contemporary popular non-fiction will confirm, the paradoxes of self-referring systems of representation are seemingly endless.[6]

Thus, what was meant to be modern became increasingly alienated from the mass of the people. What seemed to assert greater ideological sway over the nation were newer forms of conservatism. And yet these seemingly conservative movements in thought were themselves premised on the same presuppositions—'modern' presuppositions—as those of the 'renaissance'. Nowhere are these paradoxes more baffling than in the history of the so-called 'revivalism' of the late nineteenth century. To this day, they have continued to embarrass our progressive intelligentsia.

Consider Bankimchandra Chattopadhyay, a man who regarded himself as 'a Young Bengal' and wrote his first novel in English. Rationalist to the core, his early social essays are marked by an explicit acceptance of the basic tenets of mid-nineteenth-century European

---

[6] For instance, Douglas R. Hofstadter, *Gödel, Escher, Bach: An Eternal Golden Braid* (Harmondsworth: Penguin, 1980).

social thought—positivist sociology as well as utilitarian political economy. Arguing from those theoretical premises, he quite naturally identified the cause of India's poverty and subjection in the absence from our culture of those attributes that have made the European culturally equipped for power and progress. The overwhelming part of religious beliefs in India, he argued, was based on *vairagya*, on otherworldliness and fatalism. This was wholly in contradiction with the requirements of progress in the modern world. If India was to progress, she would have to change her archaic beliefs and outmoded social institutions. The conditions for such a transformation had been created by British rule. It had established a finer and more impersonal legal and judicial system, brought greater access, at least in principle, for the lower castes to positions of power and status, and had made available the means for Indians to acquire the benefits of Western science and literature.[7] In order to qualify ourselves for progress and liberty, therefore, it was necessary to transform our culture, to bring into being a new national religion suited to the modern world. And to achieve this transformation, we would have to learn from the West, indeed to a large extent to imitate the West.[8]

But how, then, would we retain our own cultural identity, those distinctive cultural traits which made us different from all other nations in the world? How could we prevent ourselves from being submerged completely by the dominant culture of the West? By imitating the West, we might become modern, but what about our national character? How were we to preserve the latter? This was the central question of our emergent nationalist thought. And Bankim's answer to this question typified the intellectual premises which characterized virtually the whole of our national movement. Bankim's answer did not deny that the West and the East were essentially different. It also did not deny that in the conditions of the modern world the cultural values of the West were intrinsically superior to those of the East. Only, this superiority was partial; it related to only one sphere of culture. The superiority of the West was in the materiality of its culture. The West had achieved progress, prosperity, and freedom because it had placed Reason at the heart of its culture. The distinctive

---

[7] See, in particular, 'Bharatbarser Svadhinata Ebam Paradhinata', *Bankim Racanabali*, vol. 2 (Calcutta: Sahitya Samsad, 1955), pp. 241–5.

[8] See 'Anukaran', ibid., pp. 200–4.

culture of the West was its science, its technology, and its love of progress. But culture did not consist only of the material aspect of life. There was the spiritual aspect too, and here the European Enlightenment had little to contribute. In the spiritual aspect of culture the East was superior: there it was undominated.

There were three kinds of knowledge, Bankim argued: knowledge of the world, of the self, and of God. Knowledge of the world consisted of mathematics, astronomy, physics, and chemistry. These, one would have to learn from the West. Knowledge of self meant biology and sociology. These, too, one would have to learn from the West. Finally, knowledge of God. In this field, the Hindu sastra contained the greatest human achievements—the Upanishads, the *darsana*, the Puranas, and, principally, the *Gita*.[9] The true national religion would have to be a synthesis of the best achievements in these three aspects of knowledge. As the Guru explains in 'Dharmatattva': 'The day the European industries and sciences are united with Indian dharma, man will be god . . . Soon you will see that with the spread of the doctrine of pure bhakti, the Hindus will gain new life and become powerful like the English at the time of Cromwell or the Arabs under Muhammad.'[10] We need not concern ourselves here with the precise details of Bankim's attempted synthesis.[11] The point is that this wave of religious revivalism, usually regarded as a 'backlash', a 'reaction' to the progressive phase of modernism which had preceded it, was itself based on exactly the same intellectual presuppositions as those of the earlier phase. Like the modernists, the new conservatives admitted, first of all, the essential cultural difference between East and West; second, the importance of the material sphere of culture in the conditions created by the modern world; third, the innate superiority of Western culture in the material aspects of life; and fourth, the need to learn from and emulate the West in those material aspects. However, they also proposed an answer to the modernists' dilemma: by learning from the West we did not necessarily risk losing our national cultural identity as long as we were careful to distinguish between the two aspects of culture. We would learn our science and technology from the West, for

[9] 'Dharmatattva', ibid., p. 630.

[10] Ibid., pp. 630, 633.

[11] I have discussed this at much greater length in my book, *Nationalist Thought and the Colonial World* (London: Zed Books, 1986).

there the West was superior. But we must at the same time revive, retain, and strengthen our own spiritual heritage, for there we were second to none. That would preserve our national identity *vis-à-vis* the West.

It is also an undeniable fact that it was this ideological solution, and not the modernism of the early 'renaissance', that created the possibility of the emergence in Bengal of a nationalist vanguard. It was a solution which directly confronted the problem of modernity without evading, as the 'renaissance' did, the problem of power. It urged the new middle class to regenerate and reform the institutions of national culture—the national 'religion', as Bankim called it—and to do it as a *political* task. The spiritual conception of the nation evoked powerful sentiments in the minds of the new nationalist intelligentsia. The nation became the Mother, once resplendent in wealth and beauty, now in tatters, exhorting her sons, those of them who were brave and enlightened, to vanquish the enemy and win back her honour. The nation acquired a utopian meaning, dreamlike and yet passionately real, charged with a deeply religious semiotic. It conveyed the acute sense of anguish of a small, alienated middle class, daily insulted by the realities of political subjection and yet powerless to hit back, summoning up from the depths of its soul the will and the courage to deliver the ultimate sacrifice that would save the honour of the nation.

It was also a singularly elitist solution. The task of cultural synthesis could be performed only by a supremely refined intellect—learned, wise, agile, and religious. So also the political task of freeing the nation. Only the enlightened and the brave could be entrusted with it. It is in no way surprising that the direct political disciples of Bankim were the revolutionary terrorists of the early twentieth century. The elitism of their intellectual conceptions was reflected in the rigid exclusiveness of their organization, their distaste, indeed contempt, for mass politics, their mistrust of the peasantry and the lower castes, and, of course, of the Muslims—ignorant, superstitious, bigoted, treacherous.

The Uniqueness of West Bengal

But surely, we could object, all this changed in the 1920s and 1930s? The nineteenth-century renaissance, it is true, was limited. It could hardly have been otherwise under conditions of colonialism. Yet, despite its limitations, it did succeed in implanting in our consciousness the ideas of reason, rationality, and progress which were the hallmarks of the new democratic age. True again, the revivalist phase was marked by excessive emphasis on religion, by a championing of conservative values, and by sectarian exclusiveness. But despite all these limitations, it nevertheless succeeded in inspiring an emerging political leadership with the spirit of nationalism. It united a much broader section of the middle classes into an uncompromising, militant, and organized struggle against foreign rule. And the limitations from which both these phases of the movement suffered were overcome in the second and third decades of the present century when radical sections of the middle-class political leadership actively sought to forge organized links with the working class and the peasantry, both within and outside the platform provided by the nationalist struggle. Why, then, should we continue to harp on the limitations of the earlier phase when these had been superseded by our more recent political history?

It is an important objection, and one which the critique of the 1970s, restricted by the terms of its analogical reasoning, does not answer satisfactorily. That critique had sought to expose the invalidity of the conclusions drawn by the proponents of the 'renaissance' argument from the application of European analogues to nineteenth-century Indian history. If the historical analogy was to be applied, these critics had argued, it would only show that there was no renaissance in nineteenth-century India, no laying of the intellectual foundations for a bourgeois and a national revolution. Our present objection, however, would put the ball back in their court. Fair enough, we could reply; let us accept that the alleged renaissance in India did not have the same significance for the emergence of capitalism and the modern nation-state as the comparable intellectual and cultural movements in Europe. But this is only a negative demonstration. Looking back on the history of India in the last century and a half, it is surely undeniable that something significant did happen. What was it? We could indeed throw the challenge back at these critics and say: analogue or no analogue, explain to us in positive terms the course of our intellectual and cultural development leading up to the country's independence, the creation of a post-colonial state and the rapid growth of democratic and Left movements in various parts of the country.

Once again, it is paradoxical that the nationalist argument, originally built upon a historical analogue, should now want to vindicate itself by asserting the irrelevance of that analogue. But let that pass. Let us consider the theoretical requirements for an answer to our objection. The objection would, in fact, force us to re-examine some of the central conceptual terms of our discourse. Instead of adopting an analytical framework which demonstrates the various ways in which developments in India *do not fit* the more well-known historical models, we would be required to construct other concepts and other theoretical relations so as to adequately understand the *specific* historical developments in India.

On the face of it, this may seem an obvious enough requirement. Unfortunately, in the field of historical scholarship it is not all that simple. Involved in this is the gigantic problem of opening our theoretical constructs to the constant interplay between generalities formulated at the level of universal history and particularities discovered at the level of the historically specific. The former seem to emerge as abstracted generalizations over a large number of particular cases, thus constituting our framework of understanding. And yet, the inadequacy of the framework is exposed as soon as particular cases are re-examined within the unity of the theory. This, then, calls for a re-examination of the general framework itself. But the problem with historical knowledge is its own presence as an active element within human consciousness which in turn creates both history and historical knowledge. This problem of self-reference makes it extremely difficult to identify, and then to make sense of, the divergences between the universal and the particular. Understanding demands a unification of knowledge, while the urge not to overlook the historically specific seems to make understanding impossible.

Yet it is this ceaseless tension itself that sustains the quest for historical knowledge. This is what makes it a powerful and creative element in our consciousness of ourselves. Let us, therefore, accept the risk of gross oversimplification and hazard a few tentative comments by way of suggesting an alternative framework for understanding our intellectual history in the last 150 years. What, in the first place, are the main elements which may be said to define the hegemonic 'national' cultural form within the Bengali nationality? To what extent does this represent the intellectual–moral achievement of the leading strata among the Bengali people? And how is this development related to the evolving structures of the Indian state formation?

To start with, we should note the fact that there now exists a fairly well-defined, standard form of the Bengali language, for speech as well as for writing, applicable with minor modifications to West Bengal and Bangladesh. This, it can safely be asserted, is largely the creation of the Calcutta-based intelligentsia; this work of standardization is pursued to this day, at least for West Bengal, from that metropolis through the vastly expanded media of the press, school textbooks, radio and television, theatre and cinema, and gramophone records. With the help of this standardized language, there has also grown since the nineteenth century a considerable body of literature, artistic as well as theoretical, perhaps less distinguished in the academic disciplines and particularly the natural sciences, but nevertheless wide enough in range to cover virtually every significant intellectual movement in the world. The most outstanding feature of this literature is its undoubted modernity. Not only does it reflect, in the main, the social, intellectual, and artistic concerns and tastes of a relatively well-educated, largely urban, middle class, it also reveals a consistent urge to 'keep up' with the most advanced cultural trends in the rest of the world, more specifically in Europe. An avantgardism of this sort is evident from the time of the Derozians, and as early as in the middle of the century Krishnakamal Bhattacharya could scoff at the positivist pandits of Bengal because they could not read Comte in the original French; Bankim, he alleged, had only a second-hand familiarity with his supposed mentor.[12] Bankim, in turn, did not bother to hide his contempt for the 'backward' views of most of his contemporaries on scientific and philosophical matters.

This intellectual attitude of Bengal's cultural leaders, undoubtedly born out of the peculiarities of the colonial situation, produced, at one and the same time, an urge to find a distinct and authentic cultural identity for nationality as well as an urge for cosmopolitanism. Paradoxical as this may sound, it was the two together, and not just the first—the claim, that is, that it was not merely national but comparable with the most advanced international standards—that provided this culture of the middle classes with the standard of legitimacy which made it the accepted cultural norm for the entire nationality—the dominant, the 'standard' form of its culture. In a sense, the intellectual and creative tension between the two demands, for indigenous authenticity on the one hand and cosmopolitanism on the other, was born out of the more fundamental contradiction encountered by the new middle class in its entire colonial experience—the contradiction between

[12] See Bipinbihari Gupta, *Puratan Prasanga* (1913; rpnt. Calcutta: Bidyabharati, 1967), pp. 11–84.

the national and the modern. But the cultural resolution of this contradiction attempted by the Bengali intelligentsia was, in many ways,
quite unique in the overall Indian context. It has a lot to do, it seems
to me, with the uniqueness, one might even say marginality, of the
West Bengal case in the evolving pattern of present-day Indian politics.

There did, of course, exist a rather unique socio-economic situation
in Bengal. The very size of the middle class was, by the early decades
of the twentieth century, much larger than anywhere else in India.
Culturally, it was fairly homogeneous, being predominantly upper-
caste Hindu, until there emerged in the twentieth century a significant
Muslim middle class. But the latter development was interrupted by
largely exogenous historical circumstances as Bengal's politics was
drawn into the vortex of all-India political developments, culminating
in the partition of the province. Looking back, it now appears as one
of those quirks of history that through all the devastation and blood-
shed of the partition, the upper-caste Hindu middle class of Bengal
should have received, as it were, a whole new lease of life in the now
truncated state of West Bengal. For there, once again, its claim to a
position of natural leadership of the entire nationality became virtually
unassailable. There was no Bengali capitalist class which could seize
the new opportunities opened up by the withdrawal of British capital
or by state support for private capitalist expansion. Historically, the industrial working class too was very largely from outside Bengal; when
a sizeable Bengali working class was formed in the 1950s and 1960s its
culture became a virtual extension of that of the urban middle class.
The middle class itself, having lost its last surviving ties with the land
as a result of partition and the abolition of the zamindari form of
landownership, became a much more distinctly urban class than ever
before. It also became much more 'radical' in its politics.

This specific combination of urbanism and radicalism in the ideological orientation of the political leadership in West Bengal has given
a distinctive character to the politics of the state. In the sphere of
agrarian politics, for instance, unlike in most other states in India, the
middle-class political leadership of West Bengal, irrespective of party
affiliation, has intervened through the state machinery or through
party organizations, not as a contending element in the agrarian class
struggle but as an outsider, an external force with an 'objective' consciousness of the social reality. This structural location of the middle-class
political leadership and the resultant 'objectification' of politics is

crucial to an understanding of the apparent paradox of the continued domination by an upper-caste Hindu and predominantly urban middle class in virtually every sphere of organized political and cultural life in the state and the absence of any significant caste or communal articulation of political demands. This creates the basis for the principal political strategy of Left politics in West Bengal—the alliance between urban consumers, both middle class and working class, and the small and landless peasantry in the countryside. The crucial mediating role in this political strategy is necessarily provided by the state machinery, in the form of guaranteeing a system of public distribution of food in the urban areas, statutory control of prices of essential items of consumption, protecting the poor peasant against eviction from the land, maintaining the bargaining position of landless peasants and labourers against landlords and moneylenders, and generally resisting as far as possible the destructive consequences of a full-scale capitalism in agriculture. It is significant that except for the ill-fated Bangla Congress of the late 1960s, West Bengal's politics has not seen a distinct party organization of the *kulak* interest.

The 'radical' thrust of this politics, however, necessarily culminates in an *étatisme*, but an *étatisme* which lacks the guidance and support of a fundamental 'national' class. This is where the continuity lies between the so-called renaissance of the nineteenth century and the dominant strand of politics in West Bengal today. This is also where the discontinuity lies between the politics of West Bengal and the politics that has emerged around the Indian state as a whole. As members of an enlightened intelligentsia, our nineteenth-century reformers were acting in accordance with the newly acquired dictates of reason, rationality, and freedom. In theory, this should have prepared the ideological conditions for the emergence of a capitalist order. Unfortunately, in the case of Bengal in the second half of the nineteenth century, the nationality did not possess even an emergent bourgeoisie with the will and the ability to carry forward this struggle in the sphere of civil society, more specifically the economy. The intelligentsia consequently fell back upon what now appears to us a supremely naive belief in the essential rationality and liberality of the colonial state. Nevertheless, a struggle was waged, both against medieval obscurantism ossified in the traditional hierarchical order and against the vulgar profligacy of the comprador rich who dominated the social life of Calcutta in the early decades of the nineteenth century. In the process, a new ethic came to acquire a position of dominance in Bengali society—a dominance backed by a wholly new claim to moral legitimacy. It was the ethic of the new middle class in which social respectability was based not on birth or wealth but primarily on education, an ethic which demanded hard work, devotion to learning, professional excellence, and a somewhat self-righteous contempt for easy wealth. It was an ethic which gave the middle class its dignity and self-respect, and even a pride in having emulated the English in the best aspects of their knowledge and culture but having done so without losing its distinct cultural identity. It was this ethic, undoubtedly elitist, even exclusive in its own social context, which sustained the political will of the Bengali middle class in the difficult years of revolutionary terrorism. It was the central moral core of the same ethic which later gave sustenance to the new phase of anti-capitalist radicalism from the late 1930s.

It was, one might be tempted to say, a puritan ethic, innately *bourgeois* in its constitutive elements. Of all the dominant regional cultures in twentieth-century India, the culture of the Bengali middle class is arguably the most bourgeois in the classical European sense. It is the moral legitimacy of this aspect of its culture which enables progressive circles in West Bengal today to proclaim with justified pride the modernity of its artistic tastes, the rationality of its social beliefs, the 'civilized' nature of its treatment of women, and the secular character of its public life. And yet, crucially, the moral power of this legitimacy, from its very birth, has lacked support in any positive principles of economic activity. In its social and political mission its predominant form of activity has been purely étatist. One might say that the historical culmination of this mission, begun in the middle of the nineteenth century, was reached with the formation of the Left Front government in West Bengal. There the mission has met its final impasse.

For what has happened to the all-India economy and the Indian state in the last fifty years has quite effectively, and one has reason to suspect irreversibly, marginalized the political role of Bengal's middle class. In this period, one has seen the creation of an organized political alliance within the Indian national movement of the aspiring ruling classes; one has then seen the end of colonial rule and the inauguration of a post-colonial state. Looking back on this recent history, it seems nothing less than a 'passive revolution', in Gramsci's sense of the term, led by an all-India bourgeoisie clearly unable to rule except in alliance with other dominant classes, particularly in the countryside, but nevertheless capable of maintaining a directing role in the central structures of the economy and at the highest levels of the state. The main ideological axis of this 'passive revolution' is also étatist, for the hegemonic role of the bourgeoisie in Indian society as a whole is clearly much too weak and fragmented for it to rule within a fully liberal, free-enterprise type of state framework. Not only does the Indian bourgeoisie have to share power with other dominant classes, it necessarily has to operate in an economy that permits a considerable degree of state intervention, state control, and state initiative. The main ideological props for such a politics are nationalism, planning, mixed economy, modern science and technology, 'national integration', and 'secularism', together constituting an ideology of 'progressivism', the acknowledged origins of which lie in the Bengal 'renaissance' of the nineteenth century.

But, of course, in the onward march of Indian capitalism in the last three decades, it is West Bengal which has been systematically marginalized. It has not had its own representation within the dominant class alliance for it to have grabbed, by those means, an adequate chunk of the investments for development. Instead, the dominant political mood of the state has turned into a pervasive anger, sometimes sullen, sometimes violent, but always negative, against the quite perceptible process of decay and the utter injustice of it all. The political leadership has voiced this anger and has received the support of the people in its stance of militant opposition to those who rule so unfairly the destiny of the country as a whole. Meanwhile, the process of capitalist accumulation and its consequences on an all-India scale has moved on relentlessly. The very cultural and moral basis of the leadership of the progressive intelligentsia is now threatened, not by any significant political challenge from within but as a result of changes in the sheer technological scale of cultural production which have made the older forms of newspaper, magazine and book publishing, or the theatre and the cinema, economically non-viable, unless undertaken on entirely new commercial premises. The moral legitimacy of virtually every aspect of the cultural edifice built by the Bengali intelligentsia over the last hundred years is now under constant assault, on the one hand by the new cosmopolitanism of the 'English medium' to which the class itself has almost wholly succumbed, once again a helpless submission to the economic laws of the job market, and on the other by the vulgarity of mass-produced commercial entertainment. The only answer to this has been state patronage of culture, on a scale so woefully inadequate as to be almost irrelevant to the overall situation.

What this reveals, as indeed does nearly every other aspect of the political experiment carried out in West Bengal in the last few years, is the inability of the political leadership to articulate its ethic of modernity and national pride into a social programme of productive economic renewal. Despite the radicalism of its politics and the decades of bitter political struggle, the failure of this leadership to formulate a feasible programme of economic transformation in West Bengal, to identify appropriate social agents, and to organize them politically for this task has necessarily led to a hollow *étatisme* whose limits are exposed almost as soon as one is brought face to face with the true realities of power in the all-India context. This is a very poor improvement on the naiveté of the nineteenth-century social reformers who had fondly believed that one only needed to persuade the enlightened English law-maker and progress would be ordained by law. The wheel has come full circle. Today a radical Bengali intelligentsia finds its own ideological resources being appropriated by a capitalist order which benignly lets it rule over a nationality whose fate the intelligentsia is powerless to decide.

5

Of Diaries, Delirium, and Discourse (1996)

From the Journal of Kamalakanta Chakravarti
(*as rediscovered recently by Partha Chatterjee and translated by him from the Bengali*)

I am not in the habit of reading books. Many years ago, I read a book in which it was said that although the British were rogues and bloodthirsty murderers, they nevertheless united India and by giving it the railways and the rule of law and *Palgrave's Golden Treasury* made it a modern country. And now that India was free, after sterling sacrifices by the nation's leaders, we should march ahead and build dams and aircraft carriers and spread the message of Vedanta and thereby take our place among the front-ranking nations of the world. I never read a book after that.

Two weeks ago, however, a strange thing happened to me. For those who do not know me, I should explain that I am afflicted by a certain addiction for which I am somewhat ignobly dependent upon the favours of a woman by the name of Prasanna. Her ostensible livelihood is the selling of milk and milk products, all of doubtful quality, for which she nevertheless appears to enjoy a steady custom. On request, she is not averse to supplying much else, whose range and variety I will not detail here. Suffice it to say that she supplies me with most of the meagre luxuries that barely manage to lift my earthly existence to the level of cultured human living.

Well, on this particular day two weeks ago, in one of her periodic fits of exuberance, she presented me with a scoop of her not-too-fresh cottage cheese wrapped in a piece of newsprint. Since this represented a rare supplement to my daily diet, I proceeded that evening to combine my ration of opium with Prasanna's humble munificence. I remember that I particularly relished the fare, and before long I slipped into a delicious stupor. Suddenly I heard an unfamiliar voice call out my name. I looked around me and saw no one. Irritated by this unexplained disturbance, I tried to push it away from my mind and resume my reverie. But it was of no use. There were letters jumping up and down before my eyes, printed letters that looked like they had leaped out of a newspaper. Soon they formed words, long words that danced in front of me, dribbling, feinting, taunting me with their surprising sinuosity. *Liminality, transgression, adjectival equilibrium, hermeneutic structure of underlyingness, metonymic reminder of a metaphysical inscription.* The words jumped to and fro, changing places, forming new phrases, each more threatening than the other. Then the voice came back. This time I saw a face, a youngish face, bearded, but touched by the pallor of wisdom. It uttered my name, and then let loose a string of expletives that left me dumbfounded. 'You debased renouncer', the face said. 'Classless sayer of the unsayable! Non-linear spectacle of the internal repertory of laughter! You Austinian performative! Disrupter of the English rationalist language game! Diagonally constructed utterer of *vakrokti* par excellence! You non-autochthonous illustrator of subalternity in Hegel's *Phenomenology*!' Surprisingly, the face showed no trace of anger. The eyes that peered at me through a pair of thick glasses were kind, even admiring, and the voice was gentle, almost chuckling to itself as it described my incomprehensible attributes.

I don't know how long this continued, but afterwards I spent a restless night, feeling angry and bewildered. The first thing I noticed in the morning was a ball of paper lying on the floor. It was the same scrap torn from a newspaper in which Prasanna had wrapped her cheese and which I had rolled up and thrown away. The words leaped out at me again, but now, in the clear sobriety of daylight, I made better sense of them. A young pundit, I gathered, had written a book about Bankimchandra, a writer I had heard of and even seen once or twice in the Goldighi area of Calcutta, but whose writings, I must confess, I have never read. I knew, of course, that having long run out of worthwhile subjects, people were now writing books about books, and even about people who write books. I was not, therefore, surprised by the contents of this particular volume which a reviewer had summarized in the newspaper article I was holding in my hand. What was utterly astounding, however, was my discovery that a large part of the book was about—yes, hold your breath—about a certain Kamalakanta, Brahmin by caste and opium-eater by choice, whose journal, and even the man himself, the aforesaid Bankimchandra had apparently passed off as products of his own fictional imagination.

I am not normally an excitable person, but this was altogether too much. I decided I must get hold of the book and explore the matter further. Prasanna, of course, was my only window on the world, my material auxiliary, solitary, if somewhat unpredictable, helpmate. Later that morning, when she came round to deliver her mug of copiously diluted cow's milk, I began to explain to her what it was that I wanted. I had anticipated a prolonged and frustrating session, but almost as soon as I had begun she snatched the piece of paper from my hand and said, 'Say no more, dearie!' Then putting her fingers under my chin and swinging my face gently from side to side, she said, 'I can always tell what you want, even before you've opened your mouth.' And then, with an imperious undulation of her hips, she was gone. (*The original Bengali phrases used by Prasanna suggest an extraordinary combination of indulgence and disdain and are virtually untranslatable.—P.C.*)

For several days I heard nothing more of this matter, nor did I bring up the subject myself. Suddenly, three days ago, Prasanna's head popped up at my window. 'Is this the book you wanted?' she asked as she tossed a slim clothbound volume on my bed. I inspected the book and found to my astonishment that it was indeed the one that had been written about in the newspaper. Prasanna had a mysterious smile on her face. 'I've never failed you, have I?' she asked. I tried to find out how, unlettered as she was, she had managed to locate the exact title I wanted. With a haughtiness only she can muster, Prasanna said that she had a grandnephew who was going to college, what sort of family did I think she had raised? I didn't dare ask for further explanations.

I have spent all of the last three days reading this book written by the young Mr Kaviraj.[1] (*The author of the book is throughout referred to by Kamalakanta as 'Kaviraja mahasaya' or 'kobiraj moshai'.—P.C.*) I must say that I approached it at first with considerable trepidation, knowing it to be an English book written by a pundit of great erudition. I anticipated a very dense, obscure, and difficult book. When

---

[1] Sudipta Kaviraj, *The Unhappy Consciousness: Bankimchandra Chattopadhyay and the Formation of Nationalist Discourse in India* (Delhi: Oxford University Press, 1995).

I finished reading it, I realized that it was nothing of the kind. It is actually a very simple and lucid book about the writer Bankimchandra whose works Mr Kaviraj has analysed in much detail. At the end of the book, Mr Kaviraj asks: 'What kind of a person was he? What sort of historical discourse did he live inside? . . . What sort of history did he set in motion, or contribute to?' Mr. Kaviraj, with the modesty becoming of a true pundit, does not make any bold claims about his own discoveries. From my reading of his book, however, the answers are as clear as crystal. Bankimchandra was a lying, thieving, deceitful rascal, a shameless plagiarist who pretended to speak in many voices when all he was doing was lifting other people's words and passing them off as his own. He is famous, or so at least I gathered from Mr Kaviraj's book, mostly for his novels which are about beautiful women who get into strange situations (the young pundit somewhat coyly calls them 'transgressions') like having to pretend to be mistresses of their husbands, or even more ridiculously, to be *sannyasinis*. He also wrote essays trying to prove that Krishna was more clever, more just, and more powerful than Christ (doesn't take much doing, as far as I can see) or that Bengalis, no matter how hard they try, will always be bad historians (which is little more than stating the obvious). What redeems this undistinguished and only moderately interesting literary output is the so-called *daptar* which contains, as Mr Kaviraj calls it, 'the secret autobiography of Bankimchandra Chattopadhyay'. It is under the pseudonym of Kamalakanta Chakravarti, in the guise of a disreputable and intemperate crank, that this man Bankimchandra, celebrated as the founder of modern Bengali literature, achieves all that is clever, subtle, and worthwhile in his works.

I have always known that criminals were the greatest creative artists in the world. Compared to them, critics are like police *darogas*, following in their trail, picking up clues, and more often than not getting lost. I cannot blame the young Mr Kaviraj. He is an outstanding daroga—methodical, conscientious, and possessing a very balanced judgement. He is also a daroga with a philosophical bent of mind. He is immensely learned in the European *sastras* but, most uncharacteristically for a young pundit in these degenerate times, he has a lively curiosity about our own aesthetic disciplines and takes them seriously. It is his misfortune that he has fallen in the clutches of a sinister blackguard who, even a hundred years after his death, continues to dupe intelligent people.

It is obvious that our Mr Kaviraj has taken a great liking to the opium-eating diarist, albeit under the sadly mistaken assumption that Kamalakanta is Bankim Babu's *alter ego.* Reading his prose, now coldly analytical, now mildly sardonic, often deeply poetic, I felt a certain communion with the young man. I sensed that he too was terribly lonely, suffering the loneliness of one who can see through the commonsensical. For such a person, the only means of survival is to write, not for a public, not for popularity or fame, but simply to establish a dialogue with an imaginary interlocutor. Somehow, thinking about him, I got the feeling that Mr Kaviraj had written this book to me. He is a brilliant man, having passed many examinations. May the combined blessings of all 330 million gods and goddesses be showered upon him. May he continue to brighten the hapless face of Bengal.

If I ever meet him, I will suggest to him another means by which he might lighten his sorrows. Even in faraway London, which is where I understand Mr Kaviraj teaches, it might be possible to get hold of the fruit of a certain plant by the name of *Papaver somniferum* of the family *Papaveraceae.* Being, so to speak, the centre of the world, it might even be possible there to secure a regular supply of the variety grown in the Shan states of Burma, a variety that unfortunately is no longer available here. Perhaps then we might have something more on which to exchange notes.

The mystery of how the diabolical Bankim Babu managed to get his hands on my journal, however, continued to bother me. I resolved to ask Prasanna if she had ever supplied milk to the house of a deputy magistrate. But when I saw her this afternoon, I found myself trying to explain to her the intricacies of the tragic sensibility; of the secret inner pain that can find a rational outlet only in the language of laughter; of how this Bengali professor in London had written a book on the subject. She came up and stood in front of me, and cupping a hand over my lips . . .

(*Unfortunately, the journal abruptly breaks off here. To date, there are no further entries that I have been able to find.—P.C.*)

6

The Nationalist Resolution of the Women's Question
(1989)

The 'women's question' was a central issue in some of the most controversial debates over social reform in early- and mid-nineteenth-century Bengal—the period of the so-called 'renaissance'. Rammohun Roy's historical fame is largely built around his campaign against *satidaha* (widow immolation), Vidyasagar's around his efforts to legalize widow remarriage and abolish Kulin polygamy; the Brahmo Samaj was split twice in the 1870s over questions of marriage laws and the 'age of consent'. What has perplexed historians is the rather sudden disappearance of such issues from the agenda of public debate towards the close of the century. From then onwards, questions regarding the position of women in society do not arouse the same degree of passion and acrimony as they did only a few decades before. The overwhelming issues now are directly political ones—concerning the politics of nationalism.

Was this because the women's question had been resolved in a way satisfactory to most sections of opinion in Bengal? Critical historians today find it difficult to accept this answer. Indeed, the hypothesis of critical social history today is that nationalism could not have resolved those issues; rather, the relation between nationalism and the women's question must have been problematic.

Ghulam Murshid states the problem in its most obvious, straightforward, form.[1] If one takes seriously, i.e. in their liberal, rationalist,

[1] See Ghulam Murshid, *Reluctant Debutante: Response of Bengali Women to Modernization, 1849–1905* (Rajshahi: Rajshahi University Press, 1983).

and egalitarian content, the mid-nineteenth-century attempts in Bengal to 'modernize' the condition of women, then what follows in the period of nationalism must be regarded as a clear retrogression. 'Modernization' began in the first half of the nineteenth century because of the 'penetration' of Western ideas. After some limited success, there was a perceptible decline in the reform movements as 'popular attitudes' towards them 'hardened'. The new politics of nationalism glorified India's past and tended to defend everything traditional; all attempts to change customs and lifestyles began to be seen as the aping of Western manners and thereby regarded with suspicion. Consequently, nationalism fostered a distinctly conservative attitude towards social beliefs and practices. The movement towards modernization was stalled by nationalist politics.

This critique of the social implications of nationalism follows from rather simple and linear historical assumptions. Murshid not only accepts that the early attempts at social reform were impelled by the new nationalist and progressive ideas imported from Europe, he also presumes that the necessary historical culmination of such reforms in India ought to have been, as in the West, the full articulation of liberal values in social institutions and practices. From these assumptions, a critique of nationalist ideology and practices is inevitable. It would be the same sort of critique as that of the so-called 'neo-imperialist' historians who argue that Indian nationalism was nothing but a scramble for sharing political power with the colonial rulers, its mass following only the successful activization of traditional patron–client relationships, its internal debates the squabbles of parochial factions, its ideology a garb for xenophobia and racial exclusiveness. The point to note is that the problem lies in the original structure of assumptions. Murshid's study is a telling example of the fact, now increasingly evident, that if one only scrapes away the gloss, it is hard to defend many ideas and practices of nationalism in terms of rationalist and liberal values.

Of course, that original structure of assumptions has not gone unchallenged in recent critical history. The most important critique in our field is that of the Bengal renaissance.[2] Not only have questions

---

[2] See, for example, Sumit Sarkar, 'The Complexities of Young Bengal', *Nineteenth Century Studies*, 4 (1973), pp. 504–34, and idem, 'Rammohun Roy and the Break with the Past', in *Rammohun Roy and the Process of Modernization in India,* ed.

limitations under colonial rule

been raised about the strictness and consistency of the liberal ideas propagated by the 'renaissance' leaders of Bengal, it has also been asked whether the fruition of liberal reforms was at all possible under conditions of colonial rule. In other words, the incompleteness and contradictions of 'renaissance' ideology were shown to be the necessary result of the impossibility of thoroughgoing liberal reform under colonial conditions.

From that perspective, the problem of the diminished importance of the women's question in the period of nationalism deserves a different answer from the one given by Murshid. Sumit Sarkar has considered this problem.[3] His argument is that the limitations of nationalist ideology in pushing forward a campaign for liberal and egalitarian social change cannot be seen as a retrogression from an earlier radical reformist phase. Those limitations were in fact present in the earlier phase as well. 'The 'renaissance' reformers, he shows, were highly selective in their acceptance of liberal ideas from Europe. Fundamental elements of social conservatism such as the maintenance of caste distinctions and patriarchal forms of authority in the family, acceptance of the sanctity of the *shastra* (ancient scriptures), preference for symbolic rather than substantive change in social practices—all of them were conspicuous in the reform movements of the early and mid-nineteenth century. Specifically on the question of the social position of women, he shows the fundamental absence in every phase of any significant autonomous struggle by women themselves to change relations within or outside the family. In fact, Sarkar throws doubt upon the very assumption that the early attempts at reform were principally guided by any ideological acceptance of liberal or rationalist values imported from the West. He suggests that the concern with the social condition of women was far less an indicator of such ideological preference for liberalism and more an expression of certain 'acute problems

V.C. Joshi (Delhi: Vikas, 1975); Asok Sen, 'The Bengal Economy and Rammohun Roy', in *Rammohun Roy*, ed. Joshi, and *Iswar Chandra Vidyasagar and His Elusive Milestones* (Calcutta: Riddhi India, 1977); and Ranajit Guha, 'Neel Darpan: The Image of the Peasant Revolt in a Liberal Mirror', *Journal of Peasant Studies*, 2, no. 1 (1974), pp. 1–46.

[3] Sumit Sarkar, 'The Women's Question in Nineteenth Century Bengal', in *Women and Culture*, ed. Kumkum Sangari and Sudesh Vaid (Bombay: SNDT Women's University, 1985), pp. 157–72.

of interpersonal adjustments within the family' on the part of the early generation of Western-educated males. Faced with 'social ostracism and isolation', their attempts at 'a limited and controlled emancipation of wives' were 'a personal necessity for survival in a hostile social world'. Whatever changes have come about since that time in the social and legal position of women have been 'through objective socio-economic pressures, some post-Independence legislation, rather than clear-cut ideology or really autonomous struggle. Mental attitudes and values have consequently changed very much less.' The pattern, therefore, is not, as Murshid suggests, one of radical liberalism in the beginning followed by a conservative backlash in the period of nationalism; Sarkar argues that in fact the fault lies with the very inception of our modernity.

The curious thing, however, is that Sarkar too regards the social reform movements of the last century and a half as a failure—failure to match up to the liberal ideals of equality and reason. It is from this standpoint that he can show, quite legitimately, the falsity of any attempt to paint a picture of starry-eyed radicalism muzzled by a censorious nationalist ideology. But a new problem crops up. If we are to say that the nineteenth-century reform movements did not arise out of an ideological acceptance of Western liberalism, it could fairly be asked: from what then did they originate? The answer that they stemmed from problems of personal adjustment within the family can hardly be adequate. After all, the nineteenth-century debates about social reform generally, and the women's question in particular, were intensely ideological. If the paradigm for those debates was not that of Western liberalism, what was it? Moreover, if we cannot describe that paradigm in its own terms, can we legitimately apply once again the Western standards of liberalism to proclaim the reform movements, pre-nationalist as well as nationalist, as historical failures? Surely the new critical historiography will be grossly one-sided if we are unable to represent the nineteenth-century ideology in its relation to itself, i.e. in its self-identity.

It seems to me that Sarkar's argument can be taken much further. We need not shy away from the fact that the nationalist ideology did indeed tackle the women's question in the nineteenth century. To expect the contrary would be surprising. It is inconceivable that an ideology which claimed to offer a total alternative to the 'traditional' social order as well as to the Western way of life should fail to have something distinctive to say about such a fundamental aspect of social institutions and practices as the position of women. We should direct our search within that nationalist ideology itself.

We might, for a start, pursue Sarkar's entirely valid observation that the nineteenth-century ideologues were highly selective in their adoption of liberal slogans. How did they select what they wanted? What, in other words, was the ideological sieve through which they put the newly imported ideas from Europe? Once we have reconstructed this framework of the nationalist ideology, we will be in a far better position to locate where exactly the women's question fitted in with the claims of nationalism. We will find, if I may anticipate my argument in the following sections, that nationalism did in fact face up to the new social and cultural problems concerning the position of women in 'modern' society and that it did provide an answer to the problems in terms of its own ideological paradigm. I will claim, therefore, that the relative unimportance of the women's question in the last decades of the nineteenth century is not to be explained by the fact that it had been censored out of the reform agenda or overtaken by the more pressing and emotive issues of political struggle. It was because nationalism had in fact resolved 'the women's question' in complete accordance with its preferred goals.

II

I have elaborated elsewhere a framework for analysing the contradictory pulls on nationalist ideology in its struggle against the dominance of colonialism and the 'resolution' it offered to these contradictions.[4] In the main, this resolution was built around a separation of the domain of culture into two spheres—the material and the spiritual. It was in the material sphere that the claims of Western civilization were the most powerful. Science, technology, rational forms of economic organization, modern methods of statecraft, these had given the European countries the strength to subjugate non-European peoples and to impose their dominance over the whole world. To overcome this domination, the colonized people must learn these superior techniques of organizing material life and incorporate them within their own cultures. This was one aspect of the nationalist project of rationalizing

[4] See Partha Chatterjee, *Nationalist Thought and the Colonial World* (Delhi: Oxford University Press, 1986).

and reforming the 'traditional' culture of their people. But this could not mean imitating the West in every aspect of life, for then the very distinction between the West and the East would vanish—the self-identity of national culture would itself be threatened. In fact, as Indian nationalists in the late nineteenth century argued, not only was it not desirable to imitate the West in anything other than the material aspects of life, it was not even necessary to do so, because in the spiritual domain the East was superior to the West. What was necessary was to cultivate the material techniques of modern Western civilization while retaining and strengthening the distinctive spiritual essence of the national culture. This completed the formulation of the nationalist project, and as an ideological justification for the selective appropriation of Western modernity it continues to hold sway to this day (*pace* Rajiv Gandhi's juvenile fascination for space-age technology).

We need not concern ourselves here with the details of how this ideological framework shaped the course of nationalist politics in India. What is important is to note that nationalism was not simply about a political struggle for power; it related the question of political independence of the nation to virtually every aspect of the material and spiritual life of the people. In every case, there was a problem of selecting what to take from the West and what to reject. And in every case the questions were asked: Is it desirable? Is it necessary? The answers to these questions are the material of the debates about social reform in the nineteenth century. To understand the self-identity of nationalist ideology in concrete terms, we must look more closely at the way in which these questions were answered.

The discourse of nationalism shows that the material/spiritual distinction was condensed into an analogous, but ideologically far more powerful, dichotomy: that between the outer and the inner. The material domain lies outside us—a mere external, which influences us, conditions us, and to which we are forced to adjust. But ultimately it is unimportant. It is the spiritual which lies within, which is our true self; it is that which is genuinely essential. It follows that as long as we take care to retain the spiritual distinctiveness of our culture, we could make all the compromises and adjustments necessary to adapt ourselves to the requirements of a modern material world without losing our true identity. This was the key which nationalism supplied for resolving the ticklish problems posed by issues of social reform in the nineteenth century.

Now apply the inner/outer distinction to the matter of concrete day-to-day living and you get a separation of the social space into *ghar* and *bahir*, the home and the world. The world is the external, the domain of the material; the home represents our inner spiritual self, our true identity. The world is a treacherous terrain of the pursuit of material interests, where practical considerations reign supreme. It is also typically the domain of the male. The home in its essence must remain unaffected by the profane activities of the material world—and woman is its representation. And so we get an identification of social roles by gender to correspond with the separation of the social space into ghar and bahir.

Thus far we have not obtained anything that is different from the typical conception of gender roles in any 'traditional' patriarchy. If we now find continuities in these social attitudes in the phase of social reforms in the nineteenth century, we are tempted to put this down as 'conservatism', a mere defence of 'traditional' norms. But this would be a mistake. The colonial situation, and the ideological response of nationalism, introduced an entirely new substance to these terms and effected their transformation. The material/spiritual dichotomy, to which the terms 'world' and 'home' corresponded, had acquired, as we have noted before, a very special significance in the nationalist mind. The world was where the European power had challenged the non-European peoples and, by virtue of its superior material culture, had subjugated them. But it had failed to colonize the inner, essential, identity of the East which lay in its distinctive, and superior, spiritual culture. That is where the East was undominated, sovereign, master of its own fate. For a colonized people, the world was a distressing constraint, forced upon it by the fact of its material weakness. It was a place of oppression and daily humiliation, a place where the norms of the colonizer had perforce to be accepted. It was also the place, as nationalists were soon to argue, where the battle would be waged for national independence. The requirement for this was for the subjugated to learn from the West the modern sciences and arts of the material world. Then their strengths would be matched and ultimately the colonizer overthrown. But in the entire phase of the national struggle, the crucial need was to protect, preserve, and strengthen the inner core of the national culture, its spiritual essence. No encroachments by the colonizer must be allowed in that inner sanctum. In the world, imitation of and adaptation to Western norms was a necessity; at home, they were tantamount to annihilation of one's very identity.

Once we match this new meaning of the home/world dichotomy with the identification of social roles by gender, we get the ideological framework within which nationalism answered the women's question. It would be a grave error to see in this, as we are apt to in our despair at the many marks of social conservatism in nationalist practice, a total rejection of the West. Quite the contrary. The nationalist paradigm in fact supplied an ideological principle of *selection*. It was not a dismissal of modernity; the attempt was rather to make modernity consistent with the nationalist project.

III

It is striking how much of the literature on women in the nineteenth century was concerned with the theme of the threatened westernization of Bengali women. It was taken up in virtually every form of written, oral, and visual communication, from the ponderous essays of nineteenth-century moralists, to novels, farces, skits, and jingles, to the paintings of the *patua* (scroll painter). Social parody was the most popular and effective medium of this ideological propagation. From Iswarchandra Gupta and the *kabiyal* (popular versifiers) of the early nineteenth century to the celebrated pioneers of modern Bengali theatre—Michael Madhusudan Dutt, Dinabandhu Mitra, Jyotirindranath Tagore, Upendranath Das, Amritalal Bose—everyone picked up the theme. To ridicule the idea of a Bengali woman trying to imitate the ways of a European woman or memsahib—and it was very much an idea, for it is hard to find historical evidence even in the most westernized families of Calcutta in the mid-nineteenth century of women who even remotely resembled these gross caricatures—was a sure recipe calculated to evoke raucous laughter and moral condemnation in both male and female audiences. It was, of course, a criticism of manners: of new items of clothing such as the blouse, the petticoat, and shoes—all, curiously, considered vulgar, although they clothed the body far more fully than the single length of fabric or sari which was customary for Bengali women, irrespective of wealth and social status, until the middle of the nineteenth century; of the use of Western cosmetics and jewellery; of the reading of novels—the educated Haimabati in Jyotirindranath's *Alikbabu* speaks, thinks, and acts like the heroines of historical romances; of needlework, considered a useless and expensive pastime; of riding in open carriages. What made the ridicule stronger was the constant suggestion that the westernized woman was fond of idle luxury and cared little for the well being of the home. One can hardly miss in all this a criticism—reproach mixed with envy—of the wealth and luxury of the new social elite emerging around the institutions of colonial administration and trade.

This literature of parody and satire in the first half of the nineteenth century clearly contained much that was prompted by a straightforward defence of 'tradition' and outright rejection of the new. The nationalist paradigm had still not emerged in clear outline. With hindsight, this—the period from Rammohun to Vidyasagar—appears as one of great social turmoil and ideological confusion among the literati. And then, drawing from various sources, a new discourse began to be formed in the second half of the century—the discourse of nationalism. Now the attempt was made to define the social and moral principles for locating the position of women in the 'modern' world of the nation.

Let us take as an example one of the most clearly formulated tracts on the subject: Bhudev Mukhopadhyay's *Paribarik Prabandha* (Essays on the Family) published in 1882. Bhudev states the problem in his characteristic matter-of-fact style:

> Because of our hankering for the external glitter and ostentation of the English way of life . . . an upheaval is under way within our homes. The men learn English and become sahibs. The women do not learn English but nevertheless try to become bibis. In households which manage on an income of a hundred rupees, the women no longer cook, sweep or make the bed . . . everything is done by servants and maids; [the women] only read books, sew carpets, and play cards. What is the result? The house and furniture get untidy, the meals poor, the health of every member of the family is ruined; children are born weak and rickety, constantly plagued by illness—they die early.
>
> Many reform movements are being conducted today; the education of women, in particular, is constantly talked about. But we rarely hear of those great arts in which women were once trained—a training which if it had still been in vogue would have enabled us to tide over this crisis caused by injudicious imitation. I suppose we will never hear of this training again.[5]

The problem is put here in the empirical terms of a positive sociology, a genre much favoured by serious Bengali writers of Bhudev's time. But

[5] Bhudev Mukhopadhyay, 'Grhakaryer Vyavastha', in *Bhudev Racanasambhar*, ed. Pramathanath Bisi (Calcutta: Mitra and Ghosh, 1969), p. 480. Translations from Bengali to English are my own.

the sense of crisis which he expresses was very much a reality. Bhudev is voicing the feelings of large sections of the newly emergent middle class in Bengal when he says that the very institutions of home and family are threatened under the peculiar conditions of colonial rule. A quite unprecedented external condition has been thrust upon us; we are being forced to adjust to those conditions, for which a certain degree of imitation of alien ways is unavoidable. But could this wave of imitation be allowed to enter our homes? Would that not destroy our inner identity? A mere restatement of the old norms of family life would not suffice: they were breaking down by the inexorable force of circumstance! New norms were needed which would be more appropriate to the external conditions of the modern world and yet not a mere imitation of the West. What were the principles by which these new norms could be constructed?

Bhudev supplies the characteristic nationalist answer. In an essay on modesty entitled 'Lajjasilata' he talks of the natural and social principles which provide the basis for the 'feminine' virtues.[6] Modesty, or decorum in manner and conduct, he says, is a specifically human trait; it does not exist in animal nature. It is human aversion to the purely animal traits which gives rise to virtues such as modesty. In this aspect, human beings seek to cultivate in themselves, and in their civilization, spiritual or godlike qualities wholly opposed to forms of behaviour which prevail in animals. Further, within the human species women cultivate and cherish these godlike qualities far more than men. Protected to a certain extent from the purely material pursuits of securing a livelihood in the external world, women express in their appearance and behaviour the spiritual qualities which are characteristic of civilized and refined human society.

The relevant dichotomies and analogues are all here. The material/spiritual dichotomy corresponds to that between animal/godlike qualities, which in turn corresponds to masculine/feminine virtues. Bhudev then invests this ideological form with its specifically nationalist content:

> In a society where men and women meet together, converse together at all times, eat and drink together, travel together, the manners of women are likely to be somewhat coarse, devoid of spiritual qualities and relatively prominent in animal traits. For this reason, I do not think the customs of

[6] 'Lajjasilata', in ibid., pp. 445–8.

such a society are free from all defect. Some argue that because of such close association with women, the characters of men acquire certain tender and spiritual qualities. Let me concede the point. But can the loss caused by coarseness and degeneration in the female character be compensated by the acquisition of a certain degree of tenderness in the male?[7]

The point is then hammered home:

> Those who laid down our religious codes discovered the inner spirituality which resides within even the most animal pursuits which humans must perform, and thus removed the animal qualities from those actions. This has not happened in Europe. Religion there is completely divorced from [material] life. Europeans do not feel inclined to regulate all aspects of their life by the norms of religion; they condemn it as clericalism. . . . In the Arya system there is a preponderance of spiritualism, in the European system a preponderance of material pleasure. In the Arya system, the wife is a goddess. In the European system, she is a partner and companion.[8]

The new norm for organizing family life and determining the right conduct for women in the conditions of the 'modern' world could now be deduced with ease. Adjustments would have to be made in the external world of material activity, and men would bear the brunt of this task. To the extent that the family was itself entangled in wider social relations, it too could not be insulated from the influence of changes in the outside world. Consequently, the organization and ways of life at home would also have to be changed. But the crucial requirement was to retain the inner spirituality of indigenous social life. The home was the principal site for expressing the spiritual quality of the national culture, and women must take the main responsibility of protecting and nurturing this quality. No matter what the changes in the external conditions of life for women, they must not lose their essentially spiritual (i.e. feminine) virtues; they must not, in other words, become *essentially* westernized. It followed, as a simple criterion for judging the desirability of reform, that the essential distinction between the social roles of men and women in terms of material and spiritual virtues must at all times be maintained. There would have to be a marked *difference* in the degree and manner of westernization of women, as distinct from men, in the modern world of the nation.

[7] Ibid., p. 446.
[8] Ibid., p. 447.

IV

This was the central principle by which nationalism resolved the women's question in terms of its own historical project. The details were not, of course, worked out immediately. In fact, from the middle of the nineteenth century right up to the present day there have been many controversies about the precise application of the home/world, spiritual/material, feminine/masculine dichotomies in various matters concerning the everyday life of the 'modern' woman—her dress, food, manners, education, her role in organizing life at home, her role outside the home. The concrete problems arose out of the rapidly changing situation—both external and internal—in which the new middle-class family found itself; the specific solutions were drawn from a variety of sources—a reconstructed 'classical' tradition, modernized folk forms, the utilitarian logic of bureaucratic and industrial practices, the legal idea of equality in a liberal democratic state. The content of the resolution was neither predetermined nor unchanging, but its form had to be consistent with the system of dichotomies which shaped and contained the nationalist project.

The 'new' woman defined in this way was subjected to a *new patriarchy*. In fact, the social order connecting the home and the world in which nationalism placed the new woman was contrasted not only with that of modern Western society; it was explicitly distinguished from the patriarchy of indigenous tradition. Sure enough, nationalism adopted several elements from 'tradition' as marks of its native cultural identity, but this was a deliberately 'classicized' tradition—reformed, reconstructed. Even Gandhi said of the patriarchal rules laid down by the scriptures: 'it is sad to think that the *Smritis* contain texts which can command no respect from men who cherish the liberty of woman as their own and who regard her as the mother of the race . . . The question arises as to what to do with the *Smritis* that contain texts . . . that are repugnant to the moral sense. I have already suggested . . . that all that is printed in the name of scriptures need not be taken as the word of God or the inspired word.'[9] The new patriarchy was also sharply distinguished from the immediate social and cultural condition in which the majority of the people lived, for the 'new' woman was quite the reverse of the 'common' woman who was coarse, vulgar, loud,

[9] M.K. Gandhi, *Collected Works*, vol. 64 (Delhi: Publications Division, 1970).

quarrelsome, devoid of superior moral sense, sexually promiscuous, subjected to brutal physical oppression by males. Alongside the parody of the westernized woman, this other construct is repeatedly emphasized in the literature of the nineteenth century through a host of lower-class female characters who make their appearance in the social milieu of the new middle class—maidservants, washerwomen, barbers, pedlars, procuresses, prostitutes. It was precisely this degenerate condition of women which nationalism claimed it would reform, and it was through these contrasts that the new woman of nationalist ideology was accorded a status of cultural superiority to the westernized women of the wealthy parvenu families spawned by the colonial connection as well as the common women of the lower classes. Attainment by her own efforts of a superior national culture was the mark of woman's newly acquired freedom. This was the central ideological strength of the nationalist resolution of the women's question.

We can follow the form of this resolution in several specific aspects in which the lives and conditions of middle-class women have changed over the last hundred years or so. Take the case of 'female education', that contentious subject which engaged so much of the attention of social reformers in the nineteenth century.[10] Some of the early opposition to the opening of schools for women was backed by an appeal to 'tradition' which supposedly prohibited women from being introduced to bookish learning, but this argument hardly gained much support. The threat was seen to lie in the fact that the early schools, and arrangements for teaching women at home, were organized by Christian missionaries; there was thus the fear of both proselytization and the exposure of women to harmful Western influences. The threat was removed when from the 1850s Indians themselves began to open schools for girls. The spread of formal education among middle-class women in Bengal in the second half of the nineteenth century was remarkable. From 95 girls' schools with an attendance of 2500 in 1863, the figures went up to 2258 schools in 1890 with a total of more than 80,000 students.[11]

10. See the survey of these debates in Murshid, *Reluctant Debutante*, pp. 19–62, and Meredith Borthwick, *The Changing Role of Women in Bengal, 1849–1905* (Princeton, N.J.: Princeton University Press, 1984).

11 Murshid, *Reluctant Debutante*, p. 43. In the area of higher education, Chandramukhi Bose and Kadambini Ganguli were celebrated as examples of what Bengali women could achieve in formal learning: they took their BA degrees from the

The quite general acceptance of formal education among middle-class women was undoubtedly made possible by the development of an educational literature and teaching materials in the Bengali language. The long debates of the nineteenth century on a proper 'feminine curriculum' now seem to us somewhat quaint, but it is not difficult to identify the real point of concern. Much of the content of the modern school education was seen as important for the 'new' woman, but to administer it in the English language was difficult in practical terms, irrelevant in view of the fact that the central place of the educated woman was still at home, and threatening because it might devalue and displace that central site where the social position of women was located. The problem was resolved through the efforts of the intelligentsia who made it a fundamental task of the nationalist project to create a modern language and literature suitable for a widening readership which would include newly educated women. Through textbooks, periodicals, and creative works an important force which shaped the new literature of Bengal was the urge to make it accessible to women who could read only one language—their mother-tongue.

Formal education became not only acceptable but in fact a requirement for the new *bhadramahila* (respectable woman) when it was demonstrated that it was possible for a woman to acquire the cultural refinements afforded by modern education without jeopardizing her place at home. Indeed, the nationalist construct of the new woman derived its ideological strength from the fact that it was able to make the goal of cultural refinement through education a personal challenge for every woman, thus opening up a domain where woman was an autonomous subject. This explains to a large extent the remarkable degree of enthusiasm among middle-class women to acquire and use for themselves the benefits of formal learning. It was a purpose which they set for themselves in their personal lives as the object of their will; to achieve it was to achieve freedom. Indeed, the achievement was marked by claims of cultural superiority in several different aspects:

University of Calcutta in 1883, before any British university agreed to accept women on their examination rolls. On Chandramukhi and Kadambini's application, the University of Calcutta granted full recognition to women candidates at the First of Arts examination in 1878. London University admitted women to its degrees later that year (Borthwick, *Changing Role of Women*, p. 94). Kadambini then went on to medical college and became the first professionally schooled woman doctor.

superiority over the Western woman for whom, it was believed, education meant only the acquisition of material skills in order to compete with men in the outside world and hence a loss of feminine (spiritual) virtues; superiority over the preceding generation of women in their own homes who had been denied the opportunity for freedom by an oppressive and degenerate social tradition; and superiority over women of the lower classes who were culturally incapable of appreciating the virtues of freedom.

It is this particular nationalist construction of reform as a project of both emancipation and self-emancipation of women (and hence a project in which both men and women must participate) which also explains why the early generation of educated women themselves so keenly propagated the nationalist idea of the 'new woman'. Recent historians of a liberal persuasion have often been somewhat embarrassed by the profuse evidence of women writers of the nineteenth century, including those at the forefront of the reform movements in middle-class homes, justifying the importance of the so-called 'feminine virtues'. Radharani Lahiri, for instance, wrote in 1875, 'Of all the subjects that women might learn, housework is the most important . . . whatever knowledge she may acquire, she cannot claim any reputation unless she is proficient in housework.'[12] Others spoke of the need for an educated woman to 'develop' such womanly virtues as chastity, self-sacrifice, submission, devotion, kindness, patience, and the labours of love.[13] The ideological point of view from which such protestations of 'femininity' (and hence the acceptance of a new patriarchal order) were made inevitable was given precisely by the nationalist resolution of the problem, and Kundamala Debi, writing in 1870, expressed this well when she advised other women: 'If you have acquired real knowledge, then give no place in your heart to *memsahib*-like behaviour. That is not becoming in a Bengali house-wife. See how an educated woman can do housework thoughtfully and systematically, in a way unknown to an ignorant, uneducated woman. And see how if God had not appointed us to this place in the home, how unhappy a place the world would be!'[14] Education then was meant to inculcate in women the

---

[12] Cited in Murshid, *Reluctant Debutante*, p. 60.

[13] See, for instance, Kulabala Debi, *Hindu Mahilar Hinabastha*, cited in Murshid, *Reluctant Debutante*, p. 60.

[14] Cited in Borthwick, *Changing Role of Women*, p. 105.

virtues—the typically 'bourgeois' virtues characteristic of the new social forms of 'disciplining'—of orderliness, thrift, cleanliness, and a
personal sense of responsibility, the practical skills of literacy, accounting,
and hygiene, and the ability to run the household according to the new
physical and economic conditions set by the outside world. For this
she would also need to have some idea of the world outside the home
into which she could even venture as long as it did not threaten her
'femininity'. It is this latter criterion, now invested with a characteristically nationalist content, which made possible the displacement of
the boundaries of 'the home' from the physical confines earlier defined
by the rules of purdah (i.e. seclusion) to a more flexible, but culturally
nonetheless determinate domain set by the *differences* between socially
approved male and female conduct. Once the essential 'femininity' of
women was fixed in terms of certain culturally visible 'spiritual' qualities, they could go to schools, travel in public conveyances, watch public entertainment programmes, and in time even take up employment
outside the home. But the 'spiritual' signs of her femininity were now
clearly marked: in her dress, her eating habits, her social demeanour,
her religiosity; the specific markers were obtained from diverse sources,
and in terms of their origins each had its specific history. The dress of
the bhadramahila, for instance, went through a whole phase of ex-
perimentation before what was known as the *brahmika* sari (a form of
wearing the sari in combination with blouse, petticoat, and shoes
made fashionable in Brahmo households) became accepted as standard
for middle-class women.[15] Here too the necessary differences were
signified in terms of national identity, social emancipation, and cultural refinement, differences, that is to say, with the memsahib, with
women of earlier generations, and with women of the lower classes.
Further, in this, as in other aspects of her life, the 'spirituality' of her
character had also to be stressed in contrast with the innumerable sur-
renders which men were having to make to the pressures of the material
world. The need to adjust to the new conditions outside the home had
forced upon men a whole series of changes in their dress, food habits,
religious observances, and social relations. Each of these capitulations
now had to be compensated by an assertion of spiritual purity on the
part of women. They must not eat, drink, or smoke in the same way
as men; they must continue the observance of religious rituals which

[15] Ibid., pp. 245–56.

men were finding it difficult to carry out; they must maintain the cohesiveness of family life and solidarity with the kin to which men could not now devote much attention. The new patriarchy advocated by nationalism conferred upon women the honour of a new social responsibility, and by associating the task of 'female emancipation' with the historical goal of sovereign nationhood, bound them to a new, and yet entirely legitimate, subordination.

As with all hegemonic forms of exercise of dominance, this patriarchy combined coercive authority with the subtle force of persuasion. This was expressed most generally in an inverted ideological form of the relation of power between the sexes: the adulation of woman as goddess or as mother. Whatever be its sources in the classical religions of India or in medieval religious practices, it is undeniable that the specific ideological form in which we know the Sati–Savitri–Sita construct in the modern literature and arts of India today is wholly a product of the development of a dominant middle-class culture coeval with the era of nationalism. It served to emphasize with all the force of mythological inspiration what had in any case become a dominant characteristic of femininity in the new woman, namely, the 'spiritual' qualities of self-sacrifice, benevolence, devotion, religiosity, etc. This spirituality did not, as we have seen, impede the chances of the woman moving out of the physical confines of the home; on the contrary, it facilitated it, making it possible for her to go out into the world under conditions that would not threaten her femininity. In fact, the image of woman as goddess or mother served to erase her sexuality in the world outside the home.

V

I conclude this essay by pointing out another significant feature of the way in which nationalism sought to resolve the women's question in accordance with its historical project. This has to do with the one aspect of the question which was directly political, concerning relations with the state. Nationalism, as I have said before, located its own subjectivity in the spiritual domain of culture, where it considered itself superior to the West, and hence undominated and sovereign. It could not permit an encroachment by the colonial power into that domain. This determined the characteristically nationalist response to proposals for effecting social reform through the legislative enactments of the colonial state. Unlike the early reformers from Rammohun to Vidya-sagar, nationalists of the late nineteenth century were in general opposed to such proposals, for such a method of reform seemed to deny the ability of the 'nation' to act for itself even in a domain where it was sovereign. In the specific case of reforming the lives of women, consequently, the nationalist position was firmly based on the premise that this was an area where the nation was acting on its own, outside the purview of the guidance and intervention of the colonial state.

We now get the full answer to the historical problem I raised at the beginning of this essay. The reason why the issue of 'female emancipation' seems to disappear from the public agenda of nationalist agitation in the late nineteenth century is not because it was overtaken by the more emotive issues concerning political power. Rather, the reason lies in the refusal of nationalism to make the women's question an issue of political negotiation with the colonial state. The simple historical fact is that the lives of middle-class women, coming from that demographic section which effectively constituted the 'nation' in late colonial India, changed most rapidly precisely during the period of the nationalist movement—indeed, so rapidly that women from each generation in the last hundred years could say quite truthfully that their lives were strikingly different from those led by the preceding generation. These changes took place in the colonial period mostly outside the arena of political agitation, in a domain where the nation thought of itself as already free. It was after Independence, when the nation had acquired political sovereignty, that it became legitimate to embody the ideas of reform in legislative enactments about marriage rules, property rights, suffrage, equal pay, equality of opportunity, etc.

Another problem on which we can now obtain a clearer perspective is that of the seeming absence of any autonomous struggle by women themselves for equality and freedom. We would be mistaken to look for evidence of such a struggle in the public archives of political affairs, for, unlike the women's movement in nineteenth- and twentieth-century Europe, that is not where the battle was waged here in the era of nationalism. The domain where the new idea of womanhood was sought to be actualized was the home, and the real history of that change can be constructed only out of evidence left behind in autobiographies, family histories, religious tracts, literature, theatre, songs, paintings, and such other cultural artefacts that depict life in middle-class homes. It is impossible that, in the considerable transformation of the middle-class home in India in the last hundred years, women played a wholly passive part, for even the most severe system of domination seeks the consent of the subordinate as an autonomous being.

The location of the state in the nationalist resolution of the women's question in the colonial period has yet another implication. For sections of the middle class which felt themselves culturally left out of the specific process of formation of the 'nation', and which then organized themselves as politically distinct groups, the relative exclusion from the new nation-state would act as a further means of displacement of the legitimate agency of reform. In the case of Muslims in Bengal, for instance, the formation of a middle class occurred with a lag, for reasons which we need not go into here. Exactly the same sorts of ideological concerns typical of a nationalist response to issues of social reform in a colonial situation can be seen to operate among Muslims as well, with a difference in chronological time.[16] Nationalist reform does not, however, reach political fruition in the case of Muslims in independent India, since to the extent that the dominant cultural formation among them considers the community excluded from the state, a new colonial relation is brought into being. The system of dichotomies of inner/outer, home/world, feminine/masculine is once again activated. Reforms which touch upon the 'inner essence' of the identity of the community can only be carried out by the community itself, not by the state. It is instructive to note here how little institutional change has been allowed in the civil life of Indian Muslims since Independence and compare it with Muslim countries where nationalist cultural reform was a part of the successful formation of an independent nation-state. The contrast is striking if one compares the position of middle-class Muslim women in West Bengal today with that in neighbouring Bangladesh.

The continuance of a distinct cultural 'problem' of the minorities is an index of the failure of the Indian nation to effectively include within its body the whole of the demographic mass which it claimed to represent. The failure assumes massive proportions when we note, as I have tried to do throughout this discussion, that the formation of a hegemonic 'national culture' was *necessarily* built upon a system of exclusions. Ideas of freedom, equality, and cultural refinement went

---

[16] See Murshid, *Reluctant Debutante*.

hand in hand with a set of dichotomies which systematically excluded from the new life of the nation the vast masses of people whom the dominant elite would represent and lead, but who could never be culturally integrated with their leaders. Both colonial rulers and their nationalist opponents conspired to displace in the colonial world the original structure of meanings associated with Western bourgeois notions of right, freedom, equality, etc. The inauguration of the national state in India could not mean a universalization of the bourgeois notion of 'man'.

The new patriarchy which nationalist discourse set up as a hegemonic construct culturally distinguished itself not only from the West but also from the mass of its own people. It has generalized itself among the new middle class, admittedly a widening class and large enough in absolute numbers to be self-reproducing, but is irrelevant to the large mass of subordinate classes. This raises important questions regarding the issue of women's rights today. We are all aware that the forms and demands of the women's movement in the West are not generally applicable in India. This often leads us to slip back into a nationalist framework for resolving such problems. A critical historical understanding will show that this path will only bring us to the dead end which the nationalist resolution of the women's question has already reached. The historical possibilities here have already been exhausted. A renewal of the struggle for the equality and freedom of women must, as with all democratic issues in countries like India, imply a struggle against the humanistic construct of 'rights' set up in Europe in the post-Enlightenment era and include within it a struggle against the false essentialisms of home/world, spiritual/material, feminine/masculine propagated by nationalist ideology.

7

Our Modernity
(1994)

There are a few unusual features I have noticed about this lecture.[1] First of all, I was stunned by the discovery that, unknown to me, I had somehow acquired the standards of sagacity, antiquity, and grandiloquence usually expected of people who are asked to deliver formal lectures of this kind. Second, there can be nothing more unusual than the fact that I am delivering a lecture in memory of Srijnan Halder who was my student and barely old enough to be a younger brother. Indeed, had Srijnan been delivering a lecture in my memory, it would have been far more in conformity with the laws of nature as well as with social convention. Third, in a short but dramatic life marked by his long battle against an incurable disease, and in a still more dramatic death, Srijnan has left behind for us unforgettable evidence of his deep intellectual curiosity, an unshakeable commitment to his own beliefs and principles, and his irrepressible love for life. I have neither the language nor the thoughts to match that evidence. There may not be anything very unusual in this but, faced with Srijnan's memory, I must, before I begin my lecture, own up to a feeling of utter inadequacy.

Conceptualizing Our Modernity

My subject is 'modernity', but more specifically, 'our' modernity. In making the distinction, I am trying to point out that there might be modernities that are not ours, or, to put it another way, that there are

[1] The Srijnan Halder Memorial Lecture, 1994, delivered in Bengali in Calcutta on 3 September 1994. The author's translation.

certain peculiarities about our modernity. It could be the case that what others think of as modern, we have found unacceptable, whereas what we have cherished as valuable elements of our modernity, others do not consider modern at all. Whether we should be proud of these differences or embarrassed by them is a question I will take up later. For the moment, let us consider how we have conceived of our modernity.

In 1873, Rajnarayan Basu attempted a comparative evaluation of 'those days and these' in *Se Kal ar E Kal* (Those Days and These Days),[2] meaning by these two terms the period before and after the full-fledged introduction of English education in India. The word *adhunik*, in the sense in which we now use it in Bengali to mean 'modern', was not in use in the nineteenth century. The word then used was *nabya* (new): the 'new' was that which was inextricably linked to Western education and thought. The other word much in use was *unnati*, an equivalent of the nineteenth-century European concept of 'improvement' or 'progress', an idea we will today designate by the word *pragati*.

Rajnarayan Basu, needless to say, was educated in the nabya or new manner; he was a social reformer and very much in favour of modern ideas. Comparing 'those days' with 'these days', he spoke of seven areas where there had been either improvement or decline. These seven areas were health, education, livelihood, social life, virtue, polity, and religion. His discussion on these subjects is marked by the recurrence of some familiar themes. Thus, for instance, the notion that whereas people of 'those days' were simple, caring, compassionate, and genuinely religious, religion now is mere festivity and pomp, and that people have become cunning, devious, selfish, and ungrateful: 'Talking to people nowadays, it is hard to decide what their true feelings are. . . . Before, if there was a guest in the house, people were eager to have him stay a few days more. Before, people even pawned their belongings in order to be hospitable to their guests. Nowadays, guests look for the first opportunity to leave' (Basu, p. 82). Rajnarayan gives several such examples of changes in the quality of sociability.

But the subject on which Rajnarayan spends the longest time in comparing those days with these is that of the *sarir*, the body. I wish to present this matter a little elaborately, because in it lies a rather curious aspect of our modernity.

---

[2] Rajnarayan Basu, *Se Kal ar E Kal*, eds. Brajendranath Bandyopadhyay and Sajanikanta Das (Calcutta: Bangiya Sahitya Parishat, 1956). Subsequent references in brackets are to this work.

Ask anyone and he will say, 'My father and grandfather were very strong men.' Compared with men of those days, men now have virtually no strength at all. . . . If people who were alive a hundred years ago were to come back today, they would certainly be surprised to see how short in stature we have become. We used to hear in our childhood of women who chased away bandits. These days, let alone women, we do not even hear of men with such courage. Men these days cannot even chase away a jackal. (Basu, pp. 37–8)

On the whole, people—and Rajnarayan adds here 'especially *bhadra-lok*', respectable people—have now become feeble and sickly, and live shorter lives.

Let us pause for a minute to consider what this means. If by 'these days' we mean the modern age, the age of a new civilization inaugurated under English rule, then is the consequence of that modernity a decline in the health of the people? On ethics, religion, sociability, and other such matters there could conceivably be scope for argument. But how, in relation to our biological existence—that most mundane of worldly matters—could the thought occur to someone that people in the present age are weaker and have shorter life-spans than those in an earlier age?

If my historian friends are awake at this moment, they will of course point out straightaway that we are talking here of 1873, when modern medicine and health services in British India were still confined to the narrow limits of the European expatriate community and the army, and had not even begun to reach out towards the larger population. How could Rajnarayan be expected in 1873 to make a judgement on the miraculous advances of modern medicine in the twentieth century? If this be the objection, then let us look at a few more examples. Addressing the All-India Sanitary Conference in 1912, Motilal Ghosh, founder of the famous nationalist daily the *Amrita Bazar Patrika*, said that sixty years ago, that is to say, more or less at the time Rajnarayan referred to as 'these days', the Bengal countryside of his childhood was almost entirely free from disease. The only illnesses were common fevers which could be cured in a few days by an appropriate diet. Typhoid was rare and cholera not heard of. Smallpox occurred from time to time, but indigenous inoculators using traditional techniques were able to cure patients without much difficulty. There was no shortage of clean drinking water. Food was abundant and villages 'teemed with healthy, happy and robust people, who spent their days in manly sports.'[3] I can produce more recent examples. Reminiscing in 1982 on her childhood in Barisal, Manikuntala Sen, the Communist leader, writes, 'The thought brings tears to my eyes. Oh Allah, why did you give us this technological civilization? Weren't we content then with our rice and *dal*, fish and milk? Now I hear there is no hilsa fish in all of Barisal!'[4] Even more recently, Kalyani Datta in her *Thod Badi Khada* (1992) tells so many stories of her childhood pertaining to food and eating habits that the people Rajnarayan Basu talks of as having lived in the late eighteenth century seem to have been very much around in the inner precincts of Calcutta houses in the 1930s. After having a full meal, she says, people would often eat thirty or forty mangoes as dessert.[5]

Examples can be easily multiplied. In fact, if I had suitably dressed up Rajnarayan's words and passed them off as the comments of one of our contemporary writers, none of you would have suspected anything, because we ourselves speak all the time about how people of an earlier generation were so much stronger and healthier than ourselves.

The question is: why have we held on to this factually baseless idea for the last hundred years? Or could it be the case that we have been trying all along to say something about the historical experience of our modernity which does not appear in the statistical facts of demography? Well, let us turn to the reasons that Rajnarayan gives for the decline in health from 'those days' to 'these days'.

The first reason, Rajnarayan says, is change in the environment: 'Before, people would travel from Calcutta to Tribeni, Santipur and other villages for a change. Now those places have become unhealthy because of the miasma known as malaria. . . . For various reasons it appears that there is a massive environmental change taking place in India today. That such change will be reflected in the physical strength of the people is hardly surprising' (Basu, pp. 38–9). The second reason is food: the lack of nutritious food, the consumption of adulterated and harmful food, and an excess of drink: 'We have seen and heard in our childhood of numerous examples of how much people could eat in those days. They cannot do so now.' The third reason is labour:

[3] Cited in David Arnold, *Colonizing the Body: State Medicine and Ayurvedic Disease in Nineteenth-Century India* (Berkeley: University of California Press, 1993), pp. 282–3.

[4] Manikuntala Sen, *Sediner Katha* (Calcutta: Nabapatra, 1982), p. 10.

[5] Kalyani Datta, *Thod Badi Khada* (Calcutta: Thema, 1992), esp. pp. 26–48.

excess of labour, untimely labour, and lack of physical exercise. 'There is no doubt that with the advent of English civilization in our country, the need to labour has increased tremendously. We cannot labour in the same way as the English; yet the English want us to do so. English labour is not suited to this country. . . . The routine now enforced by our rulers of working from ten to four is in no way suitable for the conditions of this country' (Basu, p. 39). The fourth reason is the change in the way of life. In the past, people had few wants, which is why they were able to live happily. Today there is no end to our worries and anxieties. 'Now, European civilization has entered our country, and with it European wants, European needs, and European luxuries. Yet the European way of fulfilling those wants and desires, namely industry and trade, is not being adopted.' Rajnarayan here makes a comparison between two old men, one a 'vernacular old man', the other an 'anglicized old man':

> The anglicized old man has aged early. The vernacular old man wakes up when it is still dark. Waking up, he lies in bed and sings religious songs: how this delights his heart! Getting up from bed, he has a bath: how healthy a habit! Finishing his bath, he goes to the garden to pick flowers: how beneficial the fragrance of flowers for the body! Having gathered flowers, he sits down to pray: this delights the mind and strengthens both body and spirit. . . . The anglicized old man, on the other hand, has dinner and brandy at night and sleeps late; he has never seen a sunrise and has never breathed the fresh morning air. Rising late in the morning, he has difficulty in performing even the simple task of opening his eyelids. His body feels wretched, he has a hangover, things look like getting even worse! In this way, subjected to English food and drink and other English manners, the anglicized old man's body becomes the home of many diseases. (Basu, pp. 49–50)

Rajnarayan admits that this comparison is exaggerated. But there is one persistent complaint in all the reasons he cites for the decline in health from the earlier to the present age: not all the particular means we have adopted for becoming modern are suitable for us. Yet, by imitating uncritically the forms of English modernity, we are bringing upon us environmental degradation, food shortages, illnesses caused by excessive labour, and an uncoordinated and undisciplined way of life. Rajnarayan gives many instances of an uncritical imitation of English manners as, for instance, the following story on the lack of nutritious food:

Two Bengali gentlemen were once dining at Wilson's Hotel. One of them was especially addicted to beef. He asked the waiter, 'Do you have veal?' The waiter replied, 'I'm afraid not, sir.' The gentleman asked again, 'Do you have beefsteak?' The waiter replied, 'Not that either, sir.' The gentleman asked again, 'Do you have ox tongue?' The waiter replied, 'Not that either, sir.' The gentleman asked again, 'Do you have calf's-foot jelly?' The waiter replied, 'Not that either, sir.' The gentleman said, 'Don't you have anything from a cow?' Hearing this, the second gentleman, who was not so partial to beef, said with some irritation, 'Well, if you have nothing else from a cow, why not get him some dung?' (Basu, p. 44)

The point which this story is supposed to illustrate is that 'beef is much too heat-producing and unhealthy for the people of this country.' On the other hand, the food that is much more suitable and healthy, namely milk, has become scarce: English officials, Muslims, and a few beef-eating Bengalis 'have eaten the cows, which is why milk is so dear.'

Many of Rajnarayan's examples and explanations will seem laughable to us now. But there is nothing laughable about his main project, which is to prove that there cannot be just one modernity irrespective of geography, time, environment, and social conditions. The forms of modernity will have to vary among different countries depending upon specific circumstances and social practices. We could in fact stretch Rajnarayan's comments a bit further to assert that true modernity consists in determining the particular forms of modernity that are suitable in particular circumstances; that is, applying the methods of reason to identify or invent the specific technologies of modernity that are appropriate for our purposes. Or, to put this another way, if there is any universal or universally acceptable definition of modernity, it is this: that by teaching us to employ the methods of reason, universal modernity enables us to identify the forms of our own particular modernity.

Western Modernity Representing Itself

How is one to employ one's powers of reason and judgement to decide what to do? Let us listen to the reply given to this question by Western modernity itself. In 1784, Immanuel Kant wrote a short essay, *Aufklärung*, which we know in English as the Enlightenment, i.e. *alokprapti*.[6]

---

[6] Immanuel Kant, *On History*, ed. Lewis White Beck (Indianapolis: Bobbs-Merrill, 1963), pp. 3–10.

According to Kant, to be enlightened is to become mature, to reach adulthood, to stop being dependent on the authority of others, to become free and assume responsibility for one's own actions. When man is not enlightened, he does not employ his own powers of reasoning but rather accepts the guardianship of others and does as he is told. He does not feel the need to acquire knowledge about the world, because everything is written in the holy books. He does not attempt to make his own judgements about right and wrong; he follows the advice of his pastor. He even leaves it up to his doctor to decide what he should or should not eat. Most men in all periods of history have been, in this sense, immature. And those who have acted as guardians of society have wanted it that way; it was in their interest that most people should prefer to remain dependent on them rather than become self-reliant. It is in the present age that for the first time the need for self-reliance has been generally acknowledged. It is also now, for the first time, generally agreed that the primary condition for putting an end to our self-imposed dependence is freedom, especially civil freedom. This does not mean that everyone in the present age is enlightened or that we are now living in an enlightened age. We should rather say that our age is the age of Enlightenment.

The French philosopher Michel Foucault has an interesting discussion on this essay by Kant.[7] What is new in the way in which Kant describes the Enlightenment? The novelty lies, Foucault says, in the fact that for the first time we have a philosopher making an attempt to relate his philosophical inquiry to his own age and concluding that it is because the times are propitious that his inquiries have become possible. In other words, this is the first time that a philosopher makes the character of his own age a subject of philosophical investigation, the first time that someone tries from within his own age to identify the social conditions favourable for the pursuit of knowledge.

What are the features that Kant points out as characteristic of the present age? Foucault says that this is where the new thinking is so distinctive. In marking out the present, Kant is not referring to some revolutionary event which ends the earlier age and inaugurates the age of Enlightenment. Nor is he reading in the characteristics of the present age the signs of some future revolutionary event in the making.

---

[7] Michel Foucault, 'What is Enlightenment?', in Paul Rabinow, ed., *The Foucault Reader* (New York: Pantheon, 1984), pp. 32–50.

Nor indeed is he looking at the present as a transition from the past to some future age that has not yet arrived. All these strategies of describing the present in historical terms have been in use in European thought from a long time before Kant, from at least the Greek age, and their use has not ceased since the age of Kant. What is remarkable about Kant's criteria of the present is that they are all negative. Enlightenment means an exit, an escape: escape from tutelage, coming out of dependence. Here, Kant is not talking about the origins of the Enlightenment, or about its sources, or its historical evolution. Nor indeed is he talking about the historical goal of the Enlightenment. He is concerned only with the present in itself, with those exclusive properties that define the present as different from the past. Kant is looking for the definition of Enlightenment, or more broadly, of modernity, in the difference posed by the present.

Let us underline this statement and set it aside for the moment; I will return to it later. Let us now turn to another interesting aspect of Foucault's essay. Suppose we agree on the fact that autonomy and self-reliance have become generally accepted norms. Let us also grant that freedom of thought and speech is acknowledged as the necessary condition for self-reliance. But freedom of thought does not mean that people are free to do just as they please at every moment and in every act of daily life. To admit that would be to deny the need for social regulation and to call for total anarchy. Obviously, the philosophers of the Enlightenment could not have meant this. While demanding individual autonomy and freedom of thought, they also had to specify those areas of personal and social living where freedom of thought would operate and those other areas where, irrespective of individual opinions, the directives or regulations of the recognized authority would have to prevail. In his essay 'What is Enlightenment?' Kant did specify these areas.

The way he proceeds to do this is by separating two spheres of the exercise of reason. One of these Kant calls 'public', where matters of general concern are discussed and where reason is not mobilized for the pursuit of individual interests or for the support of a particular group. The other is the sphere of the 'private' use of reason which relates to the pursuit of individual or particular interests. In the former sphere, freedom of thought and speech is essential; in the second, it is not desirable at all. Illustrating the argument, Kant says that when there is a 'public' debate on the government's revenue policy, those who are knowledgeable in that subject must be given the freedom to express their opinions. But as a 'private' individual, I cannot claim that since I disagree with the government's fiscal policy I must have the freedom not to pay taxes. If there is a 'public' discussion on military organization or war strategy, even a soldier can participate, but on the battlefield his duty is not to express his free opinions but to follow orders. In a 'public' debate on religion, I may, even as a member of a religious denomination, criticize the practices and beliefs of my order, but in my 'private' capacity as a pastor my duty is to preach the authorized doctrines of my sect and observe its authorized practices. There cannot be any freedom of speech in the 'private' domain.

This particular use by Kant of the notions of 'public' and 'private' did not gain much currency in later discussions. On the contrary, the usual consensus in liberal social philosophy is that it is in the 'private' or personal sphere that there should be unrestricted freedom of conscience, opinion, and behaviour, whereas the sphere of 'public' or social interaction should be subject to recognized norms and regulations that must be respected by all. But no matter how unusual Kant's use of the public–private distinction, it is not difficult for us to understand his argument. When my activities concern a domain in which I as an individual am only a part of a larger social organization or system, a mere cog in the social wheel, there my duty is to abide by regulations and follow the directives of the recognized authority. But there is another domain of the exercise of reason which is not restricted by these particular or individual interests, a domain that is free and universal. That is the proper place for free thought, for the cultivation of science and art—the proper place, in one word, for 'enlightenment'.

It is worth pointing out that in this universal domain of the pursuit of knowledge—the domain which Kant calls 'public'—it is the individual who is the subject. The condition for true enlightenment is freedom of thought. When the individual in search of knowledge seeks to rise above his particular social location and participate in the universal domain of discourse, his right to freedom of thought and opinion must be unhindered. He must also have the full authority to form his own beliefs and opinions, just as he must bear the full responsibility for expressing them. There is no doubt that Kant is here claiming the right of free speech only for those who have the requisite qualifications for engaging in the exercise of reason and the pursuit of knowledge and those who can use that freedom in a responsible manner. In discussing Kant's essay, Foucault does not raise this point, although he might well have done so, given the relevance of this theme in his own work. It is the theme of the rise of experts and the ubiquitous authority of specialists, a phenomenon which appears alongside the general social acceptance of the principle of unrestricted entry into education and learning. We say, on the one hand, that it is wrong to exclude any individual or group from access to education or the practice of knowledge on grounds of religion or any other social prejudice. On the other hand, we also insist that the opinion of such and such a person is more acceptable because he is an expert in the field. In other words, just as we have meant by enlightenment an unrestricted and universal field for the exercise of reason, so have we built up an intricately differentiated structure of authorities which specifies who has the right to say what on which subjects. As markers of this authority, we have distributed examinations, degrees, titles, insignia of all sorts. Just think how many different kinds of experts we have to allow to guide us through our daily lives, from birth, indeed from before birth, to death and even afterwards. In many areas, in fact, it is illegal to act without expert advice. If I do not myself have a medical degree or licence, I cannot walk into a pharmacy and say: 'I hope you know that there is unrestricted access to knowledge, because I have read all the medical books and I think I need these drugs.' In countries with universal schooling, it is mandatory that children go to officially recognized schools; I could not insist that I will educate my children at home. There are also fairly precise identifications of who is an expert in which subject. At this particular meeting today, for instance, I am talking on history, social philosophy, and related subjects, and you have come here to listen to me, either out of interest or plain courtesy. If I had announced that I would be speaking on radiation in the ionosphere or the DNA molecule, I would most definitely have had to speak to an empty room and some of my well-wishers would probably have run to consult experts on mental disorders.

Needless to say, the writings of Foucault have in recent years taught us to look at the relation between the practices of knowledge and the technologies of power from a very new angle. Kant's answer two hundred years ago to the question 'What is Enlightenment?' might seem at first sight to be an early statement of the most commonplace self-representation of modern social philosophy. And yet, now we can see embedded in that statement the not-very-well-acknowledged ideas of differential access to discourse, the specialized authority of experts, and the use of the instruments of knowledge for the exercise of power.

The irresistible enthusiasm that one notices in the writings of Western philosophers of the Enlightenment about a modernity that would bring in the era of universal reason and emancipation does not seem to us, witness to the many barbarities of world history in the last two hundred years—and I say this with due apologies to the great Immanuel Kant—as mature in the least. Today our doubts about the claims of modernity are out in the open.

A Modernity that is National

But I have not yet given you an adequate answer to the question with which I began this discussion. Why is it the case that for more than a hundred years the foremost proponents of our modernity have been so vocal about the signs of social decline rather than of progress? Surely, when Rajnarayan Basu spoke about the decline in health, education, sociability, and virtue, he did not do so out of some post-modern sense of irony. There must be something in the very process of our becoming modern that continues to lead us, even in our acceptance of modernity, to a certain scepticism about its values and consequences.

My argument is that because of the way in which the history of our modernity has been intertwined with the history of colonialism, we have never quite been able to believe that there exists a universal domain of free discourse, unfettered by differences of race or nationality. Somehow, from the very beginning, we have made a shrewd guess that given the close complicity between modern knowledges and modern regimes of power, we would forever remain consumers of universal modernity; never would we be taken seriously as its producers. It is for this reason that we have tried, for over a hundred years, to take our eyes away from this chimera of universal modernity and clear a space where we might become the creators of our own modernity.

Let us take an example from history. One of the earliest learned societies in India devoted to the pursuit of the modern knowledges was the Society for the Acquisition of General Knowledge, founded in Calcutta in 1838 by some former students of Hindu College, several of whom had been members of 'Young Bengal', that celebrated circle of radicals that had formed in the 1820s around the freethinking rationalist Henry Derozio. In 1843, at a meeting of this society held at Hindu College, a paper was being read on 'The Present State of the East India Company's Criminal Judicature and Police'. D.L. Richardson, a well-known teacher of English literature at Hindu College, got up angrily and, according to the Proceedings, complained that 'To stand up in a hall which the Government had erected and in the heart of a city which was the focus of enlightenment, and there to denounce, as oppressors and robbers, the men who governed the country, did in his opinion, amount to treason. . . . The College would never have been in existence, but for the solicitude the Government felt in the mental improvement of the natives of India. He could not permit it, therefore, to be converted into a den of treason, and must close the doors against all such meetings.' At this, Tarachand Chakrabarti, himself a former student of Hindu College who was chairing the meeting, rebuked Richardson: 'I consider your conduct as an insult to the society . . . if you do not retract what you have said and make due apology, we shall represent the matter to the Committee of the Hindoo College, and if necessary to the Government itself. We have obtained the use of this public hall, by leave applied for and received from the Committee, and not through your personal favour. You are only a visitor on this occasion, and possess no right to interrupt a member of this society in the utterance of his opinions.'[8]

This episode is usually recounted in the standard histories as an example of early nationalist feelings among the new intelligentsia of Bengal. Not that there is no truth in this observation, but it does not lie in the obvious drama of an educated Indian confronting his British teacher. Rather, what is significant is the separation between the domain of government and that of 'this society' and the insistence that, as long as the required procedures had been followed, the rights of the members of the society to express their opinions—no matter how critical of government—could not be violated. We could say that at this founding moment of modernity we did genuinely want to believe that in the new public domain of free discourse there was no bar of colour or of the political status of one's nationality; that if one could produce proof of one's competence in the subjects under discussion one had an unrestricted right to voice one's opinions.

It did not take long for the disillusionment to set in. By the second half of the nineteenth century we see the emergence of 'national' societies for the pursuit of the modern knowledges. The learned

---

[8] A report on this meeting that appeared in the *Bengal Hurkaru*, 13 February 1843, is reprinted in Goutam Chattopadhyay, ed., *Awakening in Bengal in Early Nineteenth Century (Select Documents)*, vol. 1 (Calcutta: Progressive Publishers, 1965), pp. 389–99.

societies of the earlier era had both European and Indian members. The new institutions were exclusively for Indian members and devoted to the cultivation and spread of the modern sciences and arts among Indians, if possible in the Indian languages. They were, in other words, institutions for the 'nationalization' of the modern knowledges, located in a space somewhat set apart from the field of universal discourse, a space where discourse would be modern, and yet 'national'.

[handwritten margin note: nationalization of knowledge]

This is a project that is still being pursued today. Its successes vary from field to field. But unless we can state why the project was at all considered feasible and what conditions governed its feasibility, we will not be able to answer the question I had asked at the beginning of this talk about the peculiarities of our modernity. We could take as an example our experience with practising any one of the branches of the modern knowledges. Since I began this talk with a discussion on the body and its health, let me tell you the story of our acquaintance with the modern science of medicine.

In 1851, a Bengali section was opened at the Calcutta Medical College in order to train Indian students in Western medicine without requiring them first to go through a course of secondary education in English. The Licentiate and Apothecary courses in Bengali were a great success. Beginning with a mere 22 students in its first year, it overtook the English section in 1864, and in 1873 it had 772 students compared to 445 in the English section. Largely because of the demand from students, nearly 700 medical books were published in Bengali between 1867 and 1900.[9]

But while the courses remained popular, complaints began to be heard from around the 1870s about the quality of training given to students in the vernacular sections. It was alleged that their lack of facility in English made them unsuitable for positions of assistants to European doctors in public hospitals. This was the time when a hospital system had begun to be put in place in Bengal and professional controls were being enforced in the form of supervision by the General Medical Council of London. From the turn of the century, with the institutionalization of the professional practices of medicine in the form of hospitals, medical councils, and patented drugs, the Bengali section in the medical school died a quick death. Since 1916 all medical education in our country has been exclusively in English.

---

[9] Computed from list supplied by Binaybhusan Ray, *Unis Sataker Bamlay Bijnan Sadhana* (Calcutta: Subarnarekha, 1987), pp. 252–77.

But the story does not end there. Curiously, this was also the time when organized efforts were on, propelled by nationalist concerns, to give to the indigenous Ayurvedic and Yunani systems of medicine a new disciplinary form. The All India Ayurveda Mahasammelan, which is still the apex body of ayurvedic practitioners, was set up in 1907. The movement which this organization represented sought to systematize the knowledge of ayurvedic clinical methods, mainly by producing standard editions of classical and recent texts, to institutionalize the methods of training by formalizing, in place of the traditional family-based apprenticeship, a college system consisting of lectures, textbooks, syllabuses, examinations, and degrees, and to standardize the medicines and even promote the commercial production of standard drugs by pharmaceutical manufacturers. There have been debates within the movement about the extent and form of adoption of Western medicine within the curricula of ayurvedic training, but even the purists now admit that the course should have 'the benefit of equipment or the methods used by other systems of medicine . . . since, consistent with its fundamental principles, no system of medicine can ever be morally debarred from drawing upon any other branch of science . . . unless one denies the universal nature of scientific truths.'[10]

The very idea of the universality of science is being used here to carve out a separate space for ayurvedic medicine, defined according to the principles of a 'pure' tradition, and yet reorganized as a modern scientific and professional discipline. The claim here is not that the field of knowledge is marked out into separate domains by the fact of cultural difference; it is not being suggested that ayurveda is the appropriate system of medicine for 'Indian diseases'. It is rather a claim for an alternative science directed at the same objects of knowledge.

We have of course seen many attempts of this sort in the fields of literature and the arts to construct a modernity that is different. Indeed, we might say that this is precisely the cultural project of nationalism: to produce a distinctly national modernity. Obviously, there is no general rule that determines which should be the elements of modernity and which the emblems of difference. There have been

---

[10] *Report of the Shuddha Ayurvedic Education Committee* (Delhi, 1963), cited in Paul R. Brass, 'Politics of Ayurvedic Education: A Case Study of Revivalism and Modernization in India', in Susanne Hoeber Rudolph and Lloyd I. Rudolph, eds, *Education and Politics in India* (Cambridge, Mass.: Harvard University Press, 1972), pp. 342–71.

many experiments in many fields; they continue even today. My argument was that these efforts have not been restricted only to the supposedly cultural domains of religion, literature, and the arts. The attempt to find a different modernity has been carried out even in the presumably universal field of science. We should remember that a scientist of the standing of Prafulla Chandra Ray, a Fellow of the Royal Society (FRS), thought it worth his while to write *A History of Hindu Chemistry*, while Jagadis Chandra Bose, also an FRS, believed that the researches he carried out in the latter part of his career were derived from insights he had obtained from Indian philosophy. In particular, he believed that he had found a field of scientific research that was uniquely suited to an Indian scientist. These researches of Jagadis Bose did not get much recognition in the scientific community. But it seems to me that if we grasp what it was that led him to think of a project such as this, we will get an idea of the principal driving force of our modernity.

Present History in the Age of Globalization

Whenever I think of enlightenment, I am reminded of the unforgettable first lines of Kamalkumar Majumdar's novel *Antarjali Yatra*.[11] 'Light appears gradually. The sky is a frosty violet, like the colour of pomegranate. In a few moments from now, redness will come to prevail and we, the plebeians of this earth, will once more be blessed by the warmth of flowers. Gradually, the light appears' (p. 1). Modernity is the first social philosophy which conjures up in the minds of the most ordinary people dreams of independence and self-rule. The regime of power in modern societies prefers to work not through the commands of a supreme sovereign but through the disciplinary practices that each individual imposes on his or her own behaviour on the basis of the dictates of reason. And yet, no matter how adroitly the fabric of reason might cloak the reality of power, the desire for autonomy continues to range itself against power; power is resisted. Let us remind ourselves that there was a time when modernity was put forward as the strongest argument in favour of the continued colonial subjection of India: foreign rule was necessary, we were told, because Indians must first become enlightened. And then it was the same logic of modernity

[11] Kamalkumar Majumdar, *Antarjali Yatra* (Calcutta: Kathasilpa, 1962).

which one day led us to the discovery that imperialism was illegitimate; independence was our desired goal. The burden of reason, dreams of freedom; the desire for power, resistance to power: all of these are elements of modernity. There is no promised land of modernity outside the network of power. Hence one cannot be for or against modernity; one can only devise strategies for coping with it. These strategies are sometimes beneficial, often destructive; sometimes they are tolerant, perhaps all too often they are fierce and violent. We have, as I said before, had to abandon the simple faith that because something was modern and rational, it must necessarily be for the good.

At the end of Kamalkumar's novel, a fearsome flood, like the unstoppable hand of destiny, sweeps away a decadent Hindu society. With it, it also takes that which was alive, beautiful, affectionate, kind. The untouchable plebeian cannot save her, because he is not entitled to touch that which is sacred and pure. 'A single eye, like the eye mirrored on hemlock, kept looking at her, the bride seeking her first taste of love. The eye is wooden, because it is painted on the side of a boat; but it is painted in vermilion, and it has on it drops of water from the waves now breaking gently against the boat. The wooden eye is capable of shedding tears. Somewhere, therefore, there remains a sense of attachment' (p. 216). This sense of attachment is the driving force of our modernity. We would be unjust to ourselves if we think of it as backward-looking, as a sign of resistance to change. On the contrary, it is our attachment to the past which gives birth to the feeling that the present needs to be changed, that it is our task to change it. We must remember that in the world arena of modernity, we are outcastes, untouchables. Modernity for us is like a supermarket of foreign goods, displayed on the shelves: pay up and take away what you like. No one there believes that we could be producers of modernity. The bitter truth about our present is our subjection, our inability to be subjects in our own right. And yet, it is because we want to be modern that our desire to be independent and creative is transposed on to our past. It is superfluous to call this an imagined past, because pasts are always imagined. At the opposite end from 'these days' marked by incompleteness and lack of fulfilment, we construct a picture of 'those days' when there was beauty, prosperity, and a healthy sociability, and which was, above all, our own creation. 'Those days' for us is not a historical past; we construct it only to mark the difference posed by the present. All that needs to be noticed is that whereas Kant, speaking at the founding moment of Western modernity, looks at the present as the site of one's escape from the past, for us it is precisely the present from which we feel we must escape. This makes the very modality of our coping with modernity radically different from the historically evolved modes of Western modernity.

Ours is the modernity of the once-colonized. The same historical process that has taught us the value of modernity has also made us the victims of modernity. Our attitude to modernity, therefore, cannot but be deeply ambiguous. This is reflected in the way we have described our experiences with modernity in the last century and a half, from Rajnarayan Basu to our contemporaries today. But this ambiguity does not stem from any uncertainty about whether to be for or against modernity. Rather, the uncertainty is because we know that to fashion the forms of our own modernity we need to have the courage at times to reject the modernities established by others. In the age of nationalism, there were many such efforts which reflected both courage and inventiveness. Not all were, of course, equally successful. Today, in the age of globalization, perhaps the time has come once more to mobilize that courage. Maybe we need to think now about 'those days' and 'these days' of our modernity.

8

A Tribute to the Master
(2001)

This is a fragment from a text of the Mahabharata found in a remote village in the Faridpur district of Bangladesh. The episode described here is not included in any of the standard editions of the epic. In this text, the episode occurs in the Drona Parva of the great battle at Kurukshetra. Bhishma, who was commanding the Kaurava troops, has just been slain. Stunned and grieved by the loss, the Kaurava princes confer and elect Drona, the unrivalled master of the arts of warfare, to lead them in battle the next day. Though he had chosen to stay on the side of the Kauravas, Drona had also been teacher to the Pandava princes. Much disturbed by the prospect of having to plan the downfall of his favourite pupils, Drona sends an emissary to Arjuna, the third of the Pandava brothers, and arranges to meet him in secret that night. Marshalling the enormous array of his erudition and wisdom, Drona delivers to Arjuna a lecture on the subject of world history.[1] The white-skinned philosophers of the barbarian nations of the West, he says, have corrupted our souls by preaching the false doctrine that the prose of history is merely the rational narrative of the state. Bemused by their pretensions to hegemony, we too had narrowed our sights exclusively to the domain of the state. In the process, we had forgotten the true prose of the world, which is coextensive with historicality itself, with the entirety of the human condition. Immersed in violent and futile constestations over the state, we have forgotten to listen to the sighs and whispers of everyday human life.

Janamejaya said, 'But tell us, O regenerate sage Vaisampayana, how did the blind king Dhritarashtra react when he heard that the master Drona, commander of his troops, had secretly met the most brilliant warrior of the rival camp?'

This piece was written in 2001 and is published here for the first time.
[1] Ranajit Guha, *History at the Limit of World-history* (New York: Columbia University Press, 2002).

Vaisampayana said, 'Hearing of Drona's meeting with his favourite pupil Arjuna and of his attempt to turn the young warrior's attention away from the concerns of the state to the joys and sorrows of the everyday, the monarch Dhritarashtra grew most perturbed. Displaying all the signs of restlessness, he turned his head in the direction of Sanjaya, who had just come back from the camp to the city called after the elephant [Hastinapur], and said, "Tell me, O son, what did the third Pandava say after he heard his teacher's dissertation on history and the state?"'

Sanjaya said, 'Listen, O king, with undivided attention, to me as I recite the reply of Partha, the third Pandava, to his preceptor Drona who, for his mastery of the arts of war, was also known by the name Ranajit.' After the master had concluded his erudite and sonorous speech, the young prince sat silently for several moments, apparently bewildered by the impact of the powerful words he had just heard. Then, slowly collecting his thoughts, he began his reply.

'O revered teacher', Arjuna said, 'all the knowledges I have acquired in my life—all the arts and sciences, the philosophies and literatures, the worldly wisdoms and spiritual virtues—I have learnt while sitting attentively at your feet. All my skills of mental and physical proficiency are the results of the generous gifts you have showered on me. Tonight, as I ponder over the many sentences you have just spoken to me, and while all around us the soldiers of our armies sleep fitfully, not knowing the fortunes and calamities that lie in store for them in tomorrow's battle, I find myself at a loss for words. For what you have said to me tonight seems utterly at odds with the many lessons you once taught me. Indeed, it appears to me that all that I hold to be valuable and true, in philosophy as well as in life, is preparing to rebel against your arguments.'

'Fear not, O son', Drona quickly interjected in a reassuring tone. 'Do not hold back your doubts for fear of displeasing me. I sought this conversation tonight solely to hear you respond to my thoughts. So, my dear prince, do proceed without hesitation to air your objections.'

'Master', said Arjuna, 'allow me to begin with what is probably the least consequential objection I have to your lecture. It concerns a point of merely empirical interest and could, if you accept it, be easily accommodated into your argument without significantly altering its main structure. The relevant questions are: first, was Ramram Basu, writing *Raja Pratapaditya Caritra* in 1801 at the behest of his superiors at the

Fort William College in Calcutta, producing, as you say, "the first work on Indian history, written by an Indian in his own language, but in conformity with the Western model of historical writing?" And second, once again your question, "how could the first Indian historians of the colonial era learn to write history if history had been altogether unknown to them prior to the advent of colonialism?" On the first question, I do not wish to list here the many rival claims that might be made to the somewhat dubiously distinguished position of the first Indian historian writing according to the Western model. As you well know, I am no expert on this subject and I can only recall here what I have heard from other scholars, many of whom have spoken of historical tracts from the 17th and 18th centuries, written in the languages of southern and western India and even in Sanskrit, that appear to satisfy most of the conventions of secular historiography. They point to the undeniable presence on the western coast of India—in Goa, Mangalore, and the Kerala ports in particular—of mercantile, religious, political, and literary influences from Europe long before a college at Fort William in Calcutta had been even dreamt of by Lord Wellesley's forefathers. And then there is the matter of Persian historiography, domesticated in India since the 12th century, producing its accounts of kings and generals, saints and preachers, and virtually making itself the model of the historical narrative in pre-British northern India. Needless to say, O great master, a great deal hangs on what you mean by "the Western model of historical writing". You could, of course, by a suitable definition, exclude all of this pre-British historiography as not conforming to the Western model. But then, you would have to show what Ramram Basu succeeded in doing that was absent in all previous historical texts produced by Indians. You have, sadly, neglected to carry out this exercise. In its place, you have, may I say, accepted entirely at face value the self-congratulatory claim made by the English missionary William Carey, repeated since then by generations of Bengali scholars, that the first book of history by an Indian was produced by his providential prompting and written, of all Indian languages, needless to say, in Bengali. Which is why, in answer to your second question, you have not so much as even paused to consider whether, in looking for narrative precedents to write the history of a 16th-century Mughal warlord and rebel, Ramram Basu might not have searched the most obvious and proximate source, namely, the Persian histories on the subject as well as the Bengali *vamsavali* literature, generously permeated by Persian historiography. After all, Ramram Basu, as a literate Kayastha of the 18th century—and, incidentally, the only non-Brahmin in the Bengali department at Fort William College—was undoubtedly literate in Persian. But then, to resolve this issue, we would have to go into the empirical question of the various 18th-century Persian and Bengali texts that Ramram may have used as his sources. You, however, O preceptor of mine, after having posed the historical question "how could he learn to write history?" have chosen to altogether ignore every possible historical answer to that question.'

Stopping for a moment to regain his breath, Partha, the third Pandava, continued. 'But this, as I said, is a matter of empirical history for which, I see, you have entirely lost your taste. So let me turn to that philosopher of the barbarians, known by the name Hegel, whom you have hauled over the coals. I remember very well the lessons you once gave us on the writings of that philosopher. Tonight, when you described, with that wonderful dramatic flair of which only you are capable, the task of approaching the limit of world-history from the other side, the side of emptiness into which the barbarians have sought to consign the rest of the world, it sent a thrill through my body. But when you finished your demolition job on Hegel, it appeared to me that we had been flogging a horse long dead. O great teacher, you know as well as we that the liberal writers of the West of the last hundred years have strenuously refused to own up to Hegel's statist philosophy of history. Without discarding the paradigm of experience on which their historical narratives are still based, they have rejected the statolatry and the ascriptions of divine design for which you have quite rightly castigated Hegel. They would say, I am sure, that liberal historiography as currently practised in the West cannot be held guilty of any of Hegel's crimes, not even of drawing a line through the map of the world to designate the zones of world-history from those of mere historicality. We have, of course, always suspected that this is a mere sleight of hand, that behind the gesture of universal inclusiveness is hidden a more subtle game of exclusions. Imagine my thrill, therefore, as I watched your masterly dissection of Hegel, anxiously awaiting the moment when you would demonstrate to me that, in spite of their disavowal of Hegel, the historians of the West were still engaged in writing a world-history that was, in its essentials, entirely Hegelian. That would have crowned your achievement. But alas, that moment did not come, and I am left with the sad feeling that perhaps you have given your adversaries the chance to merely smirk and say that may be it has all been a little beside the point.

'There was another question that bothered me as I followed you on your analysis of Hegel. Once again, you know better than anyone else that my knowledge of the works of that *mleccha* philosopher is perfunctory and utterly amateurish. I do not know at all his work on *Aesthetics* to which you referred; you did not teach it to us when we sat at your feet. But even going by your account of it, I find it hard to understand how you can regard Hegel's delineation of a prose of the world, free from the trammels of the prose of history—if this indeed is what it is—as anything other than a bad analytical slip. For if everyday encounters between individuals are examples of the process of mutual recognition, then how can they be exempt from the dialectics of that process? In other words, by what phenomenological reasoning could such encounters escape the clutches of the master–slave dialectic and hence of history? If Hegel does suggest that the realm of the everyday, and its prose of the world, exists independently of history, he can do so, if I may humbly submit, O revered master, only in the relative and conditional sense of a moment or a stage of the dialectic. If not, it is an error that any good Hegelian would rush to correct. For how, such a Hegelian will ask you, can you exempt your everyday world, in which individuals seek mutual recognition, from the effects of power, and if you cannot, how can you prevent the everyday from being contaminated by questions of possession, will, rights, property, law, justice— in short, by the prose of history?'

Arjuna stopped and looked questioningly at Drona. The teacher raised his bowed head, glanced up at his former pupil and asked softly, 'Have you finished?' Arjuna replied, 'I have, if I may, two more points to make on your lecture.' Drona said, 'Please continue, O son. I find your arguments very instructive.'

Partha, the third Pandava, continued with his reply. 'I would like, with your permission, to return to the question you asked about the first Indian historians: how did they learn to write history? Your answer, as far as I understood it, was as follows. To write history, they had to pass from the stage of perception to that of comprehension of the concept of history. Before the introduction of formal education in English, this could only have been possible by intuition, as in the case of Ramram Basu. How did he learn by intuition to write history? By using, as you describe it, his innate capacity to grasp a set of starting points or principles corresponding to the concept of history. These starting points, you say, citing Aristotle, the ancient philosopher of the Yavanas, are the *archai,* as they say in the language of the Yavanas. They are primary in the sense of being prior to everything else and do not depend on demonstration for their validity. What were the *archai* related to the concept of history that Ramram seized upon? They were, you say, the chronicles and stories within his own tradition of which the most ancient and continuously circulated were the Mahabharata and the Ramayana, constituting a genre known as the *itihasa.* When Ramram looked for starting points for his history of the 16th-century Mughal rebel Pratap, he found them, you say, without any hesitation, in the Mahabharata and the Ramayana. For these, you say, are the paradigmatic forms of the narrative in India.

'If you allow me to exercise my admittedly inexperienced judgment, may I say that even by Aristotelian standards, your identification of the paradigm suffers from the defect of *avyapti*—the criterion you supply does not cover all the cases. I find it an excessive generalization, some would say monstrously excessive, to assimilate all forms of proto-hist-orical narrative in India to the Mahabharata. Imagine all the genres, periods, languages, regions, classes, genders, castes, tribes, and such other collectivities among whom narratives circulate that such a criter-ion would leave out. You apply the conditions of antiquity or tradition and succession or continuous retelling in order to privilege the two Brahmanical epics over all other narrative specimens. But is this not, as we once discovered as students sitting at your feet, the same oriental-izing move with which Hindu nationalist thinkers a hundred years ago assimilated all of India's past to the pristine forms of an Aryan–Brahmanical tradition?

'You also say that the characteristic feature of the Indian narrative is that it is not based on the paradigm of experience: there is a distance between the narrator and the event. There lies its fundamental dif-ference from the Western narrative of history. In this respect, whereas the claim of history is that it is a form of true knowledge, the Indian narrative does not make any such claim, because it is a narrative of wonder. "Disengaged from experience", you say, "it does not claim to produce anything out of a given set of causes nor inform anybody of objects attainable by the common means of knowledge." If I hold on to this distinction, it explains to me why Indian logicians of all schools have over the centuries steadfastly refused to accept the *itihasa* as true knowledge, because memory, they say, not being based on direct perception of its object, cannot produce true cognition. But having made the distinction, you nevertheless go on to claim that the itihasa, a narrative of wonder, has an even higher claim to truth than history. "Neither productive nor informative by intention, it is", you assert, "still a knowledge in the most profound sense of the term. For the apprehension of *rasa* is indistinguishable from self-knowledge, and the rapture generated by *camatkara* or wonder approaches *ananda*, the most profound state of spiritual bliss."

If this is metaphysics, it is one I neither understand nor appreciate. I am prepared to put down this failure on my part to my own severely deficient spiritual attainments, but I must confess that I find it hard to understand why, having distinguished between history and itihasa, and established the difference between causal knowledge and wonder, you nevertheless find it necessary to claim the status of true knowledge for the latter. If, I might say, we have been so enraptured all this time by the narratives of wonder and have managed for so long without any use for the narratives of history, why do we now need to claim for ourselves our own version of the latter, unless it is to meet the exigencies set by history itself?

'It is in the face of that question that I find particularly perplexing your invocation of the pathos of historicality. The prose of the world, once alive and flourishing in stories that told of much that was unusual about the usual in everyday life, has been overtaken and defeated by the prose of history. The strategic alliance of the state and historiography has established its dominance even in India. Now, you say to me, we must listen to the loser's voice. But is it not a fact, O great preceptor, that we have been forced to listen to the voices of the women, the dalit, and the subaltern precisely at the moment when they have announced their refusal to accept defeat? Was it not you who taught us that it is not we who, through our tales of pathos, must inscribe the subaltern in history as the victim who deserves our sympathy, but the subaltern, herself or himself, who announces to us, even in the stories of defeat, that one day he or she will not be ruled by others? Is it not the case that there are today projects of feminist, dalit, and subaltern studies only because women, dalits, and subalterns have finally refused to live happily with their pasts? Are we now to tell them that they must not struggle to establish their place in the narrative of history but rather go back to the days when they were made to seek joy in stories from the Ramayana and the Mahabharata?

'O preceptor of mine, I must now take your leave and retire. There is a battle to be fought tomorrow. Destiny and the frailties of our own wills have conspired to now place us on opposite sides, but we must do what we each regard as rightful and just. What I do know, however, is that I will always remain your grateful and diligent pupil.'

Janamejaya said, 'But tell us, O sage Vaisampayana, what did Drona say in response to the criticisms made by the third Pandava?'

Vaisampayana said, 'Unfortunately, Sanjaya does not tell us anything further about this secret nocturnal meeting between Drona and Arjuna. Instead, he proceeds directly to narrate to the blind king Dhritarashtra the events of the next day's battle.'

9

Those Fond Memories of the Raj (2005)

There are reasons why the last surviving English gentlemen are today only to be found in India. They have brown skins, they don't speak the Queen's English, but in their hearts they are deeply appreciative of the legacies of British colonial rule. They care little for most aspects of contemporary British culture, though. They have no interest in British domestic politics. They have no taste for British art. They sneer at the British fondness for badly cooked curries. They rejoice in the fact that the best English literature today is produced by the ex-colonized. They watch the English football league on television but are fearful of the fans. It is not the real Britain of Blair and Bradford and British Rail that they think about when they speak longingly of the British connection. The Britain they conjure up in their minds is an idea that once had real referents that have now almost completely vanished from the face of Britain. Yet the myth continues to gain strength among India's elites.

One wouldn't have suspected that Prime Minister Manmohan Singh might become an articulate proponent of this myth. But then the weight of medieval ceremonies practised at Oxford convocations can have strange effects. As he admitted, it was 'a very emotional day' for him, even when he had already earned an earlier doctorate from the same university—one for which he had laboured hard. But then, come to think of it, why shouldn't Manmohan Singh believe in the supposed virtues of the British empire? He is an economist-bureaucrat, virtually untouched by the rough and tumble of electoral politics. It shouldn't surprise us if he shares the desires and prejudices of India's professional middle classes.

What is this myth of 'the beneficial consequences' of British rule? The prime minister spoke at Oxford of 'good governance', mentioning, in particular, the rule of law, constitutional government, a free press, a professional civil service, modern universities, and research laboratories. He forgot to add, however, that each of these elements of modern governance was introduced into India not in the form in which it was practised in Britain but always with crucial exceptions. Thus, the British in India resisted the jury system or even *habeas corpus* outside the Presidency towns, resisted the trial of Europeans by Indian judges, and, at every whiff of 'sedition', enacted emergency laws that would have been unthinkable in Britain. Constitutional government was introduced, but even in the last elections held before Independence less than 10 per cent of Indian adults were eligible to vote. Elected provincial ministries were allowed, but British governors had virtually unlimited powers to accept or dismiss ministers, and civil servants were required to send confidential reports directly to the governor without the knowledge of elected ministers. A free press? Yes, but only in the English language. Everywhere in India, until the last days of the Raj, the vernacular press lived under severe censorship laws. The prime minister, one gathers, is highly appreciative of the civil service, especially the district administration, created under British rule. The much celebrated steel frame epitomized the paternalist, and profoundly authoritarian, ethos of British colonial rule. Indians, it was believed, were moral infants, unable to protect or look after themselves. They had to be ruled by a benevolent master. It was a form of government that was, of course, being abandoned in Britain even as it was introduced into India. Can one imagine a twentieth-century Britain governed by district magistrates? Finally, it is astonishing that Dr Manmohan Singh believes that the modern universities and research laboratories of India were set up by the British. Of the twenty universities of pre-Independence India, the majority were funded through endowments and donations by Indians. All postgraduate departments and science institutes were set up in this way, at the initiative of Indian educationists, and against the vested interests of the colonial survey establishments. Modern education in India was a nationalist achievement, not a colonial gift.

All regimes, even the most repressive, have some beneficial effects: this is trivially true. The interesting question is when, where, and why one chooses to point them out. We are being told that it is a sign of our growing self-confidence as a nation that we can at last acknowledge, without shame or guilt, the good the British did for us. I suspect it is something else. The more popular democracy deepens in India, the more its elites yearn for a system in which enlightened gentlemen could decide, with paternal authority, what was good for the masses. The idea of an Oxford graduate of twenty-two going out to rule over the destiny of a hundred thousand peasants in an Indian district can stir up many noble thoughts in middle-class Indian hearts today. They scarcely remind themselves that the Oxford of Benjamin Jowett and Cecil Rhodes has, for good reasons, long passed into history. The historian Richard Symonds, in his book *Oxford and Empire*, describes the service of empire as Oxford's 'last lost cause'.

But then, one should not be too harsh on the prime minister. He has, one assumes, only expressed a no-longer-secret desire of the Indian elite. Mahatma Gandhi, always more perspicacious than others, had noticed it a hundred years ago. What the Indian middle classes, clamouring for self-government, really wanted, he said, was 'English rule without the Englishman'.

10

Beyond the Nation? Or Within?
(1997)

'We need to think ourselves beyond the nation', declared Arjun Appadurai in the first sentence of his 1993 essay 'Patriotism and Its Futures'.[1] Since that announcement, and indeed for some time before it, the demand has been made with increasing urgency to give clearer theoretical shape to the practices, locations, solidarities, and institutions that seem to be emerging beyond the familiar grid of the nation-state system. One obvious reason for the demand is empirical: there is little doubt that the volume of significant social phenomena that are in one way or another of a 'transnational' kind has grown considerably over the last three decades, and that these cannot be satisfactorily described or explained within a conceptual field which is still organized around the idea that a 'modern' society and people is, under normal circumstances, constituted as a nation-state. The second reason for the demand is moral-political: it is based on the perception that the authority and legitimacy of the nation-state is in crisis and that its capacity to act for the good of the people over whom it claims to exercise authority has been exhausted or irreparably undermined. The two reasons together have produced the sense of urgency behind the demand to think beyond the nation.

Address to the panel 'Culture at Large: Partha Chatterjee Meets His Interlocutors', at the American Anthropological Association meetings in San Francisco, 20–24 November 1996.

[1] Arjun Appadurai, 'Patriotism and Its Futures', *Public Culture*, 5, 3 (1993), pp. 411–29, included in Appadurai, *Modernity at Large: Cultural Dimensions of Globalisation* (Minneapolis: University of Minnesota Press, 1996), pp. 158–77. All subsequent bracketed page references to Appadurai are to this book.

I will here advance an argument that acknowledges the force of the two reasons mentioned above but that nevertheless suggests that for those very reasons we should look within the nation rather than beyond it. It could, of course, be objected that the options 'beyond or within' ought not to be posed as mutually exclusive ones, and that the proposals to think more seriously of postnational institutions or solidarities do not necessarily rule out rethinking the internal forms of the nation-state. My response to this anticipated objection is that, for certain strategic reasons which have to do with the politics of theoretical intervention, I will insist that the journey that might take us beyond the nation must first pass through the currently disturbed zones within the nation-state; and that in fact a more satisfactory resolution of the problems within could give us some of the theoretical instruments we are looking for to tackle the questions beyond.

It makes little sense for me to undertake here a review of all of the things that have been said to make the case for looking beyond the nation-state. Since Arjun Appadurai is one of the most prominent and able advocates of this proposal, I will in the following paragraphs arrange the materials for my argument through an interlocution of some of his recent writings.

II

Let us take a brief look, first of all, at some of the 'facts'. Appadurai summarizes these under two heads: electronic mediation and mass migration. The developments on this score in the last three decades or so cannot be regarded as merely quantitative enlargements of phenomena that existed in the pre-electronic age. First, 'more people than ever before seem to imagine routinely the possibility that they or their children will live and work in places other than where they were born': this creates new mythographies that are 'not just a counterpoint to the certainties of daily life' but are 'charters for new social projects' that impel ordinary people to change their daily lives (p. 6). Second, contrary to the theory of the media as the opium of the masses, there is enough evidence to show that the consumption of mass media has produced among ordinary people its own instruments of agency in the form of irony, selectivity, and resistance. Third, the collective experience of the electronic media creates the possibility of collective imaginings that are more powerful and far-reaching than the imaginative boundaries of the nation. The combination of electronic mediation and mass migration has created new diasporic public spheres that transcend the boundaries of the nation-state. These have produced in a large number of cases an awareness of cultural identity that cuts across national boundaries, movements of modern ethnicity that are transnational, and sometimes even a sense of political solidarity whose principles are non-territorial.

If these are the facts about transnational tendencies in the contemporary world, the moral conclusions have also been drawn from them. (Although Appadurai sometimes claims to be offering only a 'diagnosis' and not a 'prognosis', the shift from the one to the other is tangible enough in his writings; indeed, without the moral-political implications, the descriptions of transnational phenomena would lose much of their evidential power.) Thus, 'the nation-state, as a complex modern political form, is on its last legs . . . Nation-states, as units in a complex interactive system, are not very likely to be the long-term arbiters of the relationship between globality and modernity' (p. 19). With the nation-state having entered 'a terminal crisis', emergent 'postnational' forms of organization have moved into political spaces that were previously jealously guarded under claims of national sovereignty. Several agencies within the United Nations network and bodies such as Amnesty International now actually monitor the activities of nation-states on questions of human rights, peace-keeping, refugees, famine relief, and health. A vast network of non-governmental organizations is now providing basic support and services that nation-states in many countries of the world have failed to supply to their citizens. Religious organizations and movements of various kinds provide services across national boundaries and in addition mobilize loyalties that are not bounded by territory or citizenship. Such organizations are 'both instances and incubators of a postnational global order' (p. 168).

Of course, to seriously argue the case for postnational political forms as the emergent tendency of the age one would have to provide an alternative account of the apparent resurgence of nationalism in many places, especially in many parts of the former Soviet Union and former Yugoslavia. Appadurai does indeed offer an alternative account. He contests the description of these phenomena as a recrudescence of primordialism or tribalism: in fact, he specifically calls such descriptions 'the Bosnian fallacy'. Territorial nationalism is only 'the alibi of these movements and not necessarily their basic motive or final goal.' They 'actually contain transnational, subnational links and, more generally, nonnational identities and aspirations.' But they cannot articulate these aspirations except in the language of nationalism because 'no idiom has yet emerged to capture the collective interests of many groups in translocal solidarities, cross-border mobilizations and postnational identities . . . they are still entrapped in the linguistic imaginary of the territorial state . . . This vicious circle can only be escaped when a language is found to capture complex, nonterritorial, postnational forms of allegiance' (pp. 165–6).

In the meantime, locality continues to be produced as a structure of feeling, as a property of social life, and as an ideology of situated community, even under conditions of globalization. However, locked within the grid of the nation-state system, the production of locality has become increasingly difficult. The neighbourhood has tended to become more context-produced than context-generating. There are three reasons for this. First, the modern nation-state has increasingly resorted to greater disciplinary powers to define all neighbourhoods as owing allegiance and affiliation to it. Second, collective social movements and identities have been increasingly dissociated from territory. And third, principally because of the powers of electronic mediation, the relations between spatial and virtual neighbourhoods have been eroded. The virtual neighbourhood, where context-generating feelings of solidarity can be produced among people spatially located at different places, is at present confined to relatively small diasporic groups in which the most active component is probably the exiled intellectual. But ideas, finances, and social linkages emanating from these virtual locations also flow back to actually lived neighbourhoods and can change and reshape the structures of solidarity in those 'real' locations. These would contain the emerging forces that might produce the new postnational neighbourhoods.

III

If we are to take seriously Appadurai's proposal to rethink the linguistic imaginary of the territorial state, one of the ways might be to take a fresh look at some of the conceptual components that claim to tie together local structures of community with territorial nation-states. Let me bring these up here: family, civil society, political society, and the state. These are the classical concepts of political theory but they are used, we know, in a wide variety of senses and often with much inconsistency. I must clarify here the sense in which I find it useful to employ these concepts in talking about contemporary political forma- tions.

Hegel's synthesis, in the *Philosophy of Right,* of these elements of what he called 'ethical life' spoke of family, civil society, and the state, but had no place for a distinct sphere of political society. However, in understanding the structure and dynamics of mass political formations in twentieth-century nation-states, it seems to me useful to think of a parallel domain of institutions alongside civil society and the state. The sharpness of the nineteenth-century distinction between state and civil society, developed along the tradition of European anti-absolutist thinking, has the analytical disadvantage today of either regarding the domain of the civil as a depoliticized one—in contrast with the poli- tical domain of the state—or of blurring the distinction altogether by claiming that all civil institutions are political. Neither emphasis is of help in understanding the complexities of political phenomena in large parts of the contemporary world.

I find it useful to retain the term civil society for those characteristic institutions of modern associational life originating in Western societies that are based on equality, autonomy, freedom of entry and exit, con- tract, deliberative procedures of decision-making, recognized rights and duties of members, and such other principles. Obviously, this is not to deny that the history of modernity in non-Western countries contains numerous examples of the emergence of what could well be called civil-social institutions which nevertheless do not always conform to these principles. Rather, it is precisely to identify these marks of difference, to understand their significance, to appreciate how by the continued invocation of a 'pure' model of origin—the institutions of modernity as they were meant to be—a normative discourse can still continue to energize and shape the evolving forms of social institutions in the non-Western world, that I would prefer to retain the more clas- sical sense of the term civil society rather than adopt any of its recent revised versions. [2] Indeed, for theoretical purposes, I even find it useful

---

[2] An account of some of these versions is given in Jean L. Cohen and Andrew Arato, *Civil Society and Political Theory* (Cambridge, Massachusetts: MIT Press, 1994).

to hold on to the sense of civil society used in Hegel and Marx as bourgeois society (*bürgerliche gesellschaft*).

An important consideration in thinking about the relation between civil society and the state in the modern history of formerly colonial countries such as, for example, India is the fact that whereas the legal-bureaucratic apparatus of the state was able, by the late colonial and certainly in the postcolonial period, to reach as the target of many of its activities virtually all of the population that inhabits its territory, the domain of civil social institutions as conceived above is still restricted to a fairly small section of 'citizens'. This hiatus is extremely significant because it is the mark of non-Western modernity as an always incomplete project of 'modernization' and of the role of an enlightened elite engaged in a pedagogical mission in relation to the rest of society.

But then, how are we to conceptualize the rest of society that lies outside the domain of modern civil society? The most common approach has been to use a traditional/modern dichotomy. One difficulty with this is the trap, not at all easy to avoid, of dehistoricizing and essentializing 'tradition'. The related difficulty is one of denying the possibility that this other domain, relegated to the zone of the traditional, could find ways of coping with the modern that might not conform to the (Western bourgeois, secularized Christian) principles of modern civil society. I think a notion of political society lying alongside civil society and the state could help us see some of these historical possibilities.

By political society, I mean a domain of institutions and activities where several mediations are carried out. In the classical theory, the family is the elementary unit of social organization: by the nineteenth century this is widely assumed to mean the nuclear family of modern bourgeois patriarchy. (Hegel, we know, strongly resisted the idea that the family was based on contract, but by the late nineteenth century the contractually formed family becomes the normative model of most social theorizing in the West as well as of reformed laws of marriage, property, inheritance, and personal taxation. Indeed, the family becomes a product of contractual arrangements between individuals who are the primary units of society.) In countries such as India, it would be completely unrealistic to assume this definition of the family as obtaining universally. In fact, what is significant is that in formulating its policies and laws that must reach the greater part of the population, even the state does not make this assumption.

The conceptual move that seems to have been made very widely, even if somewhat imperceptibly, is from the idea of society as constituted by the elementary units of homogeneous families to that of a *population*, differentiated but classifiable, describable, and enumerable. Foucault has been more perceptive than other social philosophers of recent times in noticing the crucial importance of the new concept of population for the emergence of modern governmental technologies. Perhaps we should also note the contribution here of colonial anthropology and colonial administrative theories.

Population, then, constitutes the material of political society. Unlike the family in classical theory, the concept of population is descriptive and empirical, not normative. Indeed, population is assumed to contain large elements of 'naturalness' and 'primordiality'; the internal principles of the constitution of particular population groups is not expected to be rationally explicable since they are not the products of rational contractual association but are, as it were, pre-rational. What the concept of population does, however, is make available for governmental functions (economic policy, bureaucratic administration, law, and political mobilization) a set of rationally manipulable instruments for reaching large sections of the inhabitants of a country as the targets of 'policy'.

Civil social institutions, on the other hand, if they are to conform to the normative model presented by Western modernity, must necessarily exclude from its scope the vast mass of the population. Unlike many radical theorists, I do not think that this 'defect' of the classical concept needs to be rectified by revising the definition of civil society in order to include within it social institutions based on other principles. Rather, I think retaining the older idea of civil society actually helps us capture some of the conflicting desires of modernity that animate contemporary political and cultural debates in countries such as India.

Civil society in such countries is best used to describe those institutions of modern associational life set up by nationalist elites in the era of colonial modernity, though often as part of their anticolonial struggle. These institutions embody the desire of this elite to replicate in its own society the forms as well as the substance of Western modernity. It is a desire for a new ethical life in society, one that is in conformity with the virtues of the enlightenment and of bourgeois freedom and whose known cultural forms are those of secularized

Western Christianity. These are apparent in most of the arguments used by early nationalist elites in colonial countries when setting up new institutions of secular public life. It is well recognized in those arguments that the new domain of civil society will long remain an exclusive domain of the elite, that the actual 'public' will not match up to the standards required by civil society, and that the function of civil social institutions in relation to the public at large will be one of pedagogy rather than free association.

Countries with relatively long histories of colonial modernization and nationalist movements often have quite an extensive and impressive network of civil social institutions of this kind. In India, most of them survive to this day, not as quaint remnants of colonial modernity but often as serious protagonists of a project of cultural modernization still to be completed. However, in more recent times they seem to be under a state of siege.

To understand this, we will need to historicize more carefully the concepts of civil society, political society, and the state in colonial and postcolonial conditions.

IV

The explicit form of the postcolonial state in India is that of a modern liberal democracy. It is often said, not unjustifiably, that the reason why liberal democratic institutions have performed more creditably in India than in many other parts of the formerly colonial world is the strength of the civil social institutions within it that are relatively independent of the political domain of the state. But one needs to be more careful about the precise relationships involved here.

Before the rise of mass nationalist movements in the early twentieth century, nationalist politics in India was largely confined to the same circle of elites that was then busy setting up the new institutions of 'national' civil society. These elites were thoroughly wedded to the normative principles of modern associational public life and criticized the colonial state precisely for not living up to the standards of a liberal constitutional state. In talking about this part of the history of nationalist modernity, we do not need to bring in the notion of a political society located alongside civil society and the state.

However, entwined within this process of the formation of modern civil social institutions, something else was also happening. I have explained elsewhere how the various cultural forms of Western modernity were put through a nationalist sieve and only selectively adopted, and then combined with the reconstituted elements of what was claimed to be indigenous tradition.[3] Dichotomies such as spiritual/material, inner/outer, alien/indigenous, etc. were applied to justify and legitimize these choices from the standpoint of a nationalist cultural politics. What I wish to point out here in particular is that even as the associational principles of secular bourgeois civil institutions were adopted in the new civil society of the nationalist elite, the possibility of a different mediation between the population and the state was already being imagined, *one that would not ground itself on a modernized civil society.*

The impetus here was directly political. It had to do with the fact that the governmental technologies of the colonial state were already seeking to bring within its reach large sections of the population as the targets of its policies. Nationalist politics had to find an adequate strategic response if it was not to remain immobilized within the confines of the 'properly constituted' civil society of the urban elites. The cultural politics of nationalism supplied this answer by which it could mediate politically between the population and the nation-state of the future. In the Indian case, the most dramatic and effective form of this mediation was represented by what I have elsewhere described as the Gandhian moment of manoeuvre.[4]

This mediation between the population and the state takes place on the site of a new political society. It is built around the framework of modern political associations such as political parties. But, as researches on nationalist political mobilizations in the Gandhian era have shown repeatedly, elite and popular anticolonial politics, even as they came together within a formally organized arena such as that of the Indian National Congress, diverged at specific moments and spilled over the limits laid down by the organization.[5] This arena of nationalist politics, in other words, became a site of strategic manoeuvres, resistance, and appropriation by different groups and classes, many of those contests remaining unresolved even in the present phase of the postcolonial

[3] *The Nation and Its Fragments: Colonial and Postcolonial Histories* (Princeton: Princeton University Press, 1994).

[4] *Nationalist Thought and the Colonial World* (London: Zed Books, 1986).

[5] One set of studies of Indian nationalist politics that explicitly addresses this 'split in the domain of politics' is contained in the volumes of *Subaltern Studies* and in several monographs written by historians contributing to that series.

state. The point is that the practices that activate the forms and methods of mobilization and participation in political society are not always consistent with the principles of association in civil society.

What then are the principles that govern political society? The question has been addressed in many ways in the literature on mass mobilizations, electoral politics, ethnic politics, etc. In light of the conceptual distinctions I have made above between population, civil society, political society, and the state, we will need to focus more clearly on the mediations between population on the one hand and political society and the state on the other. The major instrumental form here in the postcolonial period is that of the developmental state which seeks to relate to various sections of the population through the governmental function of *welfare*. Correspondingly, if we have to give a name to the major form of mobilization by which political society (parties, movements, non-party political formations) tries to channellize and order popular demands on the developmental state, we should call it *democracy*. The institutional forms of this emergent political society are still unclear. Just as there is a continuing attempt to order these institutions in the prescribed forms of liberal civil society, there is probably an even stronger tendency to strive for what are perceived to be democratic rights and entitlements by violating those institutional norms. I have suggested elsewhere that the uncertain institutionalization of this domain of political society can be traced to the absence of a sufficiently differentiated and flexible notion of community in the theoretical conception of the modern state.[6] In any case, there is much churning in political society in the countries of the postcolonial world, not all of which are worthy of approval, which nevertheless can be seen as an attempt to find new democratic forms of the modern state that were not thought out by the post-enlightenment social consensus of the secularized Christian world.

V

In order to look more closely at what I see as the new movement of political society and the desire for democracy it represents, and also to bring the discussion back to the supposed crisis of the nation-state and the possibility of postnational formations, let me put forward three theses that might be pursued further. These are three theses that arise from the historical study of modernity in non-Western societies.

---

[6] *The Nation and Its Fragments*, ch. 11.

(1) The most significant site of transformations in the colonial period is that of civil society; the most significant transformations occurring in the postcolonial period are in political society.

(2) The question that frames the debate over social transformation in the colonial period is that of modernity. In political society of the postcolonial period, the framing question is that of democracy.

(3) In the context of the latest phase of the globalization of capital, we may well be witnessing an emerging opposition between modernity and democracy, i.e. between civil society and political society.

The implications of these theses will, I believe, diverge in important ways from the proposals for creating postnational forms of government. If one looks closely at the descriptions of the crisis-ridden nation-state in different parts of the contemporary world, one will find two sets of interrelated arguments. One is about the failure of effective governability. This has to do, in terms of the functions listed above, with the failure of the state to provide for the 'welfare' of populations. The second set of arguments relates to the decay or lack of appropriate civil social institutions that could provide a secure foundation for a proper relationship between autonomous individual lives in society and the collective political domain of the state. This is where complaints are made about the authoritarian or tyrannical role of the nation-state. The two sets of arguments are often collapsed into a single prognosis, as in Appadurai, about the failure of nation-states to arbitrate between globality and modernity. I will argue that there are actually two kinds of mediation that are being expected here—one, between globality and modernity, and the other between globality and democracy. The two—at least apparently—cannot be performed by the same set of institutions. This, as I see it, is the current crisis of the nation-state.

We can trace this crisis, in terms of the conceptual elements I have set out above, for at least two different sites—one, the old nation-states and liberal democracies of the West (including Australia and New Zealand), and the other, the countries, mostly ex-colonial, of Asia and Africa and those of the former socialist bloc in Eastern Europe and Central Asia. In the first case, the historical yardstick is provided by a description (abstract and often idealized) of a sort of normative equilibrium where civil society and state were well demarcated and properly balanced. This is the liberal description of the 'constitution' that supposedly provides both an abstract universal theory and a historically embedded, nation-specific, instance of the actual and more or less permanent substantive content of political life. This relatively stable normative equilibrium is now often seen as having been disturbed by the new immigration of the last three decades. As residents, the new immigrants have free access to the institutions of civil society, but are often insufficiently educated in or unappreciative of its practices. As populations, they are beneficiaries of governmental welfare activities but do not always have a commitment to or solidarity with the political community of the host nation. As citizens, their political loyalties are seen as being suspect and many do not even want citizenship if they can enjoy the economic and social advantages of residence. Here, transnational solidarities among immigrant groups, in fact, become evidence for the charge that they are inappropriate subjects of the nation's civic and political life. This has created a crisis both for the universalist assumptions of civil society and for the particular cultural content of nationhood. One response to this has been to recognize the change in historical situation and redefine the substantive content of civic and political life through an active effort at 'multiculturalism'. But there has also been the attempt to curb immigration, deny citizenship to many immigrants, and even restrict the access of residents to (the presumably universalist) civil social and welfare institutions.

In the case of the formerly colonial countries of Asia and Africa, the dominant approach is to apply the same yardstick of the abstract model of the modern nation-state and place the different actually existing states on a scale of 'development' or 'modernization'. The overwhelming theme is one of lack, sometimes with an additional story that describes the recent decay of a moderately satisfactory albeit inadequate set of institutions. But the lack, as I said before, is of two kinds—one in the domain of governmentality, the other in that of an effective civil society. For a considerable part of the 1960s and 1970s modernization demanded primarily, often exclusively, a rapid expansion of the governmental functions of the developmental state, legitimized by its claims to represent and strengthen the nation as a whole. By the 1980s the complaints were getting stronger that the absence of an autonomous domain of civil social institutions had made the nation-state tyrannical. And where the nation-state was failing to perform even its governmental functions, as in many countries in Africa, the situation was one of anarchy and massive social disaster. Proper modernization would have to ensure a more balanced development of both state and civil social institutions.

A considerable part of transnational activities today takes place in the domain of non-state institutions under the sign of the modernization of civil social formations. These are the activities of a transnational public sphere whose moral claims derive from the assumed existence of a domain of universal civil society. Many United Nations agencies, non-governmental organizations, peace-keeping missions, human rights groups, women's organizations, and free speech activists operate in this moral terrain. As such, they act as an *external* check on the sovereign powers of the nation-state and occupy the critical moral position of a global civil society assessing the incomplete modernity of particular national political formations. This is the standpoint that produces the most aggressive charges of the nation-state failing to successfully mediate between globality and modernity.

The charges derive their ideological power from a universalist conception of the rights of autonomous and self-determining individuals balanced against the powers of the state and, by extension, of the rights of autonomous groups against the dominance of large political formations. Often these arguments are used with blatant cynicism, as in US political interventions in different parts of the world. But many transnational activities and movements pursuing demands for social and cultural rights for individuals or groups seek to open up and institutionalize precisely such a sphere of global intervention, framed by a universalist notion of rights and grounded in a global civil society.

Even though there is much celebratory rhetoric and high moral passion associated with these visions of global modernity, the political-strategic implications of a move from 'transnational tendencies' to postnational formations are largely elided. Comparing our present world-historical moment with that of, let us say, 'the expansion of Europe' two or three centuries ago, it would not be far-fetched at all to notice similarities in the moral-cultural drive to spread 'modernity' throughout the world. The contrary tendencies I am pointing to—those that look within rather than beyond the nation-state—are also strong features of the contemporary world. In particular, they are tendencies that operate in the very heart of Western nation-states and liberal democracies, just as they are the driving force of politics in many non-Western countries. They are located on a different site—not the moral-cultural ground of modernity and the external institutional domain of a global civil society but rather the ground of democracy and the internal domain of national political society. What these tendencies in many countries around the world show up are the glaring inadequacies of the old forms of democratic representation, not only in the less modernized countries of the non-Western world but in Western democracies themselves. There is much contestation over new claims and entitlements, those that were not part of the earlier liberal consensus on state–civil society relations. In many cases the new claims directly contradict and violate universal 'modern' conventions of civil society. The historical task that has been set by these movements is to work out new forms of democratic institutions and practices in the mediating field of political society that lies between civil society and the nation-state.

The framework of global modernity will, it seems to me, inevitably structure the world according to a pattern that is profoundly colonial; the framework of democracy, on the other hand, will pronounce modernity itself as inappropriate and deeply flawed. An important observation that Appadurai often makes concerns the way in which transnational tendencies have made deep inroads into contemporary Western societies and rendered currently existing nation-state forms inadequate. In particular, talking about the cities of the Western world, Holston and Appadurai have recently noticed the abandonment of the notion of shared public space as an attribute of citizenship and the retreat into segregated private spaces. They have also correctly perceived this as an issue that is directly connected with the question of the democratic negotiation of citizenship under conditions of globalization.[7] My argument here is that it is only by separating the two interrelated issues of civil society–modernity and political society–democracy that we will begin to see the dimensions of power and political strategy that underlie this question. Without this awareness, the proposals to 'move beyond the nation' are quite likely to strengthen inequalities and defeat the struggle for democracy the world over.

[7] James Holston and Arjun Appadurai, 'Cities and Citizenship', *Public Culture*, 8, 2 (Winter 1996), pp. 187–204.

II
Democracy

11

Democracy and the Violence of the State: A Political Negotiation of Death (2001)

I begin with a word on Saadat Hasan Manto whose Urdu short story 'Toba Tek Singh' will feature in the final section of this essay on the violence of the state. Like most Bengalis of my generation, I was brought up to believe that there did not exist, in any other language of India, any semblance of a literature that could even be vaguely construed as representing a modern aesthetic sensibility. However, to the credit of my embarrassingly narrow-minded and chauvinistic compatriots, I have to confess that I first came across Manto in the late 1970s in a Bengali translation of 'Toba Tek Singh'. I distinctly remember the experience of reading those eight or ten pages of sparse, unornamented, newsreport-like prose. It shook me up, and as I began to absorb the full impact of Manto's deadly irony, I knew I was in the presence of a great craftsman of words. Since that time I have read a fair amount of his works in Bengali and English translations, have followed some of the critical literature on him that has appeared in recent years, and have come to accept, without the slightest sense of contradiction with my incurable Bengaliness, that Manto is arguably the greatest modernist prose writer of our subcontinent.

It is modernity that I will talk about. And also violence, which is a theme that etches itself so strongly in Manto's stories. In some ways, I will talk about the violence of modernity. But since I do not have the

Delivered as the Saadat Hasan Manto Lecture at the Centre for the Study of Developing Societies, Delhi, in January 2000.

facility to draw large conclusions from the singular evidence of fictional narratives, I need a different site to ground my thoughts. I will do so in the much-talked-about field of Indian democracy. I will speak about state and society in India as they come together in the democratic process. On that ground, I will talk about modernity, religion, and the violence of the state.

There is now a large literature examining the relation between state institutions and society in India. Rudolph and Rudolph have suggested that the balance has shifted periodically from a 'demand polity', in which societal demands expressed as electoral pressure dominate over the state; and a 'command polity', where state hegemony prevails over society.[1] The late M.S.A. Rao, in his last work done jointly with Francine Frankel, had suggested that public institutions such as the bureaucracy and organized industry, which had previously been the centres of dominance, were now under pressure from the rising power, especially of the lower castes, in political institutions such as the legislatures and the political parties.[2] From the periodic swings of the Rudolphs' model, the narrative here has become one of the decline of a political order. Further underscoring the theme of decline, Atul Kohli has described the recent history of Indian politics as one in which, by surrendering to the immediate electoral pressures exercised by various social groups, democratic state institutions have been allowed to decay, leading to an all-round crisis of governability.[3]

One problem I have had with the existing literature, framed as it is largely within the confines of a modernization narrative, whether of a Weberian or a Marxian type, is that the conceptual domains of state and society have either had to be sharply distinguished, with the central state institutions carrying the burden of an interventionist project of modernizing traditional social institutions and practices, or collapsed entirely so that state practices become completely moulded by the pulls and pressures of prevailing social institutions. With the unquestioned spread and deepening of electoral politics in India in the last three

[1] Lloyd I. Rudolph and Susanne Hoeber Rudolph, *In Pursuit of Lakshmi: The Political Economy of the Indian State* (Chicago: University of Chicago Press, 1987).

[2] M.S.A. Rao and Francine Frankel, *Dominance and State Power in India: Decline of a Social Order*, 2 vols (Delhi: Oxford University Press, 1990).

[3] Atul Kohli, *Democracy and Discontent: India's Growing Crisis of Governability* (Cambridge: Cambridge University Press, 1991).

decades, it has become difficult to locate the sites, if any, of an interventionist project of changing society, or indeed of the transformations
that have been brought about by the expansion of democracy itself.

In a series of recent papers, I have attempted to sketch out a conceptual field where some of these questions could be tackled.[4] One
move I have suggested is to think of a field of practices mediating
between state institutions and civil society. I have favoured retaining
the old idea of civil society as bourgeois society, in the sense used by
Hegel and Marx, and of using it in the Indian context as an actually
existing arena of institutions and practices inhabited by a relatively
small section of the people whose social locations can be identified
with a fair degree of clarity. In terms of the *formal* structure of the state
as given by the constitution and the laws, all of society is civil society;
everyone is a citizen with equal rights and therefore to be regarded as
a member of civil society; the political process is one where the organs
of the state interact with members of civil society in their individual
capacities or as members of associations. In actual fact, this is not how
things work. Most of the inhabitants of India are only tenuously, and
even then ambiguously and contextually, rights-bearing citizens in the
sense imagined by the constitution. They are not, therefore, proper
members of civil society and are not regarded as such by the institutions
of the state. However, it is not as though they are outside the reach of
the state or even excluded from the domain of politics. As populations within the territorial jurisdiction of the state, they have to be both
looked after and controlled by various governmental agencies. These
activities bring these populations into a certain *political* relationship
with the state. But this relationship does not always conform to what
is envisaged in the constitutional depiction of the relation between the
state and members of civil society. Yet these are without doubt political relations that may have acquired, in specific historically defined
contexts, a widely recognized systematic character, and perhaps even

---

[4] Partha Chatterjee, 'Beyond the Nation? Or Within?' *Social Text*, Autumn 1998.
Reproduced in the present book as ch. 10 above; idem, 'Community in the East',
Economic and Political Weekly, January 1998; idem, 'The Wages of Freedom', in
Partha Chatterjee, ed., *The Wages of Freedom: Fifty Years of the Indian Nation-State*
(Delhi: Oxford University Press, 1998); idem, 'Two Poets and Death: On Civil and
Political Society in the Non-Christian World', in Tim Mitchell and Lila Abu-Lughod,
eds, *Questions of Modernity* (Minneapolis: University of Minnesota Press, 2000).

certain conventionally recognized ethical norms, even if subject to varying degrees of contestation. How are we to begin to understand these processes?

It is to tackle questions of this kind that I proposed the idea of a *political society* occupying a zone that is distinct from both the state and civil society. Faced with similar problems, some analysts have favoured expanding the idea of civil society to include virtually all existing social institutions that lie outside the strict domain of the state.[5] This practice has become rampant in the recent rhetoric of international financial institutions, aid agencies, and non-governmental organizations, among whom the spread of a neo-liberal ideology has authorized the consecration of every non-state organization as the precious flower of the associative endeavours of free members of civil society. I have preferred to resist these unscrupulously charitable theoretical gestures, principally because I feel it is important not to lose sight of the vital and continually active project that still informs many of the state institutions in India to transform traditional social authorities and practices into the modular forms of bourgeois civil society. That civil society as an *ideal* continues to energize an interventionist political project, and that as an *actually existing form* it is demographically limited, are both facts that I think must be borne in mind when considering the relation between modernity and democracy in India.

You may recall a framework used in the early phase of the Subaltern Studies project in which we talked about a split in the domain of politics between an organized elite domain and an unorganized subaltern domain. The idea of the split, of course, was intended to mark a faultline in the arena of nationalist politics in the three decades before Independence during which the Indian masses, especially the peasantry, were drawn into organized political movements and yet remained distanced from the evolving forms of the postcolonial state. To say that there was a split in the domain of politics was to reject the notion, common in both liberal and Marxist historiographies, that the peasantry lived in some 'pre-political' stage of collective action. It was to say that peasants in their collective actions were also being political, except that they were political in a way different from the elites. Since those early experiences of the imbrication of elite and subaltern politics in the

[5] For arguments of this kind, see Jean L. Cohen and Andrew Arato, *Civil Society and Political Theory* (Cambridge, MA: MIT Press, 1992).

context of the anticolonial movements, the democratic process in India has come a long way in bringing under its influence the lives of the subaltern classes. It is to understand these relatively recent forms of the entanglement of elite and subaltern politics that I am proposing the notion of a political society.

In illustrating what I mean by political society and how it works, I have earlier used the example of a squatter settlement in the city of Calcutta and the efforts of the members of this settlement to assert their presence in urban life.[6] This they do through a body that has the form of a voluntary association but which uses a moral rhetoric of kinship and family loyalty. Since the settlement is premised on the illegal occupation of public land and therefore on the collective violation of property laws and civic regulations, the state authorities cannot treat it on the same footing as other civic associations following more legitimate social and cultural pursuits. Yet state agencies and non-governmental organizations cannot ignore it either, since it is but one of hundreds of similar bodies representing groups of population whose very livelihood or habitation involves violation of the law. These agencies therefore deal with the settlers' association not as a body of citizens but as a convenient instrument for the administration of welfare to a marginal and underprivileged population group.

The squatters on their part accept that their occupation of public land is both illegal and contrary to good civic behaviour, but they make a claim to a habitation and a livelihood as a matter of right. They profess a readiness to move out if they are given suitable alternative sites for resettlement. The state agencies recognize that these population groups do have some claim on the welfare programmes of the government, but those claims could not be regarded as justiciable rights since the state did not have the means to deliver those benefits to the entire population of the country. To treat those claims as rights would only invite further violation of public property and civic laws.

What happens then is a negotiation of these claims on a political terrain where, on the one hand, governmental agencies have a public obligation to look after the poor and the underprivileged and, on the other, particular population groups receive attention from those agencies according to calculations of political expediency. The squatter community I talked about has to pick its way through this uncertain

---

[6] This example is discussed in Chatterjee, 'Community in the East', *Economic and Political Weekly*, 33, 6 (7 February 1998).

terrain by making a large array of connections outside the group—
with other groups in similar situations, with more privileged and influential groups, with government functionaries, with political parties
and leaders, etc. In the course of its struggles over almost five decades,
the squatters have managed to hold on to their settlement, but it is an
extremely insecure hold since it is entirely dependent on their ability
to operate within a field of strategic politics. I make the claim that this
is the stuff of democratic politics as it takes place on the ground in
India. It involves what appears to be a constantly shifting compromise
between the normative values of modernity and the moral assertion of
popular demands.

Civil society then, restricted to a small section of culturally equipped citizens, represents—in countries like India—the high ground of
modernity. So does the constitutional model of the state. However, in
practice, governmental agencies must descend from that high ground
to the terrain of political society in order to renew their legitimacy as
providers of well being and there confront whatever is the current
configuration of politically mobilized demands. In the process, one is
liable to hear complaints from the protagonists of civil society and the
constitutional state that modernity is facing an unexpected rival in the
form of democracy.

II

I explore this theme further by providing one more example from the
domain of popular politics in the Indian city.[7] On 5 May 1993, in the
early hours of dawn, a man died in a Calcutta hospital. He had been
admitted a few days before and was being treated for *diabetes molutus*,
renal failure, and cerebro-vascular accident. His condition had deterio-
rated rapidly in the previous twenty-four hours and, although the
doctors attending him struggled through the night, their efforts were
in vain. A senior doctor of the hospital signed the death certificate.

The name of the man who died was Birendra Chakrabarti, but he
was better known as Balak Brahmachari, leader of the Santan Dal, a
religious sect with a large following in the southern and central districts
of West Bengal. The sect itself is no more than fifty years old, although

[7] I am grateful to Ashok Dasgupta and Debashis Bhattacharya of *Ajkal* for their
generous help in researching the story of Balak Brahmachari's death.

it probably has its antecedents in earlier sectarian movements among the lower-caste, especially Namasudra, peasants of central Bengal. Its religious doctrines are highly eclectic, consisting entirely of the views of Balak Brahmachari himself as expressed in his sayings, but they are characterized in particular by a curious involvement in political matters. The sect's mouthpiece, *Kara Chabuk* (The Strong Whip), regularly published its leader's comments on current political subjects in which there was the recurrent theme of 'revolution', a cataclysmic churning that would surgically cleanse a corrupt and putrid social order. The sect, in fact, first came into the public spotlight in the period 1967–71, when it participated in political demonstrations in support of the Left parties and against Congress rule. Santan Dal activists, with many women in their ranks, some in saffron clothes, holding aloft their tridents and shouting their slogan 'Ram Narayan Ram', were an incongruous element in Leftist demonstrations in Calcutta at the time, and could not but attract attention. But no one accused the sect of opportunistic political ambitions because it made no claims to electoral representation or recognition as a political party. Since then, many of the followers of the sect have been known to be sympathizers and even activists of the Left, especially of the Communist Party of India (Marxist)—CPI(M)—the leading partner in the Left Front that has ruled West Bengal since 1977.

On this particular morning in May 1993, the followers of Balak Brahmachari refused to accept that their spiritual leader was dead. They recalled that, several years ago, in 1967, he had gone into *samadhi* for twenty-two days during which, to all outward appearances, he was dead. But he had woken up from his trance and returned to normal life. Now once more, they said, their Baba had gone into *nirvikalpa samadhi*, a state of suspension of bodily functions that could be achieved only by those with the highest spiritual powers. The members of Santan Dal took the body of Balak Brahmachari from hospital to their ashram in Sukhchar, a northern suburb of Calcutta, and began to keep what they said would be a long vigil.

Soon the matter became a *cause célèbre* in Calcutta. The press picked it up, publishing reports of how the body was being kept on slabs of ice under heavy airconditioning and of the defensiveness of the Dal spokesmen against hostile criticism. One Bengali daily, *Ajkal*, pursued the story with particular vigour, turning it into a fight for rational values in public life and against obscurantist beliefs and practices.

It accused the local authorities and the health department of the West Bengal government of failing to implement their own rules regarding the disposal of dead bodies and of conniving in the making of a serious public hazard. Soon the authorities were forced to respond. On the thirteenth day of the vigil, the Panihati municipality clarified that it had served the Santan Dal leaders with a notice asking them to cremate the body immediately, but that under the municipal laws it had no powers to carry out a forcible cremation.[8] On behalf of the Santan Dal, Chitta Sikdar, the secretary, kept up a regular defensive campaign in the press, maintaining that the spiritual phenomenon of nirvikalpa samadhi was beyond the understanding of medical science and that Balak Brahmachari would soon resume his normal bodily life.

The standoff continued. *Ajkal* raised the tempo of its campaign, opening its columns to prominent intellectuals and public figures who deplored the persistence of such superstitious and unscientific beliefs among the people. Groups of activists from progressive cultural organizations, the popular science movement, and the rationalist society began to hold demonstrations in front of the Santan Dal headquarters in Sukhchar. *Ajkal* spared no efforts to provoke the spokesmen of the Dal and ridicule their statements, refusing to refer to the dead leader by his sectarian name of Balak Brahmachari and instead calling him 'Balak Babu'—a nonsensical 'Mr Balak'. There were some heated confrontations at the gate of the Santan Dal ashram, with the Dal activists reportedly stocking arms and preparing for a showdown. One night, some crackers and handmade bombs exploded outside the ashram and a group of Dal activists came out and shouted over their loudspeakers: 'The revolution has begun.'[9]

Nearly a month after the official death of Balak Brahmachari, his body still lay on ice slabs in an airconditioned room with his followers waiting for him to break his samadhi. *Ajkal* claimed that there was an unbearable stench in the entire neighbourhood of Sukhchar and that the residents of the area had had enough. Now it began to be openly alleged that it was because of electoral reasons that the government was reluctant to intervene. The elections to the local government bodies in rural West Bengal, the crucial panchayats, which had become the backbone of Left Front support, were scheduled for the last week

---

[8] *Ajkal*, 18 May 1993.
[9] Ibid., 21 June 1993.

of May. Any action against the Dal could antagonize a lot of Left Front supporters in at least four districts of West Bengal. It was also suggested that some important leaders of the CPI(M) were sympathetic to the Santan Dal and that one minister in particular, Subhas Chakrabarti, the minister in charge of tourism and sports, was regarded by Dal members as a fraternal supporter.

On 25 June 1993, fifty-one days after the official death of Balak Brahmachari, the health minister of West Bengal announced that a medical team consisting of leading specialists in medicine, neurology, and forensic medicine would examine the body of Balak Brahmachari and submit a report to the government. The Indian Medical Association, the apex professional body of medical practitioners, immediately protested, saying that to call for a new examination implied a lack of confidence in the death certificate issued from the hospital. It pointed out that no scientific grounds had been furnished to question the original judgement of the hospital doctors. The government doctors went ahead nevertheless and returned from Sukhchar to say that they had not been allowed to touch the body. They reported that the body had been putrefied and carried signs of mummification and that it had not decayed completely because of the extremely low temperature at which it had been kept.[10]

By this time, Subhas Chakrabarti had been given charge by the CPI(M) leadership to devise a solution to the impasse. Accompanied by the local CPI(M) leaders, he visited the Sukhchar ashram and later told journalists that he was trying to persuade the followers of the Baba to cremate the body. He agreed that there was no scientific reason for doctors to re-examine a body that had been certified as dead, but insisted that this was a necessary part of the process of persuasion. He pointed out that 'Babadom' was still prevalent in the country and that thousands of people were followers of these religious leaders. He warned that it was dangerous to take religious fanaticism lightly. It was the government's view, he said, that applying force could provoke fanaticism. When asked if he was aware of the health hazard that had been created in the neighbourhood of Sukhchar, he claimed that he had smelt nothing, but that was probably because he was a habitual inhaler of snuff.[11]

[10] Ibid., 26 June 1993.
[11] Ibid.

On 30 June, in a four-hour operation beginning at two in the morning, a force consisting of 5000 policemen stormed the Santan Dal headquarters, took charge of the body, and removed it to a nearby crematorium. *The Telegraph* reported that the last rites were performed by the guru's brother 'as the security cordon pushed back wailing women who still believed their departed cult leader would be resurrected. The state government, severely criticised for soft-pedalling the issue, heaved a sigh of relief.' The police force, which was attacked by Dal activists with acid bulbs, knives, tridents, glass bottles, and chilli powder, used teargas shells to immobilize the defenders and gas-cutters to make its way through window grilles and collapsible gates into the heavily fortified headquarters. But it did not resort to shooting. Many Dal activists as well as policemen were hurt, but, as the official press release put it, 'there were no casualties'.[12]

The minister Subhas Chakrabarti congratulated the police and local administration for carrying out a very difficult and sensitive operation. He referred to the popular Hindi film *Jugnu* and said the job was more difficult than what the actor Dharmendra had faced in that film. 'Of course', he said to journalists, 'you think all that is lumpen culture, but I think it is an apt example.' The following day, *Ajkal* in its editorial announced: 'We have come to the end of that age in West Bengal when lumpen culture could be called lumpen culture. Progressive West Bengal has seen the end of the age of reason. Now begins the age of *Jugnu*.'[13]

Despite the relatively smooth and successful conclusion of the matter, the controversy did not die down. Chitta Sikdar, the secretary of the Santan Dal, protested to the chief minister against what he described as an authoritarian and undemocratic action of the government. He said the treatment received by Balak Brahmachari at the hands of the rulers of society would be remembered in history in the same way as the trials of Jesus Christ, Galileo, and Socrates. On the other hand, opinions such as that of *Ajkal* condemned as opportunistic the attempt by sections of the government and the ruling party to target the second-rank leaders of the sect for misleading their innocent followers and profiting from their overexcited religious sentiments but not criticizing the sects and the so-called 'godmen' themselves for spreading unreason and superstition. Twelve days after the cremation

[12] *The Telegraph*, 1 July 1993; *The Statesman*, 1 July 1993.
[13] *Ajkal*, 2 July 1993.

of Balak Brahmachari, the secretary of the Santan Dal and eighty-two others were arrested and charged with rioting, assault, obstruction of justice, and other offences.[14]

Members of the Santan Dal continued for several months to write letters to newspapers portraying themselves as victims of an undemocratic and illegal police action. They asked what laws of the land the Baba's followers had broken by believing that he would come back to life. Did a religious belief in extraordinary spiritual powers deserve blows from the policeman's truncheon? And was it not the case that the Dal followers were finally subjected to police action because most of them were low-caste peasants whose marginal political value had evaporated after the local government elections were over? While public memory might be short, one letter warned, the memory of victimhood was merciless. The perpetrators of injustice would one day meet their day of judgement.[15]

The case illustrates, I think, several of the points I have raised so far about the relation between modernity and democracy in a country like India. Modernity is a project located in the historical desires of certain elite sections of Indians. The specific story of the emergence and flowering of those desires and their sources in colonial projects has been much discussed. There was a time when the country was under colonial rule, when it was believed by these elites that the crucial transformative processes that would change the traditional beliefs and practices of the people and fashion a new modern national self must be kept out of the reach of the colonial state apparatus. With the end of colonial rule and the coming to power of these classes in the postcolonial state, that transformative project became firmly located in the dynamic potential of the organs of the new national state. That those organs were now part of a constitutional system of representative democracy made the modernizing project an expression of the will of the people and thus gloriously consistent with the legitimizing norms of modernity itself.

Religion came under the sway of this transformative project in a major way. In the colonial period, the transformation was carried out through a variety of social institutions, including new sectarian movements of reformed religion, both Hindu and Islamic, using all of the new cultural technologies of print and pedagogy. In the process, a

[14] Ibid., 13 July 1993.
[15] *Dainik Pratibedan*, 5 February 1994.

certain cultural consensus emerged among the elite sections of Indians on the norms of religious practice in modern life. These norms made it possible for the leading groups in society to make distinctions between acceptable ritual behaviour or doctrinal belief, and unacceptable superstition and irrationality. Following Independence, the normalizing of religious practice was carried out most ambitiously through the legal organs of the state in the constitution itself and also in the set of legislations known as the Hindu Code Bill. Minority religious practices were left largely untouched by this exercise, not because they were not thought to be in need of reform but because of uncertainty as to whether the will of the people, as expressed by a parliamentary majority, carried an adequate measure of legitimacy for the minority communities. In other words, there was already a nuanced and differentiated notion of representation built into the idea of democratic legitimacy, even though the idea of the separate representation of minorities was anathema.

This project of cultural transformation through the powers of a democratically constituted state has become considerably muted in the last two decades. A crucial experience that, I think, defined the new limits of state action in Indian democracy was that of Indira Gandhi's 'Emergency' regime in 1975-7. That brought home to India's elites the fact that modernizing agendas could be made the political pretext for setting up an authoritarian regime which was little more than a perversion of the so-called will of the people. Such a regime put at risk all of the legal-political guarantees for a large, complex, and differentiated bourgeois civic life, even if it did not directly threaten the well being of the bourgeoisie as a class. Moreover, the 'Emergency' regime also failed to prove that it could sustain itself as a self-reproducing structure, as in other authoritarian systems in the postcolonial world, in face of the various impediments it faced from both within and outside the country. Following the collapse of that regime in 1977, a consensus emerged among modernizers of both the Left and the Right that it was unwise to push through projects of social change by means of state intervention unless these were first negotiated through certain mediating processes between state and society.

Although many of the sites and activities characteristic of the arena that I have called political society can be shown to have emerged within the spectrum of nationalist political mobilizations in the colonial period, I would say that it has taken on something like a distinct form only since the 1980s. Two conditions have facilitated this process. One is the rise to dominance of a notion of governmental performance that emphasizes the welfare and protection of populations—the 'pastoral' functions of government, as Foucault called it—using similar governmental technologies all over the world but largely independent of considerations of active participation by citizens in the sovereignty of the state. This has enabled the mutual recognition by state agencies and population groups that governments are obliged to deliver certain benefits even to people who are not proper members of civil society or of the republican body of true citizens. The second condition is the widening of the arena of political mobilization, even if only for electoral ends, from formally organized structures—such as political parties with well-ordered internal constitutions and coherent doctrines and programmes—to loose and often transient mobilizations, building on communication structures that would not ordinarily be recognized as political (for instance, religious assemblies or cultural festivals, or, more curiously, even associations of cinema fans, as in many of the southern states).

The proliferation of activities in this arena of political society has caused much discomfort and apprehension in progressive elite circles in India in recent years. The comment about 'lumpen culture' in the *Ajkal* editorial cited earlier is typical. The complaint is widespread in middle-class circles today that politics has been taken over by mobs and criminals. The result is the abandonment—or so the complaint goes—of the mission of the modernizing state to change a backward society. Instead, what we see is the importing of the disorderly, corrupt, and irrational practices of unreformed popular culture into the very hallways and chambers of civic life, all because of the calculations of electoral expediency. The noble pursuit of modernity appears to have been seriously compromised because of the compulsions of parliamentary democracy.

III

Given a history in India of more than a hundred years of modern representative institutions, we can now see a pattern of evolution of this familiar Tocquevillean problem.[16] Early liberals, such as Dadabhai Naoroji and Gopal Krishna Gokhale, or even Muhammad Ali Jinnah

---

[16] Sudipta Kaviraj has explicitly formulated this as a Tocquevillean problem in 'The Culture of Representative Democracy', in Chatterjee, ed., *The Wages of Freedom*.

in the early phase of his political life, were entirely convinced of the inherent value of those institutions, but they were also hugely circumspect about the conditions in which they could function. As good nineteenth-century liberals they would have been the first to specify requirements such as education and a proved commitment to civic life that would have to be met before a people could be considered fit, in their language, 'to receive parliamentary institutions'. If we look at it from another angle, we might say that for men such as Naoroji or Gokhale democracy was a good form of government only when it could be adequately controlled by men of status and wisdom. With the rise of the so-called Extremists in nationalist politics, especially with the Khilafat and Non-cooperation movements, there came into organized political life in India many forces and many ideas that did not care too much about the niceties of parliamentary politics. It was Gandhi, of course, who in this period intervened decisively in the political arena created by the new representative institutions of the late colonial order. Even as he claimed to reject parliamentary institutions along with all of the other trappings of modern civilization, he was more instrumental than anyone else in bringing about the mobilization that would, in the end, make the Indian National Congress the ruling political organization of independent India. As has been shown in many studies, Gandhi's words and actions are shot through by the parallel themes of unleashing popular initiative and controlling it at the same time.[17] With the formalization of Congress rule in the first decade and a half after Independence, control became the dominant motif in the close interweaving of state initiative and electoral approval in the so-called Congress system of the Nehru period.

The journey from the Nehru period to the crisis of the mid-1960s to the re-establishment of Congress dominance in the state populism of the first Indira Gandhi regime is a trajectory not unfamiliar to the historical experience of many third-world countries. What was distinctive in the life of Indian democracy is, I think, the defeat of Indira Gandhi's 'Emergency' regime in a parliamentary election. It brought about a decisive shift in all subsequent discussion about the essence and appearance of democracy, its form and content, its inner nature and outward appearance. Whatever may be the judgement of historians

---

[17] The writings of the *Subaltern Studies* group of historians have explored these themes most elaborately. See in particular Ranajit Guha, *Dominance Without Hegemony* (Cambridge, MA: Harvard University Press, 1998).

on the 'real' causes of the collapse of the 'Emergency' regime, the 1977 elections established in the arena of popular mobilizations in India the capacity of the vote and of representative bodies of government to give voice to popular demands of a kind that had never before been allowed to disturb the order and tranquillity of the proverbial corridors of power. One cannot but wonder if this is not the momentous experience that separates the popular understanding of democracy in India from that in Pakistan, where it is possible today for both elites and subalterns to say in unison that electoral democracy is a fake and that the path to true democracy may have to pass through a spell of military dictatorship.

However, before we in India are too quick to congratulate ourselves, let me restate what I have been arguing so far. The contrary themes of popular legitimacy and elite control remained embedded in the conception of Indian democracy from the very beginning. They have not gone away, nor have they been resolved or superseded. They have only taken new forms as a result of the ongoing struggles between elite and popular conceptions of democracy. They are being played out once again in the recent debates over democratic modernization in India. On the one hand, the uncertain demands of popular ratification have led committed modernizers to throw up their hands and lament that the age of reason had been brought to an end by the political surrender to the forces of disorder and irrationality. They read the many compromises with electoral compulsions as signs of the abandonment of enlightened politics. Generally less noticed are the transformative effects of these contrary mobilizations among the supposedly unenlightened sections of the population. Since this is an area that is only beginning to be studied, I can only make certain preliminary remarks on it. However, this constitutes, I believe, the most profound and significant set of social changes being produced by the democratic process in India today.

In one of my recent writings dealing with the question of minority rights and the secular state in India, I suggested that the more democratic strategy would be to promote representative processes *within* the minority communities themselves.[18] It has been objected that this is 'too strong' a requirement, that it is a concession to religious-communitarian politics itself, and that it smacks of the 'separate electorates' system in British India or even (some have said) to the

---

[18] Partha Chatterjee, 'Secularism and Toleration', in idem, A *Possible India: Essays in Political Criticism* (Delhi: Oxford University Press, 1997), pp. 228–62.

millet system in Ottoman Turkey. I could give a range of answers to these objections, but the one that will be most pertinent here is the following. All of these objections spring from the inability to recognize a domain of politics that is located neither within the constitutional limits of the state nor in the orderly transactions of bourgeois civil society, even though it is *about* both. The encounter with the constitutional state and the normative requirements of civil society has engendered a certain demand for representativeness within the various communities that *are* the social forms of populations in India. This is the most tangible effect of democratization in this country. Even as population groups both engage with and resist the agencies of the state, they give rise to an internal process in which community leaderships are criticized, new voices are heard, other examples of other communities are cited, and the demand raised for greater representativeness within the community. These processes have occurred most visibly in recent years in the mobilizations among the Dalits and the so-called Other Backward Castes. However, they have also occurred among tribal populations and indeed among the religious minorities. In addition, if one looks to the immensely rich and productive debate coming out of the women's movement in India, one cannot fail to notice the importance of the strategic question: legal reform through state initiative from the top, or mobilization of initiatives within the relatively immobilized spaces of the communities themselves? To choose the former is to underscore the moral primacy of the modernizing state. To advocate the latter is to accept the risks of walking through a normatively uncertain political terrain. If my critics demand that I state my preference between the two, I would say that while the former strategy has not necessarily exhausted itself, I believe that the real challenge lies in exploring the possibilities of the latter.

Let me also say that there has already evolved among the governing classes in India one response to this strategic choice. I see this as a variant of the colonial strategy of indirect rule. This involves a suspension of the modernization project, walling in the protected zones of bourgeois civil society and dispensing the governmental functions of law and order and welfare through the 'natural leaders' of the governed populations. The strategy, in other words, seeks to preserve the civil virtues of bourgeois life from the potential excesses of electoral democracy. I am convinced that this was the attitude taken by the economically dominant groups in Bombay, the industrial and financial capital of India and the apex of its urban cosmopolitan culture, towards the political leadership of the Shiv Sena, the most overtly fascist element in the Hindu right-wing formation that, until two years ago, ruled the state of Maharashtra.

The other response is less cynical, even as it is more pragmatic. It does not abandon the project of enlightenment, but attempts to steer it through the thicket of contestations in what I have called *political society*. It takes seriously the functions of direction and leadership of a vanguard, but accepts that the legal arm of the state in a country like India cannot reach into a vast range of social practices that continue to be regulated by other beliefs and administered by other authorities. However, it also knows that those dark zones are being penetrated by the welfare functions of modern governmental practices, producing those effects on claims and representation that I have called the urge for democratization. This is the zone in which the project of democratic modernity has to operate—slowly, painfully, unsurely.

In bringing up the example of the negotiations over the disposal of a dead body in Calcutta, I was not trying to provide a narrative of the correct handling of contradictions among the people. Nor am I saying that the specific form in which a local crisis of modernity-*versus*-democracy was resolved on that occasion flowed out of a conscious political project of social transformation in which the ruling parties in West Bengal are engaged. Rather, my intention was to point out the possibilities that exist in that normatively nebulous zone that I have called political society. When I use that term, I am always reminded that in his *Prison Notebooks* Gramsci begins by equating political society with the state, but soon slides into a whole range of social and cultural interventions that must take place well beyond the domain of the state. I have tried here to emphasize that even in resisting the modernizing project that is imposed on them, the subaltern classes embark on a path of internal transformation. At the same time, in carrying out their pedagogical mission in political society, the educators—enlightened people like us—might also succeed in educating themselves. That, I submit, will be the most enriching and historically significant result of the encounter between modernity and democracy in a country like India.

IV

Finally, I come to the subject of violence. Manto's distinctness, as has been pointed out many times, lies in his merciless, sometimes brutally unsentimental, handling of the theme of violence. His English translator Khalid Hasan has remarked: 'He alone of the writers of his time was able to turn the bloody events of 1947 into great literature.'[19] Few will quarrel with this judgement. But it is worth asking why others did not even try to do what Manto did. Is there some mystery here about the nature of the violence of 1947 that defied representation? I think it is useful to consider this question in the context of the complicated relationship of modernity to democracy and of the role of the violence of the modern state.

In August 1954, seven years after Partition and a year before his death, Manto is supposed to have written an epitaph for himself. 'Here lies Saadat Hasan Manto', it said. 'With him lie buried all the arts and mysteries of short story writing. Under tons of earth he lies, wondering if he is a greater story writer than God.'[20] Some may read these lines as one more example of Manto's penchant for shocking his readers by an exaggerated display of his bloated ego. What vulgar insolence, they might say, to compare the creativity of a story writer with that of god! But others—an unfortunate few, perhaps—will recognize here the condition of the modern secular mind, trapped under tonnes of political doubt. If ever there was poignancy in irony, I think it is here. It expresses the predicament of a creative human spirit that must continue the work of creation in a world which, it believes, has been permanently abandoned by god. How does it do its work?

Let us note, first of all, that the condition we are talking about here is not one that belongs to the world of the popular. The latter is suffused with the idea that the act of making the world requires powers that are much larger than what belongs to ordinary humans. The violence of human life is also made sense of, more often than not, as the violence of the gods, sometimes transparent, sometimes inscrutable. I once spent many months scouring the archives for eyewitness accounts of communal riots in Bengal. I came away with the lasting impression that even as ordinary people often described in vivid detail the disastrous things that happened to them, they tended to attribute the reasons to some externalized cause, something that was purposive

---

[19] Khalid Hasan, 'Introduction', in Saadat Hasan Manto, *Kingdom's End and Other Stories*, trans. Khalid Hasan (London: Verso, 1987), p. 8.

[20] Ibid., pp. 9–10. I was drawn to this epitaph by Aamir Mufti's reflections on it: Aamir R. Mufti, 'A Greater Story Writer than God: Gender, Genre and Minority in Late Colonial India', in Partha Chatterjee and Pradeep Jeganathan, eds, *Subaltern Studies XI* (Delhi: Permanent Black, 2000).

but beyond themselves. In one of his many famous disagreements with rationalists, Gandhi insisted after the Bihar earthquakes of 1934 that these were a 'divine chastisement' for the sin of untouchability. Deliberately taking up a position located in popular beliefs, he said, in effect, that this was a violence of God. When asked why God should inflict a punishment that did not distinguish between upper castes and untouchables, Gandhi said, 'I am not God. Therefore I have but a limited knowledge of his purpose.'[21] On the basis of what I know about the subject, I am not persuaded that there exists in popular consciousness a notion of violence that is fundamentally without reason. Violence may be committed for vengeance, for punishment, for justice, for practising an occupation, for a host of other reasons including possession by spirits, demons, gods, but rarely, perhaps never, as a senseless act without deliberate cause.

It is the modern secular consciousness, for whom—famously—the world has become a disenchanted place, that faces this peculiar problem of making sense of violence in human life. At the risk of grossly oversimplifying a huge history to which the greatest minds of the modern world have devoted their attention, let me say that at least as far as the world of modern political life is concerned, there have been two strategies that have been followed to bring reason and order to the facts of violence. One is to create a transcendental umbrella of ethics under which to shelter and domesticate the use of violence. This produces certain notions of goodness and justice that are believed to be true and, in the appropriate conditions, the use of violence is considered a legitimate instrument to achieve those transcendentally established moral goals. Justice, punishment, discipline, progress, science—there have been many notions of the just and the good that have legitimized violence in the modern world. The other strategy is to devise an economy of violence. The question here is not whether to use violence, but how much? Of what kind? To what purpose? With what results? It is not an ethical imperative that works here, but one of costs and benefits, of matching causes to effects, of efficiency.

Modern political life makes sense of violence either by measuring it against an ethical imperative or by reducing it to the grid of an economy. We can see both moves being made in the story I narrated earlier about the death of Balak Brahmachari. The protagonists of rationality

[21] M.K. Gandhi, 'Bihar and Untouchability', *Collected Works* (New Delhi: Publications Division, 1958), vol. 57, p. 87.

were complaining about the squeamishness of the government, hemmed in by electoral pressures, in imposing its own rules of public order and morality. If the government had to use force, the rationalists were saying, it should have used it, because it would have been justified. The government, in the end, did use violence, but within a carefully deployed economy of forces and effects so that it could say that no more violence was used than was necessary to produce the desired results: 'there were no casualties', it declared. The members of the Santan Dal, to the extent that they participated in this discourse of modern politics, protested against what they believed was an illegitimate use of force that violated their right to hold and practise their religious beliefs. Everyone participated in making sense of the violence of the modern state.

To the extent that I know the history and literature of the violence of 1947 in India, I believe there is a similar eagerness on all sides to make sense of it in terms of the logic of the modern nation-state. There are considerations of ethics—and of praise or blame—in the demands and concessions of different parties—the Congress, the Muslim League, and the British. What is the loss of Partition for Indians is the success of Independence for Pakistanis. And then there are the considerations of economy. Was the violence inevitable? Could it have been avoided? Were the British too hasty in wanting to get out? Could a little more state violence at the right time have avoided the uncontrolled explosion of communal violence? It is not that nothing has been said about 1947. In fact, a great deal has been said, and is still being said. It has been said within the twin parameters of ethics and economy.

Manto's uniqueness lies in the fact that he refused to accept the parameters of either ethics or economy in talking about the violence of 1947. He had no recourse to a morality that was given to him either by God or transcendental reason. Nor would he allow himself to be seduced by the economic calculations of governmental violence. For him, the violence of Partition called for a response that was, if I may put it this way, an act of pure politics, where morality and economy had to be created all at once, all by oneself, *de novo*, from the bare elements of human interaction. It was at such a moment of pure politics that Bishan Singh 'stood in no man's land on his swollen legs like a colossus'—pure politics, grounded in nothing other than its own domain. But this moment of pure politics cannot be sustained. The scope of its creative promise is too enormous, the burden of its responsibility too great. Bishan Singh, also known as Toba Tek Singh, screamed and then collapsed to the ground. 'There, behind barbed wire, on one side, lay India and behind more barbed wire, on the other side, lay Pakistan. In between, on a bit of earth which had no name, lay Toba Tek Singh.'[22] Perhaps, it is only after the fact—after the fact of life itself—buried under tonnes of earth, that one can contemplate if, at that moment of pure politics, one was a greater story writer than god. But it is not a risk many will take. In fact, my hunch is that this is the reason why no one other than Manto has even tried doing what he did. To embrace politics in its pure uncertainty, its unrelieved dangerousness, without the security of an anchor in some pre-given idea of the good, without the technical instruments of measuring costs and benefits, is terrifying. To seek refuge in history and statecraft is to return to the comfort of the familiar. That is what most of us prefer to do. We are not great story writers.

The discomfort that many feel with the goings-on in what I have called political society is, I think, because it raises the spectre of pure politics. This is a zone where, I have argued, the certainties of civil-social norms and constitutional proprieties are put under challenge. Rights and rules have to be, seemingly, negotiated afresh. Only those voices are heard that can make the loudest noise and can speak on behalf of the largest numbers. There is violence in the air. Not everything that happens here is desirable or worthy of approval. But then, how can we be sure that what we desire or approve is what is truly good? Who can decide that except those who go through the dangerously creative process of politics itself? I think Manto would have recognized these people. Those who dream of building the new democratic society must aspire to be greater story writers than god.

I do not know if in those fervid, disorderly zones of what I have called political society, the foundations of a new democratic order are being laid today. That is for historians of a future generation to analyse and describe. What I do know is that the practices of democracy have changed in India in the last four decades, that the project of state-led modernization has been drastically modified, and that the forms of involvement of the subaltern classes with governmental activities as well as with representative institutions have both expanded and deepened. There are new efforts to garner popular legitimacy in favour

[22] Manto, in Hasan, trans., *Kingdom's End*, p. 18.

of elite dominance, such as the political formation that goes under the sign of Hindutva, which has sought to demonstrate to the ruling classes of the country that it can create an alternative and more viable structure of class rule than the decrepit Congress. On the side of those who are governed, they have succeeded, in the teeth of severe opposition from the dominant sections, to bend and stretch the rules of bourgeois politics and rational bureaucracy to create forms of democratic practice that, even as they retain the names given to them by Western sociology and political theory, have become unrecognizably different. These are the creations of the Indian people. Perhaps some day a great story writer will appear to give them new names and a new language.

12

Secularism and Toleration
(1994)

There is little doubt that in the last two or three years we have seen a genuine renewal of both thinking and activism among left-democratic forces in India on the question of the fight for secularism. An important element of the new thinking is the re-examination of the theoretical and historical foundations of the liberal-democratic state in India, and of its relation to the history and theory of the modern state in Europe.and the Americas.

An interesting point of entry into the problem is provided by the parallels recently drawn between the rise of Fascism in Europe in the 1920s and 1930s, and that of the Hindu right in India in the last few years. Sumit Sarkar, among others, has noted some of the chilling simi-larities.[1] But a more careful look at precisely this comparison will, I think, lead us to ask a basic and somewhat unsettling question: is secu-larism an adequate, or even appropriate, ground on which to meet the political challenge of Hindu majoritarianism?

The Nazi campaigns against Jews and other minority groups did not call for an abandonment of the secular principles of the state in Germany. If anything, Nazi rule was accompanied by an attempt to de-Christianize public life and undermine the influence of the Catholic as well as the various Protestant Churches. Fascist ideology did not seek the union of state and religion in Italy, where the presence of a

[1] Sumit Sarkar, 'The Fascism of the Sangh Parivar', *Economic and Political Weekly*, 30 January 1993, pp. 163–7; Jan Breman, 'The Hindu Right: Comparisons with Nazi Germany', *Times of India*, 15 March 1993.

large peasant population and the hold of Catholicism might be supposed to have provided an opportune condition for such a demand—and this despite the virtually open collaboration of the Roman Church with Mussolini's regime. Nazi Germany and Fascist Italy are, of course, only two examples of a feature that has been noticed many times in the career of the modern state in many countries of the world: namely, that state policies of religious intolerance, or of discrimination against religious and other ethnic minorities, do not necessarily require the collapsing of state and religion, nor do they presuppose the existence of theocratic institutions.

The point is relevant in the context of the current politics of the Hindu right in India. It is necessary to ask why the political leadership of that movement chooses so meticulously to describe its adversaries as 'pseudo-secularists', conceding thereby its approval of the ideal as such of the secular state. None of the serious political statements made by that leadership contains any advocacy of theocratic institutions; and, notwithstanding the exuberance of a few sadhus celebrating their sudden rise to political prominence, it is unlikely that a conception of the 'Hindu Rashtra' will be seriously propagated which will include, for instance, a principle that the laws of the state be in conformity with this or that *samhita* or even with the general spirit of the *Dharmasastra*. In this sense, the leading element in the current movement of the Hindu right can be said to have undergone a considerable shift in position from, let us say, that of the Hindu Mahasabha at the time of the debate over the Hindu Code Bill some forty years ago. Its position is also quite unlike that of most contemporary Islamic fundamentalist movements, which explicitly reject the theoretical separation of state and religion as 'Western' and un-Islamic. It is similarly unlike the fundamentalist strand within the Sikh movements in recent years. The majoritarianism of the Hindu right, it seems to me, is perfectly at peace with the institutional procedures of the 'Western' or 'modern' state.

Indeed, the mature and most formidable statement of the new political conception of 'Hindutva' is unlikely to pit itself at all against the idea of the secular state. The persuasive power, and even the emotional charge, that the Hindutva campaign appears to have gained in recent years does not depend on its demanding legislative enforcement of ritual or scriptural injunctions, a role for religious institutions in legislative or judicial processes, compulsory religious instruction, state support for religious bodies, the censorship of science, literature, and art in order to safeguard religious dogma, or any other similar demand undermining the secular character of the existing Indian state. This is not to say that in the frenzied mêlée produced by the Hindutva brigade such noises will not be made; the point is that anti-secular demands of this type are not crucial to the political thrust, or even the public appeal, of the campaign.

Indeed, in its most sophisticated forms the campaign of the Hindu right often seeks to mobilize on its behalf the will of an interventionist modernizing state in order to erase the presence of religious or ethnic particularisms from the domains of law or public life, and to supply, in the name of 'national culture', a homogenized content to the notion of citizenship. In this role, the Hindu right in fact seeks to project itself as a principled modernist critic of Islamic or Sikh fundamentalism, and to accuse the 'pseudo-secularists' of preaching tolerance for religious obscurantism and bigotry. The most recent example of this is the Allahabad High Court pronouncement on divorce practices among Muslims by a judge well known for his views on the constitutional sanctity of Lord Rama.

Thus, the comparison with Fascism in Europe points to the very real possibility of a Hindu right locating itself quite firmly within the domain of the modernizing state, and using all of the ideological resources of that state to lead the charge against people who do not conform to its version of the 'national culture'. From this position, the Hindu right can not only deflect accusations of being anti-secular, but can even use the arguments for interventionist secularization to promote intolerance and violence against minorities.

As a matter of fact, the comparison with Nazi Germany also extends to the exact point that provides the Hindutva campaign with its venomous charge: as Sarkar notes, 'the Muslim here becomes the near exact equivalent of the Jew.' The very fact of belonging to this minority religious community is sufficient to put a question mark against the status of a Muslim as a citizen of India. The term 'communal', in this twisted language, is reserved for the Muslim, whereas the 'pseudo-secular' is the Hindu who defends the right of the Muslim citizen. (Note once more that the term 'secular' itself is not made a target of attack.) Similarly, on the vexed question of migrants from Bangladesh, the Hindu immigrant is by definition a 'refugee' while the Muslim is an 'infiltrator'. A whole series of stereotypical features, now sickeningly familiar in their repetitiveness, are then adduced in order to declare as dubious the historical, civil, and political status of the Muslim within the Indian state. In short, the current campaign of the Hindu right is directed not against the principle of the secular state, but rather towards mobilizing the legal powers of that state in order to systematically persecute and terrorize a specific religious minority within its population.

The question then is as follows: is the defence of secularism an appropriate ground for meeting the challenge of the Hindu right? Or should it be fought where the attack is being made, i.e. should the response be a defence of the duty of the democratic state to ensure policies of religious toleration? The question is important because it reminds us that not all aggressive majoritarianisms pose the same sort of problem in the context of the democratic state: Islamic fundamentalism in Pakistan or Bangladesh, or Sinhala chauvinism in Sri Lanka, do not necessarily have available to them the same political strategies as the majoritarian politics of the Hindu right in India. It also warns us of the very real theoretical possibility that secularization and religious toleration may sometimes work at cross-purposes.[2] It is necessary therefore to be clear about what is implied by these concepts.

The Meaning of Secularism

At the very outset, let us face up to a point that will be invariably made in any discussion on 'secularism' in India: namely, that in the Indian context the word has very different meanings from its standard use in English. This fact is sometimes cited as confirmation of the 'inevitable'

---

[2] Ashis Nandy makes a distinction between religion-as-faith, by which he means a way of life that is operationally plural and tolerant, and religion-as-ideology which identifies and enumerates populations of followers fighting for non-religious, usually political and economic, interests. He then suggests, quite correctly, that the politics of secularism is part of the same process of formation of modern state practices which promotes religion-as-ideology. Nandy's conclusion is that rather than relying on the secularism of a modernized elite we should 'explore the philosophy, the symbolism, and the theology of tolerance in the various faiths of the citizens and hope that the state systems in South Asia may learn something about religious tolerance from everyday Hinduism, Islam, Buddhism, and/or Sikhism . . .': 'The Politics of Secularism and the Recovery of Religious Tolerance', in Veena Das, ed., *Mirrors of Violence: Communities, Riots and Survivors in South Asia* (Delhi: Oxford University Press, 1990), pp. 69–93. I am raising the same doubt about whether secularism necessarily ensures toleration, but, unlike Nandy, I am here looking for political possibilities *within* the domain of the modern state institutions as they now exist in India.

difference in the meanings of a concept in two dissimilar cultures. ('India is not Europe: secularism in India cannot mean the same thing as it does in Europe.') At other times, it is used to underline the 'inevitable' shortcomings of the modern state in India. ('There cannot be a secular state in India because Indians have an incorrect concept of secularism.')

Of course, it could also be argued that this comparison with European conceptions is irrelevant if our purpose is to intervene in the Indian debate on the subject. What does it matter if secularism means something else in European and American political discourse? As long as there are reasonably clear and commonly agreed referents for the word in the Indian context, we should go ahead and address ourselves to the specifically Indian meaning of secularism.

Unfortunately, the matter cannot be settled that easily. The Indian meanings of secularism did not emerge in ignorance of the European or American meanings of the word. I also think that in its current usage in India, with apparently well-defined 'Indian' referents, the loud and often acrimonious Indian debate on secularism is never entirely innocent of its Western genealogies. To pretend that the Indian meaning of secularism has marked out a conceptual world all its own, untroubled by its differences with Western secularism, is to take an ideological position which refuses either to recognize or justify its own grounds.

In fact, I wish to make an even stronger argument. Commenting upon Raymond Williams' justly famous *Keywords*, Quentin Skinner points out that a concept takes on a new meaning not when (as one would usually suppose) arguments that it should be applied to a new circumstance succeed, but rather when such arguments fail.[3] Thus, if one is to consider the 'new' meaning acquired by the word 'secularism' in India, it is not as though the plea of the advocates of secularism— that the concept bears application to modern Indian state and society— has won general acceptance, and that the concept has thereby taken on a new meaning. If that had been the case, the 'original' meaning of the word as understood in its standard sense in the West would have remained unmutilated; it would only have widened its range of referents by including within it the specific circumstances of the Indian

[3] Quentin Skinner, 'Language and Political Change', in Terence Gall, James Fair, and Russell L. Hanson, eds, *Political Innovation and Conceptual Change* (Cambridge: Cambridge University Press, 1989), pp. 6–23.

situation. The reason why arguments have to be made about 'secularism' having a new *meaning* in India is because there are serious difficulties in applying the standard meaning of the word to the Indian circumstances. The 'original' concept, in other words, will not easily admit the Indian case within its range of referents.

This, of course, could be a good pretext for insisting that Indians have their own concept of secularism which is different from the Western concept bearing the same name; that, it could be argued, is exactly why the Western concept cannot be applied to the Indian case. The argument then would be about a difference in concepts: if the concept is different, the question of referential equivalence cannot be a very crucial issue. At the most, it would be a matter of family resemblances, but conceptually Western secularism and Indian secularism would inhabit entirely autonomous discursive domains.

That, it is needless to say, is hardly the case. We could begin by asking why, in all recent discussions in India on the relation between religion and the state, the central concept is named by the English words 'secular' and 'secularism', or in the Indian languages by neologisms such as *dharma-nirapekshata* which are translations of those English words and are clearly meant to refer to the range of meanings indicated by the English terms. As far as I know, there does not exist in any Indian language a term for 'secular' or 'secularism' which is standardly used in talking about the role of religion in the modern state and society, and whose meaning can be immediately explicated without having recourse to the English terms.

What this implies is that although the use of dharma in dharma-nirapekshata or *mazhab* in *ghair-mazhabi* might open up conceptual or referential possibilities in Indian discourse which were unavailable to the concept of secularism in the West, the continued use of an awkward neologism, besides of course the continued use of the English term itself, indicates that the more stable and well-defined reference for the concept lies in the Western political discourse about the modern state.[4] In fact, it is clear from discussions among the Indian political

[4] Even in the mid-1960s, Ziya-ul Hasan Faruqi was complaining about the use of *ghair-mazhabi* and *la-dini*. 'Ghair mazhabi means something contrary to religious commandments and *la dini* is irreligious or atheistic . . . The common man was very easily led to conclude that the Indian state was against religion. It is, however, gratifying to see that the Urdu papers have started to transliterate the word "secular" . . .':

and intellectual elite at least from the 1920s that the proponents of the secular state in India never had any doubt at all about the meaning of the concept of secularism; all the doubts were about whether that concept would find a congenial field of application in the Indian social and political context. The continued use of the term 'secularism' is, it seems to me, an expression of the desire of the modernizing elite to see the 'original' meaning of the concept actualized in India. The resort to 'new meanings' is, to invoke Skinner's point once more, a mark of the failure of this attempt.

It might prove instructive to do a 'history of ideas' exercise for the use of the word 'secularism' in Indian political discourse in the last hundred years, but this is not the place for it. What is important for our purposes is a discussion of how the nationalist project of putting an end to colonial rule and inaugurating an independent nation-state became implicated, from its very birth, in a contradictory movement with regard to the modernist mission of secularization.

British Rule, Nationalism, and the Separation of State and Religion

Ignoring the details of a complicated history, it would not be widely off the mark to say that by the latter half of the nineteenth century British power in India had arrived at a reasonably firm policy of not involving the state in matters of religion. It tried to stay neutral on disputes over religion and was particularly careful not to be seen as promoting Christianity. Immediately after the assumption of power by the crown in 1858, the most significant step was taken in instituting equality before the law by enacting uniform codes of civil and criminal law. The area left out, however, was that of personal law, which continued to be governed by the respective religious laws as recognized and interpreted by the courts. The reason why personal law was not brought within the scope of a uniform civil code was, precisely, the reluctance of the colonial state to intervene in matters close to the very heart of religious doctrine and practice. In the matter of religious endowments, while British power in its early years took over many of

'Indian Muslims and the Ideology of the Secular State', in Donald Eugene Smith, ed., *South Asian Politics and Religion* (Princeton: Princeton University Press, 1966), pp. 138–49.

the functions of patronage and administration previously carried out by Indian rulers, by the middle of the nineteenth century it largely renounced those responsibilities and handed them over to local trusts and committees.

As far as the modernizing efforts of the Indian elite are concerned, nineteenth-century attempts at 'social reform' by soliciting the legal intervention of the colonial state are well known. In the second half of the nineteenth century, however, the rise of nationalism led to a refusal on the part of the Indian elite to let the colonial state enter into areas that were regarded as crucial to the cultural identity of the nation. This did not mean a halt to the project of 'reform': all it meant was a shift in the agency of reform—from the legal authority of the colonial state to the moral authority of the national community.[5] This shift is crucial: not so much because of its apparent coincidence with the policy of non-intervention of the colonial state in matters of religion in the late nineteenth century, but because of the underlying assumption in nationalist thinking about the role of state legislation in religion— legal intervention in the cause of religious reform was not undesirable *per se*, but it was undesirable when the state was colonial.

As it happened, there was considerable change in the social beliefs and practices of the sections that came to constitute the new middle class in the period leading up to Independence in 1947. Not only was there change in the actual practices surrounding family and personal relations—and even in many religious practices—without there being any significant change in the laws of the state, but, perhaps more important, there was an overwhelming tide in the dominant attitudes among these sections in favour of the legitimacy of 'social reform'. These reformist opinions affected the educated sections in virtually all parts of the country, and found a voice in most religious and caste communities.

One of the dramatic results of this accumulation of reformist desire within the nationalist middle class was the sudden spate of new legislation on religious and social matters immediately after Independence. This is actually an extremely significant episode in the development of the nation-state in India, and its deeply problematic nature has been seldom noticed in the current debates over secularism. It needs to be described in some detail.

[5] I have discussed the point more elaborately in *The Nation and Its Fragments: Colonial and Postcolonial Histories* (Princeton: Princeton University Press, 1993).

Religious Reform and the Nation-State

Even as the provisions of the new constitution of India were being discussed in the Constituent Assembly, some of the provincial legislatures had begun to enact laws for the reform of religious institutions and practices. One of the most significant of these was the Madras *Devadasis* (Prevention of Dedication) Act, 1947, which outlawed the institution of dedicating young girls to temple deities and prohibited 'dancing by a woman . . . in the precincts of any temple or other religious institution, or in any procession of a Hindu deity, idol or object of worship . . .'[6] Equally important was the Madras Temple Entry Authorization Act, 1947, which made it a punishable offence to prevent any person on the ground of untouchability from entering or worshipping in a Hindu temple. This act was immediately followed by similar legislation in the Central Provinces, Bihar, Bombay, and other provinces, and finally by the temple entry provisions in the constitution of India.

Although in the course of the debates over these enactments views were often expressed about the need to 'remove a blot on the Hindu religion', it was clearly possible to justify some of the laws on purely secular grounds. Thus, the devadasi system could be declared unlawful on the ground that it was a form of bondage or enforced prostitution. Similarly, 'temple entry' was sometimes defended by extending the argument that the denial of access to public places on the ground of untouchability was unlawful. However, a contradiction appeared in this 'civil rights' argument since all places of worship were not necessarily thrown open to all citizens; only Hindu temples were declared open for all Hindus, and non-Hindus could be, and actually still are, denied entry. But even more problematically, the right of worship 'of all classes and sections of Hindus' at 'Hindu religious institutions of public character', as Article 25(2) of the constitution has it, necessarily implies that the state has to take up the onus of interpreting even doctrinal and ritual injunctions in order to assert the *religious* legitimacy of forms of worship that would not be discriminatory in terms of caste.[7]

[6] Cited in Donald Eugene Smith, *India as a Secular State* (Princeton: Princeton University Press, 1963), p. 239.

[7] In fact, the courts, recognizing that the right of a religious denomination 'to manage its own affairs in matters of religion' [Article 26(b)] could come into conflict

Still more difficult to justify on non-religious grounds was a re-formist law like the Madras Animal and Bird Sacrifices Abolition Act, 1950. The view that animal sacrifices were repugnant and represented a primitive form of worship was clearly the product of a very specific religious interpretation of *religious* ritual, and could be described as a sectional opinion even among Hindus. (It might even be described as a view that was biased against the religious practices of the lower castes, especially in southern India.) Yet in bringing about this 'puri-fication' of the Hindu religion, the legislative wing of the state was seen as the appropriate instrument.

The period after Independence also saw, apart from reformist legislation of this kind, an enormous increase in the involvement of the state administration in the management of the affairs of Hindu tem-ples. The most significant enabling legislation in this regard was the Madras Hindu Religious and Charitable Endowments Act, 1951, which created an entire department of government devoted to the administration of Hindu religious endowments.[8] The legal argument

---

with the right of the state to throw open Hindu temples to all classes of Hindus [Arti-cle 25(2)(b)], have had to come up with ingenious, and often extremely arbitrary, arrangements in order to strike a compromise between the two provisions. Some of these judgements are referred to in Smith, *India as a Secular State*, pp. 242–3. For a detailed account of a case illustrating the extent of judicial involvement in the interpretation of religious doctrine and ritual, see Arjun Appadurai, *Worship and Conflict under Colonial Rule: A South Indian Case* (Cambridge: Cambridge University Press, 1981), pp. 36–50.

[8] Actually, the increased role of the government in controlling the administration of Hindu temples in Madras began with the Religious Endowments Acts of 1925 and 1927. It is interesting to note that there was nationalist opposition to the move at the time: S. Satyamurthi said during the debates in the provincial legislature in 1923 that 'the blighting hand of this Government will also fall tight on our temples and *maths*, with the result that they will also become part of the great machinery which the Hon'ble Minister and his colleagues are blackening every day.' During the debates preceding the 1951 Act, on the other hand, T.S.S. Rajan, the law minister, said: 'the fear of interfering with religious institutions has always been there with an alien Government but with us it is very different. Ours may be called a secular Government, and so it is. But it does not absolve us from protecting the funds of the institutions which are meant for the service of the people.' For an account of these changes in law, see Chandra Y. Mudaliar, *The Secular State and Religious Institutions in India: A Study of the Administration of Hindu Public Religious Trusts in Madras* (Wiesbaden: Fritz Steiner Verlag, 1974).

here is, of course, that the religious denomination concerned still retains the right to manage its own affairs in matters of religion, while the secular matters concerned with the management of the property of the endowment is taken over by the state. But this is a separation of functions that is impossible to maintain in practice. Thus, if the administrators choose to spend the endowment funds on opening hospitals or universities rather than on more elaborate ceremonies or on religious instruction, then that choice will affect the way in which the religious affairs of the endowment are managed. The issue has given rise to several disputes in court about the specific demarcation between the religious and secular functions, and to further legislation, in Madras as well as in other parts of India. The resulting situation led one commentator in the early 1960s to remark that 'the commissioner for Hindu religious endowments, a public servant of the secular state, today exercises far greater authority over Hindu religion in Madras state than the Archbishop of Canterbury does over the Church of England.'[9]

Once again, it is possible to provide a non-religious ground for state intervention in the administration of religious establishments, namely, prevention of misappropriation of endowment funds and ensuring the proper supervision of what is after all a public property. But what has been envisaged and actually practised since Independence goes well beyond this strictly negative role of the state. Clearly, the prevailing views about the reform of Hindu religion saw it as entirely fitting that the representative and administrative wings of the state should take up the responsibility of managing Hindu temples in, as it were, the 'public interest' of the general body of Hindus.

The reformist agenda was, of course, carried out most comprehensively during the making of the constitution and subsequently in the enactment in 1955 of what is known as the Hindu Code Bill.[10] During the discussions, objections were raised that in seeking to change personal law the state was encroaching upon an area protected by the right to religious freedom. B.R. Ambedkar's reply to these objections summed up the general attitude of the reformist leadership:

[9] Smith, *India as a Secular State*, p. 246.
[10] Actually, a series of laws called the Hindu Marriage Bill, the Hindu Succession Bill, the Hindu Minority and Guardianship Bill, and the Hindu Adoptions and Maintenance Bill.

The religious conceptions in this country are so vast that they cover every aspect of life from birth to death. There is nothing which is not religion and if personal law is to be saved I am sure about it that in social matters we will come to a standstill . . . There is nothing extraordinary in saying that we ought to strive hereafter to limit the definition of religion in such a manner that we shall not extend it beyond beliefs and such rituals as may be connected with ceremonials which are essentially religious. It is not necessary that the sort of laws, for instance, laws relating to tenancy or laws relating to succession, should be governed by religion . . . I personally do not understand why religion should be given this vast expansive jurisdiction so as to cover the whole of life and to prevent the legislature from encroaching upon that field.[11]

Impelled by this reformist urge, the Indian parliament proceeded to cut through the immensely complicated web of local and sectarian variations that enveloped the corpus known as 'Hindu law' as it had emerged through the colonial courts, and to lay down a single code of personal law for all Hindu citizens. Many of the new provisions were far-reaching in their departure from traditional brahmanical principles. Thus, the new code legalized inter-caste marriage; it legalized divorce and prohibited polygamy; it gave to the daughter the same rights of inheritance as the son, and permitted the adoption of daughters as well as sons. In justifying these changes the proponents of reform not only made the argument that 'tradition' could not remain stagnant and needed to be reinterpreted in the light of changing conditions, but they also had to engage in the exercise of deciding what was or was not essential to 'Hindu religion'. Once again, the anomaly has provoked comments from critical observers: 'An official of the secular state [the law minister] became an interpreter of Hindu religion, quoting and expounding the ancient Sanskrit scriptures in defence of his bills.'[12]

Clearly, it is necessary here to understand the force and internal consistency of the nationalist-modernist project which sought, in one and the same move, to rationalize the domain of religious discourse and to secularize the public domain of personal law. It would be little more than reactionary to rail against the 'Western-educated Hindu' who is scandalized by the profusion of avaricious and corrupt priests

[11] *Constituent Assembly Debates* (New Delhi: Government of India, 1946–50), vol. 7, p. 781.
[12] Smith, *India as a Secular State*, pp. 281–2.

at Hindu temples, and who, influenced by Christian ideas of service and piety, rides roughshod over the 'traditional Hindu notions' that a religious gift was never made for any specific purpose; that the priest entrusted with the management of a temple could for all practical purposes treat the property and its proceeds as matters within his personal jurisdiction; and that, unlike the Christian church, a temple was a place 'in which the idol condescends to receive visitors, who are expected to bring offerings with them, like subjects presenting themselves before a maharaja.'[13] More serious, of course, is the criticism that by using the state as the agency of what was very often only religious reform, the political leadership of the new nation-state flagrantly violated the principle of separation of state and religion.[14] This is a matter we will now consider in detail, but it is nevertheless necessary to point out that the violation of this principle of the secular state was justified precisely by the desire to secularize.

Anomalies of the Secular State

What are the characteristics of the secular state? Three principles are usually mentioned in the liberal-democratic doctrine on this subject.[15] The first is the principle of *liberty* which requires that the state permit the practice of any religion, within the limits set by certain other basic rights which the state is also required to protect. The second is the principle of *equality* which requires that the state not give preference to one religion over another. The third is the principle of

[13] See, for instance, J. Duncan M. Derrett, 'The Reform of Hindu Religious Endowments', in Smith, ed., *South Asian Politics and Religion*, pp. 311–36.

[14] The two most comprehensive studies on the subject of the secular state in India make this point. V.P. Luthera in *The Concept of the Secular State and India* (Calcutta: Oxford University Press, 1964) concludes that India should not properly be regarded as a secular state. D.E. Smith in *India as a Secular State* disagrees, arguing that Luthera bases his conclusion on too narrow a definition of the secular state, but nevertheless points out the numerous anomalies in the current situation.

[15] For a recent exchange on this matter, see Robert Audi, 'The Separation of Church and State and the Obligations of Citizenship', *Philosophy and Public Affairs*, 18, 3 (Summer 1989), pp. 259–96; Paul J. Weithman, 'Separation of Church and State: Some Questions for Professor Audi', *Philosophy and Public Affairs*, 20, 1 (Winter 1991), pp. 52–65; Robert Audi, 'Religious Commitment and Secular Reason: A Reply to Professor Weithman', *Philosophy and Public Affairs*, 20, 1 (Winter 1991), pp. 66–76.

neutrality which is best described as the requirement that the state not give preference to the religious over the non-religious, and which leads, in combination with the liberty and equality principles, to what is known in US constitutional law as the 'wall of separation' doctrine: namely, that the state not involve itself with religious affairs or organizations.[16]

Looking now at the doctrine of the secular state as it has evolved in practice in India, it is clear that whereas all three principles have been invoked to justify the secular state, their application has been contradictory and has led to major anomalies. The principle of liberty, which implies a right of freedom of religion, has been incorporated in the constitution which gives to every citizen—subject to public order, morality, and health—not only the equal right to freedom of conscience but also, quite specifically, 'the right freely to profess, practise, and propagate religion'. It also gives 'to every religious denomination or any section thereof certain collective rights of religion.' Besides, it specifically mentions the right of all minorities, whether based on religion or language, to establish and administer their own educational institutions. Limiting these rights of freedom of religion, however, is the right of the state to regulate 'any economic, financial, political or other secular activity which may be associated with religious practice', to provide for social welfare and reform, and to throw open Hindu religious institutions to all sections of Hindus. This limit to the liberty principle is what enabled the extensive reform under state auspices of Hindu personal law, and of the administration of Hindu temples.

The liberal-democratic doctrine of freedom of religion does recognize, of course, that this right will be limited by other basic human rights. Thus, for instance, it would be perfectly justified for the state to deny that—let us say—human sacrifice or causing injury to human beings, or, as we have already noted in the case of devadasis, enforced servitude to a deity or temple, constitutes permissible religious practice. However, it is also recognized that there are many grey areas

[16] The US Supreme Court defined the doctrine as follows: 'Neither a state nor the federal government can set up a church. Neither can pass laws which aid one religion, aid all religions, or prefer one religion over another . . . Neither a state nor the federal government can, openly or secretly, participate in the affairs of any religious organization or groups and vice versa.' *Everson* v. *Board of Education*, 330 U.S. 1 (1947), cited in Smith, *India as a Secular State*, pp. 125–6.

where it is difficult to lay down the limit. A case very often cited in this connection is the legal prohibition of polygamy even when it may be sanctioned by a particular religion: the argument that polygamy necessarily violates other basic human rights is often thought of as problematic.

But no matter where this limit is drawn, it is surely required by the idea of the secular state that the liberty principle be limited only by the need to protect some other *universal* basic right, and not by appeal to a particular interpretation of religious doctrine. This, as we have mentioned before, has not been possible in India. The urge to undertake by legislation the reform of Hindu personal law and Hindu religious institutions made it difficult for the state not to transgress into the area of religious reform itself. Both the legislature and the courts were led into the exercise of interpreting religious doctrine on religious grounds. Thus, in deciding the legally permissible limits of state regulation of religious institutions, it became necessary to identify those practices that were *essentially* of a religious character; but, in accordance with the judicial procedures of a modern state, this decision could not be left to the religious denomination itself but had to be determined 'as an objective question' by the courts.[17] It can be easily seen that this could lead to the entanglement of the state in a series of disputes mainly religious in character.

It could, of course, be argued that given the dual character of personal law—inherited from the colonial period as religious law that had been recognized and codified as the laws of the state—and in the absence of appropriate institutions of the Hindu religion through which religious reform could be organized and carried out outside the arena of the state, there was no alternative to state intervention in this matter. Which other agency was there with the requisite power and legitimacy to undertake the reform of religious practices? The force and persuasiveness of this argument for the modernist leadership of independent India can hardly be overstated. The desire was in fact to initiate a process of rational interpretation of religious doctrine, and to find a representative and credible institutional process for the reform of religious practice. That the use of state legislation to achieve this modernist purpose must come into conflict with another modernist principle, of

[17] *Durgah Committee* v. *Hussain, A.* 1961 S.C. 1402 *(1415)*, cited in Durga Das Basu, *Constitutional Law of India* (New Delhi: Prentice-Hall of India, 1977), p. 84.

the freedom of religion, is one of the anomalies of the secular state in India.

The second principle—that of equality—is also explicitly recognized in the Indian constitution, which prohibits the state from discriminating against any citizen on the basis only of religion or caste, except when it makes special provisions for the advancement of socially and educationally backward classes or for scheduled castes and scheduled tribes. Such special provisions in the form of reserved quotas in employment and education, or of reserved seats in representative bodies, have of course led to much controversy in India in the last few decades. But these disputes about the validity of positive discrimination in favour of underprivileged castes or tribes have almost never taken the form of a dispute about equality on the ground of religion. Indeed, although the institution of caste itself is supposed to derive its basis from the doctrines of brahmanical religion, recent debates in the political arena about caste discrimination usually do not make any appeals at all to religious doctrine. There is only one significant way in which the question of positive discrimination in favour of scheduled castes is circumscribed by religion: in order to qualify as a member of a scheduled caste, a person must profess to be either Hindu or Sikh; a public declaration of the adoption of any other religion would lead to disqualification. However, in some recent provisions relating to 'other backward classes', especially in the much-disputed recommendations of the Mandal Commission, attempts have been made to go beyond this limitation.

The problem with the equality principle which concerns us more directly is the way in which it has been affected by the project of reforming Hindu religion by state legislation. All the legislative and administrative measures mentioned above concern the institutions and practices of the Hindus, including the reform of personal laws and religious endowments. That this was discriminatory was argued in the 1950s by the socially conservative sections of Hindu opinion, and by political parties like the Hindu Mahasabha which were opposed to the idea of reform itself. But the fact that the use of state legislation to bring about reforms in only the religion of the majority was creating a serious anomaly in the very notion of equal citizenship was pointed out by only a few lone voices within the progressive sections. One such belonged to J.B. Kripalani, the socialist leader, who argued: 'If we are a democratic state, I submit we must make laws not for one community alone . . . It is not the Mahasabhites who alone are communal: it is the government also that is communal, whatever it may say.' Elaborating, he said: 'If they [Members of Parliament] single out the Hindu community for their reforming zeal, they cannot escape the charge of being communalists in the sense that they favour the Hindu community and are indifferent to the good of the Muslim community or the Catholic community . . . Whether the marriage bill favours the Hindu community or places it at a disadvantage, both ways, it becomes a communal measure.'[18] The basic problem here was obvious. If it was accepted that the state could intervene in religious institutions or practices in order to protect other social and economic rights, then what was the ground for intervening only in the affairs of one religious community and not others? Clearly, the first principle—that of freedom of religion—could not be invoked here only for the minority communities when it had been set aside in the case of the majority community.

The problem has been got around by resorting to what is essentially a pragmatic argument. It is suggested that, for historical reasons, there is a certain lag in the readiness of the different communities to accept reforms intended to rationalize the domain of personal law. In any case, if equality of citizenship is what is desired, it already stands compromised by the very system of religion-based personal laws inherited from colonial times. What should be done, therefore, is to first declare the desirability of replacing the separate personal laws by a uniform civil code; but to proceed towards this objective in a pragmatic way, respecting the sensitivity of the religious communities about their freedom of religion, and going ahead with state-sponsored reforms only when the communities themselves are ready to accept them. Accordingly, there is an item in the non-justiciable Directive Principles of the constitution which declares that the state should endeavour to provide a uniform civil code for all citizens. On the other hand, those claiming to speak on behalf of the minority communities tend to take a firm stand in the freedom of religion principle, and to deny that the state should have any right at all to interfere in their religious affairs. The anomaly has, in the last few years, provided some of the most potent ammunition to the Hindu right in its campaign against what it describes as the 'appeasement' of minorities.

It would not be irrelevant to mention here that there have also occurred, among the minority religious communities in India, not entirely dissimilar movements for the reform of religious laws and

---

[18] Cited in Smith, *India as a Secular State*, pp. 286, 288.

institutions. In the earlier decades of this century, there were organized attempts, for instance, to put an end to local customary practices among Muslim communities in various parts of India and replace them with a uniform Muslim personal law. This campaign, led in particular by the Jamiyat al-ulama-i Hind of Deoband—well known for its closeness to the Indian National Congress—was directed against the recognition by the courts of special marriage and inheritance practices among communities such as the Mapilla of southern India, the Memon of western India, and various groups in Rajasthan and Punjab. The argument given was not only that such practices were 'un-Islamic'; specific criticisms were also made about how these customs were backward and iniquitous, especially in the matter of the treatment of women. The preamble to a bill to change the customary succession law of the Mapilla, for instance, said— using a rhetoric not unlike that used later for the reform of Hindu law—'The Muhammadan community now feels the incongruity of the usage and looks upon the prevailing custom as a discredit to their religion and to their community.'[19]

The reform campaigns led to a series of new laws in various provinces and in the central legislature, such as the Mapilla Succession Act 1918, the Cutchi Memons Act 1920 and 1938, and the NWFP Muslim Personal Law (Shari'at) Application Act 1935 (which was the first time that the terms 'Muslim personal law' and shari'a were used interchangeably in law). The culmination of these campaigns for a uniform set of personal laws for all Muslims in India was reached with the passing of the so-called Shari'at Act by the Central legislature in 1937. Interestingly, it was because of the persistent efforts of Muhammad Ali Jinnah, whose political standing was in this case exceeded by his prestige as a legal luminary, that only certain sections of this act were required to be applied compulsorily to all Muslims; on other matters its provisions were optional.

The logic of completing the process of uniform application of Muslim personal law has continued in independent India. The optional clauses in the 1937 act have been removed. The act has been applied to areas that were earlier excluded: especially the princely states that merged with India after 1947, the latest in that series being Cooch

[19] Cited in Tahir Mahmood, *Muslim Personal Law: Role of the State in the Indian Subcontinent* (Nagpur: All India Reporter, 1983), p. 21.

Behar where the local customary law for Muslims was superseded by the shari'at laws through legislation by the Left Front government of West Bengal in 1980.

Thus, even while resisting the idea of a uniform civil code on the ground that this would be a fundamental encroachment on the freedom of religion and destructive of the cultural identity of religious minorities, the Muslim leadership in India has not shunned state intervention altogether. One notices, in fact, the same attempt to seek rationalization and uniformity as one sees in the case of Hindu personal law or Hindu religious institutions. The crucial difference after 1947 is of course that, unlike the majority community, the minorities are unwilling to grant to a legislature elected by universal suffrage the power to legislate the reform of their religions. On the other hand, there do not exist any other institutions which have the representative legitimacy to supervise such a process of reform. That, to put it in a nutshell, is the present impasse on the equality principle.

The third principle we have mentioned of the secular state—that of the separation of state and religion—has also been recognized in the constitution, which declares that there shall be no official state religion, no religious instruction in state schools, and no taxes to support any particular religion. But, as we have seen, the state has become entangled in the affairs of religion in numerous ways. This was the case even in colonial times; but the degree and extent of the entanglement, paradoxically, has increased since Independence. Nor is this involvement limited only to the sorts of cases we have mentioned before, which were the results of state-sponsored religious reform. Many of the older systems of state patronage of religious institutions, carried out by the colonial government or by the princely states, still continue under the present regime. Thus, Article 290A of the constitution makes a specific provision of money to be paid every year by the governments of Kerala and Tamil Nadu to the Travancore Devaswom Fund. Article 28(2) says that although there will be no religious instruction in educational institutions wholly maintained out of state funds, this will not apply to those institutions where the original endowment or trust requires that religious instruction be given. Under this provision, Benaras Hindu University and Aligarh Muslim University, both central universities, do impart religious instruction. Besides, there are numerous educational institutions all over the country run by religious denominations which receive state financial aid.

The conclusion is inescapable that the 'wall of separation' doctrine of US constitutional law can hardly be applied to the present Indian situation (as indeed it cannot in the case of many European democracies; but there at least it could be argued that the entanglements are politically insignificant, and often obsolete remnants of older legal conventions). This is precisely the ground on which the argument is sometimes made that 'Indian secularism' has to have a different meaning from 'Western secularism'. What is suggested in fact is that the cultural and historical realities of the Indian situation call for a *different* relationship between state and civil society than what is regarded as normative in Western political discourse, at least in the matter of religion. Sometimes it is said that in Indian conditions the neutrality principle cannot apply; the state will necessarily have to involve itself in the affairs of religion. What must be regarded as normative here is an extension of the equality principle, i.e. that the state should favour all religions equally. This argument, however, cannot offer a defence for the selective intervention of the state in reforming the personal laws only of the majority community. On the other hand, arguments are also made about secularism having 'many meanings',[20] suggesting thereby that a democratic state must be expected to protect cultural diversity and the right of people to follow their own culture. The difficulty is that this demand cannot be easily squared with the homogenizing secular desire for, let us say, a uniform civil code.

Where we end up then is a quandary. The desire for a secular state must concede defeat even as it claims to have discovered new meanings of secularism. On the other hand, the respect for cultural diversity and different ways of life finds it impossible to articulate itself in the unitary rationalism of the language of rights. It seems to me that there is no viable way out of this problem within the given contours of liberal-democratic theory, which must define the relation between the relatively autonomous domains of state and civil society always in terms of individual rights. As has been noticed for many other aspects of the emerging forms of non-Western modernity, this is one more instance where the supposedly universal forms of the modern state turn out to be inadequate for the post-colonial world.

To reconfigure the problem posed by the career of the secular state in India, we will need to locate it on a somewhat different conceptual ground. In the rest of this essay I will suggest the outlines of an alter-

[20] Sarkar, 'The Fascism of the Sangh Parivar'.

native theoretical argument which holds the promise of taking us outside the dilemmas of the secular-modernist discourse. In this, I will not take the easy route of appealing to an 'Indian exception'. In other words, I will not trot out yet another version of the 'new meaning of secularism' argument. But to avoid that route, I must locate my problem on a ground which will include, at one and the same time, the history of the rise of the modern state in both its Western and non-Western forms. I will attempt to do this by invoking Michel Foucault.

Liberal-Democratic Conundrum

But before I do that, let me briefly refer to the current state of the debate over minority rights in liberal political theory, and why I think the problem posed by the Indian situation will not find any satisfactory answers within the terms of that debate. A reference to this theoretical corpus is necessary because, first, left-democratic thinking in India on secularism and minority rights shares many of its premises with liberal-democratic thought; and second, the legally instituted processes of the state and the public domain in India have clearly avowed affiliations to the conceptual world of liberal political theory. Pointing out the limits of liberal thought will also allow me, then, to make the suggestion that political practice in India must seek to develop new institutional sites that cut across the divide between state sovereignty on the one hand and people's rights on the other.

To begin with, liberal political theory in its strict sense cannot recognize the validity of any collective rights of cultural groups. Liberalism must hold as a fundamental principle the idea that the state, and indeed all public institutions, will treat all citizens equally, regardless of race, sex, religion, or other cultural particularities. It is only when everyone is treated equally, liberals argue, that the basic needs of people, shared universally by all, can be adequately and fairly satisfied. These universal needs will include not only 'material' goods such as livelihood, health care, and education, but also 'cultural' goods such as religious freedom, free speech, free association, etc. But in order to guarantee freedom and equality at the same time, the locus of rights must be the individual citizen, the bearer of universal needs; to recognize rights that belong only to particular cultural groups within the body of citizens is to destroy both equality and freedom.

Needless to say, this purist version of the liberal doctrine is regarded as unduly rigid and narrow by many who otherwise identify with the values of liberal-democratic politics. But the attempts to make room, within the doctrines of liberalism, for some recognition of collective cultural identities have not yielded solutions that enjoy wide acceptance. I cannot enter here into the details of this controversy which, spurred on by the challenge of 'multiculturalism' in many Western countries, has emerged as perhaps the liveliest area of debate in contemporary liberal philosophy. A mention only of the principal modes of argument, insofar as they are relevant to the problems posed by the Indian situation, will have to suffice.

One response to the problem of fundamental moral disagreements caused by a plurality of conflicting—and sometimes incommensurable—cultural values is to seek an extension of the principle of neutrality in order to preclude such conflicts from the political arena. The argument here is that, just as in the case of religion, the existence of fundamentally divergent moral values in society would imply that there is no rational way in which reasonable people might resolve the dispute; and since the state should not arbitrarily favour one set of beliefs over another, it must not be asked to intervene in such conflicts. John Rawls and Thomas Nagel, among others, have made arguments of this kind, seeking thereby to extend the notions of state impartiality and religious toleration to other areas of moral disagreement.[21]

Not all liberals, however, like the deep scepticism and 'epistemic abstinence' implied in this view.[22] More relevant for us, however, is the criticism made from within liberal theory that these attempts to cope with diversity by taking the disputes off the political agenda are 'increasingly evasive. They offer a false impartiality in place of social recognition of the persistence of fundamental conflicts of value in our society.'[23] If this is a judgement that can be made for societies where the 'wall of separation' doctrine is solidly established, the remoteness of these arguments from the realities of the Indian situation hardly needs to be emphasized.

[21] John Rawls, 'Justice as Fairness: Political not Metaphysical', *Philosophy and Public Affairs*, 14 (1985), pp. 248–51; John Rawls, 'The Priority of the Right and Ideas of the Good', *Philosophy and Public Affairs*, 17 (1988), pp. 260–4; Thomas Nagel, 'Moral Conflict and Political Legitimacy', *Philosophy and Public Affairs*, 16 (1987), pp. 218–40.

[22] For instance, Joseph Raz, 'Facing Diversity: The Case of Epistemic Abstinence', *Philosophy and Public Affairs*, 19 (1990), pp. 3–46.

[23] Amy Gutmann and Dennis Thompson, 'Moral Conflict and Political Consensus', *Ethics*, 101 (October 1990), pp. 64–88.

However, rather than evade the question of cultural diversity, some theorists have attempted to take up the 'justice as fairness' idea developed by liberals such as John Rawls and Ronald Dworkin, and extend it to cultural groups. Justice, according to this argument, requires that undeserved or 'morally arbitrary' disadvantages should be removed or compensated for. If such disadvantages attach to persons because they were born into particular minority cultural groups, then liberal equality itself must demand that individual rights be differentially allocated on the basis of culture. Will Kymlicka has made such a case for the recognition of the rights of cultural minorities whose very survival as distinct groups is in question.[24]

We should note, of course, that the examples usually given in this liberal literature to illustrate the need for minority cultural rights are those of the indigenous peoples of North America and Australia. But in principle there is no reason why the argument about 'being disadvantaged' should be restricted only to such indubitable cases of endangered cultural groups; it should apply to any group that can be reasonably defined as a cultural minority within a given political entity. And this is where its problems as a liberal theory become insuperable. Could a collective cultural right be used as an instrument to perpetuate thoroughly illiberal practices within the group? Would individual members of such groups have the right to leave the group? If an individual right of exit is granted, would that not in effect undermine the right of the group to preserve its identity? On the other hand, if a right of exit is denied, would we still have a liberal society?[25]

Clearly, it is extremely hard to justify the granting of substantively different collective rights to cultural groups on the basis of liberalism's commitment to procedural equality and universal citizenship. Several recent attempts to make a case for special rights for cultural minorities and oppressed groups have consequently gone on to question the idea of universal citizenship itself: in doing this, the arguments come fairly close to upholding some sort of cultural relativism. The charge that is made against universal citizenship is not merely that it forces everyone into a single homogeneous cultural mould, thus threatening the

[24] Will Kymlicka, *Liberalism, Community and Culture* (Oxford: Oxford University Press, 1989).

[25] See, for example, the following exchange: Chandran Kukathas, 'Are There Any Cultural Rights?' and Will Kymlicka, 'The Rights of Minority Cultures', *Political Theory*, 20, 1 (February 1992), pp. 105–46; Kukathas, 'Cultural Rights Again', *Political Theory*, 20, 4 (November 1992), pp. 674–80.

distinct identities of minority groups; but that the homogeneous mould itself is by no means a neutral one, being invariably the culture of the dominant group, so that it is not everybody but only the minorities and the disadvantaged who are forced to forego their cultural identities. That being the case, neither universalism nor neutrality can have any moral priority over the rights of cultural groups to protect their autonomous existence.

Once again, arguments such as this go well beyond the recognized limits of the liberal doctrine; and even those who are sympathetic to the demands for the protection of plural cultural identities feel compelled to assert that the recognition of difference cannot mean the abandonment of all commitment to a universalist framework of reason.[26] Usually, therefore, the 'challenge of multiculturalism' is sought to be met by asserting the value of diversity itself for the flowering of culture, and making room for divergent ways of life *within* a fundamentally agreed set of universalist values. Even when one expects recognition of one's 'right to culture', therefore, one must always be prepared to act within a culture of rights and thus give reasons for insisting on being different.[27]

None of these liberal arguments seems to have enough strength to come to grips with the problems posed by the Indian situation. Apart from resorting to platitudes about the value of diversity, respect for other ways of life, and the need for furthering understanding between different cultures, they do not provide any means for relocating the institutions of rights or refashioning the practices of identity in order to get out of what often appears to be a political impasse.

Governmentality

I make use of Foucault's idea of governmentality not because I think it is conceptually neat or free of difficulties. Nor is the way in which I will use the idea here one that, as far as I know, Foucault has advanced

---

[26] See, for example, Charles Taylor, *Multiculturalism and 'The Politics of Recognition'* (Princeton: Princeton University Press, 1992); Amy Gutmann, 'The Challenge of Multiculturalism in Political Ethics', *Philosophy and Public Affairs*, 22 (1993), pp. 73–206.

[27] Rajeev Bhargava has sought to make the case for the rights of minorities in India in these terms. See 'The Right to Culture', in K.N. Panikkar, ed., *Communalism in India: History, Politics and Culture* (New Delhi: Manohar, 1991), pp. 165–72.

himself. I could have, therefore, gone on from the preceding paragraph to set out my own scheme for re-problematizing the issue of secularism in India, without making this gesture towards Foucault. The reason I think the reference is necessary, however, is that by invoking Foucault I will be better able to emphasize the need to shift our focus from the rigid framework laid out by the concepts of sovereignty and right, to the constantly shifting *strategic* locations of the politics of identity and difference.

Foucault's idea of governmentality reminds us, first, that cutting across the liberal divide between state and civil society there is a very specific form of power that entrenches itself in modern society, having as its goal the well being of a population, its mode of reasoning a certain instrumental notion of economy, and its apparatus an elaborate network of surveillance.[28] True, there have been other attempts at conceptualizing this ubiquitous form of modern power: most notably in Max Weber's theory of rationalization and bureaucracy, or more recently in the writings of the Frankfurt School, and in our own time in those of Jürgen Habermas. However, unlike Weberian sociology, Foucault's idea of governmentality does not lend itself to appropriation by a liberal doctrine characterizing the state as a domain of coercion ('monopoly of legitimate violence') and civil society as the zone of freedom. The idea of governmentality—and this is its second important feature—insists that by exercising itself through forms of representation, and hence by offering itself as an aspect of the self-disciplining of the very population over which it is exercised, the modern form of power, whether inside or outside the domain of the state, is capable of allowing for an immensely flexible braiding of coercion and consent.

If we bear in mind these features of the modern regime of power, it will be easier for us to grasp what is at stake in the politics of secularization. It is naive to think of secularization as simply the onward march of rationality, devoid of coercion and power struggles. Even if secularization as a process of the decreasing significance of religion in public life is connected with such 'objective' social processes as mechanization or the segmentation of social relationships (as sociologists

[28] See, in particular, Michel Foucault, 'Governmentality', in Graham Burchell, Colin Gordon, and Peter Miller, eds, *The Foucault Effect: Studies in Governmentality* (Chicago: University of Chicago Press, 1991), pp. 87–104; and 'Politics and Reason', in Foucault, *Politics, Philosophy, Culture: Interviews and Other Writings 1977–1984* (New York: Routledge, 1988), pp. 57–85.

such as Bryan Wilson have argued),[29] it does not necessarily evoke a uniform set of responses from all groups. Indeed, contrary phenomena such as religious revivalism, fundamentalism, and the rise of new cults have sometimes also been explained as the consequence of the same processes of mechanization or segmentation. Similarly, arguments about the need to hold on to a universalist framework of reason even as one acknowledges the fact of difference ('deliberative universalism' or 'discourse ethics') tend to sound like pious homilies because they ignore the strategic context of power in which identity or difference is often asserted.

The limit of liberal-rationalist theory is reached when one is forced to acknowledge that, within the specific strategic configuration of a power contestation, what is asserted in a collective cultural right is in fact *the right not to offer a reason for being different*. Thus, when a minority group demands a cultural right, it in fact says, 'We have our own reasons for doing things the way we do, but since you don't share the fundamentals of our worldview, you will never come to understand or appreciate those reasons. Therefore, leave us alone and let us mind our own business.' If this demand is admitted, it amounts in effect to a concession to cultural relativism.

But the matter does not necessarily end there. Foucault's notion of governmentality leads us to examine the other aspect of this strategic contestation. Why is the demand made in the language of rights? Why are the ideas of autonomy and freedom invoked? Even as one asserts a basic incommensurability in frameworks of reason, why does one nevertheless say, 'We have our own reasons'?

Consider then the two aspects of the process that Foucault describes as the 'governmentalization of the state': juridical sovereignty on the one hand, governmental technology on the other. In his account of this process in Western Europe since the eighteenth century, Foucault tends to suggest that the second aspect completely envelops and contains the first.[30] That is to say, in distributing itself throughout the

---

[29] Bryan Wilson, *Religion in Secular Society* (London: Watts, 1966); idem, *Religion in Sociological Perspective* (Oxford: Oxford University Press, 1982). Also, David Martin, *A General Theory of Secularization* (Oxford: Basil Blackwell, 1978).

[30] 'Maybe what is really important for our modernity—that is, for our present— is not so much the *étatisation* of society, as the "governmentalization" of the state . . . This governmentalization of the state is a singularly paradoxical phenomenon, since if in fact the problems of governmentality and the techniques of government have

social body by means of the technologies of governmental power, the modern regime no longer retains a distinct aspect of sovereignty. I do not think, however, that this is a necessary implication of Foucault's argument. On the contrary, I find it more useful—especially of course in situations where the sway of governmental power is far from general—to look for a disjuncture between the two aspects, and thus to identify the sites of application of power where governmentality is unable to successfully encompass sovereignty.

The assertion of minority cultural rights occurs on precisely such a site. It is because of a contestation on the ground of sovereignty that the right is asserted *against governmentality*. To say 'We will not give reasons for not being like you' is to resist entering that deliberative or discursive space where the technologies of governmentality operate. But then, in a situation like this, the only way to resist submitting to the powers of sovereignty is literally to declare oneself unreasonable.

Toleration and Democracy

It is necessary for me to clarify here that in what follows I will be concerned exclusively with finding a defensible argument for minority cultural rights in the given legal–political situation prevailing in India. I am not therefore proposing an abstract institutional scheme for the protection of minority rights in general. Nor will I be concerned with hypothetical questions such as: 'If your proposal is put into practice, what will happen to national unity?' I am not arguing from the position of the state; consequently, the problem as I see it is not what the state, or those who think and act on behalf of the state, can grant to the minorities. My problem is to find a defensible ground for a strategic politics, both within and outside the field defined by institutions of the state, in which a minority group, or one who is prepared to think from the position of a minority group, can engage in India today.

When a group asserts a right against governmentality, i.e. a right not to offer reasons for being different, can it expect others to respect its

---

become the only political issue, the only real space for political struggle and contestation, this is because the governmentalization of the state is at the same time what has permitted the state to survive, and it is possible to suppose that if the state is what it is today, this is so precisely thanks to this governmentality, which is at once internal and external to the state. . . .': Foucault, 'Governmentality', p. 103.

230 *Empire and Nation: Essential Writings 1985–2005*

autonomy and be tolerant of its 'unreasonable' ways? The liberal understanding of toleration will have serious problems with such a request. If toleration is the willing acceptance of something of which one disapproves, then it is usually justified on one of three grounds: a contractualist argument (persons entering into the social contract cannot know beforehand which religion they will end up having, and hence will agree to mutual toleration);[31] a consequentialist argument (the consequences of acting tolerantly are better than those of acting intolerantly);[32] or an argument about respect for persons.[33] We have already pointed out the inappropriateness of a contractualist solution to the problems posed by the Indian situation. The consequentialist argument is precisely what is used when it is said that one must go slow on the uniform civil code. But this is only a pragmatic argument for toleration, based on a tactical consideration about the costs of imposing what is otherwise the right thing to do. As such, it always remains vulnerable to righteous moral attack. The principle of respect for persons does provide a moral argument for toleration. It acknowledges the right of the tolerated, and construes toleration as something that can be claimed as an entitlement. It also sets limits to toleration and thereby resolves the problem of justifying something of which one disapproves: toleration is required by the principle of respect for persons, but practices which fail to show respect for persons need not be tolerated. Applying this principle to the case of minority cultural rights, one can easily see where the difficulty will arise. If a group is intolerant towards its own members and shows inadequate respect for persons, how can it claim tolerance from others? If indeed the group chooses not to enter into a reasonable dialogue with others on the validity of its practices, how can it claim respect for its ways?

Once again, I think that the strategic location of the contestation over cultural rights is crucial. The assertion of a right to be different does not exhaust all of the points where the contestation is grounded. Equally important is the other half of the assertion: 'We have our own

[31] The best-known such argument is in John Rawls, *A Theory of Justice* (London: Oxford University Press, 1971), pp. 205–21.

[32] See, for instance, Preston King, *Toleration* (London: George Allen and Unwin, 1976); D.D. Raphael, 'The Intolerable', in Susan Mendus, ed., *Justifying Toleration: Conceptual and Historical Perspectives* (Cambridge: Cambridge University Press, 1988), pp. 137–53.

[33] For instance, Joseph Raz, 'Autonomy, Toleration and the Harm Principle', in Mendus, ed., *Justifying Toleration*, pp. 155–75.

reasons for doing things the way we do.' This implies the existence of a field of reasons, of processes through which reasons can be exchanged and validated, even if such processes are open only to those who share the viewpoint of the group. The existence of this autonomous discursive field may only be implied and not activated, but the implication is a necessary part of the assertion of cultural autonomy as a matter *of right*.[34]

The liberal doctrine tends to treat the question of collective rights of cultural minorities from a position of externality. Thus, its usual stand on tolerating cultural groups with illiberal practices is to advocate some sort of right of exit for individual dissident members. (One is reminded of the insistence of the liberal Jinnah that not all sections of the Shari'at Bill should apply compulsorily to all Muslims.) The argument I am advancing would, however, give a very different construction to the concept of toleration. Toleration here would require one to accept that there will be political contexts where a group could insist on its right not to give reasons for doing things differently, provided it explains itself adequately in its own chosen forum. In other words, toleration here would be premised on autonomy and respect for persons, but it would be sensitive to the varying political salience of the institutional contexts in which reasons are debated.

To return to the specificities of the Indian situation, then, my approach would not call for any axiomatic approval to a uniform civil code for all citizens. Rather, it would start from the historically given reality of separate religion-based personal laws and the intricate involvement of state agencies in the affairs of religious institutions. Here, equal citizenship already stands qualified by the legal recognition of religious differences; the 'wall of separation' doctrine cannot be strictly applied either. Given the inapplicability of the neutrality principle, therefore, it becomes necessary to find a criterion by which state

[34] In some ways, this is the obverse of the implication which Ashis Nandy derives from his Gandhian conception of tolerance. His 'religious' conception of tolerance 'must impute to other faiths the same spirit of tolerance. Whether a large enough proportion of those belonging to the other religious traditions show in practice and at a particular point of time and place the same tolerance or not is a secondary matter. Because it is the imputation or presumption of tolerance in others, not its existence, which defines one's own tolerance . . .' Nandy, 'The Politics of Secularism'. My search is in the other direction. I am looking for a 'political' conception of tolerance which will set out the practical conditions I must meet in order to demand and expect tolerance from others.

involvement, when it occurs in the domain of religion, can appear to the members of a religious group as both legitimate and fair. It seems to me that toleration, as described above, can supply us with this criterion.

Let us construct an argument for someone who is prepared to defend the cultural rights of minority religious groups in India. The 'minority group', she will say, is not the invention of some perverse sectarian imagination: it is an actually existing category of Indian citizenship—constitutionally defined, legally administered, and politically invoked at every opportunity. Some people in India happen to be born into minority groups; a few others choose to enter them by conversion. In either case, many aspects of the status of such people as legal and political subjects are defined by the fact that they belong to minority groups. If there is any perversity in this, our advocate will point out, it lies in the specific compulsion of the history of the Indian state and its nationalist politics. That being so, one could not fairly be asked to simply forget one's status as belonging to a minority. What must be conceded instead is one's right to negotiate that status in the public arena.

Addressing the general body of citizens from her position within the minority group, then, our advocate will demand toleration for the beliefs of the group. On the other hand, addressing other members of her group, she will demand that the group publicly seek and obtain from its members consent for its practices, insofar as those practices have regulative power over the members. She will point out that if the group was to demand and expect toleration from others, it would have to satisfy the condition of representativeness. Our advocate will therefore demand more open and democratic debate within her community. Even if it is true, she will say, that the validity of the practices of the religious group can be discussed and judged only in its own forums, those institutions must satisfy the same criteria of publicity and representativeness that members of the group demand of all public institutions having regulatory functions. That, she will insist, is a necessary implication of engaging in the politics of collective rights.

She will not of course claim to have a blueprint of the form of representative institutions which her community might develop, and she will certainly resist any attempt by the state to legislate into existence representative bodies for minority groups as prerequisites for the protection of minority rights. The appropriate representative bodies, she will know, could only achieve their actual form through a political process carried out primarily within each minority group. But by resisting, on the one hand, the normalizing attempt of the national state to define, classify, and fix the identity of minorities on their behalf (the minorities, while constituting a legally distinct category of citizens, can only be acted upon by the general body of citizens; they cannot represent themselves), and demanding, on the other, that regulative powers within the community be established on a more democratic and internally representative basis, our protagonist will try to engage in a strategic politics that is neither integrationist nor separatist. She will in fact locate herself precisely at that cusp where she can face, on the one side, the assimilationist powers of governmental technology and resist, on the grounds of autonomy and self-representation, its universalist idea of citizenship; and, on the other side, struggle, once again on the grounds of autonomy and self-representation, for the emergence of more representative public institutions and practices within her community.

Needless to say, there will be many objections to her politics, even from her own comrades. Would not her disavowal of the idea of universal citizenship mean a splitting up of national society into mutually exclusive and rigidly separated ethnic groups? To this question, our protagonist could give the abstract answer that universal citizenship is merely the form offered by the bourgeois-liberal state to ensure the legal-political conditions for the deployment and exploitation of differences in civil society; universal citizenship normalizes the reproduction of differences by pretending that everyone is the same. More concretely, she could point out that nowhere has the sway of universal citizenship meant the end of either ethnic difference or discrimination on cultural grounds. The lines of difference and discrimination dissolve at some points, only to reappear at others. What is problematic here is not so much the existence of bounded categories of population, which the classificatory devices of modern governmental technologies will inevitably impose, but rather the inability of people to negotiate, through a continuous and democratic process of self-representation, the actual content of those categories. That is the new politics that one must try to initiate within the old forms of the modern state.

She will also be asked whether, by discounting universal citizenship, she is not throwing away the possibility of using the emancipatory potential of the ideas of liberty and equality. After all, does not the liberal-secular idea of equal rights still hold out the most powerful ideological means to fight against unjust and often tyrannical practices within many religious communities, especially regarding the treatment of women? To this, the answer will be that it is not a choice of one or the other. To pursue a strategic politics of demanding toleration, one would not need to oppose the liberal-secular principles of the modern state. One would, however, need to rearrange one's strategic priorities. One would be rather more sceptical of the promise that an interventionist secular state would, by legislation or judicial decisions, bring about progressive reform within minority religious groups. Instead, one would tend to favour the harder option, which rests on the belief that if the struggle is for progressive change in social practices sanctioned by religion, then that struggle must be launched and won within the religious communities themselves. There are no historical shortcuts here.

A strategic politics of demanding toleration does not require one to regurgitate the tired slogans about the universality of discursive reason. Instead, it takes seriously the possibility that at particular conjunctures and on specific issues there could occur an honest refusal to engage in reasonable discourse. But it does not, for that reason, need to fully subscribe to a theory of cultural relativism. Indeed, it could claim to be agnostic in this matter. All it needs to do is to locate itself at those specific points where universal discourse is resisted (remembering that those points could not exhaust the whole field of politics: e.g. those who will refuse to discuss their rules of marriage or inheritance in a general legislative body might be perfectly willing to debate in that forum the rates of income tax or the policy of public health); and then engage in a twofold struggle—resist homogenization from the outside, and push for democratization inside. That, in brief, would be a strategic politics of toleration.

Contrary to the apprehensions of many who think of minority religious groups as inherently authoritarian and opposed to the democratization of their religious institutions, it is unlikely, I think, that the principal impediment to the opening of such processes within the religious communities will come from the minority groups themselves. There is considerable historical evidence to suggest that when collective cultural rights have been asserted on behalf of minority religious groups in India, they have often been backed by the claim of popular consent through democratic processes. Thus, the campaign in the

1920s for reform in the management of Sikh gurdwaras was accompanied by the Akali demand that Sikh shrines and religious establishments be handed over to elected bodies. Indeed, the campaign was successful in forcing a reluctant colonial government to provide, in the Sikh Gurdwaras and Shrines Bill 1925, for a committee elected by all adult Sikhs, men and women, to take over the management of Sikh religious places.[35] The Shiromani Gurdwara Prabandhak Committee (SGPC) was perhaps the first legally constituted public body in colonial India for which the principle of universal suffrage was recognized. It is also important to note that the so-called 'traditional' ulema in India, when campaigning in the 1920s for the reform of Muslim religious institutions, demanded from the colonial government that officially appointed bodies such as Wakf committees be replaced by representative bodies elected by local Muslims.[36] The persuasive force of the claim for representativeness is often irresistible in the politics of collective rights.

The more serious opposition to this proposal is likely to come from those who will see in the representative public institutions of the religious communities a threat to the sovereign powers of the state. If such institutions are to be given any role in the regulation of the lives and activities of its members, then their very stature as elected bodies representative of their constituents will be construed as diminishing the sovereignty of the state. I can hear the murmurs already: 'Remember how the SGPC was used to provide legitimacy to Sikh separatism? Imagine what will happen if Muslims get their own parliament!' The deadweight of juridical sovereignty cannot be easily pushed aside even by those who otherwise subscribe to ideas of autonomy and self-regulating civil social institutions.

I do not, therefore, make these proposals for a reconfiguration of the problem of secularism in India and a redefinition of the concept of toleration with any degree of optimism. All I can hope for is that, faced with a potentially disastrous political impasse, some at least will prefer to err on the side of democracy.

---

[35] For this history, see Mohinder Singh, *The Akali Movement* (Delhi: Macmillan, 1978).

[36] Tahir Mahmood, *Muslim Personal Law*, pp. 66–7.

13

Satanic? Or the Surrender of the Modern?
(1988)

Is the Government of India seeking directly to interfere with the right of free speech? Is it trying to control what will be written and what will be read? Is it trying to create a climate where no uncomfortable question or dangerous thought will raise its head?

On the face of it, this must be the explanation behind the decision by the government to ban Salman Rushdie's novel. The book was banned as soon as it was published, before most people had a chance to read it. In other words, even before its literary or other qualities could be judged, an executive fiat declared the book unfit to be bought or read. If this decision is accepted without protest, it will be tantamount to a death warrant on artists, writers, and scientists in this country.

Who decides on the quality of a serious literary work? Who is to pronounce judgement on a writer's social or political views? The literary readership, or a political leader or bureaucrat? By banning *The Satanic Verses* the Government of India has declared that if there is sufficient political opposition, a literary work, irrespective of its artistic merits, will not reach its intended readership.

The menace contained in this move hardly requires explication. Yet, this virtual truism now has to be stated afresh. This is because the principal argument that is being offered in support of the government's decision is political realism. It is the old argument about a situation of emergency: the times are dangerous, there are too many risks of

Anandabajar Patrika, 27 October 1988 (translated from the Bengali).

violence. At such times, one must above all be practical. There will be occasions in future for the pure contemplation of moral principles; now, one must tackle the immediate situation, if necessary even by conceding a little bit to the enemy. Those journalists—official hacks—who only a few days ago were forced to shut up when faced with the storm of protest over the Defamation Bill, are now declaiming on the principles of political realism. And listening to these lectures on the intricate methods of determining the volatility of a political situation, even many of the progressives have been left without an answer. Publicly, they are silent about the ban; in private, they will confess their anxieties: 'You never know, these communal matters are highly inflammable. It's best to stay out of them.'

The ban is not part of a planned authoritarian assault. It is the sign of extreme insecurity, when rulers appeal to realism and practicality to cover up their weakness. This politics of immediate solutions to immediate problems is shortsighted and vacuous, and more dangerous because it would have everyone ignore the consequences. It is being argued that if Rushdie's book had been allowed to be sold, there would have been riots. Interestingly, none of those who demanded the ban or imposed it had read the book. Syed Shahabuddin has made the weighty pronouncement that to tell that a drain is a drain, one does not need to jump into it. In his case, of course, the task was simple. He had heard it being said: 'Here is a drain.' Where did he hear it? From some time before *The Satanic Verses* was actually published, there were stories about it in the papers. Not literary reviews, but news stories: that is to say, sensational speculations, half-truths, and assorted misrepresentations. That was sufficient grist to Shahabuddin's mill. His politics consists of sniffing around for drains. As soon as he finds one, he shouts: 'There it is, it's polluting everything. Clean it up.' Looking for impurities and cleaning them up: that is the politics of fundamentalism. No matter what the religion or ideology, it thrives on an obsessive and intolerant search for polluting influences. Shahabuddin needed a drain; he found it. If it hadn't been this one, he would have found something else. The cry went up immediately: 'We will not tolerate this satanic conspiracy. Ban the book.' The demand found a few supporters from among that group whose only identity in democratic India is that of being 'secular Muslims'. 'Secular', and hence part of the so-called nationalist mainstream, yet 'Muslim', and hence different. They have tried all these years to keep their distinct identity intact while swimming with the mainstream—with pathetic results. Of course, being the trusted advisers of the government on Muslim matters, their sense of political realism is especially sharp. They were the ones who persuaded the government that the communal situation in northern India was so serious that with the impending general elections, etc., etc. . . .

I have read *The Satanic Verses*. I was fortunate in having bought a copy soon after the book appeared, not knowing at that time, of course, that it would be banned the next day. Having begun reading it, I could not put it down. I pushed aside all other work and read the book at a stretch over three days. Soon, I will read it once more. A narrative that is meticulously crafted, that shows unparalleled skills in the use of language, that has a complex structure, that does not sweep one away in a flood of emotion but ignites one's intelligence, that conceals at every turn the possibility of discovering some unexpected meaning: I like reading books such as this. Needless to say, the work of an author like Rushdie, steeped in the traditions of Western literary modernism and with skills virtually unsurpassed today in the innovative use of English prose, is exceedingly sophisticated. Woven into the dramatic twists and turns of the narrative is Rushdie's running conversation with other authors—comments, debates with Goethe, Dickens, Tolstoy, Joyce, Brecht, Borges, Márquez: I am sure I will notice many more when I read the book again. This is a serious book written with much effort and care: it deserves care and effort on the part of the reader.

Those who say that the book is meant to defame Prophet Muhammad are either lying (because they have not read the book), or they are being deceitful, or else they are plain ignorant. The subject of the novel is not the life of Prophet Muhammad; the subject is Salman Rushdie himself. One of the two principal characters of the story is Saladin Chamchawalla. Born in Bombay, his nationalist Congress-supporting father, like many others of his generation, believed that now that the sahibs had left, his son would become a sahib and run the country. The boy Saladin was sent off to England, to study in the sahibs' school. His effort to become a sahib was earnest. He thought he would churn the ocean of European civilization and drink the pure nectar of freethinking modernity, and in the process wipe out his inherited marks of race, nationality and culture. The other character is Gibreel Farishta. He is a superstar, known all over India for his roles in blockbuster mythologicals. He is in love with the good life, with luxury and modern technology, addicted in equal measure to Scotch whisky and the company of white women. But his words are pure swadeshi, reflecting his unshakeable conviction about the decay and imminent destruction of a shallow, materialistic, spiritually vacuous Western civilization.

Gibreel and Saladin are two sides of the same self—two sides of Indian modernity, the one inseparable from the other. Suddenly, by a stroke of providence, Gibreel acquires the powers of an angel, while the hapless Saladin becomes the embodiment of Satan. Now, Saladin is made to see through the façade of British liberalism and discover the reality of racial discrimination in the land of his dreams. He sees that in London neighbourhoods torn by race riots, he is just one of a thousand other Indians, Pakistanis, Bangladeshis, Caribbeans. And Gibreel? He decides to take his new role as an angel seriously. He proceeds to redeem Western society from its million sins. Gibreel, angel of god, is slowly transformed into Azreel, the angel of death. In his mad desire to purify the world, he ignites a devastating fire of violence, hatred, and destruction.

Needless to say, this is not the whole story of *The Satanic Verses*. It is narrative that sustains this massive book of 547 pages, and even two long paragraphs cannot provide a summary. The section that has caused such an uproar actually occupies a small portion of the book. Both Gibreel and Saladin are Muslim. Having been reborn, they ask themselves, 'What is religion? What is truth? What is the good?' Buried for so long under the layers of their consciousness, the words of the Koran are now interrogated afresh. If the Mahound described in this novel is the Prophet Muhammad, I have to say that in Rushdie's telling of his story he appears as a political figure of immense nobility: noble, but human, tortured by doubt, uncertain about the complex claims of right and wrong, courageous enough to admit his mistakes. The twelve prostitutes over whom there is so much protest are, in the novel, hardly the 'wives' of the Mahound; they are just prostitutes. It is the vengeful Salman Farsi and the poet Baal who, seeking to bring Muhammad to disrepute, spread the rumour that they might be the wives of the Prophet. And of course, it is the madam of the brothel who seeks to make a little business out of religion. Mahound, who is otherwise forgiving even in his moment of triumph, cannot forgive these transgressors. Waiting for his execution, Baal, the eternal unbeliever (one can hardly fail to recognize here the hero of Brecht's first play), says to Muhammad: 'Whores and writers. We are the people you can't forgive.' Muhammad replies, 'Writers and whores. I see no difference here.'

The Satanic Verses is a story of the contradictions, anxieties, and crisis of a rationalist consciousness in independent India. This consciousness is touched by the magical certainty of folk belief, but it can never accept folk religion as its own. (One can hear Rushdie's debate with Márquez on this subject.) The days of divine revelation are past. Whether awake or in our dreams, never again will we hear another prophet. At least, not unless we deceive ourselves. And if we do, there are two choices. We could, like Saladin Chamcha, shut our eyes and say, 'It's fine the way it is, don't upset things too much.' This is the deception of political realism. Or else, we could make a prophetic declaration that the world will have to be cleansed of the pollution of evil, and like Gibreel Farishta, send thousands of innocent people to their doom. This is the deception of fundamentalism. Two sides of the same self: the two sides of Indian modernity, the one inseparable from the other.

I have heard a few 'secular Muslims' complaining about why the minorities were being singled out as overly sensitive. If a book like this had been written about Hinduism, they ask, would Hindus have tolerated it? The complaint is justified. Among the frightened and cowardly adherents of modernity in India, there are no differences between Hindus and Muslims. If today, a man called Michael Madhusudan Dutt were to write a book called *Meghnadbadh* and declare, 'I despise Rama and his rabble', I have no doubt the book would be proscribed. It is the good fortune of Bengali literature that the colonial state of the nineteenth century banned books only when they went against colonial interests, and not at the request of their native subjects.

14

Development Planning and the Indian State

(1994)

Although it is a virtual truism that the state is the central actor in any programme for planned economic development, its role in planning is not for that reason any less problematic. What does it mean to say that 'the state' acts? Does it act on its own? Do others act through it? Who does it act upon? On other entities outside the state? Or does it act upon itself? To talk about the state as an 'actor' is to endow it with a will; to say that is acts according to coherent and rational principles of choice is further to endow it with a consciousness. How is this will and consciousness produced?

These are not, one would presumably agree, questions with which the economic literature on planning has concerned itself. For the most part, that literature has taken what it calls 'socio-political conditions' as parametric for its exercise. What the state thinks as politically necessary or feasible is 'given' to the planner; it is determined by a process of politics that is extraneous to the planning exercise *per se*. The task of the planner is to work out the consistencies between different objectives, weigh the costs and benefits of different alternatives, and suggest an efficient or optimal mix of strategies. Planning, many would say, is an exercise in instrumental rationality. And yet, it is curious that when debates about planning have led to fundamental disagreements within the discipline, economists have not managed to hold themselves back from arguing about the relative priorities among 'socio-political' objectives or about their political feasibility and have defended or attacked particular planning strategies by appealing to considerations that are presumably external to their practice.

As someone whose professional preoccupation is to marvel at the ways in which logic becomes perpetually implicated in rhetoric, knowledge in power, I am not surprised by this transgression of avowed disciplinary boundaries.[1] My own practice within my happily ill-defined discipline has taught me (notwithstanding the fact that some of my colleagues still go on pretending that they can usefully do for politics what the economists have done for the economy: may they remain at peace with their intellects!) that not only are instruments chosen according to goals that are desired, but goals themselves are very often fixed because certain instruments have to be used. Indeed, instruments in politics can become goals in themselves, just as the very declaration of an objective can become an instrument for something else. The once-fashionable debate about the separability of means and ends was, as far as I can understand it, only another way of establishing their unity. To me, then, the interesting question is not whether the idea of a domain of instrumental rationality clearly demarcated from the disorderly terrain of political squabble can be logically sustained. Rather, the interesting question is how this very assertion of a technical discipline of planning can become an instrument of politics, i.e. of the exercise and contestation of power.

I will address my question directly to the experience of Indian planning. But in order to do that, let me begin with a bit of history.

Planning for Planning[2]

In August 1937 the Congress Working Committee at its meeting in Wardha adopted a resolution recommending 'to the Congress Ministries the appointment of a Committee of experts to consider urgent and vital problems the solution of which is necessary to any scheme of national reconstruction and social planning. Such solution will require extensive survey and the collection of data, as well as a clearly defined social objective.' The immediate background to this resolution was the formation by the Congress, under the new constitutional arrangements,

---

[1] I am grateful to Asok Sen, Gautam Sen, the participants of the London conference, and my colleagues in the Kankurgachhi Hegel Club for their comments on earlier drafts of this essay.

[2] This section is largely based on Raghabendra Chattopadhyay, 'The Idea of Planning in India, 1930–1951', unpublished Ph.D. thesis, Australian National University, Canberra, 1985, pp. 82–127.

of ministries in six (later eight) provinces of India and the questions raised, especially by the Gandhians (including Gandhi himself), about the responsibility of the Congress in regulating (more precisely, restricting) the growth of modern industries. The Left within the Congress, including its two stalwarts, Jawaharlal Nehru and Subhas Chandra Bose, sought to put aside this nagging ideological debate by arguing that the whole question of Congress policy towards industries must be resolved within the framework of an 'all-India industrial plan' which this committee of experts would be asked to draw up. Accordingly, Bose in his presidential speech at the Haripura Congress in February 1938 declared that the national state 'on the advice of a Planning Commission' would adopt 'a comprehensive scheme for gradually socializing our entire agricultural and industrial system in the sphere of both production and appropriation.' In October that year Bose summoned a conference of the ministers of industries in the Congress ministries and soon after announced the formation of a National Planning Committee with Nehru as chairman. Of the fifteen members of the committee, four (Purushottamdas Thakurdas, A.D. Shroff, Ambalal Sarabhai, and Walchand Hirachand) were leading merchants and industrialists; five were scientists (Meghnad Saha, A.K. Saha, Nazir Ahmed, V.S. Dubey, and J.C. Ghosh); two were economists (K.T. Shah and Radhakamal Mukherjee)—or rather three, if we include M. Visvesvaraya who had just written a book on planning; and three had been invited on their political credentials—J.C. Kumarappa the Gandhian, N.M. Joshi the labour leader, and Nehru himself. The committee began work in December 1938.

The National Planning Committee, whose actual work virtually ceased after about a year and a half following the outbreak of the war, the resignation of the Congress ministries, and finally Nehru's arrest in October 1940, was nevertheless the first real experience of the emerging state leadership of the Congress, and of Nehru in particular, with working out the idea of 'national planning'. Before making a brief mention of the actual contents of the discussions in that committee, let us take note of the most significant aspects of the form of this exercise.

First, planning appears as a form of determining *state* policy, initially the economic policies of the provincial Congress ministries, but almost immediately afterwards the overall framework of a co-ordinated and consistent set of policies of a national state that was already being envisioned as a concrete idea. In this respect, planning was not only a part of the anticipation of power by the state leadership of the Congress, it was also an anticipation of the concrete forms in which that power would be exercised within a national state. Second, planning as an exercise in state policy already incorporated its most distinctive element: its constitution as a body of *experts* and its activity as one of the technical evaluation of alternative policies and the determination of choices on 'scientific' grounds. Nehru, writing in 1944-5, mentioned this as a memorable part of his experience with the NPC: 'We had avoided a theoretical approach, and as each particular problem was viewed in its larger context, it led us inevitably in a particular direction. To me the spirit of co-operation of the members of the Planning Committee was particularly soothing and gratifying, for I found it a pleasant contrast to the squabbles and conflicts of politics.'[3] Third, the appeal to a 'committee of experts' was in itself an important instrument in resolving a political debate which, much to the irritation of the emerging state leadership of the Congress, was still refusing to go away. This leadership, along with the vast majority of the professional intelligentsia of India, had little doubt about the central importance of industrialization for the development of a modern and prosperous nation. Yet the very political strategy of building up a mass movement against colonial rule had required the Congress to espouse Gandhi's idea of machinery, commercialization, and centralized state power as the curses of modern civilization, thrust upon the Indian people by European colonialism. It was industrialism itself, Gandhi argued, rather than the inability to industrialize which was the root cause of Indian poverty. This was, until the 1940s, a characteristic part of the Congress rhetoric of nationalist mobilization. But now that the new national state was ready to be conceptualized in concrete terms, this archaic ideological baggage had to be jettisoned. J.C. Kumarappa brought the very first session of the NPC to an impasse by questioning its authority to discuss plans for industrialization. The national priority as adopted by the Congress, he said, was to restrict and eliminate modern industrialism. Nehru had to intervene and declare that most members of the committee felt that large-scale industry ought to be promoted as long as it did not 'come into conflict with the cottage industries'. Emphasizing the changed political context in which the Congress was working, Nehru added significantly: 'Now that the

---

[3] Jawaharlal Nehru, *Jawaharlal Nehru's Speeches*, vol. 2 (New Delhi: 1954), p. 405.

Congress is, to some extent, identifying itself with the State it cannot ignore the question of establishing and encouraging large-scale industries. There can be no planning if such planning does not include big industries . . . [and] it is not only within the scope of the Committee to consider large-scale industries, but it is incumbent upon it to consider them.'

Kumarappa kept up his futile effort for a while after virtually every other member disagreed with his view and finally dropped out. Gandhi himself did not appreciate the efforts of the NPC, or perhaps he appreciated them only too well. 'I do not know', he wrote to Nehru, 'that it is working within the four corners of the resolution creating the Committee. I do not know that the Working Committee is being kept informed of its doings . . . It has appeared to me that much money and labour are being wasted on an effort which will bring forth little or no fruit.'[4] Nehru in turn did not conceal his impatience with such 'visionary' and 'unscientific' talk and grounded his own position quite firmly on the universal principles of historical progress: 'We are trying to catch up, as far as we can, with the Industrial Revolution that occurred long ago in Western countries.'[5]

The point here is not so much whether the Gandhian position had already been rendered politically unviable, so that we can declare the overwhelming consensus on industrialization within the NPC as the 'reflection' of an assignment of priorities already determined in the political arena outside. Rather, the very institution of a process of planning became a means for the determination of priorities on behalf of the 'nation'. The debate on the need for industrialization, we may say, was politically resolved by successfully constituting planning as a domain outside 'the squabbles and conflicts of politics'. As early as the 1940s, planning had emerged as a crucial institutional modality by which the state would determine the material allocation of productive resources within the nation: a modality of political power constituted outside the immediate political process itself.

The Rationality of the New State

Why was it necessary to devise such a modality of power that could operate both inside and outside the political structure constructed by

[4] M.K. Gandhi, *Collected Works*, vol. 70 (New Delhi: 1958), p. 56.
[5] Nehru, *Speeches*, vol. 2, p. 93.

the new post-colonial state? An answer begins to appear as soon as we discover the logic by which the new state related itself to the 'nation'. For the emerging state leadership (and as the bearer of a fundamental ideological orientation this group was much larger than simply a section of the leaders of the Congress, and in identifying it the usual classification of Left and Right is irrelevant), this relation was expressed in a quite distinctive way. By the 1940s the dominant argument of nationalism against colonial rule was that it was impeding the further development of India: colonial rule had become a historical fetter that had to be removed before the nation could proceed to develop. Within this framework, therefore, the economic critique of colonialism as an exploitative force creating and perpetuating a backward economy came to occupy a central place. One might ask what would happen to this nationalist position if (let us say, for the sake of argument) it turned out from historical investigation that by every agreed criterion foreign rule had indeed promoted economic development in the colony. Would that have made colonialism any more legitimate or the demand for national self-government any less justified? Our nationalist would not have accepted a purely negative critique of colonial rule as sufficient and would have been embarrassed if the demand for self-rule was sought to be filled in by some primordial content such as race or religion. Colonial rule, he would have said, was illegitimate not because it represented the political domination by an alien people over the indigenes: alienness had acquired the stamp of illegitimacy because it stood for a form of *exploitation* of the nation (the drain of national wealth, the destruction of its productive system, the creation of a backward economy, etc.). Self-government consequently was legitimate because it represented the historically necessary form of national development. The economic critique of colonialism then was the foundation from which a positive content was supplied for the independent national state: the new state represented the only legitimate form of exercise of power because it was a necessary condition for the development of the nation.

A developmental ideology then was a constituent part of the self-definition of the post-colonial state. The state was connected to the people-nation not simply through the procedural forms of representative government, it also acquired its representativeness by directing a programme of economic development on behalf of the nation. The former connected, as in any liberal form of government, the legal-political sovereignty of the state with the sovereignty of the people. The latter connected the sovereign powers of the state directly with the economic well being of the people. The two connections did not necessarily have the same implications for a state trying to determine how to use its sovereign powers. What the people were able to express through the representative mechanisms of the political process as their will was not necessarily what was good for their economic well being; what the state thought important for the economic development of the nation was not necessarily what would be ratified through the representative mechanisms. The two criteria of representativeness, and hence of legitimacy, could well produce contradictory implications for state policy.

The contradiction stemmed from the very manner in which a developmental ideology needed to cling to the state as the principal vehicle for its historical mission. 'Development' implied a linear path, directed towards a goal, or a series of goals separated by stages. It implied the fixing of priorities between long-run and short-run goals and conscious choice between alternative paths. It was premised, in other words, upon a *rational* consciousness and will, and, insofar as 'development' was thought of as a process affecting the whole of society, it was also premised upon *one* consciousness and will—that of the whole. Particular interests needed to be subsumed within the whole and made consistent with the general interest. The mechanisms of civil society, working through contracts and the market, and hence defining a domain for the play of the particular and the accidental, were already known to be imperfect instruments for expressing the general. The one consciousness, both general and rational, could not simply be assumed to exist as an abstract and formless force, working implicitly and invisibly through the particular interests of civil society. It had, as Hegel would have said, to 'shine forth', appear as an existent, concretely expressing the general and the rational.

Hegel's penetrating logic has shown us that this universal rationality of the state can be concretely expressed at two institutional levels—the bureaucracy as the universal class and the monarch as the immediately existent will of the state. The logical requirement of the latter was taken care of, even under the republican constitutional form adopted in India, by the usual provisions of embodying the sovereign will of the state in the person of the Head of State. In meeting the former requirement, however, the post-colonial state in India faced a problem that was produced specifically by the form of the transition from colonial rule. For various reasons that were attributed to political contingency (whose historical roots we need not explore here), the new state chose to retain in a virtually unaltered form the basic structure of the civil service, the police administration, the judicial system including the codes of civil and criminal law, and the armed forces as they existed in the colonial period. As far as the normal executive functions of the state were concerned, the new state operated within a framework of rational universality whose principles were seen as having been contained (even if they were misapplied) in the preceding state structure. In the case of the armed forces, the assertion of unbroken continuity was rather more paradoxical, so that even today one is forced to witness such un-lovely ironies as regiments of the Indian army proudly displaying the trophies of colonial conquest and counter-insurgency in their barrack-rooms, or the Presidential Guards celebrating their birth two hundred years ago under the governor-generalship of Lord Cornwallis! But if the ordinary functions of civil and criminal administration were to continue within forms of rationality which the new state had not given to itself, how was it to claim its legitimacy as an authority that was specifically different from the old regime? This legitimacy, as we have mentioned before, had to flow from the nationalist criticism of colonialism as an alien and unrepresentative power that was exploitative in character and from the historical necessity of an independent state that would promote national development. It was in the universal function of 'development' of national society as a whole that the post-colonial state would find its distinctive content. This was to be concretized by embodying within itself a new mechanism of developmental administration, something which the colonial state, because of its alien and extractive character, never possessed. It was in the administration of development that the bureaucracy of the post-colonial state was to assert itself as the universal class, satisfying in the service of the state its private interests by working for the universal goals of the nation.

Planning therefore was the domain of the rational determination and pursuit of these universal goals. It was a bureaucratic function, to be operated at a level above the particular interests of civil society, and institutionalized as such as a domain of policy-making outside the normal processes of representative politics and of execution through a developmental administration. But as a concrete bureaucratic function, it was in planning above all that the post-colonial state would claim its legitimacy as a single will and consciousness—the will of the nation—

pursuing a task that was both universal and rational—the well being of the people as a whole.

It is in its legitimizing role, therefore, that planning, constituted as a domain outside politics, was to become an instrument of politics. If we then look at the process of politics itself, we will discover the specific ways in which it would also become implicated in the modalities of power.

Planning and Implementing

We could first describe the political process in its own terms and then look for the connections with the process of planning. But this would take us into a lengthy excursion into a wholly different disciplinary field. Let us instead start with the received understanding of the planning experience in India and see how the political process comes to impinge upon it. Sukhamoy Chakravarty has given us a summary account of this experience from within the theoretical boundaries of development planning. From this perspective, the political process appears as a determinate and changing existent when the question arises of 'plan implementation'. Chakravarty discusses the problems of plan implementation by treating the 'planning authorities' as the central directing agency, firmly situated outside the political process itself and embodying, one might justifiably say, the single, universal and rational consciousness of a state which is promoting the development of the nation as a whole.[6] An implementational failure, Chakravarty says, occurs when (a) the planning authorities are inefficient in gathering the relevant information, (b) when they take so much time to respond that the underlying situation has by then changed, and (c) when the public agencies through which the plans are to be implemented do not have the capacities to carry them out and the private agencies combine in 'strategic' ways to disrupt the expectations about their behaviour which the planners had taken as 'parametric'. Chakravarty adds that the last possibility—that of strategic action by private actors—has greatly increased in recent years in the Indian economy.

Let us look a little more closely at this analysis. What does it mean to say that plans may fail because of the inadequacy of the information

---

[6] Sukhamoy Chakravarty, *Development Planning: The Indian Experience* (Oxford: Clarendon Press, 1987), pp. 40–2.

which planners use? The premise here is that of a separation between the planner on the one hand and the objects of planning on the other, the latter consisting of both physical resources and human economic agents. 'Information' is precisely the means through which the objects of planning are constituted for the planner: they exist 'out there', independently of his consciousness and can appear before it only in the shape of 'information'. The 'adequacy' of this information then concerns the question of whether these objects have been constituted 'correctly', i.e. constituted in the planner's consciousness in the same form as they exist outside it, in themselves. It is obvious that on these terms an entirely faultless planning would require in the planner nothing less than omniscience. But one should not use the patent impossibility of this project to turn planning into a caricature of itself. While the epistemological stance of apprehending the external objects of consciousness in their intrinsic and independent truth continues, as is well known, to inform the expressly declared philosophical foundations of the positive sciences, including economics, the actual practice of debates about planning is more concerned with those objects as they have been constituted by the planning exercise itself. Thus, if it is alleged that planners have incorrectly estimated the demand for electricity because they did not take into account the unorganized sector, the charge really is that whereas the 'unorganized sector' was already an object of planning since it was *known* that it too was a consumer of electricity, it had not been explicitly and specifically constituted as an object since its demand had not been estimated. The point about all questions of 'inadequate information' is not whether one knows what the objects of planning are: if they are not known the problem of information cannot arise. The question is whether they have been explicitly specified as objects of planning.

It is here that the issue of the modalities of knowledge and implementation become central to the planning exercise. All three conditions which Chakravarty mentions as leading to faulty implementation concern the ways in which the planner, representing the rational consciousness of the state, can produce a knowledge of the objects of planning. In this sense, even the so-called implementing agencies are the objects of planning for they represent not the will of the planner but determinate 'capacities': a plan which does not correctly estimate the capacities of the implementing agencies cannot be a good plan. Consequently, these agencies—bureaucrats or managers of public enterprises—become entities which act in determinate ways according to specific kinds of 'signals' and these the planner must know in order to formulate his plan. The planner even needs to know how long his own machinery will take to implement a plan, or else the information on the basis of which he plans may become obsolete.

If one is not to assume omniscience on behalf of the planner, how is this information ever expected to be 'adequate'? It is here that the rationality of planning can be seen to practise a self-deception—a necessary self-deception, for without it it could not constitute itself. Planning, as the concrete embodiment of the rational consciousness of a state promoting economic development, can proceed only by constituting the objects of planning as objects of knowledge. It must *know* the physical resources whose allocation is to be planned, it must *know* the economic agents who act upon these resources, *know* their needs, capacities and propensities, *know* what constitutes the signals according to which they act, *know* how they respond to those signals. When the agents relate to each other in terms of power, i.e. relations of domination and subordination, the planner must *know* the relevant signals and capacities. This knowledge would enable him to work upon the total configuration of power itself, use the legal powers of the state to produce signals and thereby affect the actions of agents, play off one power against another to produce a general result in which everybody would be better off. The state as a planning authority can promote the universal goal of development by harnessing within a single interconnected whole the discrete subjects of power in society; it does this by turning those subjects of power into the objects of a single body of knowledge.

This is where the self-deception occurs. For the rational consciousness of the state embodied in the planning authority does not exhaust the determinate being of the state. The state is also an existent—as a site at which the subjects of power in society interact, ally, and contend with one another in the political process. The specific configuration of power that is constituted within the state is the result of this process. Seen from this perspective, the planning authorities themselves are objects for a configuration of power in which others are subjects. Indeed, and this is the paradox which a 'science' of planning can never unravel from within its own disciplinary boundaries, the very subjects of social power which the rational consciousness of the planner seeks to convert into objects of its knowledge by attributing to them discrete capacities and propensities can turn the planning authority itself into an object of their power. Subject and object, inside and outside—the relations are reversed as soon as we move from the domain of rational planning, situated outside the political process, to the domain of social power exercised and contested within that process. When we talk of the state, we must talk of both these domains as its constituent fields, and situate one in relation to the other. Seen from the domain of planning, the political process is only an external constraint, whose strategic possibilities must be known and objectified as parameters for the planning exercise. And yet, even the best efforts to secure 'adequate information' leave behind an unestimated residue, which works imperceptibly and often perversely to upset the implementation of plans. This residue, as the irreducible, negative and ever-present 'beyond' of planning, is what we may call, in its most general sense, politics.

The Politics of Planning—I

Let us return to history, this time of more recent vintage. Chakravarty says that in the early 1950s, when the planning process was initiated in India, there was a general consensus on a 'commodity-centred' approach.[7] That is to say, everyone agreed that more goods were preferable to less goods and a higher level of capital stock per worker was necessary for an improved standard of living. Obviously, the central emphasis of development was meant to be placed on accumulation. But this was not all. Chakravarty also says that in the specific context in which planning was taken up in India, accumulation had to be reconciled with legitimation. 'Adoption of a representative form of government based on universal adult suffrage did have an effect on the exercise of political power, and so did the whole legacy of the national movement with its specifically articulated set of economic objectives.'[8] These two objectives—accumulation and legitimation—produced two implications for planning in India. On the one hand, planning had to be 'a way of avoiding the *unnecessary rigours* of an industrial transition in so far as it affected the masses resident in India's villages.' On the other hand, planning was to become 'a positive instrument for *resolving conflict* in a large and heterogeneous subcontinent' (emphases mine). What did these mean in terms of the relation between the state and the planning process?

[7] Ibid., p. 7.
[8] Ibid., pp. 2–3.

In the classical forms of capitalist industrialization, the original accumulation required the use of a variety of coercive methods to separate a large mass of direct producers from their means of production. This was the 'secret' of the so-called 'primitive accumulation', which was not the result of the capitalist mode of production but its starting point, and in a concrete historical process it meant 'the expropriation of the agricultural producer, of the peasant, from the soil.'[9] The possibility and limits of original accumulation were set by the specific configuration in each country of the political struggle between classes in the pre-capitalist social formation, but in each case a successful transition to capitalist industrialization required that subsistence producers be 'robbed of all their means of production and of all the guarantees of existence afforded by the old feudal arrangements.'[10] Whatever the political means adopted to effect this expropriation of direct producers, and with it the destruction of pre-capitalist forms of community concretely embodying the unity of producers with the means of production, they could not have been legitimized by any active principle of universal representative democracy. (It is curious that in the one country of Europe where a 'bourgeois' political revolution was carried out under the slogan of liberty, equality, and fraternity, the protection of small-peasant property after the revolution meant the virtual postponement of industrialization by some five or six decades.)

Once in place, accumulation under capitalist production proper could be made legitimate by the equal right of property and the universal freedom of contract on the basis of property rights over commodities. Original accumulation having already effected the separation of the direct producer from the means of production, labour power was now available as a commodity owned by the labourer who was entitled to sell it according to the terms of a free contract with the owner of the means of production. As a political ideology of legitimation of capitalist accumulation, this strictly liberal doctrine of 'freedom', however, enjoyed a surprisingly short life. But by the third and fourth decades of the nineteenth century, when the first phase of the Industrial Revolution had been completed in Britain, the new context of political

[9] Karl Marx, *Capital*, vol. 1, trans. Samuel Moore and Edward Aveling (Moscow: 1971), pp. 667–70.

[10] T.H. Aston and C.H.E. Philpin, eds, *The Brenner Debate: Agrarian Class Structure and Economic Development in Pre-Industrial Europe* (Cambridge: 1971), p. 1.

254	Empire and Nation: Essential Writings 1985–2005

conflict made it necessary to qualify 'freedom' by such notions as the rights to subsistence, proper conditions of work, and a decent livelihood. In time, this meant the use of the legal powers of the state to impose conditions on the freedom of contract (on hours of work, on minimum wages, on physical conditions of work and living) and to curtail the free enjoyment of returns from the productive use of property (most importantly by the taxation on higher incomes to finance public provisions for health, education, housing, etc.). While this may be seen as being consistent with the long-term objectives of capitalist accumulation, on the ground that it facilitated the continued reproduction of labour power of a suitable concretized quality, it must also be recognized that it was a political response to growing oppositional movements and social conflict. As a political doctrine of legitimation this meant, first, the creation of a general content for social good which combined capitalist property ownership with the production of consent through representative political processes; and second, the determination of this content not mediated through the particular acts of economic agents in civil society, but directly through the activities of the state. The course of this journey from the strictly liberal concept of 'freedom' to that of 'welfare' is, of course, coincidental with the political history of capitalist democracy in the last century and a half. What we need to note here is the fact that as a universal conception of the social whole under capitalist democracy, the elements of a concept of 'welfare' had already superseded those of pure freedom and were available to the political leadership in India when it began the task of constructing a state ideology.

The 'unnecessary rigours' of an industrial transition, consequently, meant those forms of expropriation of subsistence producers associated with original accumulation which could not be legitimized through the representative processes of politics. This was, our planner would say, a parametric condition set by the political process at the time when planning began its journey in India. Yet accumulation was the prime task if industrialization was to take place. Accumulation necessarily implied the use of the powers of the state, whether directly through its legal and administrative institutions, or mediated through the acts of some agents with social power over others, to effect the required degree of dissociation of direct producers from their means of production. As Chakravarty says, the development model first adopted in India was a variant of the Lewis model, with a 'modern' sector breaking down and superseding the 'traditional' sector, the two significant variations being that the modern sector itself was disaggregated into a capital goods and a consumer goods sector, and instead of capitalists in the modern sector the major role was assigned to a development bureaucracy.[11] Despite these variations, the chosen path of development still meant conflicts between social groups and the use of power to attain the required form and rate of accumulation. Since the 'necessary' policies of the state which would ensure accumulation could not be left to be determined solely through the political process, it devolved upon the institution of planning, that embodiment of the universal rationality of the social whole standing above all particular interests, to lay down what in fact were the 'necessary rigours' of industrialization. Given its location outside the political process, planning could then become 'a positive instrument for resolving conflict' by determining, within a universal framework of the social good, the 'necessary costs' to be borne by each particular group and the 'necessary benefits' to accrue to each. But who was to use it in this way as a 'positive instrument'? We have still to address this question.

The specific form in which this twin problem of planning—accumulation with legitimation—was initially resolved, especially in the Second and Third Five Year Plans, is well known. There was to be a capital-intensive industrial sector under public ownership, a private industrial sector in light consumer goods, and a private agricultural sector. The first two were the 'modern' sectors which were to be financed by foreign aid, low interest loans, and the taxation of private incomes mainly in the second sector. The third sector was seen as being mainly one of petty production, and it was there that a major flaw of this development strategy was to appear. It has been said that the Second and Third Plans did not have an agricultural strategy at all, or even if they did there was gross overoptimism about the long-term ability of traditional agriculture to contribute to industrialization by providing cheap labour and cheap food.[12] The problem is often posed as one of alternative planning strategies, with the suggestion that if suitable land reforms had been carried out soon after Independence, a quite different development path may have been discovered which would have avoided the 'crisis' in which the planning process found

[11] Chakravarty, *Development Planning*, p. 14.
[12] Ibid., p. 21.

itself in the middle of the 1960s. The difficulty with this suggestion, if we are to look at it from a political standpoint, is precisely the confusion it entails regarding the effective relation between the whole and the part, the universal and the particulars, in the acts of a state promoting and supervising a programme of planned capitalist development. To discover the nature of this relation, we need to look upon planned industrialization as part of a process of what may be called the 'passive revolution of capital'.

Passive Revolution

Antonio Gramsci has talked of the 'passive revolution' as one in which the new claimants to power, lacking the social strength to launch a full-scale assault on the old dominant classes, opt for a path in which the demands of a new society are 'satisfied by small doses, legally, in a reformist manner'—in such a way that the political and economic position of the old feudal classes are not destroyed, agrarian reform is avoided, and especially the popular masses are prevented from going through the political experience of a fundamental social transformation.[13] Gramsci, of course, treats this as a 'blocked dialectic', an exception to the paradigmatic form of bourgeois revolution which he takes to be that of Jacobinism. It now seems more useful to argue, however, that as a historical model passive revolution is in fact the general framework of capitalist transition in societies where bourgeois hegemony has not been accomplished in the classical way.[14] In 'passive revolution' the historical shifts in the strategic relations of forces between capital, pre-capitalist dominant groups, and the popular masses can be seen as a series of contingent, conjunctural moments. The dialectic here cannot be assumed to be blocked in any fundamental sense. Rather, the new forms of dominance of capital become understandable, not as the immanent supersession of earlier contradictions, but as parts of a constructed hegemony, effective because of the successful exercise of both coercive and persuasive power, but incomplete and fragmented at the same time because the hegemonic claims are

---

[13] Antonio Gramsci, *Selections from the Prison Notebooks*, trans. Q. Hoare and G. Nowell Smith (New York: 1971), pp. 44–120.

[14] Asok Sen, 'The Frontiers of the Prison Notebooks', *Economic and Political Weekly: Review of Political Economy*, 23, 5 (1988), pp. PE31–6.

fundamentally contested within the constructed whole.[15] The distinction between 'bourgeois hegemony' and 'passive revolution' then becomes one in which, for the latter, the persuasive power of bourgeois rule cannot be constructed around the universal idea of 'freedom'; some other universal idea has to be substituted for it.[16]

In the Indian case, we can look upon 'passive revolution' as a process involving a political-ideological programme by which the largest possible nationalist alliance is built up against the colonial power. The aim is to form a politically independent nation-state. The means involve the creation of a series of alliances, within the organizational structure of the national movement, between the bourgeoisie and other dominant classes and the mobilization, under this leadership, of mass support from the subordinate classes. The project is a reorganization of the political order, but it is moderated in two quite fundamental ways. On the one hand, it does not attempt to break up or transform in any radical way the institutional structures of 'rational' authority set up in the period of colonial rule. On the other hand, it also does not undertake a full-scale assault on all pre-capitalist dominant classes: rather, it seeks to limit their former power, neutralize them where necessary, attack them only selectively, and in general bring them round to a position of subsidiary allies within a reformed state structure. The dominance of capital does not emanate from its hegemonic sway over 'civil society'. On the contrary, it seeks to construct a synthetic hegemony over the domains of both civil society and the pre-capitalist community. The reification of the 'nation' in the body of the state becomes the means for constructing this hegemonic structure, and the extent of control over the new state apparatus becomes a precondition for further capitalist development. It is by means of an interventionist state, directly entering the domain of production as mobilizer and manager of investible 'national' resources, that the foundations are laid for industrialization and the expansion of capital. Yet the dominance of capital over the national state remains constrained in several ways. Its function of representing the 'national-popular' has to be shared with other governing groups and its transformative role restricted to

---

[15] Ajit Chaudhuri, 'From Hegemony to Counter-hegemony', *Economic and Political Weekly: Review of Political Economy*, 23, 5 (1988), pp. PE19–23; Partha Chatterjee, 'On Gramsci's "Fundamental Mistake"', *Economic and Political Weekly: Review of Political Economy*, 23, 5 (1988), pp. PE24–6.

[16] I am grateful to Kalyan Sanyal for suggesting this point.

reformist and 'molecular' changes. The institution of planning, as we have seen, emerges in this process as the means by which the 'necessary rigours' of these changes is rationalized at the level, not of this or that particular group, but of the social whole.

For the development model adopted in India, the 'modern' sector is clearly the dynamic element. Industrialization as a project emanated from the particular will of the 'modern' sector; the 'general consensus' Chakravarty refers to was in fact the consensus within this 'modern' sector. But this will for transformation had to be expressed as a general project for the 'nation', and this could be done by subsuming within the cohesive body of a single plan for the nation all of those elements which appeared as 'constraints' on the particular will of the 'modern' sector. If land reform was not attempted in the 1950s, it was not a 'fault' of planning, nor was it the lapse of a squeamish 'political will' of the rulers. It was because at this stage of its journey the ideological construct of the 'passive revolution of capital' consciously sought to incorporate within the framework of its rule not a representative mechanism solely operated by individual agents in civil society, but entire structures of pre-capitalist community taken in their existent forms. In the political field, this was expressed in the form of the so-called 'vote banks', a much-talked-about feature of Indian elections in the 1950s and 1960s, by which forms of social power based on landed proprietorship or caste loyalty or religious authority were translated into 'representative' forms of electoral support. In the economic field, the form preferred was that of 'community development' in which the benefits of plan projects meant for the countryside were supposed to be shared collectively by the whole community. That the concrete structures of existent communities were by no means homogeneous or egalitarian but were in fact built around pre-capitalist forms of social power was not so much ignored or forgotten as tacitly acknowledged, for these were precisely the structures through which the 'modernizing' state secured legitimation for itself in the representative processes of elections. It is therefore misleading to suggest as a criticism of this phase of the planning strategy that the planners 'did not realise the nature and dimension of political mobilisation that would be necessary to bring about the necessary institutional changes' to make agriculture more productive.[17] Seen in terms of the political logic of 'passive revolution', the strategy called for was precisely one of promoting

---

[17] Chakravarty, *Development Planning*, p. 21.

industrialization without taking the risk of agrarian political mobilization. This was an essential aspect of the hegemonic construct of the post-colonial state: combining accumulation with legitimation while avoiding the 'unnecessary rigours' of social conflict.

Rational strategies pursued in a political field, however, have the unpleasant habit of producing unintended consequences. Although the objective of the Indian state in the 1950s was to lay the foundations for rapid industrialization without radically disturbing the local structures of power in the countryside, the logic of accumulation in the 'modern' sector could not be prevented from seeping into the interstices of agrarian property, trade, patterns of consumption, and even production. It did not mean a general and radical shift all over the country to capitalist farming, but there were clear signs that agrarian property had become far more 'commoditized' than before, that even subsistence peasant production was deeply implicated in large-scale market transactions, that the forms of extraction of agricultural surplus now combined a wide variety and changing mix of 'economic' and 'extra-economic' power, and that a steady erosion of the viability of small-peasant agriculture was increasing the ranks of marginal and landless cultivators. Perhaps there were conjunctural reasons why the 'food crisis' should have hit the economic, and immediately afterwards the political, life of the country with such severity in the mid-1960s. But it would not be unwarranted to point out a certain inevitability of the logic of accumulation breaking into an agrarian social structure which the politics of the state was unwilling to transform.

There were other consequences of this phase of planned industrialization under state auspices which were to be of considerable political significance.

The Politics of Planning—II

The object of the strategy of 'passive revolution' was to *contain* class conflicts within manageable dimensions, to control and manipulate the many dispersed power relations in society to further as best as possible the thrust towards accumulation. But conflicts surely could not be avoided altogether. And if there were conflicts between particular interests, mobilizations based on interests were only to be expected, especially within a political process of representative democracy; in fact, the very form of legitimacy by electoral representation, in so far as it involves a *relation* between the state and the people, implies a mutual recognition by each of the organized and articulate existence of the other, the general on the one hand and the particulars on the other. Mobilizations, consequently, did take place, principally as oppositional movements and in both the electoral and non-electoral domains. The response of the state was to subsume these organized demands of particular interests within the generality of a rational strategy.

The form of this strategy is for the state to insist that all conflicts between particular interests admit of an 'economic' solution—'economic' in the sense of allocations to each part that are consistent with the overall constraints of the whole. Thus, a particular interest, whether expressed in terms of class, language, region, caste, tribe, or community, is to be recognized and given a place within the framework of the general by being assigned a priority and an allocation relative to all the other parts. This, as we have seen before, is the form which the single rational consciousness of the developmental state must take—the form of planning. It is also the form which the political process conducted by the state will seek to impose on all mobilizations of particular interests: the demands therefore will be for a reallocation or a reassignment of priorities relative to other particular interests.

It is curious to what extent a large variety of social mobilizations in the last two decades have taken both this 'economic' form and the form of demands upon the state. Mobilizations which admit of demographic solidarities defined over territorial regions can usually make this claim within the framework of the federal distribution of powers. This could be either a claim for greater shares for the federal units from out of the central economic pool, or for a reallocation of the relative shares of different federal units, or even for a redefinition of the territorial boundaries of the units or the creation of new units out of old ones. On the one hand, we therefore have a continuous process of bargaining between the union and the states over the distribution of revenues which is sought to be given an orderly and rational form by such statutory bodies as the finance commissions, but which inevitably spills over into the disorderly immediacy of contingent political considerations, such as the compulsions of party politics, electoral advantage, or the pressures of influential interest lobbies, and which takes the form of an ever-growing series of ad hoc allocations that defy rational and consistent justification. On the other hand, we also have many examples of demands for the creation of new states within the federal union.

While the solidarities over which these demands are defined are cultural, such as language or ethnic identity, the justification for statehood invariably carries with it a charge of economic discrimination within the existing federal arrangement, and is thus open to political strategies operating within the 'economic' framework of distribution of resources between the centre and the states.

For mobilizations of demographic sections which cannot claim representative status of territorial regions, the demands made upon the state are nevertheless also of an 'economic' form. This includes not only the demands made by the organizations of economic classes, but also by social segments such as castes or tribes or religious communities. Examples of the management of class demands of this kind are, of course, innumerable and form the staple of the political economy literature. They affect virtually all aspects of economic policy-making and include things like taxation, pricing, subsidies, licensing, wages, etc. But for the economic demands of 'ethnic' sections too, the state itself has legitimized the framework by qualifying the notion of citizenship by a set of discriminatory protections for culturally underprivileged and backward groups (lower castes, tribes) or minority religious communities. The framework has virtually transformed the nature of caste movements in India over the last fifty years from movements of lower castes claiming higher ritual status within a religiously sanctified cultural hierarchy to the same castes now proclaiming their ritually degraded status in order to demand protective economic privileges in the fields of employment or educational opportunities. In response, the higher castes, whose superiority has historically rested upon the denial of any notion of ritual equality with lower castes, are now defending their economic privileges precisely by appealing to the liberal notion of equality and by pointing out the economic inefficiencies of discriminatory protection.

The point could therefore be made here that the centrality which the state assumes in the management of economic demands in India is not simply the result of the large weight of the public sector or the existence of state monopolies, as argued, for instance, in Bardhan or Rudolph and Rudolph.[18] Even otherwise, a developmental

---

[18] Pranab Bardhan, *The Political Economy of Development in India* (Oxford: 1984); Lloyd H. Rudolph and Susanne Hoeber Rudolph, *In Search of Lakshmi: The Political Economy of the Indian State* (Chicago: 1987).

state operating within the framework of representative politics would necessarily require the state to assume the role of the central allocator if it has to legitimize its authority in the political domain.

The Ambiguities of Legitimation

There is no doubt that the fundamental problematic of the post-colonial state—furthering accumulation in the 'modern' sector through a political strategy of passive revolution—has given rise to numerous ambiguities in the legitimation process. In the field of economic planning these ambiguities have been noticed in the debates over the relative importance of market signals and state commands, over the efficiency of the private sector and the inefficiency of the state sector, over the growth potential of a relatively 'open' economy and the technological backwardness of the strategy of 'self-reliance', and over the dynamic productive potential of a relaxation of state controls compared with the entrenchment of organized privileges within the present structure of state dominance. It is not surprising that in these debates the proponents of the former argument in each opposed pair have emphasized the dynamic of accumulation while those defending the latter position have stressed the importance of legitimation (although there are arguments which defend the latter on the grounds of accumulation as well). We need not go into the details of each of these debates here; what should be pointed out, however, is, first, that these ambiguities are *necessary* consequences of the specific relation of the post-colonial developmental state with the people-nation; second, that it is these ambiguities which create room for manoeuvre through which the passive revolution of capital can proceed; and third, that these ambiguities cannot be removed or resolved within the present constitution of the state.

Let me briefly illustrate this point. Given the political process defined by the Indian state, the ambiguities of legitimacy are expressed in the well-known forms of 'interest-groups'. These are the variety of permanent associations of businessmen, professionals, and trade unions as well as temporary agitational mobilizations based on specific issues. There are competing demands in this sector, and the state may use both coercive and persuasive powers to allocate relative priorities in satisfying these demands. But the overall constraint here is to maintain the unity of the 'modern' sector as a whole, for that, as we have seen before, stands forth within the body of the state as the overwhelmingly dominant element of the 'nation'. The unity of the 'modern' sector is specified in terms of a variety of criteria encompassing the domains of industrial production, the professional, educational, and service sectors connected with industrial production, and agricultural production outside the subsistence sector, and also embracing the effective demographic boundaries of the market for the products of the 'modern' sector. The identification of this sector cannot be made in any specific regional terms, nor does it coincide with a simple rural/urban dichotomy. But because of its unique standing as a particular interest which can claim to represent the dynamic aspect of the nation itself, the entire political process conducted by the state, including the political parties which stake their claims to run the central organs of the state, must work towards producing a consensus on protecting the unity of the 'modern' sector. Any appearance of a fundamental lack of consensus here will resonate as a crisis of national unity itself. Thus the political management of economic demands will require that a certain internal balance—an acceptable parity—be maintained between the several fractions within the modern sector. Seen from this angle, the analysis of the 'political economy' of Indian planning as a competitive game between privileged pressure groups within a self-perpetuating 'modern' sector will appear one-sided, for it misses the fundamental ambiguity of a state process which must further accumulation while legitimizing the 'modern' sector itself as representative of the nation as a whole.

Indeed, more profound ambiguities appear in the relations between the 'modern' sector and the rest of the people-nation. On the one hand, there is the system of electoral representation on a territorial basis in the form of single-member constituencies. On the other hand, competing demands may be voiced not only on the basis of permanent 'interest-group' organizations but also as mobilizations building upon pre-existing cultural solidarities such as locality, caste, tribe, religious community, or ethnic identity. It would be wrong to assume that no representative process works here. Rather, the most interesting aspect of contemporary Indian politics is precisely the way in which solidarities and forms of authority deriving from the pre-capitalist community insert themselves into the representational processes of a liberal electoral democracy. This allows, on the one hand, for organizations and leaders to appear in the domain of the state process claiming to represent this or that 'community', and for groups of people threatened

with the loss of their means of livelihood or suffering from the consequences of such loss to use those representatives to seek the protection,
or at least the indulgence, of the state. On the other hand, the state itself
can manipulate these 'pre-modern' forms of relations between the
community and the state to secure legitimacy for its developmental
role.[19]

An instance of the latter is the shift from the earlier strategy of
'community development' to that of distributing 'poverty removal'
packages directly to selected target groups among the underprivileged
sections. The new strategy allows for the state to use a political rhetoric
in which intermediate rungs of both the social hierarchy (local power
barons, dominant landed groups) and the governmental hierarchy
(local officials and even elected political representatives) can be condemned as obstacles in the way of the state trying to reach the benefits of development to the poor and the package of benefits directly
presented to groups of the latter as a gift from the highest political
leadership.[20] From the standpoint of a rational doctrine of political
authority, these forms of legitimation doubtless appear as 'pre-modern',
harking back to what sociologists would call 'traditional' or 'charismatic'
authority. But the paradox is that the existence, the unity, and indeed
the representative character of the 'modern' sector as the leading element within the nation has to be legitimized precisely through these
means.

There is the other side to this relation of legitimation: the ambiguous
image of the state in popular consciousness. If, as has been pointed out
in some studies,[21] it is true that the state appears in popular consciousness
as an external and distant entity, then, depending upon the immediate
perception of local antagonisms, the state could be seen either as an
oppressive intruder in the affairs of the local community or as a benevolent protector of the people against local oppressors. The particular
image in which the state appears is determined contextually. But this

[19] Kalyan K. Sanyal, 'Accumulation, Poverty and the State in the Third World',
Economic and Political Weekly: Review of Political Economy, 23, 5 (1988), pp. PE27–
30.

[20] Atul Kohli, *The State and Poverty in India: The Politics of Reform* (Cambridge:
1987); Arun Patnaik, 'Gramsci's Concept of Hegemony: The Case of Development
Administration in India', *Economic and Political Weekly: Review of Political Economy*,
23, 5 (1988), pp. PE 12–18.

[21] Partha Chatterjee, *Bengal: The Land Question* (Calcutta: 1985).

again opens up the possibility for the play of a variety of political strategies of which the story of modern Indian politics offers a vast range of examples.

Such ambiguities show up the narrow and one-sided manner in which the 'science' of planning defines itself—a necessary one-sidedness, for without it the singular rationality of its practice would not be comprehensible to itself. From its own standpoint, planning will talk about the inefficiency and wastage of the public sector, about the irrationality of choosing or locating projects purely on grounds of electoral expediency, about the granting of state subsidies in response to agitational pressure. The configuration of social powers in the political process, on the other hand, will produce these inefficient and irrational results which will go down in the planning literature as examples of implementational failures. Yet, in the process of projecting the efficiency of productive growth as a rational path of development for the nation as a whole, the particular interests in the 'modern' sector must shift on to the state the burden of defraying the costs of producing a general consent for their particular project. The state sector, identified as the embodiment of the general, must bear these social costs of constructing the framework of legitimacy for the passive revolution of capital.

What we have tried to show is that the two processes—one of 'rational' planning and the other of 'irrational' politics—are inseparable parts of the very logic of this state conducting the passive revolution. The paradox in fact is that it is the very 'irrationality' of the political process which continually works to produce legitimacy for the rational exercise of the planner. While the planner thinks of his own practice as an instrument for resolving conflict, the political process uses planning itself as an instrument for producing consent for capital's passive revolution.

It is not surprising then to discover that the rational form of the planning exercise itself supplies to the political process a rhetoric for conducting its political debates. 'Growth' and 'equity'—both terms are loaded with potent rhetorical ammunition which can serve to justify as well as to contest state policies that seek to use coercive legal powers to protect or alter the existent relations between social groups. We have shown how the very form of an institution of rational planning located outside the political process is crucial for the self-definition of a developmental state embodying the single universal consciousness of the social whole. We have also shown how the wielders of power can constrain, mould, and distort the strategies of planning in order to produce political consent for their rule. What is science in the one domain becomes rhetoric in the other; what is the rational will of the whole in the one becomes the contingent agglomeration of particular wills in the other. The two together—this contradictory, perennially quarrelsome and yet ironically well-matched couple—comprise the identity of the developmental state in India today.

15

We Have Heard This Before
(1990)

When the interests of dominant minorities are threatened, the reactions are always the same.

A hundred years ago, when the demand was made that, to enable Indians to sit for the examinations to the Indian Civil Service, the age limit of applicants be raised and arrangements made for examinations to be held in India, British civil servants were aghast. 'That would bring disaster', they said. 'We could never maintain the efficiency of the service. Indians cannot have the same abilities as graduates of British universities. Besides, these jobs will be cornered by a tiny elite among Indians. What good will that do to the vast majority?' Historians today consider these opinions as reflecting the racial prejudices of the then rulers of India.

Fifty years ago, when the demand to abolish zamindari was being debated, landlords raised similar arguments. The demand was discriminatory, they said. First, to take property away from one class and give it to another violated the universal right of property. Second, not all zamindars were wealthy or oppressive. There were many who were owners of small landed property whose incomes barely provided them with a livelihood. The only class that would profit from the abolition of zamindari was the rich peasantry. This class was poorly educated, with no tradition of assuming social leadership or responsibility. If they had power, rich peasants would be far more oppressive than zamindars ever were. The poor peasant would hardly be better off.

Anandabajar Patrika, 14 September 1990 (translated from the Bengali by the author).

Third, the demand was politically motivated. It would produce conflict between classes and hatred and disorder in society. If the anti-reservationists of today take a look at the debates in the provincial legislatures of Bengal, Bihar, or UP half a century ago, they will be astonished. Whether they will be embarrassed as well, I cannot tell.

It is often true that the more substantial peasants were the ones who gained the most from the abolition of zamindari. It is also true that they are the ones who have in many regions become the oppressive rich farmers of today. But we do not for that reason claim that the abolition of zamindari was wrong. On the contrary, we often condemn the Congress governments of the time for having paid compensation to zamindars, and for allowing loopholes in the law which enabled landlords to retain their hold over much of their possessions. Of course, we forget which classes of the future were to profit from those loopholes.

The same arguments are now being repeated in the debate over the reservation of jobs for backward castes in the central government services. Three objections have been raised to the proposal. First, disregarding the criterion of merit, jobs are being reserved for one section of applicants: this is both discriminatory and harmful to administrative efficiency. Second, it is not true that everyone from the upper castes is privileged or that everyone from the lower castes is disadvantaged. If jobs are reserved by caste, the better-off among the lower castes will grab them; those who are truly disadvantaged will not gain in any way. If jobs have to be reserved, this should be done using economic criteria, not caste. Third, a politically motivated move such as this will only create new conflicts between castes. Unlike education or land reforms which are the real answers to caste discrimination, this proposal will only increase disparities, not remove them.

The same arguments, but in different contexts. The debate must therefore be carried out all over again.

Take first the question of merit. It does not require much knowledge of economic theory to see that under conditions of free competition, those who have greater initial endowments will in the end capture the market. The observation holds for the education market too. Where recruitment is by open competitive examination, if it is found that successful applicants come predominantly from a small section of society, then surely the conclusion cannot be that their merit is a natural gift. There must be social reasons for systematic disparities in 'merit'. The report of the Mandal Commission shows that of Class I positions in the central services, only 7.14 per cent are held by those from the scheduled castes or tribes (despite a reservation for them of 22.5 per cent). Other backward castes hold 2.59 per cent. Of Class II posts, scheduled castes and tribes have only 13.66 per cent. Of Class III and IV jobs, however, they hold 31 per cent, well above the reserved quota. Obviously, the upper castes are not particularly interested in these lowly jobs. Hence, the division of labour in the administrative apparatus of our modern state looks much like that recommended by the varna system of the scriptures.

Yet this is a division of labour produced by an assessment of educational merit. And it is not as if we do not know why such a result has been produced. Yes, there has been an expansion of secondary and higher education in independent India, but this expansion has brought into existence two separate educational systems. The more the educated upper castes have been ousted from landed property and turned themselves into the urban middle classes, the more strenuously have they built up their own institutions for producing professionals with 'merit'. The consequence has been that the system of public education catering to the rest of the population has been entirely dissociated from the production of 'merit'. This disparity has been less the result of state patronage and more that of the enterprise, expenditure, and infinite energy of the urban middle classes. Every city and town in India is now part of this structure, beginning with nursery schools. These institutions have better teaching, better facilities; the costs are also much higher. Needless to say, there is also far greater homogeneity in the class backgrounds of students. Every urban resident in India knows that if one can manage to put one's child into one of these 'English-medium' schools, he or she will get a headstart in the race to acquire 'merit'. Disparities in educational achievement, therefore, begin from the primary stage of schooling.

Where there is such extreme disparity in access to education, it is easy to see what open competitive examinations will perpetuate. If educational achievement is the only merit that will be tested, surely those who come from educated middle-class families and who have had the privilege of going into the elite schools will be the ones qualifying: the others will not stand a chance. If the criterion of merit is to be applied fairly, there should not only be an expansion of education but also an equalization of educational opportunities, at least up to the secondary level. In every country of the world where there is universal secondary education, the principle is not only that every child must go to school, but that, with rare exceptions, they will go to the same *kind* of school. This is not some coercive diktat of socialist regimes. Even the United States follows exactly the same system. Except for a handful who go to private or denominational schools, all children in that holy land of modern capitalism and meritocracy are educated through a universal system of public schooling. If in India today it is ruled that all children, irrespective of class, will have to attend their neighbourhood schools, I suppose middle-class parents in their despair will decide to renounce the world and retire to monastic life. There is no political force in the country which can bring about such a democratic revolution in education.

If jobs are reserved for those from socially and educationally backward castes, it is obvious that they will go to the relatively better-off sections among those castes. What else could we expect? Only those from relatively prosperous lower-caste families will have the minimum educational qualifications needed to get even reserved places in the Class I and II services—over which there is so much competition. The alternative proposal of reservation by economic criteria is entirely irrelevant to the problem of caste discrimination. If that proposal is aimed at reserving places for those who, irrespective of caste, fall below a certain level of income, we are hardly likely to find many who will be from a backward caste, from a low-income family, and at the same time possess the minimum educational qualifications for the job. Clearly, these reserved positions will then go overwhelmingly to low-income upper-caste applicants. That will only reinforce the present caste imbalance in the professional middle class; the lower castes will again be denied entry into that exclusive circle.

Hidden behind the cloud of political slogans is a very simple fact. Is it at all correct to say that the demand for reservations is a result of the lack of spread of education or the incompleteness of land reforms? To me, the truth seems to be the exact opposite. It is in fact because of the spread, however tardy, of education in rural areas and of land reforms, no matter how inadequate, that there has now grown a class of prosperous peasants in the countryside. They have even acquired some economic and political power at local levels. Their children are now making a bid to find a place among the urban middle classes which inhabit the central institutions of power in society. This has nothing to do with the removal of poverty in the country at large. The central government services, over which there is such conflict today, actually comprise only about 10 per cent of the total employment in the organized sector of the economy. If one takes the Class I and II positions, they account for less than 5 per cent. Not even an idiot will claim that by distributing these jobs the problem of poverty will be affected in any way. It is in fact the class differentiation among the peasantry and among the middle castes, brought about in the rural areas in the last few decades by economic changes and the expansion of education, that is now producing the assault on the citadels occupied for so long by the educated urban middle classes. The real question is: will the institutions of administrative, professional, and cultural power remain under the dominance of the upper castes, or will others have to be given a place? That is what the fight is all about.

It is apparent that caste conflicts will grow. Those who were complaining the most about the possibility of conflict are the ones who have now taken to violence. This is a conflict that took place in the south of the country a few decades ago. In most parts of southern India, the social dominance of the upper castes has crumbled. The conflict has now emerged in a big way in the north. To complain of political motives in this connection is strange, to say the least. Could any decision of such consequence for the structures of power in the country have been taken without strong political motivations? Were there no political motives behind the fact that the Mandal Commission report had only gathered dust in the last ten years? In terms of politics, the truth is that the National Front government has taken a daring risk. It is a tough task indeed to incur the wrath of the urban upper and middle classes and still remain in power.

The expressions of wrath are frightening. There are few things more ugly than the flaunting of the cultural superiority of dominant minorities. I am no longer surprised when I hear of the parents of anti-reservationist student agitators waxing nostalgic about the golden age of the ICS. I can see in front of my eyes the first political movement in independent India whose campaign is in English, whose slogans are in English, whose ideology too, I presume, is articulated in English. I can also see despicable vulgarities of which only the privileged are capable, from ridiculing the chief minister of Bihar on the size of his family to shining shoes for the benefit of news photographers. These are perhaps the most sublime examples of the perversities of a merit-producing education.

There is no doubt that there will be conflict. There is also no doubt that no political party and no elected government in India will ever succeed in overturning the recent decision to reserve government jobs for backward castes. Of course, there will now appear innumerable loopholes in the regulations: in whose interest, it hardly needs to be elaborated. And it is my presumption that future historians will judge the anti-reservationists of today in exactly the same way that present-day historians judge British imperialists or Indian zamindars. It may be that I am being excessively optimistic. Only the future acts of the present generation of educated youth can decide whether my presumption will prove to be correct.

III

Capital and Community

16

A Response to Taylor's 'Modes of Civil Society' (1990)

While writers in Eastern Europe have recently appealed to the concept of a civil society with an initiative and organization independent of and opposed to the state, Charles Taylor has warned us of the dangers of transposing too easily the results of a historical development specific to Western Europe to situations in other countries that do not necessarily share the same preconditions.[1] He has also pointed out that the state–civil society opposition is too simplistic an abstraction even in the case of Western liberal democracies, for it ignores the profound ways in which the state and civil society are implicated in and supportive of each other in the West.

I wish to push this point about the specificity of Western European thought. Taylor proposes to take seriously the differences in the several strands of thinking that went into the making of the concept of civil society in Europe and of the possibilities of enriching this concept so as to include within its purview processes of state–society interaction in non-European contexts. Yet the central assumption of this proposal is that it is only the concepts of European social philosophy that contain within them the possibility of universalization. This assumption implies that only by expanding and enriching these concepts can one encapsulate non-European processes as the particulars of a universal

[1] See Charles Taylor, 'Modes of Civil Society', *Public Culture*, 3, 1 (Fall 1990). The present essay was given at the Center Forum of the Center for Psychosocial Studies (Chicago), and is No. 39 of Working Papers and Proceedings of the Center For Psychosocial Studies (edited by Greg Urban and Benjamin Lee) under the title 'Response to Taylor's Invocation of Civil Society'.

history whose theoretical subject is, and will always remain, Europe.[2] I wish to contest this assumption.

Let me clarify that I am not accusing Taylor of a Eurocentrism he could have avoided simply by an act of choice. None of us engaged in the academic practices of the social sciences can make such a choice. It is in fact the very condition of our intellectual discourse—in the ways it is framed through disciplinary practices in the universities and in the international academic community—that forces us to speak in the language of European philosophy. A 'traditional' intellectual from Ghana or Iran or Thailand may have the option of speaking in a different language, but by doing so he will condemn himself to an irrevocable provincialism. The 'modern' intellectuals from these countries do not have even this choice. If we wish to do academic social philosophy, we cannot pretend to occupy an alternative subject-position merely by privileging the concepts of Ghanian or Iranian or Thai philosophy. Alternative subject-positions, if they are to emerge, must be fought for through contestations within the site of European philosophy by pushing its terms of debate beyond its own discursive boundaries. This is what I wish to attempt. I will, in short, take Taylor's arguments about the specificity of the European concept of civil society, explore the conditions and limits of that concept, and see if it might be possible to suggest ways in which that concept could be shown to be a particular form of a more universal concept. I wish, in other words, to send back the concept of civil society to where I think it properly belongs—the provincialism of European social philosophy.

I

What, then, is civil society? Taylor distinguishes three different senses in which it can be identified from within the European political tradition:

1. In a minimal sense, civil society exists where there are free associations, not under the tutelage of state power.
2. In a stronger sense, civil society exists only where society as a whole can structure itself and coordinate its actions through associations free of state tutelage.

[2] I am grateful to Dipesh Chakrabarty for pointing out to me the implications of this formulation. Chakrabarty has argued this point in his *Rethinking Working-Class History: Bengal 1890–1940* (Princeton, NJ: Princeton University Press, 1989) and in a recent unpublished essay entitled 'Post-coloniality and the Artifice of History.'

3. As an alternative or supplement to the second sense, we can speak of civil society wherever the ensemble of associations can significantly determine or inflect the course of state policy.

He then spells out five distinct ideas that historically contributed to the production in Europe of a concept of civil society separate from the idea of the state:

A. The medieval idea that society is not identical with its political organization and that political authority is only one organ among others.
B. The Christian idea of the Church as an independent society.
C. The development within feudalism of a legal notion of subjective rights.
D. The growth in medieval Europe of relatively independent, self-governing cities.
E. The secular dualism of the medieval polity, in which a monarch ruled with the intermittent and uncertain support of a body of estates.

Taylor then describes how these ideas were brought together in two quite distinct ways by Locke and Montesquieu, respectively, to produce two different conceptualizations of the state–civil society relation.

In Locke, A is interpreted to mean that society is created before government, through a first contract by which individuals in the state of nature give themselves a society. It is this society which then sets up government as a trust. The implication is that if government should violate its trust, society would recover its freedom against government. B is given the meaning of a prepolitical community constituted by a natural law received from God. This now becomes the foundation for subjective rights in C: no positive law can be valid if it contravenes these rights. This particular combination of A, B, and C produces for Locke the notion of a civil society distinguished from political authority. Much that is valuable and creative in social life, especially in the sphere of social production, is seen as belonging to the domain of civil society, outside the direction or intervention of the political authority. We can immediately notice the centrality of this notion in the ideological self-representation of English capitalism.

Since Montesquieu, on the other hand, does not presume a prepolitical natural community, he does not need to appeal to either A or B. For him, society and political authority are coeval. In order to establish his anti-absolutist doctrine, he brings together C, D, and E in a form that enables him to distinguish between central political authority on the one hand and a set of entrenched rights, defended by citizens who have a republican sense of patriotic virtue, on the other. His view of society, then, is that of a balance between two elements, neither prior to the other, which remain as it were in perpetual but creative tension, seeking always to achieve that equilibrium in which both retain their identities without destroying each other.

What is significant in this distinction drawn by Taylor between the two streams of thinking leading to the state–civil society opposition, represented by Locke and Montesquieu, respectively, is the element they share in common. This element C—the notion of subjective rights—plays a crucial role in establishing both the distinction between as well as the unity of state and civil society in both these anti-absolutist doctrines. I think this commonality is important especially because of the way in which the history of these two streams of political thinking in Europe becomes implicated in another history: the history of capital. I will return to this point later.

In the meantime, let us note another curious feature shared by both streams. Both Locke and Montesquieu defend subjective rights by appealing to the notion of a community. In Locke, this is straightforward. Subjective rights have their source in the prepolitical natural community that God creates for mankind: C is grounded in B. Men in the state of nature are already constituted as subjects by the community of natural law, even before the emergence of society. As already constituted individuals they can, therefore, proceed to create through mutual contacts first society and then government, and thereby establish the institutions for the defence of their subjective rights. In Montesquieu, although C is related in institutional terms to the equilibrating forces contained in D and E, the ultimate defence of subjective rights is *vertu*—the patriotic spirit of citizens who 'feel shame in obeying any order which derogates from their code' and who 'defend the laws to the death against internal and external threats'. One would be justified in thinking of *vertu* as the sense of community that is not prior to the establishment of political authority but coeval with it, which nevertheless regards itself as having an identity distinct from that of the political authority. Why else would the defence of subjective rights against royal encroachment be 'patriotic'?

Subjective rights and the grounding of those rights in community—these are the two features that are common to the otherwise different arguments made by Locke and Montesquieu. The problems that Taylor describes in the subsequent history of the state–civil society relation are fundamentally shaped by divergences in conceptualizing the relation between rights and community. These divergences are framed within two extreme positions: on the one hand, abolishing community altogether and thinking of rights as grounded solely in the self-determining individual will, and on the other, attributing to community a single determinate form, delegitimating all other forms of community. This subsequent history, I will argue, is intricately tied to the history of capital.

II

The two streams represented by Locke and Montesquieu, Taylor says, were brought together in its most celebrated form by Hegel. Taylor is quite right when he says that the two 'sit uneasily together' in Hegel's new concept of civil society. Let me explore the source of this tension in Hegel.

Hegel, as we know, strenuously resisted the line of argument that preferred to think of the state as having been founded by contract. Contracts follow from the accidental, and entirely contingent, agreements among individual wills. They properly belong to the domain of the system of needs, but are too fickle to be the basis of Right itself. Hegel also would not admit that the family, that first elementary moment of social life, was founded on contract. To admit this would mean having to recognize that members of a family, whether adults or children, might have rights against each other and even the right to dissociate from or dissolve the family at will. That would make the primary elements of social life subject to the transient and utterly chaotic accidents of contingent agreements. Contracts, for Hegel, belong neither to the domain of the state nor to that of the family; their place is in civil society.

How, then, is the family formed? Hegel begins the *Philosophy of Right* by first establishing subjective will in abstract right. But when he moves to the actualizing of subjective will in the concreteness of ethical life, he grounds the first moment—the family—in love, which is precisely the free surrender of will and personality. The family is ethical mind 'in its natural or immediate phase', where it 'is specifically characterized by love, which is mind's feeling of its own unity. One is in it not as an independent person but as a member.'[3] I will also quote some of the other things Hegel has to say about this 'natural or

[3] Hegel, *Philosophy of Right*, trans. T.M. Knox (London: Oxford University Press, 1967), p. 110.

immediate phase' of ethical life because I prefer to read these passages as a suppressed narrative of community, flowing through the substratum of liberal capitalist society, which those who celebrate the absolute and natural sovereignty of the individual will refuse to recognize. Hegel says:

> Love means in general terms the consciousness of my unity with another, so that I am not in selfish isolation but win my self-consciousness only as the renunciation of my independence and through knowing myself as the unity of myself with another and of the other with me. Love, however, is feeling, i.e. ethical life in the form of something natural . . . The first moment in love is that I do not wish to be a self-subsistent and independent person and that, if I were, then I would feel defective and incomplete. The second moment is that I find myself in another person, that I count for something in me. Love, therefore, is the most tremendous contradiction; the Understanding cannot resolve it since there is nothing more stubborn than this point of self-consciousness which is negated and which nevertheless I ought to possess as affirmative. Love is at once the propounding and the resolving of this contradiction. As the resolving of it, love is unity of an ethical type.[4]

The right of the family properly consists in the fact that its substantiality should have determinate existence. Thus it is a right against externality and against secessions from the family unity. On the other hand, to repeat, love is a feeling, something subjective, against which unity cannot make itself effective. The demand for unity can be sustained, then, only in relation to such things as are by nature external and not conditioned by feeling.[5]

Hegel, of course, restricts this substantial unity to the nuclear family, in which it finds its determinate existence as a right against externality and secession in, first, the family property, and, second, the male head of the family, i.e. husband and father. In doing this, Hegel leads himself into a precarious position, for no matter how hard he tries to resist the idea of the family as based on a contractual agreement in which the members retain their individual rights against each other, he cannot prevent the tide of individualism from seeping into the representations of marriage and inheritance even in the positive law

[4] Ibid., pp. 261–2.
[5] Ibid., p. 262.

of modern Western societies. Reading these passages today, Hegel's arguments on marriage, gender relations, and inheritance seem to us either quaint, if one takes a charitable view, or outrageously conservative.

I wish to argue, however, that there is another narrative in which Hegel's eloquence on the subject of love will not seem so outmoded. This is the narrative not of the bourgeois family but of the community. Think of the rhetoric in which, even in this age of the triumph of individualism, all movements that appeal to the 'natural' solidarity of community speak. They claim the right against externality and secession, they seek determinate existence in property and representation through collectively recognized heads, they speak in the language of love and of self-recognition through the free surrender of individual will to others in the community. One might object that this idea of 'natural' affiliation to a community (or an intermediate set of communities) does violence to the freedom of choice inherent in the subjective will. It is this objection which becomes the basis for the identification in European sociological theory (fed, let us remember, on large doses of Orientalist literature and colonial anthropology) of all precapitalist *gemeinschaften* as the domain of ascription, and hence unfreedom, and of modern associations as the field where freedom and choice can blossom. Hegel's arguments on the family remind us of the irreducible immediacy in which human beings are born in society: not as pure unattached individuals free to choose their social affiliations (whether gender, ethnicity, or class) but as already ascribed members of society. Liberal individualism seeks to erase this level of immediacy, where people are not free to choose the social locus of their birth. Indeed, liberalism seeks to forget that the question of choice here is itself fallacious, for human beings cannot exist as individuals before they are born, and when they are born, they are already ascribed as particular members of society. Liberal theory, then, can only deal with this phenomenon as accidents of 'natural inequality', which social policies of welfare or equal opportunity must mitigate. It can, in other words, only deal with it in bad conscience.

If I am allowed the conceit of reading Hegel against the grain, I will choose to read this subsection, 'Ethical Life', as a narrative of community where subjective rights must be negotiated within the ascribed field of the ethical life of the community. I will also recall here that Hegel makes the family the site for that other great process by which individual subjectivities could be negotiated in society, namely, the education of children.[6] That site, too, he would not be able to defend against the relentless sway of the modern disciplinary regimes of power constantly striving to produce the 'normalized' individual. Against the grain of liberal sociology, I prefer to read Hegel as saying that education properly belongs to the field of the ethical life of the community and not to the compulsory discipline of the school, the prison, the hospital, or the psychiatrist's clinic. I will not describe this field of community ethical life as one devoid of choice, nor will I give it a place at some early stage in the sequence of development of the bourgeois nuclear family.[7] Rather, I will read this as a narrative that continues to unfold to this day against the grain of that other narrative of bourgeois individualism.

To return to Hegel and civil society: families, united within themselves against the externality constituted by other families and each represented by its head—the burgher, the *bourgeois*—comprise the domain of civil society. This is the domain of particular interests, based on particular needs, and the mutual satisfaction of the needs of all through contractually mediated exchange of the products of labour. This is also the domain in which the property of each family is protected through the administration of justice. Civil society, in other words, is the well-known domain of the market economy and civil law.

Hegel, however, also includes within civil society a residual category providing for 'contingencies still lurking' in the system of needs and the administration of justice and for the 'care of particular interests as a common interest'. This residual category includes the police and the corporation. What is curious here is that in demarcating the limits of public surveillance organized by civil society (Hegel is presumably thinking of institutions such as municipal policing), he admits that 'no objective line can be drawn'. In other words, at this interface between family and civil society there is no objective line separating the private from the public. The separation can only be made contextually, taking into view specific contingencies. 'These details', Hegel says, 'are determined by custom, the spirit of the rest of the constitution, contemporary conditions, the crisis of the hour, and so forth.'[8] How is one to read this

---

[6] Ibid., *Philosophy of Right*, pp. 117–18.

[7] I am reminded here of Marx's criticism in the *Ethnological Notebooks* of Henry Maine's treatment of 'ancient forms of kinship', including the Indian 'village community', as the prehistory of the modern family. See Lawrence Krader, *The Ethnological Notebooks of Karl Marx* (Assen: Van Gorcum, 1974), pp. 287–336.

[8] Ibid., p. 146.

lack of objective separation between the civil and the familial, the public and the private? What is it that produces this zone of contingency and indeterminacy, where 'everything is subjective'? Can one read this as one more instance in which a suppressed narrative of community is seeping through the interstices of the objectively constructed, contractually regulated structure of civil society?

A final illustration: still on the subject of civil society and its residual function of taking care of particular interests as a common interest, Hegel writes:

> In its character as a universal family, civil society has the right and duty of superintending and influencing education, inasmuch as education bears upon the child's capacity to become a member of society. Society's right here is paramount over the arbitrary and contingent preferences of parents . . . Parents usually suppose that in the matter of education they have complete freedom and may arrange everything as they like . . . None the less, society has a right . . . to compel parents to send their children to school, to have them vaccinated, and so forth. The disputes that have arisen in France between the advocates of state supervision and those who demand that education shall be free, i.e. at the option of the parents, are relevant here.[9]

I wish to suggest that, once again the same suppressed narrative is raising its irrepressible head. How else can Hegel suddenly slip in the idea of civil society as a universal family? How can civil society represent itself as a family that, according to Hegel himself, is born not out of contract but out of love, the free surrender of individual wills? By reducing family to the single determinate form of the bourgeois nuclear family, he has narrowed and impoverished its scope. The gap has to be filled by civil society, arrogating to itself the role of a universal family. Ironically, by admitting this Hegel immediately opens himself to appropriation by that powerful strand of thinking which claims that this role of the universal family can be properly played by the only legitimate community in modern society—the nation—a role that must then be enforced by the disciplinary mechanisms of the nation-state. Hegel becomes complicit in this act of appropriation, not innocently but as an inevitable consequence of his own construction of the system of Right: the contingent, contractual domain of civil

[9] Ibid., pp. 148, 227.

society must, after all, be unified at the higher, universal level of the absolute idea of Right, and embodied in the state as *the* political community.

III

I am suggesting, therefore, that it is this suppression in modern European social theory of an independent narrative of community which makes possible both the posing of the distinction between state and civil society and the erasure of that distinction. At one extreme, then, we have arguments proclaiming the sovereignty of the individual will, insisting that the state has no business to interfere in the domain of individual freedom of choice and contractual arrangements. At the other extreme, there are arguments that would have the *one* political community, given the single, determinate, demographically enumerable form of the nation-state, assume the directing role in all regulatory functions of society, usurping the domain of civil society and family, and blurring the distinction between the public and the private. It is to this range of arguments that Taylor refers when he says that the state–civil society relation in Western thought is not one of simple opposition. I will argue that the possibilities of opposition as well as encapsulation arise because the concepts of the individual and the nation-state both become embedded in a new grand narrative: the narrative of capital. It is this narrative of capital that seeks to suppress the narrative of community and produce in the course of its journey both the normalized individual and the modern regimes of disciplinary power.

The historical specificity of European social thought cannot be described simply by Taylor's conditions A to E. It would not be surprising at all if one finds in the premodern histories of other, non-European countries similar features in state–society relations. It is also difficult to explain why, if European thought is indeed conditioned by these specifics, people from Poland to the Philippines to Nicaragua should appeal to those philosophers from Britain, France, or Germany to think out and justify what they do to their own societies and states. If there is one great moment that turns the provincial thought of Europe to universal philosophy, the parochial history of Europe to universal history, it is the moment of capital—capital that is global in its territorial reach and universal in its conceptual domain. It is the narrative of capital that can turn the violence of mercantilist trade, war, genocide, conquest, and colonialism into a story of universal progress, development, modernization, and freedom.

For this narrative to take shape, the destruction of community is fundamental. Marx saw this clearly when he identified as the necessary condition for capitalist production the separation of the mass of labourers from the means of labour. This so-called primitive accumulation is nothing but the destruction of precapitalist community, which in various forms had regulated the social unity of labourers with their means of production. Thus, in the narrative of capital, community becomes relegated to capital's prehistory, a natural, prepolitical, primordial stage in social evolution that must be superseded for the journey of freedom and progress to begin. And since the story of capital is universal, community, too, becomes the universal prehistory of progress, identified with medievalism in Europe and the stagnant, backward, undeveloped present in the rest of the world.

Community could not be entirely suppressed, however. The domain of civil society, ruled by 'freedom, equality, property and Bentham',[10] could not produce an adequate justification for the lack of freedom and equality within the industrial labour process itself and the continued division of society into the opposed classes of capital and labour. What Marx did not see too well was the ability of capitalist society to reunite capital and labour ideologically at the level of the political community of the nation, borrowing from another narrative the rhetoric of love, duty, welfare, and so forth. Notwithstanding its universalist scope, capital remained parasitic upon the reconstructed particularism of the nation. (It would be an interesting exercise to identify in Marx's *Capital* the places where this other narrative makes a surreptitious appearance: for instance, in money, the universal equivalent, which nevertheless retains the form of a national currency assigned a particular exchange value by the national state; or in the value of labour power, homogenous and normalized, which is nevertheless determined by specific historical and cultural particularities.)

We must remember that the rise of a public sphere in Europe, to which Taylor refers as a space outside the supervision of political authority where 'opinion could present itself as that of society', was also crucial in connecting a reconstructed cultural identity of the people with the legitimate jurisdiction of the state. It was principally in

---

[10] *Capital*, trans. Ben Fowkes, vol. 1 (Harmondsworth: Penguin, 1976), p. 280.

this public space that, through the medium of 'print-capitalism', as Benedict Anderson calls it, the homogenized forms of a national culture were forged—through the standardization of language, aesthetic norms, and consumer tastes. The public sphere, then, was not only a domain that marked the distinction of state and civil society; by creating the cultural standards through which public opinion could claim to speak on behalf of the nation, it also united state and civil society. Civil society thus became the space for the diverse life of individuals in the nation; the state became the nation's singular representative embodiment, the only legitimate form of community.

But community is not easily appropriated within the narrative of capital. Community, by definition, belongs to the domain of the natural, the primordial. Only in its sanitized, domesticated form can it become a shared subjective feeling that protects and nurtures (good nationalism). But it always carries with it the threatening possibility of becoming violent, divisive, fearsome, irrational (bad nationalism). It is not so much the state–civil society opposition but rather the capital–community opposition that seems to be the great unsurpassed contradiction in Western social philosophy. Both state and civil–social institutions have assigned places within the narrative of capital. Community, which ideally should have been banished from the kingdom of capital, continues to lead a subterranean, potentially subversive life within it because it refuses to go away.

The contradictions between the two narratives of capital and community can be seen quite clearly in the histories of anticolonial nationalist movements. The forms of the modern state are imported into these countries through the agency of colonial rule. The institutions of civil society, in the forms in which they had arisen in Europe, also make their appearance in the colonies precisely to create a public domain for the legitimation of colonial rule. This process was, however, fundamentally limited by the fact that the colonial state could only confer subjecthood on the colonized; it could not grant them citizenship. The crucial break in the history of anticolonial nationalism comes when the colonized refuse to accept membership in this civil society of subjects. They construct their national identities within a different narrative, that of the community. They do not have the option of doing this within the domain of bourgeois civil-social institutions. They create, consequently, a very different domain—a cultural domain—marked by the distinctions of the material and the spiritual, the outer and the inner. (This is something that Anderson does not recognize.) The inner domain of culture is declared the sovereign territory of the nation, to which the colonial state is not allowed entry, even as the outer domain remains surrendered to the colonial power. The rhetoric here (Gandhi is a particularly good example) is of love, kinship, austerity, sacrifice. The rhetoric is in fact antimodernist, anti-individualist, even anti-capitalist. The attempt is, if I may stay with Gandhi for a while, to find against the grand narrative of history itself the cultural resources to negotiate the terms through which people living in different contextually defined communities can coexist peacefully, productively, and creatively within large political units.

The irony is, of course, that this other narrative is again violently interrupted once the postcolonial nation-state attempts to resume its journey along the trajectory of world-historical development. The modern state, embedded as it is within the universal narrative of capital, cannot recognize within its jurisdiction any form of community except the single, determinate, demographically enumerable form of the nation. It must therefore subjugate, by the use of state violence if necessary, all such aspirations of community identity. These other aspirations, in turn, can give to themselves a historically valid justification only by claiming an alternative nationhood with rights to an alternative state.

One can see how a conception of the state–society relation, born within the parochial history of Western Europe but made universal by the global sway of capital, dogs the contemporary history of the world. I do not think that the invocation of the state–civil society opposition in the struggle against socialist-bureaucratic regimes in Eastern Europe (or, for that matter, in the Soviet republics or in China) will produce anything other than strategies seeking to replicate the history of Western Europe. The result has been demonstrated a hundred times. The provincialism of the European experience will be taken as the universal history of progress; by comparison, the history of the rest of the world will appear as the history of lack, of inadequacy—an inferior history. Appeals will be made all over again to philosophies produced in Britain, France, and Germany. The fact that these doctrines were produced in complete ignorance of the histories of other parts of the world will not matter: they will be found useful and enlightening. It would indeed be a supreme irony of history if socialist industrialization gets written into the narrative of capital as the phase when socialist-bureaucratic regimes had to step in to undertake 'primitive accumulation' and clear the way for the journey of capital to be resumed along its 'normal' course.

In the meantime, the struggle between community and capital, irreconcilable within this grand narrative, will continue. The forms of the modern state will be forced into the grid of determinate national identities. This will mean a substantialization of cultural differences, necessarily excluding as minorities those who will not conform to the chosen marks of nationality. The struggle between 'good' and 'bad' nationalism will be played out all over again.

What, then, are the true categories of universal history? State and civil society? Public and private? Social regulation and individual rights?—all made significant within the grand narrative of capital as the history of freedom, modernity, and progress? Or the narrative of community—untheorized, relegated to the primordial zone of the natural, denied any subjectivity that is not domesticated to the requirements of the modern state, and yet persistent in its invocation of the rhetoric of love and kinship against the homogenizing sway of the normalized individual?

It is clear, then: the struggle to provincialize European history becomes a struggle against universal history itself.

17

A Brief History of *Subaltern Studies* (1998)

Gramsci in India

In the form in which it is currently known, 'subaltern' historiography derives from the writings of a group of historians of modern South Asia whose work first appeared in 1982 in a series entitled *Subaltern Studies*.[1] The term 'subaltern' was borrowed by these historians from Antonio Gramsci, the Italian Marxist whose writings in prison in the period 1929–35 had sketched a methodological outline for a 'history of the subaltern classes'.[2] In these writings, Gramsci used the word 'subaltern' (*subalterno* in the Italian) in at least two senses. In one, he used it as a code for the industrial proletariat. But against the thrust of orthodox Marxist thinking, he emphasized that in its rise to power the bourgeoisie did not simply impose a domination through the coercive apparatus of the state but transformed the cultural and ideological institutions of civil society to construct a hegemony over society as a whole, even eliciting in the process the acquiescence of the subaltern

[1] The series has so far published twelve volumes of essays: Ranajit Guha, ed., *Subaltern Studies I–VI* (Delhi: Oxford University Press, 1982–9); Partha Chatterjee and Gyanendra Pandey, eds, *Subaltern Studies VII* (Delhi: Oxford University Press, 1992); David Arnold and David Hardiman, eds, *Subaltern Studies VIII* (Delhi: Oxford University Press, 1992); Shahid Amin and Dipesh Chakrabarty, eds, *Subaltern Studies IX* (Delhi: Oxford University Press, 1996); Gautam Bhadra, Gyan Prakash, and Susie Tharu, eds, *Subaltern Studies X* (Delhi: Oxford University Press, 1999); Partha Chatterjee and Pradeep Jeganathan, eds, *Subaltern Studies XI* (Delhi: Permanent Black, 2000); Shail Mayaram, M.S.S. Pandian, and Ajay Skaria, eds, *Subaltern Studies XII* (Delhi: Permanent Black, 2005).

[2] Antonio Gramsci, *Selections from the Prison Notebooks*, trans. Quintin Hoare and Geoffrey Nowell Smith (New York: International Publishers, 1971).

classes. In Gramsci's analysis of capitalist society, the central place is occupied by questions such as the relations of state and civil society, the connections between the nation, the people, the bourgeoisie, and other ruling classes, the role of intellectuals in creating the social hegemony of the bourgeoisie, strategies for building a counter-hegemonic alliance, etc.

In the second sense, Gramsci talked of the subaltern classes in precapitalist social formations. Here he was referring to the more general relationship of domination and subordination in class-divided societies. But specifically in the context of southern Italy, he wrote about the subordination of the peasantry. Gramsci was very critical of the negative and dismissive attitude of European Marxists towards the culture, beliefs, practices, and political potential of the peasantry. Positioning himself against this attitude, he wrote of the distinct characteristics of the religious beliefs and practices, the language and cultural products, the everyday lives and struggles of peasants, and of the need for revolutionary intellectuals to study and understand them. But he also highlighted the limits of peasant consciousness which, in comparison with the comprehensiveness, originality, and active historical dynamism of the ruling classes, was fragmented, passive, and dependent. Even at moments of resistance, peasant consciousness remained enveloped by the dominant ideologies of the ruling classes. These discussions by Gramsci were turned to productive use by South Asian historians writing in the 1980s.

Against Elitist Historiography

Ranajit Guha, who edited the first six volumes of *Subaltern Studies*, wrote in the introductory statement of the project: 'The historiography of Indian nationalism has for a long time been dominated by elitism— colonialist elitism and bourgeois-nationalist elitism.'[3] The objective of subaltern historiography was to oppose the two elitisms. The field of modern South Asian history was dominated in the 1970s by a debate between a group of historians principally located in Cambridge, England, and another based mainly in Delhi. The former argued that

[3] Ranajit Guha, 'On Some Aspects of the Historiography of Colonial India', in Ranajit Guha, ed., *Subaltern Studies I* (Delhi: Oxford University Press, 1982), pp. 1–8.

Indian nationalism was a bid for power by a handful of Indian elites who used the traditional bonds of caste and communal ties to mobilize the masses against British rule. The latter spoke of how the material conditions of colonial exploitation created the ground for an alliance of the different classes in Indian society and how a nationalist leadership inspired and organized the masses to join the struggle for national freedom. Guha argued that both these views were elitist—the former representing a colonial elitism and the latter a nationalist elitism. Both assumed that nationalism was wholly a product of elite action. Neither history had any place for the independent political actions of the subaltern classes.

In setting their agenda against the two elitisms, the historians of *Subaltern Studies* focused on two main issues. One was the difference between the political objectives and methods of colonial and nationalist elites on the one hand and those of the subaltern classes on the other. The second was the autonomy of subaltern consciousness. Pursuing the first question, the historians of *Subaltern Studies* showed that the claim of colonialist historians that the Indian masses had been, so to speak, duped into joining the anti-colonial movement by Indian elites using primordial ties of kinship and patron–client relations was false. They also showed that it was untrue to say, as nationalist historians did, that the political consciousness of the subaltern classes was only awakened by the ideals and inspiration provided by nationalist leaders. It was indeed a fact that the subaltern classes had often entered the arena of nationalist politics. But it was also a fact that in many instances they had refused to join, despite the efforts of nationalist leaders, or had withdrawn after they had joined. In every case, the goals, strategies, and methods of subaltern politics were different from those of the elites. In other words, even within the domain of nationalist politics, the nationalism of the elites was different from the nationalism of the subaltern classes.

The second question followed from the first. If subaltern politics was indeed different from that of elite politics, what was the source of its autonomy? What were the principles of that politics? The answer that was suggested was that subaltern politics was shaped by the distinct structure of subaltern consciousness.[4] That consciousness had

---

[4] Ranajit Guha, *Elementary Aspects of Peasant Insurgency in Colonial India* (Delhi: Oxford University Press, 1983).

evolved out of the experiences of subordination—out of the struggle, despite the daily routine of servitude, exploitation, and deprivation, to preserve the collective identity of subaltern groups. Where was one to look for the evidence of this autonomous consciousness? It could not be found in the bulk of the archival material that historians conventionally use, because that material had been prepared and preserved by and for the dominant groups. For the most part, those documents only show the subaltern as subservient. It is only at moments of rebellion that the subaltern appears as the bearer of an independent personality. When the subaltern rebels, the masters realize that the servant too has a consciousness, has interests and objectives, methods and organization. If one had to look for evidence of an autonomous subaltern consciousness in the historical archives, then it would be found in the documents of revolt and counterinsurgency.

The first phase of the work of *Subaltern Studies* was dominated by the theme of peasant revolt. Ranajit Guha's *Elementary Aspects of Peasant Insurgency in Colonial India* (1983) is the key text in this area. But most other scholars associated with the project wrote on the history of peasant revolt from different regions and periods of South Asian history. They were able to discover a few sources where the subaltern could be heard telling his or her own story. But it was always clear that there would be few such sources. What became far more productive were new strategies of reading the conventional documents on peasant revolts. The historians of subaltern politics produced several examples of ways in which reports of peasant rebellion prepared by official functionaries could be read from the opposite standpoint of the rebel peasant and thus used to shed light on the consciousness of the rebel. They also showed that when elite historians, even those with progressive views and sympathetic to the cause of the rebels, sought to ignore or rationally explain away what appeared as mythical, illusory, millenarian, or utopian in rebel actions, they were actually missing the most powerful and significant elements of subaltern consciousness. The consequence, often unintended, of this historiographical practice was to somehow fit the unruly facts of subaltern politics into the rationalist grid of elite consciousness and to make them understandable in terms of the latter. The autonomous history of the subaltern classes, or to put it differently, the distinctive traces of subaltern action in history, were completely lost in this historiography.

The Imbrication of Elite and
Subaltern Politics

The analysis of peasant insurgency in colonial India and of subaltern participation in nationalist politics by the historians of *Subaltern Studies* amounted to a strong critique of bourgeois-nationalist politics and the postcolonial state. Writing about peasant revolts in British India, Ranajit Guha and Gautam Bhadra showed how this powerful strand of anticolonial politics, launched independently of bourgeois-nationalist leaders, had been denied its place in established historiography.[5] Gyanendra Pandey, David Hardiman, Sumit Sarkar, and Shahid Amin wrote about the two domains of elite and subaltern politics as they came together in the nationalist movement led by the Congress.[6] Dipesh Chakrabarty wrote about a similar split between elite and subaltern politics in the world of the urban working class.[7] Partha Chatterjee traced the development of nationalist thought in India in terms of the separation of elite and subaltern politics and the attempts by the former to appropriate the latter.[8] The postcolonial nation-state had, it was argued, included the subaltern classes within the imagined space of the nation but had distanced them from the actual political space of the state. Although the political emphasis was not the same in each writer, there was nevertheless a strong flavour in *Subaltern Studies* of the Maoist politics that had hit many parts of India in the 1970s. Many critics thought they could detect in it a romantic

[5] Guha, *Elementary Aspects;* Gautam Bhadra, *Iman o Nishan: Banglar Krishak Chaitanyer ek Adhyay* (Faith and the Flag: An Aspect of Peasant Consciousness in Bengal) (Calcutta: Subarnarekha, 1994).

[6] Gyanendra Pandey, *The Ascendancy of the Congress in Uttar Pradesh, 1926–1934* (Delhi: Oxford University Press, 1984); David Hardiman, *Peasant Nationalists of Gujarat* (Delhi: Oxford University Press, 1984); Sumit Sarkar, *Popular Movements and Middle-class Leadership in Late Colonial India* (Calcutta: K.P. Bagchi, 1984); Gyanendra Pandey, *The Construction of Communalism in Colonial North India* (Delhi: Oxford University Press, 1990); Shahid Amin, *Event, Metaphor, Memory: Chauri Chaura 1922–1992* (Delhi: Oxford University Press, 1995).

[7] Dipesh Chakrabarty, *Rethinking Working-Class History: Bengal 1890–1940* (Princeton: Princeton University Press, 1989).

[8] Partha Chatterjee, *Nationalist Thought and the Colonial World: A Derivative Discourse?* (London: Zed Books, 1986); Chatterjee, *The Nation and Its Fragments: Colonial and Postcolonial Histories* (Princeton: Princeton University Press, 1993).

nostalgia for a peasant armed struggle that never quite took place. Others alleged that by denying the unifying force of the nationalist movement and stressing the autonomous role of the subaltern classes, the historians of *Subaltern Studies* were legitimizing a divisive and possibly subversive politics.

Another connection that was often made in the early phase of *Subaltern Studies* was with the 'history from below' approach popularized by British Marxist historians. Clearly, the work of Christopher Hill, E.P. Thompson, Eric Hobsbawm, or the *History Workshop* writers, or indeed of French social historians like Emmanuel Le Roy Ladurie, was eagerly mined by subalternist historians for methodological clues towards doing popular history. But there was a crucial difference because of which subaltern history could never be a 'history from below'. The forgotten histories of the people, pulled out from under the edifice of modern capitalist civilization in the West, had undoubtedly made the story of Western modernity more detailed and complete. But there did not seem to be any narrative of 'history from below' that could persuasively challenge the existence, stability, or indeed the historical legitimacy of capitalist modernity itself. Not surprisingly, 'history from below' was invariably written as tragedy. But in countries such as India, 'history from below' could not be confined within any such given narrative limits. The subalternist historians refused to subscribe to the historicist orthodoxy that the trajectories of the West, or of other parts of the world, had to be repeated in India. They rejected the framework of modernization as the necessary narrative of history in the formerly colonial countries. They were sceptical about the established orthodoxies of both liberal-nationalist and Marxist historiographies. As a result, they resisted in their writings the tendency to construct the story of modernity in India as the actualization of modernity as imagined by the great theorists of the Western world. This resistance, apparent even in the early phase of *Subaltern Studies*, was to be expressed later in arguments about 'other modernities'.

Reorientations

One line of argument of the early *Subaltern Studies* project that ran into serious problems concerned the existence of an autonomous subaltern consciousness. Much of the study of the insurgent peasant was a search for a characteristic structure of peasant consciousness, shaped by its experience of subordination but struggling ceaselessly to retain its autonomy. One problematic question that arose was about the historicity of this structure. If subaltern consciousness was formed within specific historical relations of domination and subordination, then could that consciousness change? If so, why could it not be said that the Indian peasantry was transformed (modernized, turned into citizens) by its experience of nationalist politics? Why the resistance to a progressive narrative of history? Or was there another narrative of a changing subaltern consciousness? It was a classic structuralist impasse to which there was no easy historical answer.

A related problem was about the notion of the subaltern as an active historical agent. Research into subaltern history had shown that the subaltern was both outside and inside the domains of colonial governance and nationalist politics. To the extent that it was outside, it had retained its autonomy. But it had also entered those domains, participated in their processes and institutions, and thereby transformed itself. Every bit of historical evidence was pointing to the fact that the subaltern was 'a deviation from the ideal'. Why then the search for a 'pure structure' of subaltern consciousness? Moreover, argued Gayatri Spivak in two influential articles, subaltern history had successfully shown that the 'man' or 'citizen' who was the sovereign subject of bourgeois history writing was in truth only the elite. Why was it necessary now to clothe the subaltern in the costume of the sovereign subject and put him on stage as the maker of history? Subaltern historiography had in fact challenged the very idea that there had to be a sovereign subject of history possessing an integral consciousness. Why bring back the same idea into subaltern history? It was only a myth that the subaltern could directly speak through the writings of the historian. In fact, the historian was only representing the subaltern on the pages of history. The subaltern, announced Spivak, cannot speak.[9]

The new turn in *Subaltern Studies* began more or less from the fifth and sixth volumes published in 1987-9. It was now acknowledged with much greater seriousness than before that subaltern histories were fragmentary, disconnected, incomplete, that subaltern consciousness

---

[9] Gayatri Chakravorty Spivak, 'Subaltern Studies: Deconstructing Historiography', in Ranajit Guha, ed., *Subaltern Studies IV* (Delhi: Oxford University Press, 1987), pp. 338–63; Spivak, 'Can the Subaltern Speak?', in Cary Nelson and Lawrence Grossberg, eds, *Marxism and the Interpretation of Culture* (Urbana, Illinois: University of Illinois Press, 1988).

was split within itself, that it was constituted by elements drawn from the experiences of both dominant and subordinate classes. Alongside the evidence of autonomy displayed by subalterns at moments of rebellion, the forms of subaltern consciousness undergoing the everyday experience of subordination now became the subject of inquiry. Once these questions entered the agenda, subaltern history could no longer be restricted to the study of peasant revolts. Now the question was not 'What is the true form of the subaltern?' The question had become 'How is the subaltern represented?' 'Represent' here meant both 'present again' and 'stand in place of'. Both the subjects and the methods of research underwent a change.

One direction in which the new research proceeded was the critical analysis of texts. Once the question of the 'representation of the subaltern' came to the fore, the entire field of the spread of the modern knowledges in colonial India was opened up for subaltern history. Much-studied subjects such as the expansion of colonial governance, English education, movements of religious and social reform, the rise of nationalism—all of these were opened to new lines of questioning by the historians of *Subaltern Studies*. The other direction of research concentrated on the modern state and public institutions through which modern ideas of rationality and science and the modern regime of power were disseminated in colonial and postcolonial India. In other words, institutions such as schools and universities, newspapers and publishing houses, hospitals, doctors, medical systems, censuses, registration bureaux, the industrial labour process, scientific institutions—all of these became subjects of subaltern history writing.

Other Modernities

A major argument that has been developed in the more recent phase of writings in and around *Subaltern Studies* is that of alternative or hybrid modernities. The focus here is on the dissemination of the ideas, practices, and institutions of Western modernity under colonial conditions. The framework of modernization theory invariably produces the history of modernity in non-Western colonial countries as a narrative of lag or catching up. As Dipesh Chakrabarty has put it, these societies seem to have been consigned for ever to 'the waiting room of history'. The universality of Western modernity erases the fact that, like all histories, it too is a product of its local conditions. When transported to other places and times, it cannot remain unaffected by other local conditions. What happens when the products of Western modernity are domesticated in other places? Do they take on new and different shapes—shapes that do not belong to the original? If they do, are we to treat the changes as corruptions? As deviations from an ideal? Or are they valid as examples of a different modernity?

To argue the latter is both to provincialize Europe and to assert the identity of other cultures even as they participate in the presumed universality of modernity. Dipesh Chakrabarty, David Arnold, Gyan Prakash, Gayatri Spivak, and Partha Chatterjee, for example, have explored various aspects of this process of the 'translation' of modern knowledges, technologies, and institutions.[10] They have tried to show that the encounter between Western forms of modernity and colonized non-Western cultures was not a simple imposition of the one on the other, nor did it lead to corrupt or failed forms of modernity. Rather, it produced different forms of modernity whose marks of difference still remain subject to unresolved contestations of power.

Here, the work of South Asian subalternist historians has often overlapped with and contributed to what has become known in the United States and Britain as postcolonial studies. The historical study of modern discourses and institutions of power in colonial India has fed into a growing literature on the production of hybrid cultural forms in many different regions of the formerly colonial world. More significantly, postcolonial studies has extended the argument about hybrid cultural forms to the understanding of contemporary cultures in the Western metropolitan countries themselves, instanced most immediately in the diasporic cultures of immigrants but also, less obviously, in the role of the colonial experience in the formation of Western modernity even in its purportedly 'original' form.[11] Historical and

[10] David Arnold, *Colonizing the Body: State Medicine and Epidemic Disease in Nineteenth-Century India* (Berkeley: University of California Press, 1993); Partha Chatterjee, ed., *Texts of Power: The Disciplines in Colonial Bengal* (Minneapolis: University of Minnesota Press, 1995); Gyan Prakash, *Another Reason* (Princeton: Princeton University Press, 1999); Gayatri Chakravorty Spivak, *A Critique of Postcolonial Reason* (Cambridge, Mass.: Harvard University Press, 1999); Dipesh Chakrabarty, *Provincializing Europe: Postcolonial Thought and Historical Difference* (Princeton: Princeton University Press, 2000).

[11] A few examples: Mary Louise Pratt, *Imperial Eyes: Travel Writing and Transculturation* (London: Routledge, 1992); Jack Goody, *The East in the West* (Cambridge:

social science disciplines have tended to merge here with the concerns and methods of the literary and cultural disciplines to break new, and still mostly uncharted, theoretical grounds.

Yet, even as the overlap between *Subaltern Studies* and postcolonial studies has often been noticed, there remains a crucial difference in emphasis that continues to be reflected in the choice of problems and topics in the two strands of history writing. Despite the reorientation of the original set of theoretical problems in *Subaltern Studies*, its historical and polemical focus continues to be set on the contemporary political debates of the countries of South Asia. Thus, in view of the religious-sectarian conflicts in India in the last two decades, subalternist historians have contributed in very distinct ways to rewriting the history of communal conflicts in colonial India or to the history of the Partition of India. The subalternist approach has been used in productive ways to reframe the history of ethnic conflicts in Sri Lanka. This has led to a serious critique of the nation-state as well as of the ideology of nationalism as they have been instituted in South Asia. But given the centrality of these questions to the everyday politics of the nation-state, even in their most 'mainstream' forms the subalternist critics have been forced to engage with the debates of the mainstream not from the relative theoretical freedom afforded by a position of marginality but with the full responsibility demanded by considerations of practicality and institutional realism. Unlike postcolonial history in the United States and Britain, where notions of hybridity or the colonial origins of Western modernity can be explored with considerable creative freedom because of the relative marginality of the discipline, subaltern history in South Asia has to work within the realist confines of national politics, even as it offers its critique. This becomes clear if we consider some of the main political issues that have featured in the recent work of *Subaltern Studies*.

Cambridge University Press, 1996); Frederick Cooper and Ann Laura Stoler, eds, *Tensions of Empire: Colonial Cultures in a Bourgeois World* (Berkeley: University of California Press, 1997); Antoinette Burton, *At the Heart of the Empire: Indians and the Colonial Encounter in Late-Victorian Britain* (Berkeley: University of California Press, 1998); Catherine Hall, *Civilising Subjects: Metropole and Colony in the English Imagination 1830–1867* (Chicago: University of Chicago Press, 2002); Chandak Sengoopta, *Imprint of the Raj: How Fingerprinting Was Born in Colonial India* (London: Macmillan, 2003).

Rethinking the Political

If we recall the initial political questions raised by subaltern history writing, where have they led? The early emphasis on peasant rebellion and consciousness had widened, even in the first phase of the project, to include the resistance of other dominated and marginalized groups in colonial society. Once the idea of a paradigmatic structure of subaltern consciousness became less persuasive, the subject of resistance began to be approached from a variety of angles and without a fixed design either of the reproduction of a traditional structure or of the necessary transition to new structures. Recent subaltern historiography has vigorously participated in three sets of South Asian debates—over religious minorities, caste, and gender. These debates have opened up the way to rethinking the political formation of the nation as well as the political process of democracy.

In India, the broader political debate over religious minorities has been carried out between two opposed groups—the Hindu chauvinists on the one hand and the secularists on the other. What the researches of subalternist historians have shown is that the debate between secularism and communalism is in no way a struggle between modernity and backwardness. Both the rival political positions are firmly planted in the soil of modern government and politics. Second, the two groups are pursuing two different strategies of consolidating the regime of the modern nation-state. Both strategies are elitist, but they involve two different modes of representation and appropriation of the subaltern. Third, faced with these rival elitist strategies, subaltern groups in India are devising, in their own ways, independent strategies of coping with communal as well as secularist politics. The recent experiences of ethnic violence and authoritarian politics in Sri Lanka and Pakistan have raised even more fundamental questions about the adequacy of the nation-form as a field where subaltern politics might be negotiated.[12]

[12] Partha Chatterjee and Pradeep Jeganathan, eds, *Subaltern Studies XI* (Delhi: Permanent Black, 2000); Gyanendra Pandey, *Remembering Partition: Violence, Nationalism and History in India* (Cambridge: Cambridge University Press, 2001); Shail Mayaram, *Resisting Regimes: Myth, Memory and the Shaping of a Muslim Identity* (Delhi: Oxford University Press, 1997); Shail Mayaram, *Against History, Against State: Counterperspectives from the Margins* (New York: Columbia University Press, 2003); Shail Mayaram, M.S.S. Pandian, and Ajay Skaria, eds, *Subaltern Studies XII* (Delhi: Permanent Black, 2005).

The second question on which there has been significant recent discussion is caste. There has been a transformation in the politics of caste in India following the agitations in 1990-1 over the Mandal Commission report. By looking at the politics of caste in its discursive aspect, it has become clear that the supposedly religious basis of caste divisions has now completely disappeared from public debate. The conflicts now are almost exclusively centred on the relative positions of different caste groups in relation to the state. Second, the debate over whether or not to recognize caste as a criterion for affirmative action by the state once again reflects two different elitist strategies of representing and appropriating the subaltern—one insisting on equality of opportunity and selection by merit, the other arguing that a phase of affirmative action is needed to compensate for the centuries of deprivation suffered by the lower castes. And subaltern groups too, in their efforts to establish social justice and self-respect, are devising various strategies of both resisting the state as well as of utilizing the opportunities offered by its electoral and developmental functions.[13] Strategies of alliance between castes at the middle and bottom rungs of the ritual hierarchy with other oppressed groups such as tribals and religious minorities have produced significant electoral successes. But with the creation of new political elites out of subaltern groups, the questions of 'who represents?' and 'to what end?' are being asked with a new urgency.

The third debate concerns the social position of women. In one sense, all women living in patriarchal societies are subalterns. Yet, it is not true that women are not identified by class, race, caste, and community. Hence, just as it is valid to analyse the subordination of women in a society ruled by men, so also is it necessary to identify how the social construction of gender is made more complex by the intervention of class, caste, and communal identities. Recent discussions on this question have focused on the Indian social reform movements of the nineteenth century, especially the various legal reforms to protect the rights of women, in the context of the colonial state and nationalist politics. Subaltern feminist writings have raised questions about the adequacy of a modernizing agenda of legal reform from the top without facing up to the challenge of reforming the actual

[13] Mayaram *et al.*, eds, *Subaltern Studies XII.*

structures of patriarchal power within the local communities which continue to flourish outside the reach of the law.[14]

The recent debates raise new questions about conceptualizing old modernist ideas such as nation, citizenship, and democracy. By virtue of these implications, recent subaltern history writings from South Asia have been productively used in writings on the history of modernity in other parts of the formerly colonized world, such as, for instance, on nationalism and gender in the Middle East, or on the politics of peasant and indigenous groups in Latin America. Having travelled from Italy to India, the idea of subaltern history has now produced a generally available methodological and stylistic approach to modern historiography that could indeed be used anywhere.

[14] Nivedita Menon, ed., *Gender and Politics in India* (Delhi: Oxford University Press, 1999); Flavia Agnes, *Law and Gender Inequality: The Politics of Women's Rights in India* (Delhi: Oxford University Press, 2001); Nivedita Menon, *Recovering Subversion: Feminist Politics Beyond the Law* (Delhi: Permanent Black, 2004).

18

The Colonial State and Peasant Resistance in Bengal, 1920–1947

(1986)

I. Colonial Rule and the Mode of Production in Agriculture

It is widely agreed that a prolonged period of modern colonial rule in pre-capitalist societies establishes the conditions for the rise of capitalist relations of production in agriculture. At a general level of analysis this is almost a truism. The task of historical analysis, however, is to look into the specific processes by which these relations emerge in different regions under colonial rule, the different ways in which pre-capitalist agrarian forms are replaced, modified, or retained, and the manner in which these differences affect the conditions within which the political struggle among classes is carried out.

There are two major and interrelated aspects to the question of the impact of colonial rule on the agrarian economy: first, changes in the legal structure of agrarian property brought about by the colonial state; and secondly, the effects of an entirely novel arrangement of market operations in agricultural products, usually known as the process of commoditization or 'commercialization' of agriculture.

On the first aspect, it has sometimes been argued, with the specific case of British India in mind, that the establishment of a 'colonial bourgeois state' with its 'bourgeois' legal and institutional framework

Presented to the *Past and Present* conference on 'Agrarian Unrest in British and French Africa, French Indo-China and British India', Oxford, 11–12 July 1982.

creates conditions in which, even if pre-capitalist forms of labour exploitation continue, their 'essential nature and significance undergoes a revolutionary transformation'.[1] The most significant part of the legislative acts of the colonial state is to transform the very nature of landed property from a 'feudal' to a 'bourgeois' type: 'The main impact of the change brought about by the colonial dispensation was the elimination of the petty sovereignties of chieftains and *zamindars* who *ruled* the land, as much as they owned it. [Thus] the "fusion of economic and political power at the point of production" . . . was dissolved and was reconstituted in the form of bourgeois landed property, under the authority of the colonial state which marked a separation of economic and political power.'[2] Specifically for the case of Bengal, it has been argued that the Permanent Settlement, the predominant legal form of property arrangements in land in eastern India, meant that 'the peasant was dispossessed of the land which now became the "property" of the zamindar . . . The *landlord* became *landowner. Land* was now "bourgeois landed property" . . .'[3]

The historical evidence on this subject, however, makes it quite clear that the 'bourgeois' character of the legal structure erected under colonial rule was profoundly contradictory and ambiguous,[4] and the 'revolutionary' nature of the transformation a far more complex question than is suggested by essentialist arguments of this kind. Here I will show the specific ways in which such an essentialist characterization can lead to a complete misunderstanding of some of the most significant aspects of the class struggle in the final phase of colonial rule in Bengal.

On the second question, there has been much debate about the characterization of the impact of commercialization on production relations in agriculture, a debate that has in fact continued into the field of developments in post-colonial India. It has been argued on the one

[1] Hamza Alavi, 'India and the Colonial Mode of Production', in John Saville and Ralph Miliband, eds, *Socialist Register 1975* (London, 1975), pp. 160–97.

[2] Hamza Alavi, 'India: Transition from Feudalism to Colonial Capitalism', *Journal of Contemporary Asia*, x (1980), pp. 359–98.

[3] Ibid., p. 371.

[4] Many of these ambiguities in the case of British India in general are pointed out in Dietmar Rothermund, *Government, Landlord and Peasant in India* (Wiesbaden, 1978); D.A. Washbrook, 'Law, State and Agrarian Society in Colonial India', *Modern Asian Studies*, xv (1981), pp. 649–721.

hand that, whereas commercialization (or commoditization) started a process of differentiation among the peasantry, it also led to a strengthening rather than weakening of 'semi-feudal' forms of bondage and exploitation. While the viability of small-peasant subsistence production was undermined, this was replaced not by capitalist agricultural production employing wage labour, but rather by the extension of effective control over an increasing part of the product of small-peasant agriculture by landlord/moneylender/traders using the debt-credit mechanism. The extension as well as the intensification of such forms of 'debt bondage' depended not only on new economic conditions (such as lack of alternative employment in a labour-surplus economy), but also, and crucially, on the ability of these 'semi-feudal' landlords to resort to extra-economic, and often extra-legal, means of coercion to secure the conditions of bondage.[5]

On the other hand it has been suggested that the continuation of such forms of exploitation of peasant labour should be seen as a case of 'formal', as distinct from 'real', subordination of labour by capital, and as the extension of capitalist domination.[6] 'Formal' subordination of labour by capital occurs when capital 'takes over' the process of production of the small producer 'as it finds it', without subjecting it to a technical transformation. Capital here subjugates the labour process of the small producer, becomes the 'immediate owner' of the process of production, converts the immediate producer into a mere

[5] The analytical statements of this argument can be found in Amit Bhaduri, 'An Analysis of Semi-feudalism in Eastern Indian Agriculture', *Frontier* (Calcutta), 29 September 1973; Amit Bhaduri, 'A Study in Agricultural Backwardness under Semi-feudalism', *Economic Journal*, lxxxiii (1973), pp. 120–37; Amit Bhaduri, 'The Evolution of Land Relations in Eastern India under British Rule', *Indian Economic and Social History Review*, xiii (1976), pp. 45–58; Nirmal K. Chandra, 'Farm Efficiency under Semi-feudalism', *Economic and Political Weekly*, ix (1974), pp. 1309–32; Utsa Patnaik, 'Class Differentiation within the Peasantry', *Economic and Political Weekly: Review of Agriculture*, xi (1976), pp. 82–101. This argument has also been spelt out for the case of colonial Bengal in Partha Chatterjee, 'Agrarian Structure in Pre-partition Bengal', in Asok Sen, Partha Chatterjee, and Saugata Mukherji, *Three Studies on the Agrarian Structure in Bengal 1850–1947* (Calcutta, 1982), pp. 113–224.

[6] Jairus Banaji, 'Capitalist Domination and the Small Peasantry: Deccan Districts in the Late Nineteenth Century', *Economic and Political Weekly*, xii (1977), pp. 1375–404; Hamza Alavi, 'Structure of Colonial Social Formations', *Economic and Political Weekly*, xvi (1981), pp. 475–86. This argument is based on a distinction suggested by Marx in a hitherto unpublished fragment of *Capital*. See Karl Marx, *Capital*, i, trans. Ben Fowkes (Harmondsworth, 1976), Appendix, pp. 1019–38.

'factor' in the production process 'which is then directed by the capitalist to produce absolute surplus-value'. It is argued, then, that this is precisely what happens to small-peasant production in colonial India when it is subsumed under mercantile usurious capital.

The difference between this position and the one of 'semi-feudalism' seems to hinge, crucially, on whether capital is seen as becoming the 'immediate owner' of the production process in the colonial period, reducing the peasant to a mere factor in that process. It could be argued, particularly from the evidence on Bengal, that the small peasant/ sharecropper, although subjected to exploitation by the moneylender/ trader, nevertheless retained a partial control over his means of subsistence, was not wholly directed by the moneylender/trader in production decisions, and was still exploited in large part in the form of an absolute ground rent by the landlord, often fused in the same person as the moneylender/trader.[7] More significantly, of course, the problem is not one of attributing essential characteristics to long historical periods, but of understanding the structural dynamics of a historical process of change. And here, the earlier argument of 'formal' subordination has been extended to suggest that a control of even a portion of the means of subsistence of the small producer by capital 'would tend to lead in the vast majority of cases to the system of formal subordination—i.e. over time, the monied capitalist would gain control over the entire means of subsistence and production of this enterprise.'[8] But this is clearly an *a priori*, unhistorical, and determinist extension of the argument of 'formal' subordination, ignoring altogether the fact that the subordination of labour to capital, whether 'formal' or 'real', in a particular society can only be the historical result of a specific historical process of class struggle. Moreover, the counterargument could be advanced emphasizing the *specific political* significance in different regions and different periods of all those structural conditions in the colonial social formation which impeded 'pre-formal' subordination

[7] See Chatterjee, 'Agrarian Structure'.

[8] Banaji, 'Capitalist Domination', p. 1376. Banaji supports this *a priori* pronouncement by remarking that Marx often assimilated cases of mercantile exploitation falling short of formal subordination (Banaji calls them, somewhat disingenuously, cases of 'pre-formal' subsumption) with formal subordination proper, implying that Marx 'did not regard the distinction as particularly important'. The distinction, however, was explicitly made by Marx himself in the course of clarifying what he did *not* mean by 'formal' subordination. See Marx, Appendix to *Capital*, i.

from becoming 'formal', or, for that matter, 'formal' subordination to capital from becoming 'real', despite 'capitalist domination' for almost two hundred years.

The point, therefore, is that the question of transition in modes of production in the period of colonial rule cannot be solved by collapsing the general historical tendency towards the extension of capitalist domination and the subordination of various pre-existing forms of labour by capital to every historically specific case, since many such cases can present quite distinct problems for historical analysis. The problem can only be confronted by analysing for each particular region in question the specific techno-economic changes in the production process in agriculture as well as the specific political forms of the struggles among contending agrarian classes seeking to redefine production relations. Perhaps we will then be in a position to make a richer, more complex, and historically more accurate formulation of the general relationship between capitalism and colonial social formations. In the following sections I will attempt to look at the two aspects of this process of change—the techno-economic and the political—in their interrelation in the specific case of Bengal in the last three decades of colonial rule.

II. Agrarian Property and the Colonial State in Bengal

The basic legal framework of landed property in colonial Bengal was laid down by the Permanent Settlement of 1793. In its intellectual origins this settlement was based on a physiocratic rationalization of the belief that a capitalist landowning class on the model of the English squirearchy could be reproduced in the richly endowed and prosperous province of Bengal.[9] In the end, as Marx remarked, it merely became 'a caricature of large-scale English landed estates', one of 'a string of futile and really absurd (in practice infamous) economic experiments' which the British carried out in India.[10]

Initially the settlement conferred on landlords what were presumed to be full rights of private proprietorship in their estates. In return the landlords were obliged to pay to the government, by a particular date

[9] A study of the ideas surrounding the making of the Permanent Settlement is Ranajit Guha, *A Rule of Property for Bengal* (Paris, 1963).
[10] Karl Marx, *Capital*, iii (Moscow, 1971), pp. 333–4.

every year, an amount of revenue 'fixed in all perpetuity'. The expectation was that since the revenue burden would be constant the landlord would have the incentive to improve the productivity of his estate and reap the benefits of increased returns. Since the initial assessment of revenue was very high and many of the existing zamindari establishments hardly equipped to organize quickly enough the increased collection of rents, a very large part of the older estates was bought off by new and presumably more 'enterprising' and 'commercially oriented' landlords. The law then conferred on them in 1799 and 1812 additional coercive powers *vis-à-vis* their tenants, so as to enable them to collect the rents in time.[11]

However, well into the first quarter of the nineteenth century the situation in most of Bengal was still one where the main problem of agricultural production was to find enough labour to cultivate the available land. The principal manner in which landlords tackled this problem was to organize a rapid extension of cultivation, mainly in the north, east, and south of the province, by subleasing portions of estates to enterprising tenants who would undertake to mobilize cultivators to clear out and settle the new lands. By the 1850s and 1860s one finds the situation reaching a fairly stable plateau; by the turn of the century there was very little cultivable land that was not already fully employed within the prevalent technical limits of production.[12] Until the middle of the century, therefore, although unfamiliar and unprecedented methods of coercing the peasantry, such as those practised by British indigo planters, met with much resentment and hostility,[13] the issue of the exact nature of 'property' under the new colonial state hardly

[11] For a detailed account of the evolution of the laws of landed property in Bengal following the Permanent Settlement, see Anil Chandra Banerjee, *The Agrarian System of Bengal*, 2 vols. (Calcutta, 1981), ii.

[12] Benoy Chowdhury, 'Agrarian Economy and Agrarian Relations in Bengal, 1859–1885', in N.K. Sinha (ed.), *The History of Bengal, 1757–1905* (Calcutta, 1967), pp. 237–336. Figures for the 1930s show that only 8 per cent of the total cultivable area was 'cultivable waste': *Report of the Land Revenue Commission, Bengal* (Chairman: F.L.C. Floud), 6 vols (Alipore, 1940), ii, p. 88. In 1944–5 Ishaque put the proportion of 'cultivable waste' at 9 per cent of the total area: H.S.M. Ishaque, *Agricultural Statistics by Plot to Plot Enumeration in Bengal, 1944–45*, 2 vols (Alipore, 1946), i, p. 7.

[13] See Benoy Chowdhury, 'Growth of Commercial Agriculture in Bengal, 1757–1900', *Indian Studies Past and Present* (Calcutta), iv (1962–3), pp. 461–508, and v (1963–4), pp. 5–87.

became a matter of political dispute, and local customary practices were considered adequate to decide the respective rights of landlords, intermediate tenure holders, tenants, and undertenants. In fact the overwhelming part of the peasantry in Bengal cultivated the land without any recorded contractual agreement setting down the conditions under which they held the land as tenants.

But with the cumulative effects of deindustrialization and rapidly increased pressures of population growth, it soon became apparent that uncontrolled 'high landlordism' would have serious consequences. In particular, the Pabna revolt of 1873 showed clearly that the economic context had changed enough to make it imperative for the colonial state to define more precisely, perhaps redefine, the legal rights of 'property' amongst different agrarian classes.[14]

The Rent Act of 1859 and the Tenancy Act of 1885 together established that the colonial state in Bengal preferred above all to protect the basic structure of small-peasant agriculture, devoted primarily to subsistence production but also responding, within the limits of the existing organization of production, to the forces of the market in order to produce a reasonable volume of commercial crops. In order to secure these conditions for an expanded process of colonial appropriation in a period of growing international trade, the state was even prepared to tamper with the presumed sanctity of zamindari property rights. But given its political constraint—the massive 'law and order' problem of large-scale evictions from the land—the state was entirely unprepared to create the conditions for a more thoroughgoing capitalist reorganization of agricultural production. It even turned the force of its legal and administrative machinery against British entrepreneurs (the indigo planters, for instance) when their activities posed too much of a threat to the stability of small-peasant agriculture.[15]

The land laws of the nineteenth century recognized the rights to occupation of various groups of tenants ('occupancy' tenants, for instance, were given the heritable right not to be ejected by the landlord) and the limits within which their rents could be enhanced. Only a

[14] On the Pabna revolt, see Kalyan Sen Gupta, *Pabna Disturbances and the Politics of Rent, 1873–1885* (New Delhi, 1974); and Binay Bhushan Chaudhuri, 'The Story of Peasant Revolt in a Bengal District', *Bengal Past and Present* (Calcutta), xcii (1973–4), pp. 220–78.

[15] On this point in particular, see Binay Bhushan Chaudhuri, 'The Agrarian Question in Bengal and the Government 1850–1900', *Calcutta Historical Journal*, i (1976–7), pp. 33–88.

section of tenants, including most of the more prosperous ones (some of whom, although tenants, were not actually cultivators but *rentiers*), got the 'occupancy' right.[16] But it was a definite restriction on the 'unfettered' proprietary rights of landlords. This started the process by which the colonial state responded to each spell of agrarian unrest by setting narrower limits on the property rights of landlords and expanding or ramifying the occupation rights of different sections of tenants. Thus the structure of land law was no longer even formally contained within the straightforward bourgeois principles of private property and freedom of contract. Property itself was ambiguously located in different persons and in different sorts of rights to the same piece of land, and freedom of contract was severely curtailed, on the one hand by 'custom'; and on the other by the ubiquitous threat to law and order lurking below the surface of 'traditional' village life.

The only clear incidence of the 'proprietary' right of landlords or tenure holders related to the right to the rent from the land, within the legal limits, not to the land itself or to the organization of production on it. Correspondingly, the quantum of exaction from the actual producer, distributed among an ever-growing number of surplus-extracting interests, was in fact dependent not on the strictly legal sanctions available on the basis of the 'freedom of contract', but to a very large extent on the instruments of domination, 'customary' and cultural as well as coercive and physical, which these rent-receiving classes could impose on their tenants.

III. Commercialization and Changes in Agrarian Structure

This evolution of the legal structure of landed property, and the specific role in it of the colonial state, must of course be seen in the context of an agrarian economy increasingly dominated by the fact of 'commercialization', because this was the specific form of the expanding process of colonial appropriation in British India from the second half of the nineteenth century. After the failure of the indigo experiment the principal export crop in Bengal became jute, cultivated on small peasant plots, mainly with family labour, in the districts of eastern and northern Bengal. Jute cultivation did not require any major structural

---

[16] For a discussion of the implications, see Asok Sen, 'Agrarian Structure and Tenancy Law in Bengal, 1850–1895', in Sen, Chatterjee, and Mukherji, *Three Studies*, pp. 1–112.

modification in the organization of production. For peasants who grew jute, it reduced somewhat their sole dependence on rice. However, the limits of jute cultivation were set by the demand in the world market; it could not be extended indefinitely. Only about 5 per cent of the net cultivated area of Bengal was under jute, but nearly 70 per cent of the total crop was grown in the districts of the Dacca and Rajshahi divisions, i.e. in eastern and northern Bengal. As much as 12 per cent of the gross cultivated area in some of these districts was under jute.[17] The trade in jute was directed almost exclusively towards the export market in raw jute and jute products, and was firmly controlled by the British-owned manufacturing houses in Calcutta. The prices of raw jute ostensibly depended upon the demand in the world market, but whether the world prices rose or fell it was always the small cultivator of jute who was hit the hardest. The peasants in northern and eastern Bengal grew jute because it helped them to maintain a certain level of subsistence, and it was the cash advanced to them by the jute trader in the lean months before a harvest which virtually forced them into an agreement with the trader to sell the crop at a stipulated price. Prices of raw jute were kept under tight monopsonistic control.[18]

The trade in paddy and rice, on the other hand, was far less organized. Paddy was essentially a subsistence crop. Only 4.5–7.5 per cent of the annual production of rice and paddy was exported out of Bengal; the bulk of the operations in the market, therefore, consisted of local and inter-district trading within the province. About 30 per cent of the total population of Bengal was said to be net buyers of rice, mainly landless labourers, other rural wage-earners, factory workers, artisans, professionals, and fixed-income groups.[19]

The relatively more centralized trading in rice was in western Bengal. Nearly 90 per cent of all rice mills in the province were located in the six districts of 24-Parganas, Burdwan, Birbhum, Midnapur,

[17] For details regarding areas, yields, productivities, and prices, see M. Mufakharul Islam, *Bengal Agriculture 1920–1947: A Quantitative Analysis* (Cambridge, 1979).

[18] For a more detailed analysis of the jute trade and the mechanism of control exercised by jute manufacturers, see Saugata Mukherji, *A Colonial Framework for Agricultural Marketing in Eastern India* (New Delhi, forthcoming); and Omkar Goswami, 'Jute Economy of Bengal 1900–1947: A Study of Interaction between Industrial, Trading and Agricultural Sectors', D.Phil. thesis, University of Oxford, 1982.

[19] *Report of the Bengal Paddy and Rice Enquiry Committee* (Chairman: M. Carbery), 2 vols (Alipore, 1940), i, p. 29.

Hooghly, and Malda.[20] It was really in these districts of western Bengal, plus Dinajpur and Rangpur, that rice played an important role as a cash crop.

The price of rice had risen steadily in Bengal up to the Depression of 1931–2. Yet small cultivators had rarely been able to derive any of the benefits, since, given their liabilities of rent payments and the debts incurred during the lean months, they were under great pressure to sell immediately after the harvest. The more substantial cultivators, on the other hand, particularly in western Bengal, 'habitually stored their surplus stock for months on end, and sometimes even for more than a year'.[21]

It was the gradual subsumption of peasant production under a market economy of this nature that brought into operation the familiar process of indebtedness leading to increasing control by the creditor over the surplus product of the small producer, leading in turn to the transfer of the small peasant's land. There was a steady increase in both sales and mortgages of small-peasant holdings in Bengal from the late nineteenth century, although in varying magnitudes and rates in different parts of the province. These rates of increase picked up substantially in the years following the Depression in the early 1930s, and outright sales of smallholdings increased dramatically after the free transferability of tenant holdings was legally recognized by the new Tenancy Act amendment in 1939.[22]

The creditors to whom the land passed were typically *jotdar*—rich peasants who also engaged in moneylending and grain-trading, and often also in small agricultural processing industries, such as rice mills.[23] Typically, once again the transferred land would be cultivated by the dispossessed small peasant, but now on a half-share-of-produce rent and with no legal rights of tenancy. This phenomenon—what has been called 'depeasantization'[24]—occurred throughout the province, but earlier than elsewhere in the western and south-western regions. In

[20] Ibid., p. 23.

[21] Ibid., p. 57.

[22] See, in particular, Binay Bhushan Chaudhuri, 'The Process of Depeasantization in Bengal and Bihar, 1885–1947', *Indian History Review* (1975–6), pp. 105–65. See also Chatterjee, 'Agrarian Structure'.

[23] See A. Ghosh and K. Dutt, *Development of Capitalist Relations in Agriculture: A Case Study of West Bengal 1793–1971* (New Delhi, 1977), especially pp. 59–87.

[24] Chaudhuri, 'Process of Depeasantization'.

the eastern districts, in particular, the availability of a jute crop sustained the viability of small-peasant subsistence production much longer than elsewhere. It was only after the Depression of the early 1930s that the fragility of small-peasant production was finally exposed in eastern Bengal.[25]

The process of colonial extraction, therefore, served to integrate peasant production to a much wider market economy. But the structural form of this integration did not favour a thoroughgoing capitalism in agriculture. It did in the 1930s lead to a major rent crisis which utterly undermined the older structures of zamindari landownership.[26] On the other hand the effect of the expanded process of colonial extraction through a commercialization of agriculture was, as Alan Smalley has recently pointed out,[27] to strengthen the conditions of surplus appropriation by the primary extracting agencies at the village level. As a consequence the dominant general tendency in the Bengal countryside was towards the emergence and sharpening of the contradiction between two broad agrarian classes: a jotdar/moneylender/trader class of primary appropriators partly rooted in production at the village level, but functioning in general as a kulak class engaged in a variety of economic activities; and a small-peasant/sharecropper/labourer class of increasingly impoverished and immiserized primary producers.

The specific political articulation of this process of class formation—that is, the decline of the older zamindari classes and the emergence of a new kulak class—however, requires a specific historical explanation, because it did not take the same form in all regions of Bengal. Indeed it is because of these specific differences in the political articulation of the class struggle in the different regions of the province that the agrarian question had a particularly decisive bearing on the political history of Bengal in the last decades of colonial rule, and arguably on the specific forms of the post-colonial state in West Bengal and East Pakistan/Bangladesh.

In order to systematize this discussion, therefore, it would be useful to bear in mind the following major elements and the relations between them: (1) a landed proprietor class in decline, faced with an old

---

[25] For a detailed discussion on regional differences, see Chatterjee, 'Agrarian Structure'.

[26] Again, for details, see ibid.

[27] Alan Smalley, 'The Colonial State and Agrarian Structure in Bengal', *Journal of Contemporary Asia*, xiii (1983), pp. 176–97.

confrontation with the mass of the peasantry and a new confrontation with a jotdar/moneylender/trader class; (2) the jotdar/moneylender/trader class challenging the erstwhile dominance of the landed proprietors and seeking greater control over the land and the produce of the rest of the peasantry; (3) a growing poor-peasant/sharecropper/labourer class formed out of the dissolution of small-peasant production; and (4) the colonial state, seeking to maintain the economic conditions for expanded colonial appropriation from the agrarian sector but faced with a major political challenge to its very survival and trying, therefore, to intervene both in the process of agricultural production and in the evolving class struggle within the colonial social formation. Later we will add to this a fifth element—a new middle-class intelligentsia, formed principally out of the ranks of the declining *rentier* classes, but playing an independent role of leadership in the political sphere.

IV. Agrarian Relations and Political 'Mobilization'

The general tendency in the process of class formation in twentieth-century Bengal has been noted, and used in different ways, in various current explanations of the political history of the province. John Gallagher, explaining the 'decline' of the Bengal Congress,[28] notes that the Congress was 'the spokesman of interests which were now on the defensive', that is to say, of the predominantly Hindu *rentier* interests with 'lines into the political leadership of Calcutta'. On the other hand, in eastern Bengal, the 'vitality of agriculture' had raised the aspirations of the more substantial peasants, both Muslim and the low-caste Namasudra. At the same time in south-western Bengal, especially in Midnapur and in Arambag in Hooghly, the richer peasantry 'exploited local grievances' against the government: 'it was their domination which gave the resistance the flavour of a mass movement in those areas'. Faced with this challenge to its traditional social dominance, and 'as the defender of interests vulnerable to social change and a wider franchise', the Bengal Congress needed to make a quick bargain with the British. But this neither the British nor the Congress outside Bengal was ready to permit.

[28] John Gallagher, 'Congress in Decline: Bengal 1930 to 1935', in J. Gallagher, G. Johnson and A. Seal, eds, *Locality, Province and Nation: Essays on Indian Politics, 1870–1940* (Cambridge, 1973), pp. 269–325.

Hitesranjan Sanyal, discussing the growth of nationalist mass movements in south-western Bengal,[29] also notes the general decline of the landed proprietor class and the rise, all over the province, of a 'new leadership' from out of 'the richer and more prosperous *raiyats* [tenants with recognized rights].' Politically, this meant a challenge to the erstwhile dominance of the English-educated *bhadralok* [respectable] classes as links between the peasants of the countryside and the expanding institutional structures of government. The newly emerging leadership from the jotdar/moneylending/trader classes now challenged the zamindari sections on the question of local control at the village level. These leaders organized the rest of the peasantry against zamindari oppression with two objectives in mind: one, to increase their own bargaining position *vis-à-vis* the zamindars; and two, to expand their sphere of dominance and control over the peasants. They then succeeded in translating their control at the village level into institutionalized power by seizing upon the new opportunities opened up by an expanding arrangement of local government, and still later by the extension of the franchise in elections to the provincial legislature. After the 1936 elections, says Sanyal, 'the representatives of the new leadership were the strongest force in the Bengal Assembly'. Sanyal also remarks that 'the emergence and spread of this new leadership was desired by the colonial government', since it was now desperately looking for 'loyal allies' among the subject population. In the specific case of south-western Bengal, however, where the mass movements were directed specifically against the colonial state, the new jotdar/moneylender/trader classes were faced with a choice: to go against the mass of the peasantry and seek support from the state, or to join the movement and use their local dominance to lead and direct it towards their own ends. In Midnapur, in particular, they opted for the latter course.

On the other hand, Badruddin Umar, discussing political developments in the eastern districts of Bengal in this period,[30] does not emphasize the contradictory nature of relations between a declining zamindari class and a rising jotdar/moneylender/trader class. Instead he regards the entire group of exploiters of the labouring peasantry as a combine of 'landlord-bourgeois classes'. His problem is to explain

[29] Hitesranjan Sanyal, 'Dakshin-paschim Banglay Jatiatabadi Andolan, I' (Nationalist Movement in South-Western Bengal, I), *Chaturanga* (Calcutta), xxxviii (1976–7), pp. 1–26.

[30] Badruddin Umar, *Chirasthayi Bandobaste Bangladesher Krishak* (Bengal Peasants under the Permanent Settlement) (Calcutta, 1978).

why the agrarian class struggle in eastern Bengal becomes 'communal'. His explanation starts with an oft-mentioned demographic fact: the majority of landlords and moneylenders in eastern Bengal were Hindu, while the majority of cultivating peasants were Muslim. Both the organized political movements in the region were led by sections of the landlord-bourgeois classes—the Hindu section controlled the Congress, the Muslim section the Krishak Praja Party/Muslim League. But since the majority of peasants were Muslim, the Muslim landlord-bourgeois leadership, in order to gain electoral support, found it necessary to back the anti-landlord demands of the peasantry, but only up to a point. More significantly, however, they were able to turn the anti-landlord movement against the majority Hindu section of exploiters and draw peasant support on a communal basis, only to betray the peasants' cause after securing their immediate political objective of gaining a share of government power. The movements of poor share-cropper/small peasants in this period, however, were free from such 'communal' distortions, and were defeated only by massive state repression.

We see, then, that these three different explanations of the course of Bengal's politics have each emphasized a different possible configuration among the four elements we listed above. It has been suggested that a rising rich-peasant class mobilized peasant support against a declining zamindari class and was supported by the state. At other times it seems to have mobilized mass support against the colonial state and not against zamindars. In mobilizing mass support, the rich peasants are said to have supported the anti-feudal demands of the bulk of the peasantry, and even that insincerely. 'Mobilization' here was thus very much a politics of manipulation. One aspect of this was the manipulation of religious and caste segmentations to mobilize as well as to divide the masses, in order to serve the interests of rival sections within the exploiting classes. On the other hand where the demands of an increasingly exploited and often dispossessed poor peasantry were articulated in clear class terms, such segmentations were apparently no longer effective; these movements were, however, crushed by the repressive acts of the colonial state supported by the exploiting classes.

It seems necessary, therefore, to place these regional variations in the evolution of political movements in colonial Bengal within a single explanatory framework that can relate a determinate agrarian economy and state structure to varying regional articulations of the class struggle.

V. Landlords, Tenants, and the State
in Eastern Bengal

Let me consider first the situation in eastern Bengal. (For our purposes, eastern Bengal will mean the districts of the Dacca and Chittagong divisions and Rajshahi, Pabna, and Bogra districts of the Rajshahi division.) Historically, the principal political antagonism in eastern Bengal had been seen for a long time as one between landlords and tenants. All tenants were not, of course, cultivating peasants. Many had held land as occupancy tenants but had actually sublet it to other subtenants at higher rents and inferior rights. At the time of the settlement operations of the early twentieth century some of them were recognized as rent-receiving intermediate tenure holders, and their tenants given the status of raiyats. The significant feature of the tenancy structure in eastern Bengal as compared to the other regions of Bengal was, however, that a far greater proportion of the land was held by occupancy raiyats on cash rents than anywhere else in the province. Moreover most qualitative evidence, and whatever little quantitative evidence exists, shows that until the 1920s there was a much smaller degree of inequality in the distribution of land among the raiyat peasantry than elsewhere in Bengal. The proportion of landless labourers in the rural workforce too was the lowest in this region.[31]

More significant was the cultural perception of the landlord–tenant divide. Eastern Bengal, of course, had a far higher proportion of Muslims in the population than other parts of the province. Thus in the districts of the Dacca and Chittagong divisions Muslims comprised between 67 and 78 per cent of the population, and in Rajshahi, Pabna, and Bogra districts the proportions were 76, 77, and 83 per cent respectively. Most Muslims were, of course, peasants. The 1911 census, however, shows that of those whose principal income was rent from land, substantial proportions in the Rajshahi, Dacca, and Chittagong divisions—37.22 per cent, 33.44 per cent, and 49.13 per cent respectively—were Muslim.[32] And yet an almost universally accepted feature of the agrarian structure in eastern Bengal was its predominantly upper-caste Hindu landlord class. True, these figures need to be qualified by the fact that there were many members of Hindu landlord

[31] For a detailed discussion, see Chatterjee, 'Agrarian Structure'.
[32] See Partha Chatterjee, 'Bengal Politics and the Muslim Masses', *Journal of Commonwealth and Comparative Politics*, xx (1982), pp. 25–41.

families whose principal incomes were no longer from rent, but from white-collar employment or trade or the professions. Nonetheless, the discrepancy between the census figures and the common understanding of the situation points to the very significant fact that in social terms 'landlordism' in eastern Bengal was generally perceived as something practised principally by upper-caste Hindu landlords. It was true, first of all, that most of the bigger and more powerful landlords were Hindu. Secondly, many Muslim rent-receivers, although they had let out much of their land, themselves often continued to cultivate and were culturally a part of the peasant community. Above all, the overwhelming cultural pattern of landlord dominance in the region was reinforced and demonstrated in terms of upper-caste Hindu superiority over a predominantly Muslim or lower-caste Hindu peasantry.

A central question in landlord–tenant relations was rent. Since a large part of the peasantry had occupancy rights, it was not so much the legal rent that was a bone of contention in the twentieth century, but the large volume of illegal exactions or *abwab*, some 'customary', others quite ad hoc, which had become a major means for landlords to get around the legal restrictions on rent enhancement. In some areas, for instance, the rate of abwab was higher than the legal rent. Such illegal exactions were, of course, directly dependent on the superiority of physical force which landlords could command, and were enforced up to the early years of the twentieth century with much high-handedness and violence. By the 1920s, however, with the fragmentation of zamindari property and rapidly rising costs of living, few except the largest landlords (and their estate managers and agents) found it possible to keep up the real levels of cash exactions by legal and illegal means. At the same time peasant opposition to abwabs was growing, and gradually this began to take on the form of a more general resistance to landlord domination.

Closely associated with the question of rent was that of interest. In general, it is true that the pure professional moneylender was much less visible on the agrarian scene of Bengal than in other parts of India. Even where they did exist, as in the case of the Marwari moneylenders of the trading towns of eastern and northern Bengal, their activities were closely tied up with the jute trade. More typically, however, moneylending and trading in agricultural produce were tied with landlordism into a single network. This was quite different from the typical 'semi-feudal' jotdari form which had grown up in other parts of Bengal, where rich peasants would extend their effective control over the land of small peasant/sharecroppers by using a combination of debt-bondage and extra-economic coercion.[33] In eastern Bengal usurious and commercial exploitation of the peasantry was generally perceived as linked inseparably with feudal exploitation, typified in cultural terms by upper-caste or trading-caste Hindu domination.

If we look at the more organized demands made on behalf of the Praja [tenants'] movement in eastern Bengal from the 1920s, the following demands keep recurring: (1) abolition of illegal exactions, (2) reduction of rent, (3) reduction of interest rates and relief from indebtedness, (4) 'honourable treatment of Muslim tenants in the zamindar's office', and (5) abolition of the landlord's fee on transfers of *raiyati* land.[34] In time, by the mid-1930s, these would be aggregated into the general demand for the abolition of the Permanent Settlement. The first four demands affected the peasantry in general. The fifth related to the fact that although many tenants now had heritable rights of occupation on their raiyati holdings, they did not have a statutory right to sell or transfer them unless this was permitted by 'local custom'. And the local custom in eastern Bengal was one where zamindars would permit such transfers only if they were paid a certain percentage of the sale price, the proportion varying from area to area according to the local relation of strength between landlords and tenants. This demand can therefore be construed as affecting in particular the richer peasantry, seeking to increase its control over the land and consequently demanding a freer land market in peasant holdings. However, in the prevailing situation in eastern Bengal, this was also a demand supported by the majority of peasants, since freer transferability and a general rise in land values would have meant easier terms for loans and smaller distress sales of land. These issues were posed much more sharply following the impact of the Depression of 1931–2 on the agrarian economy of eastern Bengal.

Politically, however, peasant resistance in eastern Bengal did not only take the form of an organized Praja movement. Particularly in the crucial period 1926–31, it erupted in a series of violent 'communal' clashes against Hindu landlords and moneylenders.[35] The evidence

[33] Sugata Bose, 'The Roots of Communal Violence in Rural Bengal: A Study of the Kishoreganj Riots, 1930', *Modern Asian Studies*, xvi (1982), pp. 463–92.

[34] Chatterjee, 'Bengal Politics and the Muslim Masses'.

[35] See Partha Chatterjee, 'Agrarian Relations and Communalism in Bengal 1926–1935', in Ranajit Guha, ed., *Subaltern Studies I: Writings on South Asian History*

on these 'riots', particularly in the districts of Pabna, Mymensingh, Dacca, and Bakarganj, suggests quite clearly the more or less general character of the resistance among the predominantly Muslim peasantry of the region. Ideologically the participants saw themselves as resisting the unjust domination and exploitation of a peasant community by external enemies. The lines of division were clear in cultural terms: peasant resistance took the form of acts of defiance against targets that symbolized the wealth and power of the dominant classes. Besides plunder and destruction of property, there occurred widespread dis-obedience of 'customary' cultural practices at religious festivals patron-ized by Hindu landlords or trading groups, desecration of idols worshipped in landlord households, and the almost ritualized burning of bonds and records of loans. The armed strength of landlords, on the other hand, was organized by Hindu zamindars, traders, and pro-fessionals living in the district towns of the region, with open political support from the Hindu Mahasabha and various quasi-political Hindu religious organizations. The identification of landlord interests with organized Hindu politics was clearly demonstrated at the time of the passing of the 1928 amendment to the Tenancy Act when the Congress-Swarajya Party in the legislature unequivocally supported the rights and privileges of landlords against every attempt to voice the demands of tenants.[36]

This, therefore, was the context in which peasant resistance to feudal domination and usurious exploitation in eastern Bengal became 'communal'. The agrarian structure and the dynamics of agrarian change, together with a specific demographic distribution, laid the conditions in which this was a distinct political possibility. The parti-cular cultural form of landlordism, and that of peasant communal resistance to landlord authority, then determined the specific political articulation of this struggle in the form of a 'communal' conflict.

In this conflict between contending agrarian classes within the colo-nial social formation, the colonial state retained a role of ambiguity. It

and Society (Delhi, 1982); Bose, 'Roots of Communal Violence'; Tanika Sarkar, 'The First Phase of Civil Disobedience in Bengal, 1930–31', *Indian Historical Review*, iv (1977–8), pp. 75–95; Tanika Sarkar, 'Communal Riots in Bengal', in Mushirul Hasan, ed., *Communal and Pan-Islamic Trends in Colonial India* (New Delhi, 1981), pp. 284–301.

[36] On this, see Partha Chatterjee, *Bengal 1920–1947: The Land Question* (Cal-cutta, 1984).

was interested in maintaining and expanding the process of colonial extraction from the agrarian sector. In this, as we have noted above, it was increasingly forced to intervene directly in the institutional structure of agrarian property and the process of agricultural production as well as in the developing class struggles within colonial society. On the first point, the general tendency of state intervention was to strengthen the hands of primary surplus-extracting agents at the village level at the expense of the rights and privileges of landlords. But in doing this the government was always careful to use the complexity and ambiguity of its land laws to balance the grant of new legal rights to sections of tenants with compensatory restatements of the 'customary' privileges of landlords. It thus attempted to present itself as a neutral arbiter in the developing agrarian class struggle, aiming to protect the 'sanctity of private property' against incipient revolutionary movements as well as to help the survival of small peasants against rapacious landlords and moneylenders. Politically the colonial government was concerned above all to prevent a broad nationalist combination against its authority. Since most organized wings of the Congress in eastern Bengal were identified with upper-caste Hindu political groups, whether Swarajya politicians defending the privileges of landlords or revolutionary terrorists leaning much more towards secret conspiratorial activities than mass mobilization, the government found it fairly easy to use the communal edge of the anti-landlord movement to split any possible nationalist combination against its authority in eastern Bengal.

In 1919–21, at the time of the Non-co-operation Khilafat movement, the most widespread popular response to the Congress call for non-co-operation came from the districts of eastern and northern Bengal. A new section of Muslim leaders joined the Congress-Khilafat movement, pronouncing every form of co-operation with the 'satanic' government a 'sin'.[37] But once the broad organizational platform of Non-co-operation Khilafat broke down with the communal riots of 1926 and the Tenancy Act amendment of 1928, the government was particularly careful to keep the rift as wide as possible. It repeatedly emphasized, on the one hand, the 'economic' nature of Muslim grievances in eastern Bengal, which would in time be set right by suitable legislative action by the state; and on the other, the self-interested and sectarian

---

[37] See Rajat K. Ray, 'Masses in Politics: The Non-Co-operation Movement in Bengal, 1920–22', *Indian Economic and Social History Review*, xi (1974), pp. 343–410.

'political' demands of Hindu nationalists. It actively promoted 'suitable Muhammadan associations' and even tenants' associations in the late 1920s, and at the time of the communal riots in Dacca and Faridpur in 1930 which coincided with the Civil Disobedience movement, blatantly manipulated the administrative and police machinery to promote the idea that while it would severely punish Hindu political agitations against the government, it was prepared to overlook violations of the law if they were aimed against Hindu Swarajists.[38]

Since the landlord–peasant antagonism was of primary significance in the agrarian struggles in eastern Bengal, the position in peasant consciousness of the third element of the triad, the colonial state, was necessarily ambiguous.[39] It was sometimes possible for political leaders in eastern Bengal to rouse the peasantry against the state on the question of taxes or Union Boards, as was done in many areas at the time of Non-co-operation Khilafat. It could also be briefly roused on the much more nebulous and distant issue of British crimes against the sultan of Turkey. But when the peasantry revolted against their lords, the state would often acquire in peasant consciousness the role of a benevolent protector. At the time of the Dacca riots people apparently believed that power had been handed over to the nawab of Dacca who 'had become the lord of thirteen districts and it was ordered by him that no person would be arrested or convicted if Hindu houses were looted and burnt in those thirteen districts for seven days.' In Kishoreganj looters were heard to have said that 'Government had given Swaraj [self-rule] to them for the space of fifteen days.' The district magistrate in his tour through the riot-torn villages found one which was practically empty and was told that 'the villagers had all gone south to demand back their deeds from mahajans [money-lenders] . . . everybody said this was the Government order promulgated about ten days previously.' A rioter wounded in a police shooting called out before he died, 'Ami British governmenter praja, dohai British government' (I am a subject of the British government, I ask for the British government's mercy) and 'could not evidently understand why he had been shot'. Sometimes there were dramatic shifts in this perceptual relation

[38] Chatterjee, *Bengal 1920–1947: The Land Question*; Tanika Sarkar, 'First Phase of Civil Disobedience'.

[39] For a more detailed consideration of the state–lord–peasant triad, see Partha Chatterjee, 'More on Modes of Power and the Peasantry', in Guha, ed., *Subaltern Studies II* (Delhi, 1983), pp. 311–49.

of the state to the peasantry. In Patuakhali in Bakarganj in 1926 Muslim peasant violence against Hindus in a dispute over processions passing before mosques had begun on the assumption that the government supported the Muslim cause. After an incident of police shooting in which fifteen Muslims were killed, the government, and the district magistrate in particular, became in the eyes of Muslim leaders a 'blood-thirsty murderer' who had to be 'suitably punished'.[40]

The fundamental class antagonism in the agrarian struggles in eastern Bengal in the 1920s was, therefore, the one between landlordism of the zamindari type and the mass of the peasantry. In structural terms this landlordism was already on the decline and facing a rent crisis of massive proportions; on the other hand, the peasantry consisted predominantly of small owner-cultivators, differentiated to a much lower degree than elsewhere in the province. But the outcome of the contest had by no means been decided: landlords were prepared to defend their power and privileges by means of party-political pressure as well as by local demonstrations of armed strength. The dominant cultural form of this class antagonism then made it possible for both the defence of landlord power and the revolt of the peasantry against landlord authority to be articulated as a 'communal' conflict. The colonial state intervened directly in the conflict, both at the level of the legal conditions of agrarian property and at the level of organized party politics, but only to project its neutrality and to derive the full manipulative advantages from the ambiguity of its position in order to prevent a broad political combination against its authority.

It is also worth pointing out here the way the landlord–tenant conflict was resolved in eastern Bengal. In the end the zamindari form of landed property was abolished in Bengal, but not before Independence and the partition of the province in 1947. And it is hardly necessary to state that the course of developments leading up to that conclusion did not bring to reality any of the millenarian dreams of a self-sufficient peasantry free from oppression and injustice. The organized Praja movement gained in strength in eastern Bengal in the decade of the 1930s, resisting excessive rent payments and demanding the abolition of the Permanent Settlement. In the meantime the Depression of the early 1930s caused a massive dislocation and subsequent restructuring of the market and credit mechanisms of the jute

---

[40] For more detailed accounts of these incidents, see Chatterjee, *Bengal 1920–1947: The Land Question.*

economy. The traditional landlord/moneylender was forced to move out and was replaced by new suppliers of credit from among the better-off sections of the cultivators themselves.[41] The usual dynamic of indebtedness leading to the transfer of small-peasant holdings was then set into full motion, helped on by the grant of full rights of transferability in raiyati lands in 1939. The process of differentiation was accelerated even further after the great famine of 1943.[42] In the meantime a section of the Praja leadership went into a coalition government in 1937 under the new constitutional reforms. The compulsions of coalition politics forced it to backtrack on its election promise of abolishing the Permanent Settlement, causing numerous splits within the Praja movement, and finally drew most sections of Muslim leadership in the province towards the movement for Pakistan. The old zamindar-Praja antagonism died a quick death in East Pakistan/Bangladesh in the years after partition, to be replaced by the now more familiar picture of differentiation between a jotdar/moneylender/trader class and a mass of increasingly impoverished small peasant/labourers.

VI. Peasants and the State in South-Western Bengal

In south-western Bengal, on the other hand, the organized thrust of the peasant movement was directed overwhelmingly against the colonial state. The principal organizers here came from the Congress, particularly from its Gandhian wing. In terms of social forces, although the Congress movement received extensive support from virtually all sections of the peasantry in the areas in which its organization was the strongest, such as in Contai and Tamluk in Midnapur, the leading force was quite clearly the jotdar section.

Hitesranjan Sanyal, who has studied the Congress movements in this region in great detail, offers the following explanation of the political motives of the jotdar class in Midnapur.[43] To start with, in Midnapur as in the rest of Bengal, given the context of the declining power

[41] Saugata Mukherji, 'Some Aspects of Commercialization of Agriculture in Eastern India 1891–1938', in Sen, Chatterjee, and Mukherji, *Three Studies*, pp. 225–315; Goswami, 'Jute Economy of Bengal 1900–1947'.

[42] Chatterjee, 'Agrarian Structure'.

[43] Sanyal, 'Dakshin-paschim Banglay Jatiatabadi Andolan, II', pp. 183–207; Hitesranjan Sanyal, 'Congress Movements in the Villages of Eastern Midnapore, 1921–1931', in Marc Gaborieau and Alice Thorner, eds, *Asie du sud: traditions et changements* (Paris, 1979), pp. 169–78.

of zamindars and *patnidars* (intermediate tenure-holding landlords), 'the new leadership emerging from out of the jotdar, moneylender and trading classes was eager to seize the opportunities opened up by the establishment of Union Boards to secure government patronage and increase their political power.' But once the mass agitation against Union Boards started by Congress leaders gained support among the bulk of the peasantry, the relatively wealthier sections were faced with a new choice:

> It now became clear that there was a distinct possibility of their gaining political power, even by opposing the government, through the medium of the new mass mobilization. If they joined the movement, it was virtually certain that its leadership at the local level of organization would fall in their hands . . . As soon as the richer peasants joined the movement, their economic and social power gave the movement considerable strength . . . Economic and social leadership had already passed into their hands; now by joining the anti-Union Board movement, they emerged as local political leaders of the new mass mobilization.[44]

This is, of course, a different course of political action from the one which the predominantly Muslim peasant leadership is said to have adopted in eastern Bengal. But given the difference in context it is an equally plausible explanation. In order to unify our understanding of political developments in the province as a whole, we should, therefore, be able to locate the class interests of the richer peasantry in south-western Bengal within the context of the triad of conflict defined by the three other elements in the struggle, that is, a declining zamindari class, an increasingly impoverished small peasantry, and the colonial state. I will attempt this analysis on the basis of the evidence of histori-cal researches into three of these movements—in Contai and Tamluk in Midnapur, in Arambag in Hooghly, and in Burdwan.

The focus of mass mobilization against the colonial state in Midna-pur was the question of increased taxes. A central point of the Congress campaign in the movement against the establishment of Union Boards in 1919 was the apprehension that local taxes would be doubled. We have noted before that one of the ways in which the colonial government in Bengal tried to obtain a share of the increased revenue from agricul-tural production was to impose a series of taxes over and above the land

---

[44] Sanyal, 'Dakshin-paschim Banglay Jatiatabadi Andolan, II', pp. 198–9.

revenue which, for most parts of the province, had been made inflexible by the Permanent Settlement. Apart from the political objective of co-opting the primary appropriating classes into the structure of governmental power in the localities, the Village Self-government Act of 1919 was also meant to raise new taxes at the village level in order to pay for the activities of local government. In the case of Midnapur there was also the special consideration that large parts of the coastal areas were outside the Permanent Settlement and in these areas the revenues from land settled on temporary leases had gone up progressively. The Congress leadership in Midnapur tried, therefore, to mobilize a broad-based nationalist opposition to the colonial government on the issue of increased taxes.

But the specific interest of the jotdar leadership of the movement was not simply the question of taxes. It was a directly political question concerning local power. Sanyal has shown that by the early twentieth century, with a much more advanced state of differentiation within the peasantry, a proliferation of kulak-type activities among the richer peasantry, and a strong cultural movement of Mahishya caste advancement encompassing the bulk of the peasantry in Contai and Tamluk under jotdar leadership, the jotdar/*mahajan* (rich peasant/moneylender) sections already enjoyed *de facto* dominance in rural society in the region.[45] The political problem which faced them in 1919 was not a contest against zamindari power, but resistance to what was seen as an encroachment by the colonial state into the affairs of village society. The entire campaign against Union Boards was, therefore, fought on two issues: refusal to pay increased taxes, and resistance to the attempts by the government to extend its bureaucratic arm into the countryside and further erode what was left of the autonomy of the peasant community. It is not surprising that the ideology and programmes of the Gandhian Congress proved so effective in the context.

This was the principal modality of anti-state resistance in Midnapur in the three major waves of nationalist upsurge in 1919–21, 1930–1, and 1942–3. The defiance of the salt laws in 1930–1 had precisely the same significance as the opposition to Union Boards in 1919–21: the peasant community was resisting what it considered the unjust interference by a colonial state in the right of peasants to manufacture an essential item of daily use from resources that were naturally available

[45] Ibid.; Sanyal, 'Congress Movements'.

in this coastal region.[46] In 1942 the front-rank Gandhian leadership of the local Congress was in prison by the time the movement got under way. The initial actions were a series of attacks by thousands of peasants against police stations, post offices, and other government buildings. With five companies of armed troops in the area, the movement then became a classic *jacquerie*, with hit-and-run attacks on troops and a corps of organizing cadres finding shelter among the village population. The Congress, in fact, set itself up as the legitimate contender for organized power in the locality, with its own institutional structure and procedures replicating in minute detail those followed by the British colonial government, imposing its own taxes, and instituting justice and punishment. Indeed, such was its claim to authority that in spite of a devastating cyclone that left more than ten thousand dead, none came to the government for relief, preferring to wait until alternative relief arrangements were set up by the rebels. But it was only a question of time—about eight months—before the armed strength of the state finally overcame this all-too-localized rebellion.[47]

In this confrontation between an oppressive colonial state and a peasant community organized and led for the most part by the richer peasantry, the older zamindari classes were largely left by the wayside. Their social power in the region had been already largely superseded. They made futile attempts locally to oppose the Congress mass movement in its initial stages. Later, as the leaders of the mass movement combined throughout the district, the hold of the zamindari classes over the Congress organization at the district level came under irresistible challenge. Soon the new district leaders, certain of their own popular bases of strength, joined the district and local levels of government. They were prepared now to utilize the benefits of the state system, but were ever conscious of the need to retain the organizational strength and readiness for an oppositional movement.

But although the principal thrust of the mass movement in Midnapur was that of a peasant community resisting the authority of the colonial state, the degree of differentiation within the peasantry inevitably gave rise to organized antagonisms within the movement. The emerging

[46] Sanyal, 'Congress Movements'.

[47] For more details, see Partha Chatterjee, 'Spontaneity and Organization in Peasant Movements in Bengal 1920–1947', in W.H. Morris-Jones and J. W. Manor, eds, *Political Violence* (London: Institute of Commonwealth Studies Seminar Papers, 1982).

forms of differentiation mainly coalesced into a conflict between a jot-dar/mahajan/trader class and a large mass of indebted small peasants and sharecroppers. Immediately after the anti-Union Board movement, demands began to be made on behalf of sharecroppers for a reduction in the various ad hoc impositions which jotdars made over and above the conventional half-share of produce. Congress leaders attempted to arrange a compromise but jotdars agreed to make only slight con-cessions. The grievances simmered.[48] At the time of the passing of the Tenancy Act amendment in 1928 the Congress legislators from Midna-pur had voted with the Swarajya Party in favour of the privileges of landlords and against attempts to strengthen the rights of tenants, although they had been elected on behalf of their local Congress orga-nization against powerful zamindar candidates backed by the Provin-cial Congress. Faced with strong criticism from their constituents, they defended their actions with one telling argument: the proposed amendments in favour of raiyats would have given legal rights of ten-ancy to sharecroppers and, as the Contai legislator put it, 'one shudders to think what a calamity this would have been for the people of Contai.'[49]

The Civil Disobedience movement, however, saw a quick resurgence of solidarity against the state. But as soon as it subsided the sharecrop-pers' agitation resumed once again. In 1932–3 it became widespread in the Contai, Bhagabanpur, Khejuri, and Pataspur areas of Contai and the Mahisadal, Nandigram, and Sutahata areas of Tamluk. Congress leaders again attempted to bring about a compromise, but *bhagchasi* (sharecropper) demands were now much more vociferous. In some areas Congress arbitration succeeded in eliciting concessions from jot-dars, but elsewhere the agitation continued and was now led by a new group of Communist peasant leaders.[50]

The separate organization of sharecropper/small-peasant interests, directed against jotdar/mahajan exploitation, began in south-western Bengal in the 1930s. It represented the sharpening of a new, and now the more dominant, class antagonism in agrarian society. What is sig-nificant, however, is that in spite of this clear articulation of demands against jotdar domination, the resurgence of peasant solidarity in the revolt against the authority of the colonial state in Contai and Tamluk

[48] Sanyal, 'Congress Movements'.
[49] Chatterjee, *Bengal 1920–1947: The Land Question.*
[50] Sanyal, 'Congress Movements'.

in 1942 seemed to be as spontaneous and widespread as ever. In the initial phase of the series of collective acts of popular violence against the physical symbols of state authority, participation in the movement was massive. With the deployment of troops and severe repression by the government, and the unprecedented ravages of the cyclone, the organizing cadres were driven underground. In time they began to resort to increasingly terroristic actions, not only against government agents but also against those they suspected of not co-operating with the rebel authority. In a context of massive food shortages leading up to the great famine of 1943, many of the terroristic acts of the rebel leaders were aimed against local jotdars. But these acts were not part of any agrarian programme, nor were they backed by demonstrations of collective support by the poor peasantry. In the period leading up to their capture the rebel leaders were isolated from their own people.[51]

The Midnapur case brings up a number of major issues concerning the development of distinct political organization of class demands in an agrarian society in the throes of rapid differentiation. In spite of clearly perceived divisions within the peasantry, one notices the continued vitality of peasant communal resistance to state authority. The crucial question, of course, is: what is the nature of the transformation in the structure and form of peasant consciousness which enables it to distinguish between the external enemies of a peasant community and internal exploiters within it, and indeed to perceive the connections between the two? What are the corresponding changes in the modalities of resistance? And finally, if there is such a transformation, is it valid to speak any more of *peasant* resistance? In other words, does such a transformation presuppose a virtual dissolution of the peasantry as a distinct social form of existence of productive labour? We will return to some of these questions in the final section.

Arambag in Hooghly, on the other hand, was an area which had been in continuous decline since the mid-nineteenth century, an isolated pocket that had seen massive destruction of traditional handicraft industries, rapid decline of irrigation and drainage systems, and large-scale depopulation owing to epidemics as late as the first two decades of the twentieth century. The political organization of the Congress in Arambag is directly attributable to the coming of outside activitists—Gandhian political workers—who came in to organize relief work in

[51] Chatterjee, 'Spontaneity and Organization'.

the area after a devastating flood in 1921. The major political movements in the area were organized by this Gandhian leadership against the state, once again against Union Boards in 1930–3 and against land survey and settlement operations in 1932. But the main plank of Congress mobilization in Arambag was not the straightforward antagonism between a peasant community and the state. It could not have been, because zamindari domination was very much a reality. Arambag was an area where agriculture had for long been in a state of chronic decay, and zamindari exploitation too was of a particularly perverse kind. Most lands were parts of very large and far-flung estates, the landlords were absentee and the business of rent collection and management was carried out by estate officials who used the full array of legal and illegal methods to squeeze out whatever was available from a deeply impoverished peasantry.

Congress mobilization in Arambag had to face up to the question of zamindari domination. Sanyal has shown that its organization among the peasantry was built up through a series of sustained agitations and resistance against illegal exactions, physical punishment and intimidation by zamindari agents, and against the confiscation of land and movable property for non-payment of rents.[52] These led in 1932 to a direct no-rent campaign to which the local Gandhian leadership gave open support. The confrontation became still sharper when candidates put up by the Arambag Congress defeated the powerful zamindars of Hooghly in the elections to the provincial assembly in 1936. But the move into the institutionalized politics of legislatures and district boards brought entirely new constraints before the Arambag leadership. A more radical section, particularly a younger Communist leadership, was pushing for an intensification of the struggle against landlords. The established leadership, on the other hand, was now keen to draw the reins and consolidate power within the structures of local government. These new political conflicts remained alive and unresolved.

There were few dramatic developments in Arambag until 1947. It was only after Independence that the leaders of the Arambag Congress were to prove their political acumen in the wider fields of provincial

---

[52] Hitesranjan Sanyal, 'Arambager Jatiatabadi Andolan (1921–1942)', *Anya Artha* (Calcutta), 6 (Sept.–Oct. 1974), pp. 6–23; 7 (November–December 1974), pp. 1–15.

and national politics. In the meantime zamindari power in Hooghly declined as it did in the rest of the province. But again it was only after Independence and Partition that, backed by substantial state patronage, agriculture regained its vitality in Arambag and a new stratum of the kulak type emerged in strength. On the other hand, the more radical organizations of the poor peasantry now became part of the province-wide extension of Communist-led peasant movements. The Burdwan case only requires a brief mention. Burdwan too was an area where the peasantry was highly differentiated. It had seen the steady growth of Congress mass organizations in the 1920s and 1930s, again under jot-dar leadership, although the movements there were nowhere near as dramatic as in neighbouring Midnapur. The issue of the large-scale movement against the government in 1936–9 was the opening of the new Damodar canal and the levy of a tax at the flat rate of 5 rupees 8 annas per acre annually. The objection to the tax was widespread. A moderate section led by lawyers and professionals and supported by many of the zamindari classes urged that the government lower the rates. The Congress opposition, led by the jotdar section but enjoying the support of the bulk of the peasantry, was predictably more massive. In December 1937 the government agreed to reduce the tax to 3 rupees per acre, and when agitations did not cease this was brought down further to 2 rupees 9 annas in May 1938. The movement had gone on for more than two years and now the Congress leadership urged acceptance of the reduced rates. A more radical Communist section pressed on for a further reduction but standing on its own, the movement did not go very far and, by the middle of 1939, fizzled out.[53]

South-western Bengal shows us, therefore, some of the complexities of agrarian struggle in a colonial social formation at a relatively advanced stage of differentiation within the peasantry. In general, it confirms the observation that the dominant tendency of agrarian change was towards the emergence of a new antagonism between a jot-dar/moneylender/trader class and an increasingly impoverished mass of small peasants/sharecroppers/labourers. Where the local power of the older landowning classes was already on the decline, jotdar dominance could be consolidated on the basis of massive movements of peasant solidarity against the encroachments of the colonial state. This

[53] For details, see B. Bhattacharyya, T.K. Banerjee, and D.K. Das, *Satyagrahas in Bengal, 1921–39* (Calcutta, 1977).

solidarity remained vital despite attempts to articulate the distinct and opposing interests of the poor peasantry and despite the absorption of the jotdar classes into the structures of governmental power at the local level. On the other hand, where zamindari power was still strong, anti-colonial mass movements could be built up only in combination with anti-feudal struggles. But despite the consolidation of jotdar dominance, the organization of poor-peasant/sharecropper demands could not easily be built upon the foundations of the anti-colonial struggle. The political organization of class struggles within the peasantry seemed to require an ideological transformation of peasant consciousness. Although the economic conditions for the emergence of new class differentiations within the peasantry were firmly established in the last decades of colonial rule in Bengal, the political and ideological resources for organizing the new class struggles were not available within the framework of the anti-colonial movement.

VII. Landlords and Sharecroppers in Northern and Southern Bengal

The difficulties are brought out even more sharply by the experience of the most powerful and heroic struggles carried out in Bengal by the peasant leadership of the Communist Party. The Tebhaga movement was conducted over the demands of sharecroppers and was directed by Communist leaders with considerable centralization of control through the Krishak Sabha, the peasant wing of the Communist Party. But it did not take firm root in areas where the emerging forms of differentiation had created a new stratum of sharecroppers from out of an impoverished small peasantry bound by debt-bondage to a class of kulak-type rich peasants. Despite the presence of Communist workers, the Tebhaga movement did not get off the ground in Burdwan or Midnapur. It became a powerful movement in those areas of northern Bengal and in the Sundarban region of southern Bengal where sharecropping was a widespread historical form of subtenancy with inferior rights.

In Jalpaiguri, Dinajpur, and Rangpur districts of northern Bengal, the crop-sharing arrangement of cultivation was both common and old, and was used by landlords irrespective of whether they held the land as rent-receiving tenure holders or cultivating raiyats. The crop-sharing *adhiars* (tenants paying half the produce as rent) in Jalpaiguri cultivated as tenants-at-will the lands of proprietors—jotdars or *chukanidars* (subinfeudators of jotdars)—on a half-share basis without any legal or customary rights. In Dinajpur the settlement operations in 1934–40 showed that a quarter of the land in the south and west of the district, the areas of the Tebhaga movement, was cultivated by adhiars.[54] In Rangpur adhiars were either poor raiyats or undertenants, or were entirely landless and did not have any rights in the *adhi* lands. But although *adhiari* was a well-recognized historical form of tenancy or subtenancy, it was clearly on the increase in the early decades of the twentieth century, and the reasons were the same as in other parts of Bengal: increased commercialization, the rising prices of agricultural commodities (particularly of rice), indebtedness, and the transfer of effective control of land to jotdar creditors. Yet despite the recent spread of adhiari, owing to these new conditions imposed on the agrarian economy of the region, this specific form of labour was clearly perceived locally within the well-recognized historical framework of jotdar–adhiar tenancy relations.

The Sundarban area of south 24-Parganas was an area of recent reclamation of forest lands. The government had settled the land here with large landholders outside the framework of the Permanent Settlement. In the Kakdwip area in particular, where Tebhaga became a powerful movement, most landlords were absentee and had appointed managers and agents to arrange the collection of produce rents from tenants, all of whom were bhagchasis. Sharecropping, in other words, was the predominant form of tenancy in the region. Not surprisingly, landlord–tenant relations in a situation such as this were marked by a host of forcible impositions over and above the half-share rent, besides physical coercion by the landlords' agents. There was also a compulsory obligation upon sharecroppers to take advances, repayable in kind at 50 per cent interest after the harvest.[55]

The sharecroppers' movements in these areas were organized by Communist cadres from the early 1940s. In Dinajpur the Krishak Sabha movement began with a campaign against levies imposed by jotdars on peasants selling their produce in village marts. Later this developed into the broader movement of adhiars demanding a reduction

[54] F.O. Bell, *Final Report on the Survey and Settlement Operations in the District of Dinajpur, 1934–40* (Alipore, 1941), p. 20.
[55] Krishnakant Sarkar, 'Kakdwip Tebhaga Movement', in A.R. Desai, ed., *Peasant Struggles in India* (Bombay, 1979), pp. 469–85.

of the landlord's share of the produce from half to a third. A similar
movement developed in the Nilphamari area of Rangpur and spread
'spontaneously'—according to Sunil Sen, the historian of Tebhaga[56]—
to the Duars area of Jalpaiguri. In the Sundarban area of South 24-
Parganas, again the organizers were Communist workers coming in for
relief work after the famine of 1943. Here too, besides a general call for
the abolition of landlordism, the specific demands were for a reduction
of the share rent to one-third of the produce; the stopping of ad hoc
impositions, fines, and punishments; and the grant of receipts against
share rents. Once again the element of 'spontaneity' in the spread of the
movement was particularly noticeable.[57]

Another area where a movement of sharecropping tenants was led
by Communist cadres in this period was the Susang area of Mymensingh. Here too the predominant mass of the peasantry cultivated the
lands of a very large zamindar under a form of tenancy-at-will known
as *tanka*. The movement began in the period 1937–9 and demanded
the recognition of tanka peasants as raiyats and for the commutation
of produce rents into a normal cash rent. The movement gained considerable strength in 1942 and for three subsequent years—according
to Pramatha Gupta, a leading Communist organizer of the movement—
the zamindar's agents and money-lenders were not allowed into the
area and *tanka* rents were virtually not paid. The tanka peasants who
were mobilized here belonged predominantly to the Hajong tribe
and the solidarity of the movement was firmly based on this tribal-
communal identity.[58]

In north Bengal, on the other hand, there were both Muslim and
Rajbangshi jotdars, just as there were Muslim and Rajbangshi adhiars.
Accounts of the Tebhaga movement particularly emphasize the point
that at the time of the movement the jotdar–adhiar confrontation was
never blurred or deflected by caste or religious divisions, despite attempts to do so by sections of the jotdars and by other organized political groups.[59] The principal organizing cadres were middle-class political
activists, who acted as independent vanguardist agents in the agrarian
class struggle. It is important to note, however, that the Communist

[56] Sunil Sen, *Agrarian Struggle in Bengal 1946–47* (New Delhi, 1972).
[57] Sarkar, 'Kakdwip Tebhaga Movement'.
[58] Jnanabrata Bhattacharyya, 'An Examination of Leadership Entry in Bengal
Peasant Revolts, 1937–1947', *Journal of Asian Studies*, xxxvii (1977–8), pp. 611–35.
[59] Sen, *Agrarian Struggle*; Umar, *Chirasthayi Bandobaste*, pp. 54–100.

leadership was particularly conscious of the political dangers of Muslim communal attempts to divide the movement: Sunil Sen speaks of the special role of Haji Mohammed Danesh, a Muslim Communist leader, in dealing with such propaganda.[60] But a major condition for the ineffectiveness of such divisive tactics was the absence of equally credible and culturally identifiable targets for peasant communal action. As we have noted before, the antagonism against the jotdar was the dominant conflict for the large mass of the adhiar peasantry in that region, an antagonism that was historically established and clearly recognized; its cultural form was not signified in terms of religion or caste divisions.

The Tebhaga movement in northern and southern Bengal was broken by direct and massive state repression, supported by the armed strength of the jotdar class. But the question of the rights of sharecroppers was to become a major, perhaps the principal, issue of Communist-led agrarian struggles in West Bengal after Independence and Partition. However, it would then have to confront the full range of problems concerning the location of sharecroppers' rights and the viability of that particular form of productive labour within the complex series of relations that had emerged from the process of differentiation among the peasantry. Given the specific nature of landlord–sharecropper relations in the areas where the Tebhaga movement occurred, and despite the undoubted bravery of those struggles, these were not questions which the leaders of the movement had to confront at the time.

VIII. Colonialism and the Agrarian Class Struggle in Bengal

It was in the period of colonial rule that the conditions were established in Bengal's agriculture for the subsumption of peasant cultivation under an expanded and more generalized process of commodity production. And yet, as in many other colonial social formations, the structural conditions of colonial extraction and colonial rule also impeded the emergence of the full social consequences of capitalist production. Despite the existence of an initial legal basis in large-scale landed property, the development of thoroughgoing landlord-capitalism never got off the ground. In the end a process of rapid decline in the economic viability of zamindari property culminated, in the face

[60] Sen, *Agrarian Struggle*, pp. 24, 37.

of growing peasant resistance, in what was to be a terminal rent crisis in the 1930s. On the other hand, attempts by the colonial state to re-organize and extend the process of extraction from agriculture led to a gradual strengthening of the position of primary surplus-appropriating agents. A new class of rich peasants operated to their advantage the lease market in peasant holdings, and by suitably altering the mode of rent from cash to kind payments and by combining usurious and trading activities, acquired an increasing control over the surplus pro-duct of the immediate producers, extending in some cases to a share in the costs of cultivation and a partial control over the labour process.

It is possible, of course, to look at this as a specific colonial form of the process of 'formal' subordination of labour by capital. Yet, knowing as we do that such specific colonial forms differ quite significantly from the better-known historical cases of the emergence of capitalism in Europe or North America or Japan, it seems vital to study much more closely not only the variety of techno-economic forms by which pre-existing labour was subordinated to capital, but equally the poli-tical forms of the accompanying struggles among contending classes. It would be a gross error of reductionism to suppose that all such processes must eventually ('in the ultimate analysis'?) lead to a complete and real subordination to the hegemonic sway of capitalism.

The analysis of the agrarian class struggles in Bengal in the last decades of colonial rule, in fact, shows us the inappropriateness of any simple linear explanations, whether of the combined resistance of all subordinate classes to colonial rule, or of the opposition between capi-talist owners and propertyless labourers. Even if we reduce these strug-gles to relations between a small number of fundamental elements, we are still left with a variety of possible alignments and combinations, differing from region to region and from period to period according to the specific structural formation and the historical conjuncture.

I suggest that this variety of political possibilities is particularly the result of the specific characteristics of peasant consciousness. I have attempted elsewhere to state some of the central analytical problems of studying the ideological aspects of peasant movements.[61] Without go-ing into the theoretical implications of that analysis, let me simply state that a fundamental feature of the class demands of a peasantry is their

[61] Chatterjee, 'More on Modes of Power'. For a detailed examination of these problems in the historical context of colonial India, see Ranajit Guha, *Elementary Aspects of Peasant Insurgency in Colonial India* (Delhi, 1983).

articulation not in terms of a shared aggregate of interests but as the demands of a community united by pre-existing bonds of solidarity, whether real or imaginary and imputed. The bonds which are believed to define the community are not immutable, and therefore it is misleading simply to call them 'primordial' or 'traditional'. These are historically evolved solidarities and are subject to change, sometimes extremely sudden change. But it is this specific modality of political action, quite different from the way politics is conceptualized within the institutionalized processes of the capitalist state, which creates the many divergent, and spatially dissociated, possibilities for the politics of peasant 'mobilization'.

This raises yet another methodological question. By looking at recent peasant movements exclusively in terms of the politics of 'mobilization', historiography has tended to describe changes in the conditions of social existence of a peasantry almost exclusively as processes imposed on the peasantry, whether as new agrarian structures or new patterns of political organization, and has denied to the peasantry any specific subjectivity in the political processes that have brought about these changes. It is important to attempt to restore this subjectivity to the peasantry, to look at its political actions not as 'primordial', 'pre-political', irrational, and hence inherently inexplicable 'spontaneous' acts, but as actions informed by its own consciousness, shaped by centuries of its own political history, structured by distinct conceptions of power and morality, and attempting to come to terms with and act within wholly new contexts of class struggle. It is an approach such as this which will give us more reliable clues to an understanding of both the strengths and the weaknesses of peasant resistance in contexts of 'modern' politics, as well as of the opportunities of 'mobilization' of a peasantry, or sections of a peasantry, by other classes and groups in a historical context which tends towards a presumably irreversible process of differentiation within the peasantry.

Indeed the analytical framework of differentiation is quite correctly designed for the study of agrarian change in situations where peasant production is in the process of being subsumed under an expanded and generalized system of commodity production. But it must tend towards a techno-economic determinism if it is assumed at the same time that the technical superiority of the capitalist mode of production will inevitably dictate its triumph over pre-existing forms of production organization and thereby dissolve the peasantry as a distinct social form of existence of labour. One would then be in danger of ignoring the specific political process of the agrarian class struggle. In particular, the experience of large agrarian societies such as India points over-whelmingly to the continued vitality of the resistance of the peasantry to forces threatening to dissolve its distinct form of social existence. It is important, therefore, to see the incomplete fruition of capitalism in societies such as colonial (or, for that matter, post-colonial) India not merely as a failure of the dominant classes that came into existence through the operations of colonial capital, or of 'dependent' or 'peripheral' native capital, but also as the result of the resistance of subordinate classes. Differentiation in such a situation is not linearly transformed into a uniquely determined form of the new class struggle in the countryside. On the contrary, differentiation creates the possibilities for the emergence of a variety of solidarities around which peasant resistance can coalesce. This not only creates entirely new possibilities for the 'mobilization' or 'manipulation' of peasants by dominant groups; it also leaves the political resolution of the class struggle in a continued state of indeterminacy.

This element of indeterminacy in agrarian class struggles can, however, create still other political possibilities. What is crucial here is the role of a middle-class intelligentsia. We have seen from our description of the class struggles in colonial Bengal the independent political role of such an intelligentsia, whether as Gandhian organizers or 'communal' agitators or Communist cadres. Perhaps this is a feature that is much more prominent in the politics of Bengal than in many other parts of India. Formed out of the ranks of a rapidly dissolving land-owning class, the middle-class intelligentsia became increasingly urbanized in its culture, but increasingly radicalized as well. From the 1920s onwards a large professional and salaried middle class was formed which had lost its last remaining ties of material interest with the land. It was this class which provided the organizing cadres of the new parties of mass mobilization. Its role in the agrarian class struggle was not as another contending agrarian party; it was intervening in that struggle from outside. As a result, it could affect the outcome in quite unforeseen ways.

Clearly such opportunities for 'conscious' intervention in the agrarian class struggle are of great historical significance in colonial and post-colonial countries such as India. In Bengal, much more than in other parts of India, such interventions have taken the form of centrally organized party-political movements. Nevertheless, the 'conscious' perspective of class struggle has remained imprisoned within the given forms of its articulation. This has considerably limited the transformative impact of middle-class intervention. Although, as we have seen, the principal tendency of class differentiation in the Bengal countryside in the last decades of colonial rule was the sharpening of the contradiction between a class of jotdar/moneylenders/traders and a class of poor peasants/sharecroppers/labourers, this did not find adequate recognition in the programmes of the 'organized' class struggle which continued to operate within the familiar state–landlord–tenant triad. In consequence, while the intervention of middle-class activists undoubtedly provided a radical edge to the anti-landlord demands of the mass of the tenantry, it has continued to display an ambivalent attitude towards the 'progressive' historical potentiality of the new contradiction.

The history of middle-class domination of organized party politics in Bengal (and in West Bengal in the period after Independence and Partition) can be shown to have resisted, much more than in other parts of India, the emergence and domination of rich capitalist farmers in the countryside and sustained to a very large extent the continued viability of small-peasant cultivation. The major thrust of Communist-led peasant movements in West Bengal, and of the legal and administrative actions of Communist-led governments, has been to extend further the logic of peasant resistance in the last days of colonial rule: to abolish the land revenue form of agrarian taxation; to protect against eviction the small producer with inferior rights of tenancy, especially sharecroppers; to control by statutory pricing, state purchases, and public distribution, the prices of agricultural commodities in favour of both urban and rural consumers; to reduce, by public work programmes and alternative organizations of credit and marketing, the subjection of small producers to local trading and usurious capital. It is also worth pointing out that all attempts to create a separate political organization of the kulak interest, of the kind which exists in most other parts of India, have been singularly unsuccessful in West Bengal.

It cannot, of course, be said that these attempts have laid the organizational or programmatic foundations for an agrarian socialism, or even that the full range of problems involved in such a programme have been formulated and understood. In fact, it could be argued that because these programmes have on the whole attempted to follow rather than transform the given forms of articulation of the agrarian class struggle, the conscious interventions of a political leadership have failed to project any viable alternative forms of agrarian transformation. The theoretical difficulties can be traced to two unresolved problems, both of which emerged in the last phase of colonial rule and continue to exist to this day: first, the reality of differentiation and yet the conviction that this cannot represent a genuinely progressive historical tendency; and secondly, the undeniable evidence of peasant communal resistance to feudal, state, and usurious exploitation and yet the failure to develop suitable forms to organize the strength of these collective solidarities within a broader political framework of struggle against capitalist domination.

19

On Religious and Linguistic Nationalisms: The Second Partition of Bengal
(1999)

The Nation at the Time of Swadeshi

It is instructive to compare the first partition of Bengal in 1905 with the second in 1947. The first partition of Bengal into two provinces—Bengal in the west and Eastern Bengal and Assam in the east—was almost exclusively the result of an administrative decision at the top. There was no mass political agitation of the kind we now associate with nationalist mobilizations, making the demand that the province be divided in accordance with cultural demography. On the contrary, the partition decision provoked what was perhaps the first mass nationalist agitation in India—the Swadeshi movement—demanding the repeal of partition on the ground that the people of Bengal were culturally one and indivisible. The reason given for the partition decision was administrative convenience: the undivided province with an area of 189,000 square miles and a population of seventy-nine million, was said to have become ungovernable. But, of course, there were important political considerations that were, as Sumit Sarkar has shown in his classic study, by no means secondary.[1] The most clearly stated of these was the need to curb the growing nationalist sentiments in Bengal, which were thought to be confined almost exclusively to the Hindu middle classes: a partition of the province, the colonial governors felt, would reduce the effect that this movement, 'unfriendly if not seditious in character', was having on

---

[1] Sumit Sarkar, *The Swadeshi Movement in Bengal, 1903–1908* (New Delhi: People's Publishing House, 1973).

'the whole tone of Bengal administration'. As H.H. Risley, the ethnographer-administrator, put it in two oft-quoted sentences: 'Bengal united is a power; Bengal divided will pull in different ways . . . One of our main objects is to split up and thereby weaken a solid body of opponents to our rule.'[2]

The political objective of the colonial administration, in other words, was pre-emptive: to disrupt what was seen as a growing nationalist opposition led by the Hindu middle classes. Curzon, the viceroy, stated the objective quite plainly:

> The Bengalis, who like to think themselves a nation, and who dream of a future when the English will have been turned out, and a Bengali Babu will be installed in Government House, Calcutta, of course bitterly resent any disruption that will be likely to interfere with the realisation of this dream. If we are weak enough to yield to their clamour now, we shall not be able to dismember or reduce Bengal again; and you will be cementing and solidifying, on the eastern flank of India, a force already formidable, and certain to be a source of increasing trouble in the future.[3]

He did not forget to mention the other part of the colonial strategy: partition 'would invest the Muhammadans in Eastern Bengal with a unity which they have not enjoyed since the days of the old Mussulman viceroys and kings.'[4]

If the first partition of 1905, therefore, is attributed primarily to a colonial strategy of divide and rule, then that strategy can already be seen to be playing with the varying possibilities of congruence between territories and culturally marked populations. The historically significant point here is not whether there already *existed* one nation of Bengalis or two. Rather, the point is that even as the project of imagining a nation into existence got under way, it found itself on a political field where contending strategies could be devised to contest or disrupt that project by enabling the rival imagining of rival nations, one on a principle of linguistic nationalism, the other that of religious nationalism.

The first partition was undone in six years. The Swadeshi movement's success in 'unsettling the settled fact' of a divided Bengal (in the celebrated words of Surendra Nath Banerjea, a principal leader of the

---

[2] Cited in ibid., pp. 17–18.
[3] Cited in ibid., pp. 19–20.
[4] Cited in ibid., p. 18.

movement) provided a major spurt to the nationalist imagination in Bengal and produced most of the ideological and organizational forms that would characterize nationalist politics there in the subsequent decades. This was the first significant occasion when the nationalist imagination in India was confronted with a concrete question about the territorial division of state jurisdictions. The idea that Bengal was one and indivisible, regardless of religious plurality, was a crucial element that shaped the notion that territory and culture were inseparably tied in a sort of 'natural history' of the nation. The same natural-historical theme once again made the encompassment of Bengal within India largely unproblematic: the culture of Bengal was seen to be 'naturally' a part of the larger cultural unity of the Indian nation.

The success of the anti-partition movement, however, barely concealed the faultlines in this unitary conception of the nation. The nationalist political leadership in Bengal at this time was overwhelmingly upper-caste Hindu. More significantly, the nationalist imagination that flourished so spectacularly at the time of the Swadeshi movement actually naturalized a conception of the nation in history that was quite distinctly Hindu. And yet, it would be wrong to suppose that this Hindu-centred view of the nation was targeted against Muslims or that it even sought to exclude them from the ambit of the nation. It is noteworthy that even though there was little political campaigning in favour of partition, the Swadeshi movement nevertheless produced an explicit rhetoric of Hindu–Muslim unity as part of its evocation of nationhood. Bipinchandra Pal, for instance, put forward the idea of a composite patriotism and a federal India of which the units would be the religious communities—Hindu, Muslim, Christian, aboriginal tribes.[5] The idea persisted into the period of mass nationalism and was applied most famously in Chittaranjan Das's Hindu–Muslim pact of the 1920s. Alongside the conception of a natural history of the nation, therefore, articulated predominantly in terms of a Hindu religious idiom, there was also the idea of unity born out of fraternal association between Hindus and Muslims. The two ideas were perhaps best expressed in a very early nationalist text, which stretched the metaphor of natural relationship to its limit:

> Although India is the true motherland only of those who belong to the Hindu jati and although only they have been born from her womb, the Muslims are not unrelated to her any longer. She has held them at her

5 Ibid., pp. 420–4.

breast and reared them. The Muslims are therefore her adopted children. Can there be no bonds of fraternity between two children of the same mother, one a natural child and the other adopted? There certainly can; the laws of every religion admit this. There has now been born a bond of brotherhood between Hindus and Muslims living in India.[6]

To sum up, the dominant form of the imagined nation produced in Bengal at the time of the Swadeshi movement contained, at one and the same time, an Indian nationalism built around a natural history of Aryan–Hindu tradition, a linguistic nationalism valorizing Bengal's cultural unity, and a rhetoric of Hindu–Muslim unity. This combination was possible because neither the place of Bengal within a state structure of the Indian nation nor the place of a Hindu minority within a Muslim-majority Bengal had yet been posed as problems. The nationalist elite of Bengal, predominantly upper-caste Hindu and belonging to the landed proprietor and urban professional classes, was still comfortably ensconced in its position as leader of the nation it had imagined into existence.

Two developments threw this situation into disarray. First, the rise of nationalist mass movements all over India from the 1920s produced an entirely new organizational structure of the all-India Congress in which the place of Bengal's nationalist leadership became either marginal or oppositional. Second, within Bengal the politics of Muslim identity found an agrarian base. The older rhetoric of Hindu–Muslim fraternity could not suffice any more unless it was able to confront the question of agrarian class relations.

Let us begin with the second development, since this is often taken to be the most crucial element of a 'structural' explanation of the second partition of Bengal.

Histories of Partition

The fact that the peasantry in eastern Bengal was predominantly Muslim and the landlords largely Hindu has long been regarded by historians, especially Marxist historians, as the crucial structural condition that allowed a class antagonism to be expressed as a conflict between religious groups and that enabled the British to manipulate the various Indian political organizations around this issue. Badruddin

---

[6] Bhudeb Mukhopadhyay, 'Svapnalabdha Bharatbarser Itihas' (1876), in Pramathanath Bisi, ed., *Bhudeb Racana Sambhar* (Calcutta: Mitra and Ghosh, 1969), pp. 341–74.

Umar, the radical Bangladeshi historian, for instance, states that the partition of Bengal in 1947 'became possible because of the presence of certain nonantagonistic contradictions in the country that were converted into antagonistic contradictions by the British rulers.'[7] Sugata Bose provides the most carefully researched elaboration of this argument.[8] He notes that the Muslim-majority districts of east Bengal consisted of a peasantry that was little differentiated. Until the early decades of the twentieth century, this peasantry had a 'symbiotic relationship' with the predominantly Hindu landlords, moneylenders, and traders who supplied the vital needs of credit in a highly monetized agrarian economy. The prolonged Depression of the 1930s, however, destroyed these networks of rural credit, leading to 'a decisive shift in the balance of class power in [the peasant's] favour.' The rentier and trading classes

> ceased to perform any useful function. Once a political challenge came within the realm of possibility, the strength of a religious identity was exploited in a readily available and, for the privileged co-religionists, a safe ideology. To the vast mass of smallholding peasants living under similar, yet very splintered, conditions of economic existence in east Bengal, religion seemed to impart a sense of 'community'; so at a critical juncture in Bengal's history, religion provided the basis of a 'national bond', however stretched, and became the rallying cry of a 'political organisation' demanding the creation of a separate Muslim homeland. Efforts by some Hindu and Muslim leaders to mobilize the Muslim peasantry under the banner of progressive nationalism and socialism proved abortive. Weighed under for decades by an economic, political, and moral order they had long ago silently rejected, the Muslim peasantry responded to the appeals of religion and gave a powerful ideological legitimation to a breakdown in social relations that had already occurred, but which was only now being formally conceded.[9]

Agrarian class conflict erupted in east Bengal in the 1930s. 'This conflict was interpreted and used by self-serving politicians for their own ends. Operating in higher-level political arenas with communal constituencies, the gift of government's successive constitutional

---

[7] Badruddin Umar, *Bangabhanga o Sampradayik Rajniti* (Calcutta: Chirayata, 1987), preface.

[8] Sugata Bose, *Agrarian Bengal: Economy, Social Structure, and Politics, 1919–1947* (Cambridge: Cambridge University Press, 1986), esp. pp. 181–232.

[9] Ibid., pp. 231–2.

reforms, these politicians unflinchingly used religion to mask an essentially economic conflict.'[10]

While not quite arguing that religion only provided a mask over class conflicts, Suranjan Das nevertheless points out that between the two partitions of Bengal a significant change in the nature of Hindu–Muslim antagonism occurred.[11] After an early period in which they were relatively unorganized, less connected with the institutional politics of parties and legislatures, and strong in class orientation, communal conflicts later showed two kinds of convergences: on the one hand class and communal identities tended to converge, and on the other elite and popular communalism also tended to converge. The result was a polarization of virtually the entire population around two communal blocs, each led by elites successfully mobilizing the masses.

What about the Hindu population? Joya Chatterji has recently made the argument that the emphasis on agrarian conflict and peasant-communal consciousness in east Bengal has tended to suggest that 'communalism in Bengal was essentially a Muslim phenomenon' and that 'a parallel Hindu communalism did not emerge, or . . . if it did, it was too limited and peripheral to have contributed in any significant way to the conflicts that led to Pakistan.'[12] She then attempts to show how a Hindu-communal identity was built up in Bengal from the 1930s, initially as an alliance of the educated and the well-to-do landed and professional classes with the lower middle class, but increasingly attempting to mobilize the 'sanskritising aspirations of low-caste groups' and having as its main political objective the refusal 'to accept the rule of the Muslim majority.'[13]

Bengalis were not passive bystanders in the politics of their province; nor were they victims of circumstances entirely out of their control, forced reluctantly to accept the division of their 'motherland'. On the contrary,

[10] Ibid., p. 277.

[11] Suranjan Das, *Communal Riots in Bengal, 1905–1947* (Delhi: Oxford University Press, 1991). Taj ul-Islam Hashmi also makes the argument that there was a 'communalization of class politics', a takeover of the peasant movement in east Bengal by the better-off tenants, and finally a takeover of the communalized Praja movement by urban elite political groups represented by the Muslim League. *Pakistan as a Peasant Utopia: The Communalization of Class Politics in East Bengal, 1920–1947* (Boulder, Colo.: Westview Press, 1992).

[12] Joya Chatterji, *Bengal Divided: Hindu Communalism and Partition, 1932–1947* (Cambridge: Cambridge University Press, 1995), p. 152.

[13] Ibid., p. 228.

346 Empire and Nation: Essential Writings 1985–2005

a large number of Hindus of Bengal, backed up by the provincial branches of the Congress and the Hindu Mahasabha, campaigned intensively
in 1947 for the partition of Bengal and for the creation of a separate Hindu
province that would remain inside an Indian union.[14]

Placed alongside each other, the two histories of Muslim and Hindu
communalism in Bengal seem to suggest a population divided right
down the middle, cutting across classes and strata, one half asserting
its political right to rule over the entire province by virtue of its being
the majority religious community, the other insisting on a political
division of the province in order to create (or perhaps to retain) a separate 'homeland' for the minority religious community. The historiography has, it seems, conditioned itself precisely to explain the 'historical
inevitability' of an unfortunate event.

It seems to me especially important that when we think about the
histories of an 'event' such as the partition of Bengal (or of India), we
take care to disentangle the many different roots of that event, running
along different levels of determination and with very different tempo-
ralities. Separate narratives can be constructed for each of these roots,
from that of the cultural construction of nationality, a story running
over more than a hundred years, to the mobilization for a partition of
the province that, properly speaking, lasted only a few months. It is the
property of foundational events such as those of August 1947 in India
that they supply each of these narratives with a closure that identifies
it as a history of partition. But they are very different histories, in which
categories such as religion or nationalism have entirely different signi-
fications.

Restricting myself to the theme of religion and nationalism, let me
go through some of the narratives that might be told of the second
partition of Bengal. At the level of popular beliefs and practices, we
could tell a long story of the spread of Islam in Bengal, of the coexistence in the everyday life of Muslim peasants of numerous Islamic and
non-Islamic practices, and of periodic attempts to 'purify' Islam.[15] At
another level, we could tell the story of the formation of a new middle-
class Muslim elite in the late nineteenth century, the conflict between
those who preferred to identify with an Urdu-speaking North Indian

[14] Ibid., p. 227.
[15] Richard M. Eaton, *The Rise of Islam amd the Bengal Frontier, 1204–1760* (Delhi:
Oxford University Press, 1994).

aristocratic culture and those who sought to build up a distinctly Bengali Muslim cultural identity, and the rapid spread of secondary and higher education in east Bengal in the early twentieth century.[16] To take up another strand, I have already mentioned the evolution in the late nineteenth century of a historicized nation whose core was supposed to consist of an Aryan/Hindu civilization. This construction went hand in hand with a new modernized hegemony of upper-caste Hindus over the entire province, as shown dramatically at the time of the Swadeshi movement. It saw little inconsistency between an Indian and a Bengali cultural identity, or indeed between its explicitly Hindu lineages and the rhetoric of Hindu–Muslim unity. This nationalist endeavour found its greatest moment of success at the time of the Khilafat–Non-cooperation movement conducted by Chittaranjan Das's Congress. Riding the crest of a mass agitation in both city and country, nationalism in Bengal in the early 1920s proudly displayed the banner of Hindu–Muslim anticolonial fraternity.

It is much too simplistic to think that when Hindu–Muslim unity broke down in the late 1920s and the Congress took a much more narrowly defined position in defence of Hindu upper-caste landed interests, there was a transformation in the long-duration ideological construction from nationalism to communalism.[17] The story of this change must be sought among political strategies adopted over much shorter durations, in institutional arenas that involve only small numbers of people. One cannot tell this story without mentioning specific meetings and negotiations, without citing statements and declarations,

---

[16] Rafiuddin Ahmed, *Bengal Muslims: The Quest for Identity, 1876–1906* (Delhi: Oxford University Press, 1982); Tazeen M. Murshid, *The Sacred and the Secular: Bengal Muslim Discourses, 1871–1977* (Calcutta: Oxford University Press, 1995).

[17] Joya Chatterji makes this argument about a shift from nationalism to communalism: 'Nationalism was directed against imperialism, and gave top priority to anti-British action. The communalism of the bhadralok was directed against their fellow Bengalis. History for the one was the struggle against British rule; for the other, it was the celebration of British rule as an age of liberation from the despotism of Muslims. Its key political objective was to prevent this "despotism" from returning when the British left India, and to deny that Muslims could be Bengalis, and by extension Indians' (*Bengal Divided*, p. 268). She marks this 'shift' from the 1930s and emphasizes it to argue that 'far from being a helpless pawn in the endgames of empire', Bengal was divided because large and powerful sections of the Hindu population, in town and countryside, actively fought for the province's partition. Her argument seems to me to flow from an astonishingly naive view of nationalist politics.

indeed without sneaking behind particular people into particular smoke-filled offices. It is precisely because of the relevance of this level of political activity that there will always remain the possibility of telling secret histories and untold stories of events such as the Partition.

To be more specific, religious identity as a demographic category became perhaps the single most crucial factor in determining the distribution of government power in Bengal under the constitutional reforms of 1935. The legislature out of which provincial ministries were to be formed was statutorily constituted so that 48 per cent of the seats were reserved for Muslims (who were 54 per cent of the population), 12 per cent for the Depressed Classes (Scheduled Castes, who were 18 per cent of the population), and 20 per cent were available as 'general' seats for Hindu candidates (Hindus, not including the Depressed Classes, were 26 per cent of the population). Significantly, as many as 10 per cent of the seats were reserved for Europeans, who amounted to only 0.04 per cent of the population, but who could nevertheless hold a crucial balance in a communally constituted house. The 'provincial autonomy' arrangements in Bengal remain one of the most obvious examples of nationalist accusations about divide and rule.

That Hindu communalism came strongly to the fore in Bengal's provincial politics in the 1930s and 1940s can hardly be denied. What is not true, however, is that organized opinion among Hindus became any less anti-British. Indeed, the allegation that the imperial power and the local British bureaucracy were promoting Muslim interests in order to curtail those of the nationalist Hindus only strengthened anti-British feelings. What is also not true is that the new atmosphere of Hindu–Muslim conflict required any significant transformation in the internal elements of the nationalist consciousness as it had been constructed since the late nineteenth century. If it was generative of slogans of Hindu–Muslim fraternity in an earlier era, it could now generate with equal ease the spectre of Muslim tyranny. We fail to see the hegemonic power of the nationalist imagination as it emerged in India if we ignore the wide range of strategic political possibilities it could yield on the question of religious identity—from Hindu dominance at one extreme to varying degrees of intercommunal fraternization to an insistence on the separation of religion and politics altogether.

Not so in the case of Muslim politics in Bengal, at least not in the decades we are considering. One of the most striking features of

Muslim-majoritarian politics in Bengal in the 1930s and 1940s is its singularly non-hegemonic ambition in relation to the Hindu minority. There is no way to explain this except by connecting Muslim politics in Bengal with that in India as a whole—where, of course, it had the character of the politics of a minority. There is not a single cultural or political endeavour in Bengal in the period that can be read as a hegemonic attempt to mobilize the consent of the Hindu minority for Muslim leadership over Bengali society. This absence, perhaps, was only an inevitable sign of the subalternity of the movement. It could also be said that there was little time for any hegemonic efforts to coalesce. Or, to be more careful, we could say that at the most promising moment for such an effort—the 1937 emergence of Fazlul Huq's peasant-populist Krishak Praja movement as the most dynamic political force in east Bengal—attempts to forge a political alliance between the Congress and the Krishak Praja Party were foiled, first by the unbending policy of the all-India Congress not to enter into coalitions in any province and, subsequently, by the systematic vigilance of the governor and the rest of the British bureaucracy against any intercommunal political alliance that might put Congress leaders in ministerial office during the war.[18] The only noteworthy, though entirely inchoate, intellectual efforts to present the Praja movement as a democratic upsurge holding out the promise of social and political transformation not just for Muslims but for Bengali society as a whole come from this brief period around 1937.[19] In the absence, however, of an intercommunal democratic alliance at the provincial level, local efforts by left-wing peasant organizers to build up agrarian bases cutting across the religious divide either remained confined to particular localities or were scuttled by the more resourceful and organized communal forces backed by a government bureaucracy.[20] The peasant-populist upsurge in east Bengal, with its powerful use of Islam as a religion of agrarian solidarity and

[18] Both these sets of facts are well documented: Shila Sen, *Muslim Politics in Bengal, 1937–1947* (New Delhi: Impex India, 1976); Kamala Sarkar, *Bengal Politics, 1937–1947* (Calcutta: Mukherjee, 1990); Leonard A. Gordon, *Brothers against the Raj: A Biography of Sarat and Subhas Chandra Bose* (New Delhi: Penguin Books India, 1990).

[19] See in particular Humayun Kabir, *Muslim Politics, 1909–1942* (Calcutta: Gupta, Rahman and Gupta, 1943); and Nareschandra Sengupta, *Yugaparikrama*, vol. 2 (Calcutta: Firma K. L. Mukhopadhyay, 1961), esp. pp. 178–253.

[20] This has been well documented for the districts of Tippera and Noakhali in Bose, *Agrarian Bengal*, pp. 181–232.

justice, could not, in the end, produce a credible democratic force that might elicit the consent of the religious minority.

Strategies and Outcomes

It is also historically inaccurate to suggest that the decision to partition the province of Bengal along religious-demographic lines actually involved the participation of masses of people. As far as opinion within Bengal was concerned, the relevant decisions were made by members of the Bengal assembly, elected on the basis of a very restricted suffrage. There was some campaigning on the issue of Partition in 1947, both in favour and against, but by the standards of mass agitation of the time they involved small numbers of people. In fact, evidence from the period suggests that the incidents that most strongly framed discussion on the subject were in fact the communal killings in Calcutta in August 1946 and those in Noakhali a few weeks later. These were perhaps the most powerful mass actions, organized by Hindu and Muslim communalists, contributing to Partition. Some people understood the unprecedented communal violence of 1946 as the cataclysmic sign of a general transition of power, with its associated feelings of anxiety as well as of anticipation. Others took it to mean that Pakistan, whatever its precise legal or constitutional form, was inevitable.

Reading through the political debates that took place in Bengal from August 1946 to August 1947, one cannot but get the sense that positions were being taken on the assumption that Pakistan was in the offing, that there was nothing left to be done to change that eventuality, and that all that remained was to strike the best bargain for each sectional interest, whether majority community, the minority community, or the Depressed Classes within the minority community. One also gets the undeniable sense that, irrespective of party or community and irrespective of the stature of the organization or leader within Bengal, every statement, whether a demand or an appeal, a promise or a threat, was addressed to an external and distant group of decision-makers; no one in Bengal saw himself as involved in taking the momentous decisions that would determine the future of the province. There is reason why the feeling would persist, in West Bengal as well as in Bangladesh, that in 1947 Bengal was merely a pawn in the hands of all-India players.

It is easy to demonstrate the highly contingent and strategic nature of the various positions taken on the question of religion and national status by organizations and individuals in the months preceding August 1947. Fazlul Huq, who was by then out of power and estranged from the Muslim League, had little qualms about stating that there was 'constitutionally speaking, no government in Bengal', since the ministers were responsible not to the legislature but 'to Mr. Jinnah as head of the Muslim League.'[21] More significantly, when the debate broke out in May 1947 over the Sarat Bose–Suhrawardy proposal for a sovereign United Bengal, Abul Hashim, campaigning for the proposal from within the provincial Muslim League, sought to justify it as being consistent with the original Lahore resolution in which Pakistan had apparently been thought of as consisting of 'independent Muslim states'. Opposing the proposal, Akram Khan took the stand that no one in the Provincial League was empowered to make statements in this matter since negotiations were being conducted on behalf of all Muslims of India by Jinnah and the central Muslim League.[22]

As far as Hindu opinion is concerned, it was clear almost as soon as the question was raised that there would be near unanimity, at least within the domain of organized opinion, from the Hindu Mahasabha on the right to the Congress in the middle to the socialists and even communists on the left.[23] Once it became apparent that Pakistan was a certainty, and especially after the Congress high command seemed to have accepted in March 1947 the idea of a partition of Punjab, the argument became unstoppable among Hindus that Bengal too must be partitioned so that the Hindu minority would have a place outside Pakistan. Apart from the straightforward communal justifications, of which there were plenty, the position was also supported by more sophisticated arguments that said, for instance, that the Indian union was more likely to uphold the modern democratic traditions built up through the nineteenth and twentieth centuries and therefore more

[21] Cited in Kalipada Biswas, *Yukta Banlar ses Adhyay* (Calcutta: Orient Book Company, 1966), pp. 386–90.

[22] The debate is extensively quoted in Umar, *Bangabhanga*, pp. 46–68.

[23] Most communists later confessed that in 1946–7, the pressure to recognize the inevitability of a communal division was overwhelming. See the survey of communist literature and reminiscences in Amalendu Sengupta, *Uttal Callis: Asamapta Biplab* (Calcutta: Pearl Publishers, 1989).

likely to safeguard the rights of all communities. The United Bengal proposal found few takers and most seemed persuaded by Shyama Prasad Mukherjee's argument that if a sovereign Bengal later decided, on the basis of its religious composition, to join Pakistan, the minority community would be left at that stage with no options.

Especially interesting is the debate between leaders of the Depressed Classes. Jogendra Nath Mandal, leader of the Scheduled Castes Federation and politically allied with the Muslim League, opposed the suggestion to partition Bengal.

> If such a thing happens, then it is a virtual certainty that Hindus from east Bengal will be forced to take shelter in west Bengal. Of course, if the leaders who are proposing the partition of Bengal intend an exchange of populations, then I have nothing to say except that only the other day the caste-Hindu leaders had vehemently criticized Dr. Ambedkar for his *Thoughts on Pakistan* and Mr. Jinnah for his suggestion that populations might be exchanged … If Bengal is partitioned, the scheduled castes will suffer the most. The caste-Hindus of east Bengal are wealthy and many have salaried jobs. They will have little difficulty in moving from east to west Bengal. Poor scheduled caste peasants, fishermen and artisans will have to remain in east Bengal where the proportion of Hindus will decline and they will be at the mercy of the majority Muslim community.

To this, Radhanath Das, a Scheduled Caste member of the Constituent Assembly, retorted:

> Today if we say to our Namasudra brothers in Noakhali that they come to west Bengal where the government of the separate province of West and North Bengal will provide them with shelter and other economic necessities, then I am prepared to swear that Jogen Babu will not be able to keep a single one of his caste brothers in Noakhali. In other words, he will not be able to make them feel secure under Muslim League rule or Muslim League protection … I say the backward Hindus will be better able than others to leave east Bengal, since they have few possessions besides their tiny huts.[24]

In the end, when the votes were taken in the Bengal assembly, only five of the thirty Scheduled Caste members voted against the partition of

[24] The debate is reprinted in Jagadischandra Mandal, *Banga-bhanga* (Calcutta: Mahapran Publishing Society, 1977).

Bengal. Clearly, when the time came for a strategic decision by a group organized as a minority within a minority, the hegemonic gestures of the Muslim League towards the Scheduled Castes proved inadequate.

We also get a sense of the extreme contingency within which the question of Partition was talked about in Bengal from writings in non-political circles. There is a small book published in April 1947 on the communal riots of the previous year titled—using the English word—*Delirium*.[25] The author, Birendranath Chattopadhyay, was a medical practitioner involved in voluntary social work, not directly affiliated with any political organization, and clearly conscious of his stature as a leading figure of the neighbourhood, looked up to with respect by the working-class poor, both Muslim and Hindu, who lived in the nearby slums of the industrial suburb of Alambazar, north of Calcutta.

Most striking about the author's description of the communal riots in his area in August 1946 is the sense of assault from the outside, carried out by powerful but anonymous forces, against which the carefully nurtured bonds of neighbourhood solidarity were no match. He talks of local Congress and Muslim League leaders jointly setting up peace committees as soon as news of rioting in Calcutta arrived. He himself went around the neighbourhood, urging people to look out for outsiders. 'We must not let these outside disturbances get into our neighbourhood.' And yet, before the night was over, the slums were in flames and people were killing one another with astonishing brutality.

The rest of the book is a series of arguments and counterarguments about why this happened and what was to come. It gives us a flavour of the animated conversations that took place in Hindu middle-class male gatherings. The full range of political arguments, now familiar to all students of modern Indian history, is presented here—blaming the British, blaming the Congress, blaming Muslim communalism and the Muslim League. What is remarkable, however, is the way in which an otherwise bewildering and deplorable set of events is sought to be made comprehensible in terms of historical necessity.

All these differences and conflicts between the League, the Congress and other parties seem to me like an elaborate theatre being performed on the political stage. Mahatmaji is the playwright and director of India's freedom struggle and the others are all experienced actors. Most Indians have still

[25] Birendranath Chattopadhyay, *Diliriyam (Sampratik Hangama)* (Alambazar: Databya Bibhag, 1947).

not understood the mysterious way in which Mahatmaji and Jinnah Saheb
have divided up their responsibilities . . . They have together taken up
the role of religious reformers and, by prevailing upon the men of religion,
have combined religious preaching with the message of freedom. Thus
have they built up their parties and the nation . . . By starting an upheaval,
they have sought to destroy stagnant minds and a decrepit society and to
produce a renaissance among ordinary people. I do not think of these
disturbances as communal. I think of this as India's last movement . . . This
is a conspiracy to eradicate for ever the demon of communalism from
this country. The clashes now taking place will soon lead to a situation
where people of both communities will get fed up with those who preach
untouchability, communal hatred, and religious hypocrisy. Perhaps then
a new nation will arise in India.[26]

The rapidly unfolding political events are also seen as unreal, devoid
of truth—events that must necessarily give way to 'real' history.

This December [1946], the Congress has accepted the British view of
things which was for so long in favour of the objectives of the Muslim
League. Now the Congress will accept the division of Bengal, the division
of Punjab, even the division of India. In time, perhaps every province of
India will be partitioned in order to accommodate the League's demand for
Pakistan. This will either lead to the strengthening of two nations, or else
it will cause so much disruption in everyday life that Hindus and Muslims
will come to see that by fighting each other and putting up fences all across
the country neither community can live in happiness . . . Even if partition is necessary today, the country cannot remain partitioned for ever.[27]

Historical necessity is the theme of another small book written at the
time of Independence and Partition published in December 1947.[28]
Partition had been made inevitable because of the nationalist Congress's
failure to forestall the aggresive politics of a 'fascist' Muslim League
whose ideology was that of 'modern totalitarianism in the garb of
medieval bigotry'.[29] 'In truth, the failure is of the Congress, the success
of the Muslim League. As a matter of fact, Congress's efforts in the last
two years to avoid the partition of India were not very conducive to

[26] Ibid., p. 18.
[27] Ibid., pp. 47–8.
[28] Satyen Sen, *Paneroi Agast* (Calcutta: City Book Company, 1947).
[29] Ibid., p. 63.

maintaining unity . . . [Mountbatten] has only done that which was inevitable, because every effort to avoid that eventuality had led to miserable failure; he has merely resolved the problem with the surgeon's scalpel.'[30]

Having thus condemned the all-India nationalist leadership for failing to resist an aggressive religious nationalism, the writer then takes a wistful look at the other failed possibility—that of linguistic nationalism.

> Bengal, which had once energetically and courageously foiled Lord Curzon's plan to divide it, is now, in 1947, proceeding to implement another plan of the same kind. Such is the irony of history! In 1905, the leadership mainly came from eastern Bengal, now it is from western Bengal. In 1905, the organizer was the Government of India, now the organizers are the Bengalis themselves. In 1905, the problem was political, now it is communal. The movement of 1905 spread the consciousness of undivided nationality throughout India; now Bengal is eager to sacrifice that glorious tradition as it looks upon others to come to its rescue.[31]

Wistful evocation of linguistic nationalism is the predominant mood of Chunilal Gangopadhyay's portrait gallery of individuals whose convictions had crumbled as a result of the Partition.[32] Written between 1946 and 1950 as a series of letters, one of his sketches is that of Khadim Islam, lifelong supporter of the Muslim League, who now says, 'It is through my fault that the land of my birth is being divided and subdued . . . Hindu-majority West Bengal will now be separated from Muslim-majority East Bengal and turned into a colony of north India.' Zainul Kabir says, 'The conspiracy of the League and the English will now turn East Bengal into a colony of Aligarh and West Bengal into a colony of Banaras. . . . When will Bengal, the land of Raja Ganesa to Subhas [Chandra Bose] and of Sultan Ilyas to Titumir, rise up again from the depths of time?' Sunil Sen of Purulia realizes in April 1949 that the rulers of Patna will mistreat the Bengalis of Bihar: 'His so-called "Indianism", fondly nurtured throughout his life, is suddenly washed away . . . Having neared the end of his life, he realizes that he has no bonds of imagination or need with the Hindus of Punjab or

[30] Ibid., p. 95.
[31] Ibid., pp. 87–8.
[32] Chunilal Gangopadhyay, *Bhangan Diner Kathamala* (n.p., n.d., possibly 1952).

the Muslims of Peshawar. Rather, he is tied by ideal and interest with the Hindus of Bankura and the Muslims of Barisal.'

Read historically, this can only appear to us as a fanciful evocation of what might have been, a sign once again of the unacceptability of the truth of Partition rather than an assertion of a new linguistic nationalism. Even the most recent historiography in West Bengal, self-consciously seeking to avoid the inherited demonologies of Indian nationalist history, is forced to conclude that the story of Partition can only be read as a Greek tragedy: 'Like insects drawn to the flame, our characters are driven by an invisible hand towards inevitable tragedy . . . Why else should the leaders of India's freedom movement, who were all [including Jinnah] resistant to the idea of partition, behave in the final act of the transition of power in such a way that partition would become inevitable?'[33] Curiously, as the trauma of Partition was gradually overcome and a massive uprooted population managed to resettle and restart their lives, the nationalism that came to predominate in West Bengal, in the period of Congress rule as well as later under the Left, was precisely the nationalism of the Swadeshi era: an Indian nationalism rooted in a Hindu civilizational past, a sense of Bengali identity firmly anchored within that nationalism (no matter how strained its strategic relations with the political centre), and a rhetoric of Hindu–Muslim unity (now called the politics of secularism). Partition, in this historiography, became an aberration, a mark of loss and of failure, and was attributed in the main to communalism, imperial machinations, and the inadequacies of the nationalist leadership. The durable construct of the imagined nation resumed its position of hegemony, claiming to have within itself a secure place for religious minorities, while allowing for a considerable range of communal discriminations, animosities, and strategic conflicts to be played out in the public arena of national life.

Across the border in the other half of Bengal, the curious development was the rise to dominance, over the next two and a half decades, of a new linguistic nationalism that took as its foundational moment not August 1947, the birth of Pakistan, but February 1952, the beginning of the movement for recognition of the Bengali language in Pakistan. The nationalism that became hegemonic in Bangladesh after

---

[33] Saileskumar Bandyopadhyay, *Jinnah, Pakistan: Natun Bhabna* (Calcutta: Mitra and Ghosh, 1988), pp. 302–3.

1971 spoke on behalf of a national community united by language and cutting across religious divisions. There too the partition of Bengal in 1947 became an aberration, a mark of loss and failure, brought on by the obduracy of Hindu leaders and the manipulations of the British.[34] The hegemonic move that was missing in the decade before Partition was successfully made in the 1970s, but only in a territory already truncated by a division along religious lines.

Despite the rejection of religious nationalism, however, there has been no significant move made on either side of the border for a reunification of Bengal and none is likely to be made in the foreseeable future. Perhaps what this demonstrates is that an event brought about by extremely contingent and short-term actions can in turn decisively and permanently shape the forms of social structures and political imaginations. I have shown that historical memory in both West Bengal and Bangladesh strenuously seeks to deny the truth of the second partition of Bengal; yet the renewed possibility of nationalist imaginings unrestricted by religious identity is crucially conditioned by the very consequences of that partition.

The case of Bengal seems to point to one aspect of modern nation-state formations that has been little recognized in the literature on nationalism. This relates to the frequent, but necessarily subterranean, presence of religion as a cultural-demographic element in the formation

---

[34] A large unanimity on this has emerged among Bangladeshi historians. An officially sponsored history, for instance, deplores the scuttling by 'obstinate Bengali Hindus' of the 'noble plan' of Suhrawardy and Abdul Hashim for a sovereign United Bengal. It also criticizes the British for giving equal weight to majority and minority opinions in granting the partition of Bengal. Mohammad Waliullah, *Amader Mukti-samgram* (Dhaka: Bangla Academy, 1978), pp. 411–12. Badruddin Umar, arguing on Leninist grounds that only a genuinely democratic federal solution could have struck an acceptable balance between communal and regional interests in a multinational country like India, blames the Congress, the Muslim League, and the British for the partition (*Bangabhanga*, pp. 104–5). Harun-Or Rashid ends his study of the demise of the Praja movement and the rise of the Muslim League in the 1940s by talking of how the all-India Muslim leadership subverted the project of an independent Bengal: 'the victory of the Khwaja group . . . including the central League leadership was not to last long. With the removal of the fear of Hindu domination, Bengali subnationalism came to be asserted more prominently in the post-1947 Pakistani polity . . . culminating in the emergence of Bangladesh as an independent state in 1971, which is the partial fulfilment of the 1940s dream of an independent Greater Bengal.' *The Foreshadowing of Bangladesh: Bengal Muslim League and Muslim Politics, 1936–1947* (Dhaka: Asiatic Society of Bangladesh, 1987), p. 346.

of hegemonic national ideologies. Religion does not sit well with the various classificatory categories with which a 'population' is defined as the target of the government activities that provide legitimacy for the post-enlightenment state. After all, of all contemporary nation-states today, only Israel and Pakistan explicitly claim a basis of nationality located primarily in religious identity. Yet it is possible to cite numerous instances of nationalisms in which a dominant religious identity has provided a major element in the cultural construction of the national identity. Indeed, one of the most surprising features of the recent emergence of scholarly interest in nationalism is the sudden discovery of religion as a constituent element of the supposedly secular nationalisms of Western European countries.[35] Perhaps nationalist ideologies lodge themselves most effectively in the body of the modern state when they are able to relegate religion to the secret history of its birth, when they can transform the gross facts of religious majoritarianism into the benign cultural common sense of everyday national life. That perhaps is the condition in which the nation-state can make its most magnanimous gestures towards religious minorities by offering them the promise of universal bourgeois citizenship, even if it is by recognizing and protecting their identities as minorities. To create that condition, a selective erasure from public memory of certain kinds of narratives appears to be a major task of nationalist historiographies.

[35] For instance, Linda Colley, *Britons: Forging the Nation, 1707–1837* (New Haven, Conn.: Yale University Press, 1992).

Index